# TRAINING AND RACING WITH A
# *Power Meter*

*2ND EDITION*

## PRAISE FOR *TRAINING AND RACING WITH A POWER METER*
### BY HUNTER ALLEN AND ANDREW COGGAN, PhD

"Training and Racing with a Power Meter *is the ultimate guide to training with power. Hunter Allen and Andrew Coggan are, without a doubt, the most knowledgeable people on the planet when it comes to power meters."*

—JOE FRIEL, WORLD-RECOGNIZED ENDURANCE SPORTS COACH
AND AUTHOR OF THE CYCLIST'S TRAINING BIBLE

*"Once mastered,* Training and Racing with a Power Meter *could help provide any cyclist with the kind of information usually available only to elite pro riders."*

—COMPETITOR MAGAZINE

"Training and Racing with a Power Meter *is a must-have for every triathlete serious about excelling in this sport. Using the steps outlined here has really helped me not only to just understand what the data means but to apply it on a daily basis. As a result, my functional threshold has raised over 30 watts!"*

—TERRA CASTRO, PROFESSIONAL TRIATHLETE, TEAM LUNA CHIX

*"When affordable power meters hit the market, I knew they had the potential to revolutionize the way we train. Anyone who could harness the exact demands of elite racing and apply that knowledge to specific training would definitely have a serious advantage.* Training and Racing with a Power Meter *is, without a doubt, the definitive manual on how to use a power meter to the fullest extent. It's an unmatched opportunity to have access to cutting-edge training methods developed by the world's leading experts. Hunter and Andy have given all cyclists an amazing opportunity to take their training to the next level. I certainly have!"*

—JEREMIAH BISHOP, PROFESSIONAL MOUNTAIN BIKER

*"By far the best instruction manual I've seen is* Training and Racing with a Power Meter. *The book has enough scientific detail and analysis to satisfy even the most demanding numbers junkie, while remaining readable and useful to even the casual power enthusiast."*

—STEPHEN CHEUNG, PhD, PEZCYCLINGNEWS.COM

*"It's been exciting to actually see my progress quantitatively for the first time in thirty years of racing."*

—PHIL WHITMAN, ACCOMPLISHED MASTERS RACER

# TRAINING AND RACING WITH A
# *Power Meter*
## *2ND EDITION*

Hunter Allen and Andrew Coggan, PhD

BOULDER, COLORADO

velopress

3002 Sterling Circle, Suite 100
Boulder, Colorado 80301-2338 USA
(303) 440-0601 · Fax (303) 444-6788 · E-mail velopress@competitorgroup.com


Distributed in the United States and Canada by Ingram Publisher Services

Library of Congress Cataloging-in-Publication Data
Allen, Hunter.
Training and racing with a power meter  / Hunter Allen and Andrew Coggan, Ph.D.—2nd ed.
          p. cm.
Includes bibliographical references and index.
ISBN 978-1-934030-55-4 (alk. paper)
1.  Cycling—Training. 2.  Triathlon—Training.  I. Coggan, Andrew. II. Title.
GV1048.A55 2010
796.6'2—dc22

2010005328


For information on purchasing VeloPress books, please call (800) 811-4210 ext. 2138 or visit www.velopress.com.


This paper meets the requirements of ANSI/NISO Z39.48-1992 (permanence of paper).

Cover & interior design by Erin Johnson
Cover photo by Tim De Frisco
Illustrations by Tom Feiza
Photographs courtesy of Hunter Allen (p. 255); Garmin® (p. 29); Brad Kaminski (p. 26); Polar (p. 21); Saris Cycling Group (p. 19, top); photographs on pp. 16, 19 (bottom), and 24 by Don Karle

15  /  10  9

# Contents

# Foreword

The first edition of *Training and Racing with a Power Meter* has been front and center on my bookshelf since it was first published in 2006. I keep it handy so I can refer to it often. In fact, there are few books I rely on as much as this one. I've learned a lot from it—and I'm not the only one. Whenever I talk with riders who train with a power meter, they nearly always tell me they also have Hunter Allen and Andrew Coggan's book. This makes sense because *Training and Racing with a Power Meter* was the first book for serious cyclists on how to train with power, and it continues as the guide for anyone using a power meter.

If you are new to training with power, you are starting in the right place by reading this book. Begin applying the lessons learned on the following pages to your training, and I'm sure you'll find what many other athletes have discovered—training with power will make you a stronger rider. And this book will show you how to do it.

If you've already read the first edition, the second edition includes some new concepts you'll want to apply to your training. Perhaps most notable is the discussion on how to create form at pivotal times in your season. Using the Performance Manager Chart (found in TrainingPeaks WKO+ Software), Allen and Coggan explain how to quantify and plan form for your best performances. In the past three years, I've come to rely on the information in this chart to help me make decisions about my clients' training.

For steady-state events such as triathlon, pacing is the key to fast racing. You will find guidelines to master this challenging skill in a new chapter dedicated to using power to train for triathlon. Other data within WKO+ that triathletes will find beneficial is running Training Stress Score (rTSS), which is introduced and explained here. When there is more than one sport to master, the Performance Manager Chart will be even more valuable to the triathlete who is attempting to achieve peak fitness in three sports.

Triathletes aren't the only ones to receive much-needed new attention for power-meter training. If you compete in cyclocross, track, ultra-endurance mountain biking, or BMX, you will now find more power-based information on the training and racing demands of your sport.

The world of power meters continues to change as new products and features are introduced. Here you will find up-to-date information on the latest power meters and a comparison guide to help you find the best fit for you.

If you want to train smarter and race faster using power, there is nothing else that even comes close to this book. This is the source for information on training and racing with a power meter.

*—Joe Friel*
*Coach, Author, and Co-Founder of TrainingPeaks*

# Preface to the Second Edition

We wrote this second edition of *Training and Racing with a Power Meter* because we wanted to teach you about the latest tools, techniques, theories, and principles emerging in power-meter technology. In this book you will find some brand-new sections along with updated and revised chapters on the basics. All of this information will enable you to use your power meter to enhance your cycling and achieve optimum performance.

As in the first edition, we will explain how to collect and analyze data from your power meter, how to use your power meter to identify your strengths and weaknesses, how to develop the best possible training plan using your power meter as a training tool, and how to use your power meter effectively in racing. We have updated the information on power-meter features and software to help you make the best possible decisions about what to purchase. We also introduce the concept of Fatigue Profiling in this book, which will allow you to choose the correct tactic in a race or spirited ride. Fatigue Profiling, along with Power Profiling, will help you expose the exact weaknesses that you need to work on in order to become even more successful.

Since the first edition was written, we have learned more about triathlon as well, and we have dedicated an entire chapter to this unique event. You will learn how best to incorporate power training in the bike leg of triathlon (and even how to use GPS devices in your running) to maximize your effort. We have also added new information on BMX, track racing, cyclocross, and ultra-endurance mountain biking. You'll learn key workouts to do on the cyclocross bike in order to be better prepared than your competition, and you'll learn strategies used by the world's best to improve your mountain biking.

Developing a training plan using power can sometimes be challenging, but we have further developed our "16-Week Threshold Improvement" plan and added an "8-Week Peak Performance" plan. These plans illustrate how power will help you become a better cyclist. It's quite possible that one of the two is a good fit for your training goals. To complement these plans, we have supplied a menu of workouts to use on a daily basis, which will guarantee that you are training at the correct level.

Peaking at the right time has been an elusive "art," understood by a few elite coaches and racers but hard to grasp by others who could hope to achieve it only through trial and error. Power-meter technology takes much of the mystery out of this aspect of training and racing, and in this edition we will teach you how to create the form that you want on the day that you want it. To that end, we'll explain how Chronic Training Load and Acute Training Load interrelate with a proper taper. Balancing your training stress is key to making sure that you peak on the exact date that you want to, and with the tools we give you in this second edition, you no longer have to just hope that things will work out.

Whatever your specialty in cycling, you will learn exactly how to apply the latest power-training principles to your own situation in order to create the watts when and where you want them. We encourage you to dig deep into this book, and we are confident that it will become your reference guide to training with a power meter. Refer to it again and again as you see your cycling abilities improve.

The power is in your hands now.

—*Hunter Allen and Dr. Andrew R. Coggan*

# Acknowledgments

We would like to thank the many people who have helped our book become a reality. First and foremost, we thank our respective spouses, Kate and Angie, without whose support and help on the home front this book would still be on the drawing board. Our parents deserve a big thank-you as well for supporting our dreams in cycling and beyond.

Many thanks to Kevin Williams, Gear Fisher, Donovan Guyot, Dirk Friel, Joe Friel, Ben Pryhoda, and Jeffrey Hovorka, who have all played a large role in the creation and support of the TrainingPeaks WKO+ Software, which really started it all for us.

Thanks to Leslie Klein and Uli Schoberer at SRM, Siegfried Gerlitzki and Gabi Allard at ergomo, Alan Cote for his help with the Polar power meter, Jesse Bartholomew at PowerTap, Jim Meyers at Quarq, Clark Foy at Metrigear, John Hamman at iBike, and Paul Smeulders for his help and hard work with the Intellicoach software.

A huge round of applause goes out to Sam Callan of USA Cycling, who has supported us from the beginning and has played a large role in helping to get the knowledge of training with a power meter out to all the coaches at USA Cycling. Thanks also to all the members of the Google groups wattage forum, who have inspired us to think more critically about training with power and, without a doubt, have contributed greatly to this book. Richard Wharton gets a big pat on the back for his undying support and great help with all the requests we made of him. Thanks to Richard Sawiris of Wheelbuilder.com for the many hours spent fiddling, machining, and customizing the PowerTap BMX wheel. Thanks to Rich Strauss and Patrick McCrann for their input on using power meters in triathlon. Thanks to Tim Cusick for his undying wisdom and great leadership. Thanks to Gary Hoffman for insisting that his 10-second sprint power was more important than his 5-second, which led to the creation of the Fatigue Profiling concept. Thanks to Becky Lambert for her editing and help with the workout menus. Charles Howe also deserves a great big thank-you for all of his work on the "FAQ for Power-Based Training" and for letting us use his Variability Index and comparison of power meters.

Thanks to Steve Karpik, Gavin Atkins, Jeremiah Bishop, Dean Golich, James Mattis, Frank Overton, Pam Maino, Sam Krieg, Dave Jordaan, Dave Harris, Dr. Dennis Ryll, Dr. Sami Srour, Joey D'Antoni, Jeff Labauve, Dr. Jim Martin, John Verheul, Bill Black, Dr. Dave Martin, and Bernie Sanders, who kindly let us incorporate some of their power data into our analyses.

Thanks to everyone who helped us along the way—from those who supported us in the feed zones of our races, to those who challenged us in the lab, to those who helped us develop new ways of implementing our training ideas and theories. Without a doubt, this book is the sum of many contributions, and we thank all of our friends.

Finally, thanks to the team at VeloPress: Renee Jardine, Kara Mannix, Jessica Jones, Dave Trendler, Kathy Streckfus, and Jen Soulé. They truly work behind the scenes in the production and promotion of every book and deserve a very big thank-you!

# Introduction

This book is designed to help you learn the step-by-step process of using a power meter for performance improvement. Though power meters have been around for a relatively long time—indoor power meters, or ergometers, first appeared in the late 1800s—recent technology and advances have made them available and accessible to a wide range of athletes. The most significant advances in power-meter technology have come about in the past fifteen years, but even today many cyclists don't know how to use them effectively. It used to be the case that knowledge about training with power meters was a secret closely guarded by top coaches and a few select, elite athletes. Our goal is to demystify the tools and techniques used by those people in the know in order to help a wide range of cyclists tap into cycling's best technology and, consequently, achieve peak performance in their training and racing. This book is geared for everyone from the recreational cycling enthusiast to the professional cyclist and also includes multisport athletes.

## HOW WE GOT OUR START

Coauthor Andrew Coggan, an exercise physiologist, first began working with ergometers in the early 1980s in his exercise physiology lab. Creating testing protocols that used specific workloads (wattage), he learned how carbohydrates work in the body and how blood-lactate levels affect an athlete's performance. He eventually wrote more than fifty scientific papers relating to the subject. As a talented cyclist himself, Andrew often took advantage of indoor ergometers to improve his own training and racing—with great success. With the introduction of a less expensive mobile power meter in the late 1990s, he began to collect even more data while racing and training outdoors. From what he had learned in the lab, he knew that this tool would benefit cyclists training in the "real world" by quantifying the demands of racing, by improving pacing, and even by tracking fitness changes. Soon, however, it became clear that this tool would provide many cyclists with more information than they could handle. Andrew set out to create a schema of training with a power meter and began teaching the coaches at USA Cycling how to use this schema, much of which you'll find in *Training and Racing with a Power Meter*.

Coauthor Hunter Allen, an elite-level cycling coach and a former professional cyclist, is the owner of the Peaks Coaching Group. He has been coaching endurance athletes since 1995 and has worked with several athletes who were early adopters of power meters in the late 1990s. As their questions about training with power multiplied, he realized he needed to explore the technology further. In 2003, Hunter Allen, Andrew Coggan, and Kevin Williams developed TrainingPeaks WKO+ Software, a valuable program that helps athletes analyze workouts, compare race data, and track progress. Hunter Allen is now known as one of the world's experts in training and coaching with a power meter, having analyzed thousands of power-meter files and successfully coached hundreds of athletes using power meters.

Now, years later, we can say with confidence that power meters are here to stay. Professional cyclists have demonstrated the value of using power meters both in training and in racing. The number of cyclists using them increases with every racing season. Power meters have become far more accessible, both in price and in practice, and the software that demonstrates their usefulness keeps getting better. There's never been a better time to incorporate power into your training.

## HOW YOU CAN GET STARTED

A power meter is probably the best tool ever developed for a cyclist who wants to reach new thresholds of achievement. By recording a second-by-second diary of your ride, a power meter can help you uncover hidden areas of weakness that never would have come to light through the use of a heart rate monitor or simple cyclometer. The ability to record the data from your ride and later download and analyze those data is the key to the power meter's usefulness.

Far from being just another gadget on your bike, the power meter is a tool that can track your improvements over any period of time. Would you like to compare this week's hill repeats to last week's? How does your best twenty minutes of effort from this year compare to your best twenty minutes from two years ago? Do you want to see if your average cadence has changed over the past three years? With a power meter and a few clicks of the mouse, you will be able to answer such questions.

Power meters can make the difference between a mediocre season and a successful one. Chapter 1 explains how using a power meter could make a difference in your own training. Chapter 2 delves into the equipment and available software. What is a power meter, and how does it work? What are the main features to look for in purchasing a power meter? If you haven't already purchased a power meter, this analysis should help you select the one that is best for you.

Chapter 3 will teach you how to find your functional threshold power and introduce the different training levels, and Chapter 4 will show you how to use a power meter to identify your strengths and weaknesses as a cyclist. You'll find some sample workouts in Chapter 5, all of which are based on wattage—time trials, hill climbs, interval training, and so on. These workouts further explain the goals of the power-based training levels.

Chapter 6 is where you will begin to learn how to interpret the data from your rides. There are plenty of sample graphs to illustrate the important concepts that you can explore using your power-meter software. Chapter 7 continues this theme, explaining how to use Normalized Power, Intensity Factor, and Training Stress Score to look deeper into your data. In Chapter 8, we see the real value of these concepts as we look at how to create and time your peak fitness using your power data.

Although the focus of this book is not on training, Chapter 9 presents two case studies on training with power. You will see how the workout menu in Appendix B can be used in your own training, and you will get a better understanding of how to develop your Power Profile and build fatigue resistance specifically where you need it most.

Chapter 10 explains what the data will mean over a longer period of time. For example, you can use the power-meter data to track long-term changes or compare races from year to year. Again, we'll give you concrete examples of how you can use your power-meter software to reach your goals.

Triathletes benefit tremendously from power meters and the insight they provide into effective pacing. Chapter 11 tells you how to train properly for both long- and short-distance events and also includes some key racing advice.

Chapter 12 goes into the specifics of using the power meter to reach your peak performance in racing. Chapter 13 discusses other cycling disciplines and how to effectively use a power meter in cyclocross, BMX, track, and ultra-endurance events. Finally, Chapter 14 summarizes the important steps.

There is a lot of terminology and technical jargon in this book. If you are anything like us, you'll love it. For the moments when you can't keep the terminology straight, use the Abbreviations (pages xvii–xviii) or the Glossary (page 313) to sort it out.

In Appendix B, you'll find more than 65 sample workouts sorted according to training level. These are just a starting point. After reading this book and figuring out your own Power and Fatigue Profiles, you'll undoubtedly want to write a few workouts of your own.

Again, this book is not a training manual—it will not explain the nuances of peaking or go into the details of exercise physiology. There are many great books that go over these concepts in detail. The goal of this book is to teach cyclists at every level of ability that training and racing with a power meter is not hard to do. You do not need a Ph.D. in exercise physiology to understand what the data mean. Furthermore, you do not have to be an elite racer to benefit from the technology the power meter offers. If you are a cyclist with an interest in improving your cycling, this book is for you, whether you have a power meter already or you are just considering purchasing one. Any athlete can benefit from being challenged to think critically about training and coming to a better understanding of the essential components that comprise peak performance.

# Abbreviations

| | |
|---|---|
| **AEPF** | average effective pedal force |
| **AT** | anaerobic threshold |
| **ATL** | Acute Training Load |
| **ATP** | adenosine triphosphate |
| **bpm** | beats per minute |
| **C** | cadence |
| **Cat. I, Cat. II, etc.** | Category I, Category II, etc. |
| **$C_dA$** | cyclist's aerodynamic drag |
| **CPV** | circumferential pedal velocity |
| **Crr** | cyclist's rolling resistance |
| **CTL** | Chronic Training Load |
| **CX** | cyclocross |
| **FTHR** | functional threshold heart rate |
| **FTp** | functional threshold pace |
| **FTP** | functional threshold power |
| **IF** | Intensity Factor |
| **J** | joule |
| **kJ** | kilojoule |
| **LT** | lactate threshold |
| **m/s** | meters per second |
| **MAOD** | maximal accumulated $O_2$ deficit |
| **MFQA** | Multi-File Quadrant Analysis |
| **MFRA** | Multi-File/Range Analysis |
| **MLSS** | maximal lactate steady state |
| **MMP** | Mean Maximal Power |
| **MTB** | mountain bike |
| **NP** | Normalized Power |
| **OBLA** | onset of blood lactate |
| **PCr** | phosphate creatine |
| **PMC** | Performance Manager Chart |
| **RM** | repetition maximum |

| | |
|---|---|
| **RPE** | rate of perceived exertion |
| **rTSS** | running Training Stress Score |
| **SX** | Super Cross |
| **TRIMP** | training impulse |
| **TSB** | Training Stress Balance |
| **TSS** | Training Stress Score |
| **TT** | time trial |
| **VI** | Variability Index |
| **W/kg** | watts per kilogram |

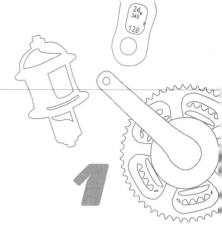

# Why Train with a Power Meter?

**At cycling events and triathlons,** in bike shops, velodromes, and anywhere else cyclists and multisport athletes gather, the power meter has become the topic that everyone wants to discuss. The consensus is the same: For cyclists, training with power is the next big step in achieving peak performance.

In our work in coaching and exercise physiology, we have seen the benefits of training with a power meter firsthand. Using a power meter can take your training to a new level and allow you to fine-tune your training program. Simply put, the power meter allows you to quantitatively track your fitness changes, more easily define your weaknesses, and then refocus your training based on those weak areas. It can be an impetus for change in your training program.

Even riders who have been racing for many years and think they "know it all" are likely to benefit from a power meter. Hunter has found this to be true again and again, even with masters riders who have been cycling for twenty or thirty years. Phil Whitman, for example, a masters 60+ rider, had seen many advances in cycling over the years and was hesitant to adopt the power meter, thinking it unlikely that it could help him improve further. However, he gave it a try and found that his power meter did help him improve. "I have seen all the little 'gadgets' that have promised improvement, and most have come and gone," he said, "so when Hunter asked me to purchase a power meter, it took some convincing. However, now that I have used it for a full season, I don't need any more convincing. I know it really helped me this year in focusing my training for specific intervals, pacing in breakaways, and also in time trials, plus it's been exciting to actually see my progress quantitatively for the first time in thirty years of racing."

By installing a power meter on your bicycle, you will gain access to more data than you can now imagine. True, the benefits accrue only when you know what to do with all that data and how to interpret it using the power-meter software. This has been a problem for many power-meter users: Seeing the graphs of all the data from your ride may seem daunting at first. That is why we have devoted Chapters 6 and 7 to explaining how to extract the information necessary to focus your training and track improvements. You also will need to understand how to implement new wattage-based workouts in your training regimen and when and how to make changes in your training. Chapters 3, 4, 5, 8, and 9 will teach you how to train effectively with a power meter and use this new technology to achieve your performance goals. By learning some simple steps, you will be well on your way to training with a power meter effectively and expertly. We are going to help you take this "fancy" bike computer and turn it from an expensive toy into a tool to be utilized completely. Truly, this is what a power meter is: a tool to be used to improve performance.

Here, we will survey the benefits that you can look forward to when you take the simple steps to improvement that are presented in this book. The benefits are many, but they generally fall into four main categories. These can be expressed in four brief phrases that sum up what you can do when you know how to use the power-meter technology properly:

- *Know Thyself:* A power meter supplies a great deal of information about your ride, and these data will enable you to identify your strengths and weaknesses.
- *Work Together:* A power meter communicates detailed information to your coach and teammates in a way that will enable everyone to work together more efficiently.
- *Focus Your Training:* With this information at your fingertips, along with good coaching and teamwork, you will identify appropriate training goals and methods.
- *Achieve Peak Performance:* With better information, better communication, and better training, you will be positioned to do your best in cycling.

As you can see, these four areas are interlocked. They build on each other. Without the data that the power meter provides, analysis of your ride, communication with your coach and teammates, and development of a training plan all remain limited to guesswork. With the data as a basis, you can move to a whole new level in all these areas.

However, let the old-timers be warned: If you do not use a cyclocomputer or heart rate monitor now, or if you are unwilling to change the way you train, then training with a power meter might not be for you. It will take some time and effort on your part, using your home computer and adjusting your training paradigm, but in the end, if you are serious about training and going faster, then a power meter will help you reach your peak performance.

Here, in more detail, are some of the reasons why.

## KNOW THYSELF
### Record Your Effort

Power meters record massive amounts of data that you can download after your ride. By literally creating a second-by-second diary of your ride, you will be able to see exactly how strong you were as you "stomped" up that hill, whether you should have eaten more snacks or rehydrated yourself better along the way, whether you had the right gearing on your bicycle when you hit that "wall" 50 miles into the ride, and so on.

A power meter records your effort from both a cardiovascular viewpoint (heart rate) and a muscular viewpoint (watts). The watts that you are able to produce are what drive the bicycle forward. Your heart rate is your body's response to the pressure you are exerting on the pedals, and by being able to quantify the exact training "dose," you will be able to better understand all the other aspects of your training and racing. You will know exactly how much time you've spent in your wattage training zone while riding. You will be able to highlight the areas of your ride where you need the most practice, concentrating, for example, on intervals, hills, sprints, or attacks during a race. By reviewing your data after the fact, you will know with certainty whether you completed your training goals or need to revise your training methods.

### Add Meaning to Heart Rate Monitoring

Heart rate monitoring alone does not tell you how much you are improving on your bicycle; it just tells you how fast your heart is pumping. Your heart rate may be affected by factors that have little to do with actual performance, however, and using only a heart monitor could easily trick you into believing a false conclusion about your fitness, mislead you about your performance, or even undermine your confidence.

Your heart rate is influenced by your level of hydration, by the air temperature, by your core temperature, by how well you slept the night before, by the level of stress in your life, and other factors. The rate at which your heart can pump depends on so many factors that sometimes you really are better off not knowing your heart rate when training or competing, and going on your "perceived exertion" instead. Although heart rate monitors can be valid and useful tools—athletes have been training with them now for more than twenty years, and certainly this has improved the level of fitness of many athletes—heart rate is just one small piece of the puzzle. How fast your heart is pumping is a response to a stimulus, whether that is you being chased by a bear in the woods, your level of anxiety before that big presentation at work, or the exertion required to push harder on the pedals as you try to latch on to the tail end of that winning breakaway. Think of your heart rate as being similar to the rpm dial (tachometer) in your car. The more you step on the gas pedal, the higher the rpms go.

How does a power meter add more meaning to heart rate data and thus allow you to improve your performance? A power meter measures your true rate of work (power), that is, how hard you are pushing on the pedals. Power is the amount of horsepower your car engine uses to cruise at 60 mph. You are the engine for your bike, and a power meter tells you how much power you are exerting in the form of watts. By comparing your heart rate response with the power output, you may find there are days when your heart rate is telling you to slow down, but your power meter is telling you to speed up because you are not making those muscles work hard enough to really create a training stimulus. Your heart is a muscle, just like any other muscle in the body, and it gets tired, too. This means that if, for example, you've been training hard for seven days, your heart rate may be lower than normal for a given wattage while you are riding. If your heart rate is normally 165 beats per minute (bpm) when you are riding at 280 watts, then after seven days of hard training it may only be 158 bpm at 280 watts. This does not necessarily mean that you should not train that day, however, because clearly you are still getting training benefits. It's highly probable that you would still be able to do the same amount of watts, or nearly the same amount, as when you were fresh at the beginning of the block. Your wattage will be the key to knowing when you truly need a rest day.

### Track Fitness Changes

Gaining the ability to track change in performance is possibly one of the most exciting reasons to train with a power meter: Over time, you will know with certainty whether your fitness is improving and by exactly how much. Is all this hard work really worth it? Are you really getting faster? Will doing all those dad-blame intervals really help you get over that last hill in the Tuesday-night group ride with the leaders?

Since you will be able to download your information directly after your ride, you will easily be able to see the differences between today's effort and the same ride last week, and the week before, and so on. Since your fitness changes continually, and you will have different strengths and weaknesses from one month to the next, it's essential to see on a regular basis exactly where you are in the bigger picture of the season. With power data, you will be able to find out whether your lactate threshold is improving, for example, or whether you are making improvements in your anaerobic capacity, and then make appropriate changes to your training regime. You will be able to look back on previous data and see how long it has taken for you to achieve a new level of fitness, which will enable you to set realistic goals. On the other side of the coin, it is also important to know when to take a rest to avoid overtraining, and this is also one of the great uses of a power meter. By tracking the overall training stress, using a method such as Training Stress Score (TSS), you will be able to make more accurate decisions about your training load.

### Analyze Your Race

Using your power meter during a race and analyzing the data later is a great way to gain an objective view of your race performance. You can use the data to examine the demands of the racecourse and to determine what would have been needed to finish well. In fact, often your best data will come from races, as you always go harder in races than in routine training.

Sometimes the most interesting data you can gather will come from a race in which you got "dropped." You can review the power-meter file, much in the same way that a football coach would review a videotape of a game, to see what changes are necessary to avoid similar problems in the future. During a very hard stage in the Gila Stage Race, for example, one of the athletes whom Hunter coaches was dropped on a particularly hard part of the climb. In reviewing the post-race data, Hunter was able to pinpoint other races in which he had been dropped from the lead pack and then compare these very critical times with each other. He found that whenever this racer had to pedal at a slower cadence than 70 rpm while producing watts at his threshold for more than five minutes, he was dropped. However, Hunter also found many cases in which the cyclist was able to stay with the same athletes at and above his threshold wattage as long as his cadence was over 95 rpm. As a result, they changed the gearing on his bike so that the largest cog had twenty-seven teeth instead of the standard twenty-three. This allowed him to "spin" at a cadence of over 100 rpm on the steepest climbs, thus maximizing his ability to produce watts based on his body's physiology. This rider benefited immensely from this change, and for the rest of the year he was able to stay in the front group of riders.

A power meter can also help you determine when you are using too much energy in a race. Could it be that you are pedaling "too much"? From the thousands of power-meter files that Hunter has analyzed, he has found that the racers who consistently win are also the ones who do not pedal as much as the rest of the peloton. How can this be? Well, the best racers just sit in the pack, watch, wait, and hide from the wind, conserving their energy. These aren't the guys who are sitting out front driving the peloton down the road for hours on end. The winners are the ones who pedal less than the rest, but when they do pedal, watch out, because they pedal harder than the rest of the pack.

In this same vein, a power meter can tell you when you "burned a match"—that is, performed a very hard effort (you have only so many matches in your "matchbook" to burn)—or whether you used too much energy in parts of the race that were not decisive. Maybe you made a tactical error in a race but didn't realize it. By analyzing the data, you can replay the race in your head while viewing your power-meter file, and understand exactly what it would have taken to make the winning break or the decisive split. Then you can take this information and use it to better focus your training.

### Pinpoint Your Strengths and Weaknesses

Ultimately, armed with this new information, some simple testing protocols, and experience with your power meter in a variety of races and training rides, you will begin to get a clearer picture of your specific strengths and weaknesses. Before the advent of power meters, cyclists had to guess at their strengths and weaknesses, and many times these guesses were wrong. Guessing can hurt your ability to improve. With a power meter, you will be able to find out whether you need to work on changing the gearing for your bike or on building your muscular strength.

Learning what your weaknesses are may not always be pleasant. Finding out that you are a Category I racer in your best 5-minute power, but a Category IV racer in your best 20-minute power, may be exciting for a track racer, but it would be a bit of a disappointment for a road racer desperately trying to improve. However, you cannot improve until you know what your weaknesses are. Each racer is different, and each racer has different goals. Just knowing your strengths and weaknesses will make a big difference in the focus of your training. What will happen if you have to do 105 percent of your threshold power for more than three minutes? Will your lungs feel like they're about to explode, or will this be easy for you? With a power meter, you can analyze your performance and training to find out what your natural talents are and where you need improvement.

## WORK TOGETHER
### Improve Interaction with Your Coach

Coaches love power meters and the information that they provide. Once a coach starts using a power meter with athletes, he or she will almost never go back to the old way of doing things. The information from the power meter is clear and concise, and it is right there on the computer screen—an objective set of facts that can't be denied. That is why most coaches who have worked with power meters will work hard to persuade all their cyclists to use them. Plain and simple, using a power meter brings you and your coach closer together.

Tim Cusick, coach for the Peaks Coaching Group, explained, "Dose and response is the key communication that goes on between coach and athlete, and power training gives us the ability to be truly analytical about our dose and response communications." With power training, Tim can "prescribe doses in clear, measurable standards" and "clearly understand the athlete's response to the prescribed dose." This leads to "greater effectiveness in reviewing daily training schedules, better assessment of progress through more in-depth discussion, improved analysis, and better result tracking over time to ensure we are meeting our goals."

With the data that you collect with your power meter, your coach will discover things about you and your riding abilities, both positive and negative, that he or she would not otherwise have been able to figure out even by racing with you. Your coach can then use these data to improve your training plan. He or she will be able to react more quickly to changes in your fitness and will be able to make adjustments to your plan accordingly.

One of the primary ways a power meter aids the coach/athlete relationship is that it improves communication between the two parties. With a power meter, there can be no "hemming and hawing" about what is going on with your fitness or whether you are on the right path. Instead, where you are with your training, and whether you are doing the workouts correctly or not, will be fairly clear-cut. Your coach will be able to see instantly what you are doing in races and training rides, and he or she will be able to make more useful suggestions for further improvements.

A power meter also should increase your accountability—that feeling you get of having to be "responsible" to someone for your training. You will know that your coach is going to see that you did only five out of the ten prescribed efforts as soon as you download and e-mail him or her your weekly data. This can also be a reason not to have a power meter: It's the equivalent of having your coach with you on every ride. A power meter doesn't lie, and sometimes, the truth can be tough to face!

One cyclist who started using a power meter, Sam Krieg, commented on how much this accountability issue helped him. He started working with a coach in his second season of training with power. Later, he said, "Combining both made my training super-focused and my racing the perfect test to see if what we were training created results. Several times during my pre-season training, I would see my workouts on my e-mail and think, 'I can't finish that.' I would start the workout saying to myself, 'When I blow up, I'll just e-mail my coach the power file and let him know I tried but just couldn't pull it off.'" However, most of the time the opposite would happen: "Minute by minute the intervals would come and go and somehow I would still be turning the pedals," Sam said. "More times than not I survived all the intervals in complete disbelief of what I had just accomplished."

One workout in particular stands out. "My coach prescribed doing 50 minutes at my threshold power, with several cadence changes and power spikes," Sam said. "I didn't think I could survive 20 minutes of this workout, much less 50. Slowly the seconds on the computer just ticked away. In the back of my mind, I knew I would have to e-mail this power file to my coach, so I figured that as long as I could sustain the prescribed wattage, I would continue. Several times during the interval I didn't think I could make it another minute, but my power and heart rate were stable so I pedaled on. Fifty minutes later I finished. I had a new 50-minute peak power, and I had mentally grown more in one workout than I had over the past three months."

This mental and physical strength translated into racing strengths throughout the season. "In one early-season race, I made the selection early on, only to get dropped out the back door of an echelon 20 minutes later. I just wanted to kick myself. Struggling to regain some composure, I was able to regroup mentally and reframe the remainder of the race into a 30-minute time trial with threshold wattage as my goal. As demented as it sounds, I was racing for a great power file, not against the racers who were up the road. I struggled for the next half hour just like I did in my winter workouts, racing my power meter minute to minute." As it turned out, Sam caught the break and managed to finish at the front of the remaining riders. "Without having to e-mail that file I would have stopped at my car and called it a day," he said. Sam carried this new level of persistence into the rest of the season: "My placing in races was not half as telling as the power files I had created during those efforts," he said. "I had won on days when I was actually weak and struggled on my strongest days of the year. It's pretty cool to have bad days that are actually great days."

### Improve Interaction with Teammates

The use of a power meter can have a profound impact on how well a cycling team works together. Many times in teams, it is not always clear who should be the leader; sometimes, it's hard to know exactly who is riding the best. When all the team members use a power meter, and with regular testing, coach and riders alike will know exactly who is riding well enough to be a protected leader and who ought to be a worker bee for the race.

While in a race, a very good rider will be able to teach by example exactly where to ride in the peloton to save the most energy. With a power meter, the leader will know just how many watts were needed to make it over the climb in the lead group. In addition, power meters can build confidence in the team when the data show that team members have the physical ability to win. It's right there on the graph if, say, three out of five riders have the necessary fitness to win the race, and having that level of certainty can really propel a team to success.

## FOCUS YOUR TRAINING
### Gain Motivation to Work Harder

As a motivator, a power meter can be very effective. For example, if you are doing a five-minute effort, and you see your average watts drop near the end of the effort, you'll pick it up just another notch in order to achieve your five-minute wattage goal. As long as the goals are set realistically—that is, they are challenging yet achievable—when you are out there training hard and pushing it to the absolute max, seeing those wattage numbers on your power meter can help you eke out just a tiny bit extra. And in the world of a sport that can be won or lost by less than a tire width, that tiny bit extra is significant.

Every athlete strives to eliminate guesswork and wasted time, and in this day and age, it seems that most athletes are too busy to train as much as they'd like. That's why every training minute must be optimized. If you are strapped for time, having a power meter and sticking to the letter of your workout will help you gain a higher fitness level more rapidly, with fewer wasted junk miles and less of your precious time.

### Improve Your Position and Aerodynamics

Your body position is the single greatest factor determining your speed while riding at a specific power output. Why risk the disadvantage of riding in a poor position when you can measure your aerodynamics and discover your fastest position? With some simple tests using a power meter, you can figure out how your current position on the bike is impacting your overall speed and exactly how to change it in order to produce the most watts and the least amount of aerodynamic drag. With the most recent wind-tunnel testing of bicycle frames, wheels, rider positioning, and other factors, it has been found that with improvements in positioning and equipment a rider should be able to pedal at approximately 30 watts less to maintain a given speed. In other words, just by optimizing your position and equipment, you may be able to gain 30 watts of power. This is incredibly significant and represents more of a gain than most cyclists see in an entire year of training.

### Pace Your Efforts

When you are out training, racing, or just riding around enjoying the countryside, a power meter allows you to pace your effort better in order to achieve your goal for that ride. Whether that's simply to finish the ride or to achieve a particular physiological stimulus, using a power meter as a pacing tool can help you to conserve energy when necessary and also to expend energy when necessary.

You can use a power meter on all of your long rides—on ultra-endurance rides, in interval workouts, on hill climbs and time trials (TTs), and so on—in order to get the most out of your effort and avoid overdoing it. Once you know your functional threshold wattage (which you'll learn how to determine in Chapter 3), you can hold to it like glue in a time trial or hill climb so that you will know that you went as hard as you could possibly go. Using a power meter for pacing in time trials is an especially good use of the technology. It can give you a "ceiling" to stay beneath to prevent you from overexerting yourself in the first five minutes of the race. During a race, knowing your wattage helps you to focus, providing a "carrot" when the going gets tough and you are pushing right on the edge of your ability. In mass-start races, pacing is equally important. You can use it in the field in order to conserve your energy until later in the race, and you can use it to judge whether the pace is right for you to attempt a breakaway or to figure out what it will take to win the race.

Randy Weintraub, a highly competitive triathlete, for example, was concerned about the lack of hills near his home and training grounds. His goal was to complete the Ironman Lake Placid in less than ten hours. The Lake Placid race is one of the toughest of the Ironman-distance races. The bike course is very hilly and includes a substantial 2-mile climb. Randy needed to figure out exactly how many hills he would have to ride up, and how long each one was, and then go back and train for those racecourse demands at home in Long Island, New York.

Randy went up to Lake Placid and rode the entire bike course for the race at very close to his goal wattage and recorded it with his power meter. First, he wanted to assess whether his goal wattage was actually correct. He had never done this triathlon before and was unsure whether he could maintain that wattage for the entire 112 miles and then still have something left for the 26.2-mile run. After his ride, he downloaded the information and found that he indeed had averaged his goal wattage. Based on his level of fatigue at the end of the bike leg, he surmised that he had enough energy left over for his run. Then, using old-fashioned pencil and paper, Randy simply counted the number of hills that took more than two minutes to complete along the course. With this information, he began to seek out new training routes near his home that would mimic that course as closely as possible. When he did not have a long enough hill, he would simply ride into the wind to simulate a longer climb. He also programmed the number of hill repeats, along with the wattages he would need to reach in order to achieve a peak performance, into his indoor trainer.

### Create a Mobile Testing Lab

A power meter allows you to test your fitness on a monthly basis so you can quantitatively see where you have made improvements and where you still need work. For serious racers, using a power meter in this way can even eliminate some of the costly testing that formerly was possible only at a lab, since they now have the mobile equipment installed right on their bikes.

A power meter measures changes in your ability to move the bicycle down the road. It tells you how much force you are putting into the pedals, not just how hard your cardio-vascular system is working. By testing your skills regularly, you will better understand your potential for improvement, and you can avoid overtraining. We all undergo changes in our fitness in different areas. Some athletes improve more quickly with shorter efforts, whereas others improve more quickly with longer efforts. With proper periodic testing, you can see exactly which physiological systems are improving and then determine whether it is the right time to focus on a particular area of training.

As Andrew often tells the athletes who consult with him: Training is testing; testing is training. Make every training session a peak performance.

### Enhance Indoor Training

With a power meter, you can use your indoor trainer to the fullest extent. One of the first things you will learn about using a power meter on the road is that your wattage will have a high degree of variability. Your wattage fluctuates on a moment-by-moment basis depending on the conditions, and sometimes this is not the best way to train. On an indoor trainer, without the outside influences of wind, hills, dogs, and so on, you can focus your intervals in exact wattage zones for optimal improvement.

In addition, indoor training gains new meaning when you can compare your intensity with on-road efforts. Indoor training also becomes more interesting, as now you have a new goal and focus to your workout. With the advent of the latest computerized indoor trainers, a cyclist with a power meter can even go out and ride a particular racecourse, come back, and download these data into the trainer to re-create this exact ride indoors. Power-meter data from indoor training sessions are also "cleaner" than from on-road efforts, as the massive wattage fluctuations caused by changes in terrain, riding with others, and just the variable nature of pedaling frequency are gone from the power file, making it easier to analyze the periods of effort.

### Quantify Your Sports Nutrition

The entire time you are riding your bike, you are expending energy based upon how much work you are doing. Knowing how much work (in kilojoules) you are doing while riding is important. If you know your kilojoule expenditure, you can easily estimate your kilocalorie usage (almost a one-to-one ratio), and this can help you determine when you need to consume additional calories or cut back.

Your production of watts will be drastically reduced if you allow your energy stores to become depleted, so making sure that you are eating often enough, and getting the right number of calories, can be a very important factor in the quality of your workout or race. By knowing your energy expenditure on the bike, you can more accurately plan your post-exercise meals to the exact kilocalorie. This especially helps if you are trying to balance your energy intake with your energy expenditure to maintain body weight during heavy training.

By eating to replenish your expended glycogen fuel stores and possibly packing in more, you should be able to recover faster from training sessions and be ready to train harder, sooner. Sami Srour, for example, a highly competitive recreational cyclist, had been planning for many months to ride a local metric century with his club. However, in each of his practice runs, he ran out of energy toward the end of the ride and had to stop at a convenience store to refuel. This routine impacted his energy levels for the next two days, and consequently, the quality of his training for those days suffered. From his two practice runs, however, Hunter figured out his total expenditure of energy in kilojoules for the entire ride.

## What Is a Kilojoule?

Almost all current power meters report the amount of work you have performed in joules in addition to measuring and recording your power in watts. Joules (J) and kilojoules (kJ) are therefore a measure of energy expenditure, or work performed. Here in the United States, however, this is usually measured in kilocalories, or Calories (1 kilocalorie, or large Calorie [with a capital "C"], is equal to 1,000 small calories [lowercase]).

By definition, there are 4.184 kJ per Calorie, so at first glance it would seem that to determine your energy expenditure using power-meter data, you would simply divide your total work in kJ by 4.184. However, this is not correct because power meters measure external work production, not the amount of energy needed to perform that work. Most of the energy expended during cycling is actually converted into "waste" heat that must be dissipated to the environment, with only a portion available to actually turn the pedals. The relationship between work performed and energy expended depends upon your thermodynamic efficiency (i.e., your ability to process food and convert it into energy) when cycling, which, for most trained cyclists, is on the order of 20–25 percent.

Thus, to estimate your energy expenditure (in Calories, or kilocalories) from the amount of work performed, using a power meter, you would need to first divide your total work in kilojoules by 4.184, but then multiply this result by either 4 (if efficiency is at 25 percent) or 5 (if efficiency is at 20 percent). These conversion factors tend to simply cancel one another out, such that you can also take the value for the total work performed in kJ as an estimate of your energy expenditure in kilocalories (or Calories). Although the exact relationship between kJ and kcal is not one to one, it probably is not worth worrying about any error this assumption creates, since an individual's efficiency can only be readily determined in a laboratory setting, and can vary depending upon the intensity and duration of training, environmental conditions, and other factors.

Then he broke the ride into segments and determined the number of kilojoules used in each segment, which allowed us also to set goals for Calorie intake in each segment. Sami was able to determine when to eat, and how much to eat, during each section of the ride, and also how much electrolyte replacement drink to use. With this new information, Hunter was also able to create a post-ride recovery protocol that gave Sami the correct levels of carbohydrates, proteins, and fats to maximize his recovery, so he would be ready and able to complete his next day of training.

## ACHIEVE PEAK PERFORMANCE

With all of the benefits that a power meter offers—greater knowledge about your riding, improved communication with your coach and teammates, and better focus for your training efforts—there is no reason why you should not be able to reach your fitness goals and achieve your peak performance at events.

Every top cycling performance in recent years has been aided by the use of power-meter training technology. In everything from the Tour de France to hour records, track records, Human-Powered Vehicle (HPV) records, mountain-bike racing, and even BMX racing, the best cyclists have used power meters to determine not only the exact physiological demands of hard stages but also exactly how powerful they are as cyclists and how they stack up against their peers. Controlling training with the latest in computer-aided scientific training tools used to be achievable only by the top cyclists in the world with the biggest budgets. Now almost any serious cyclist can gain access to the same data that the pros have and execute their workouts to the same exacting precision.

Training with a power meter is about results. Just training with a power meter is not going to bring you success. It's not the power meter that does the work: You must do the work. If you want to go faster on your bike by just throwing money at it, then go get a nicer set of aero wheels, a lighter frame, or the latest carbon-fiber widget. But eventually, you will have to push harder on those pedals if you want to ride faster. Training with a power meter is worth doing only if you are willing to work at it.

If the information you have about your training is limited, then you are limiting your ability to improve, and you are ultimately limiting your success. Using a power meter may seem intimidating at first, and learning the details of testing and training with it may entail some frustration, but give yourself some time, and soon you'll be on the way to training more effectively and efficiently using a power meter. If your training and cycling are to change (that is, improve), then you must be willing to change first. This book is about how to change your thinking about training and racing and how to gain a clear understanding of what needs to be done in order to achieve your goals.

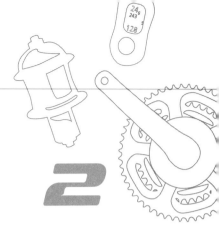

# Power Tools

**Once they hear about the power meter and its benefits**—and see their competitors racing and training with power meters on their bikes—the first thing that most cyclists and triathletes ask is this: Which one is right for me? Other questions quickly follow:

Which type of power-meter technology is the best?

What about price? Which model is most cost-effective?

Do all the models have the same features and ease of use?

Which type has the fewest problems?

Does the athlete have to have a degree in computer science or exercise physiology to understand what all those graphs mean?

Let's briefly explore the power meters on the market today and the pros and cons of each. For a checklist of features by company, see Table 2.1 later in the chapter.

## POWER HARDWARE

The power-meter hardware is currently very different from one company to the next. That is because the companies currently offering power meters all take very different approaches to the technology. Basically, the six methods have resulted in: (1) a crank-based integrated system, (2) a hub-based integrated system, (3) a chainstay-mounted sensor, (4) a bottom-bracket sensor, (5) the "opposing forces method," and (6) a pedal-based force sensor.

Advances in wireless technology have had a big impact on power meters over the past few years. DynaStream, a Canadian company acquired by Garmin in late 2006, has developed a "common language" by which power-meter measuring devices can communicate to a computer head unit. This ultra-low-power wireless transmission protocol, called ANT+, has many applications beyond cycling. But what makes it such a valuable feature for cyclists and power-meter manufacturers is its interoperability. The ANT+ technology essentially divorces the power-measuring device from the computer head unit. This allows cyclists to "mix and match" the devices they use.

In other words, you no longer have to use a computer head made by the power-meter manufacturer. An ANT+ SRM crank can talk to an ANT+ Garmin 705 computer, an ANT+ PowerTap hub can talk to an ANT+ iAero computer head, and an ANT+ MetriGear Vector pedal can talk to a PowerTap Joule computer head. All but two of the power meters described in this chapter operate on the ANT+ network—which is something you should take into consideration when purchasing a power meter. For the most part, you can now select a head unit with the features you like without worrying about whether the same company's power-meter offering is your top choice. ANT+ has given consumers the ability to choose their ideal power-meter system.

One downside to this new transmission protocol is that the power-meter manufacturers are constrained by the broadcast message definitions, which can limit the types and amount of data that can be sent and received by the computer heads and power-meter measuring units. In practical terms, this limits the data that can be received by the ANT+ head units. For example, let's say a future power meter is able to capture pronation or supination data from the foot of the cyclist (that is, determine whether the cyclist is pressing down on the inside or outside of his or her foot on the pedal). That would be a very interesting piece of the puzzle, but we would not be able to capture these data within the existing ANT+ communication protocol. Unless the ANT+ protocol expands to capture additional channels of data, or a new head unit is created that allows for raw data capture, the limits of the ANT+ protocol could hinder future product development.

### SRM

The first commercial power meter—and the one that started this technological revolution in cycling—was made by the SRM company (Schoberer Rad Messtechnik) in Germany. Ulrich Schoberer, a medical engineer, brought the measurement of wattage to the world in a product that can be used by the masses.

Schoberer developed his first prototype in the 1980s by taking old cranks, cutting off the "spyder" portion (the part between the right crank arm and the chainrings themselves), and then replacing it with a power meter, about the size of a small saucer plate, that consisted of a series of embedded strain gages. The front chainrings were then mounted onto this plate to allow for the measure-

SRM crank

ment of power as the rider applied force to the pedals. As this force is transmitted, there is a twisting, or torsion, within the plate; the strain gages measure the amount of twisting from normal. This torsion information is then sent to a microprocessor in the bicycle computer and converted into wattage. Uli Schoberer spent the ensuing years working on his ideas and building newer, more advanced models. The first models that he put on the market were incredibly pricey, reaching upward of $10,000 per unit. Greg LeMond was one of the first Americans to use a power meter. Already known for forging his cycling successes partly through the adoption of new technology, he again paved the way here.

The SRM crank power meter, called the SRM Training System, which includes a crank and chainrings, has set the standard by which all other power meters are measured. It certainly has been around the longest, has been updated and improved the most, and tends to be one of the most reliable of the power meters. Measuring wattage in the spyder of the crank is both convenient and logical, as the data incorporate the force from both legs and force is measured in the place where it occurs, right at the crank. Since the power meter is built as one unit with the crank itself, it is integrated into the bike, becoming just part of the equipment. It is also very weatherproof. SRM has models for road riders, track riders, and mountain bikers and also offers a scientific version for the lab. The company also produces indoor spin bikes for use in fitness and performance centers. The computer controller, called the PowerControl, is rechargeable—and, in the newer models, ANT+ compatible—and it mounts in front of the handlebar at handlebar height. The rider can view all the necessary data while riding, including wattage, heart rate, cadence, elapsed time, and clock time, on the same screen. This allows the rider to keep track of his or her effort while riding and pace the effort accordingly. The PowerControl can be customized to a certain degree—for example, you set your own recording rates for later download, with intervals of up to sixty seconds between saved data points, and you can choose among different options for the display.

Each time the rider uses the SRM, he or she must create a "zero-offset," or "zero-point," to ensure that the wattage will be zero when there is no load on the power meter. This is a five-second procedure and can be done throughout the ride with no detrimental effects to your data. Since the SRM uses a strain gage to measure torsion, the readings can be susceptible to changes in temperature, so if you are riding and all of a sudden the temperature changes drastically and your watts appear to be different from what you would normally expect, then the SRM might need to be "re-zeroed." Since the metal of the crank will change in size with changes in temperature, it is important that you achieve a zero-offset when the crank is at the same temperature as the ambient outside temperature. This only tends to be a problem when a bike goes from 70 degrees Fahrenheit while parked inside a house to a much colder 40–50 degrees outside. It is a good idea to park your bike outside for ten or fifteen minutes before beginning your ride so that the metal of the crank and the strain gages can adjust to the correct temperature.

The SRM computer is one of the best-designed models available, in large part due to more than twenty years of development. The ability to set your own intervals increases the amount of data that can be recorded, and the SRM has a very user-friendly method of marking these intervals while riding. (When you start [and stop] an interval, you press the "set" button on the PowerControl, and this creates a small "time stamp" in the data, so that when you download the data to your PC, you will see immediately where the interval started and stopped.) The handlebar mount of the SRM is one of the best and most secure; the screen is easy to read but unobtrusive, and because it is positioned flush and just in front of the handlebar, it is somewhat protected from damage in crashes. The rider can also easily review data while riding and thus determine when it is time to head home and when it is time to do one more hill repeat.

One of the disadvantages of the SRM is its cost. It continues to be the most expensive of the power meters. Another drawback is that the battery inside the power meter itself must be replaced by the factory when it is dead, and this requires some downtime while you mail it in and wait for it to be returned. SRM has a U.S. service center in Colorado Springs, so the turnaround time isn't unbearable.

Another problem that occurs with the SRM is that over time, as the strain gages age, the watt measurements are susceptible to "drift." If this occurs, the SRM may need to be recalibrated to ensure its accuracy. The user can do this at home by following the recalibration procedure laid out in the SRM manual, but this can be confusing for the first-timer. The SRM also does not output torque in the controller for download. This is unfortunate because the meter has the best ability to receive the correct torque of any model on the market. With torque for download, cyclists and coaches could analyze how torque loads might be affected by different types of cycling efforts.

### PowerTap

The PowerTap is a complete rear hub for the back wheel of a bicycle that houses a power meter. The hub contains a "torque tube" with strain gages similar to those used by the SRM. These strain gages measure the torsion inside the hub as it twists from the load that is applied to the pedals by the rider. The bicycle chain wraps around the cogs on the hub and, as it moves, causes small twists in the hub itself. This torque is measured and then converted into wattage at the PowerTap computer.

The wattage that is measured in the PowerTap is the wattage that is actually getting to the road, as it has to go through the drivetrain from the crank. This causes the power to be about 5–10 watts lower than what would be measured by the SRM at the crank. The PowerTap takes measurements sixty times per second, averages these figures over a one-second time period, and then records the data at intervals as short as one second.

The PowerTap was created back in 1997 by a company called Etune, which consisted of a group of four partners with a vision for the future of cycling technology. Unfortunately, they were not able to keep the cash flow going while they dealt with the issues that come up when developing hardware of this nature. Graber Products Group, now known as the Saris Cycling Group, bought the company in 2001 and has since made considerable investments in improving the unit. Along with the standard wireless ANT+ PowerTap computer head, which mounts on the handlebar, PowerTap has introduced a new, larger computer head called the Joule, expected to be released in 2010, that has more memory, carries out more functions (including displaying Training Stress Score™, Intensity Factor™, and Normalized Power™, explained in some detail in later chapters), and includes firmware that can be upgraded.

The wireless ANT+ hub and computer head unit are the flagships of the PowerTap product line, but a lower-cost wired version (the PowerTap Comp) is still available and for the price is a great option for someone looking to get into power training. Saris has expanded its product line over the years. The release of the SL hub in 2004 brought the company into a leading role in the marketplace, and with the release of the Joule, it should maintain that position for some time. Saris Cycling Group has continued to respond to customer requests and gain market share.

Joule head unit

PowerTap has also partnered with Zipp wheels to produce a disc-wheel solution for time trialing and has a mountain-bike (MTB) hub compatible with disc brakes. As power training continues to grow in popularity, more and more mountain bikers will start riding with power meters. The PowerTap MTB disc hub should help many mountain bikers gain a better understanding of the demands of their sport and how to train. There is also a solution for track riders: A company called Wheelbuilder provides a custom conversion for the PowerTap for use in track riding. Complaints about the weight of power-meter components and their durability in different kinds of weather are now a thing of the past, and bike geeks

PowerTap hub

will continue to enjoy the appearance of the PowerTap units, which incorporate carbon-fiber bits. The design of the computer head unit is also a plus, as it makes it easy to take advantage of the unit's features and review efforts while training.

One disadvantage of using the PowerTap is that you are locked into the wheel into which the hub is laced. If you want to use your super trick wheels for racing, you'll need to get an additional hub for racing and then keep your standard wheel for training.

Saris continues to make strides in hub innovations and also with its software. In 2004 the company released a spin bike, and in 2010 it released the PowerBeam Pro trainer with the PowerTap technology integrated into each, allowing participants in indoor spin classes and training indoors to have the benefits of using wattage data. This continued innovation in new markets should help Saris to gain market share in both the fitness and indoor trainer worlds. Although the pricing on PowerTap power meters is very competitive, the PowerTap is still a sizable investment, especially considering the fact that you may still have to build a wheel around the hub.

### Polar Electro

The Polar Electro power meter, which is compatible with the Polar Power Output Sensor W.I.N.D., features a unique and interesting measuring system. The technology was developed in New England by J. J. Cote, Alan Cote, and John Croy, who then sold their patent to Polar. The Polar system measures chain tension via a chainstay-mounted sensor that detects vibrational frequency; just like a guitar string, a chain vibrates faster as its tension increases. This frequency is translated into an amount of force, which is then multiplied by chain speed, as measured by a magnetic sensor mounted on the rear derailleur, to derive power output:

Power (in watts, or W) = chain tension (N) × chain velocity (in meters per second, or m/s)

Although there have been reports of inaccuracies with the Polar system on the road, the system's good accuracy and consistency have been demonstrated in numerous tests against the SRM and PowerTap systems. On an indoor trainer, the Polar system may or may not be accurate in all gears. Reports of inaccuracies with the Polar system are often related to improper installation of the system's chainstay-mounted sensor, which some riders feel is difficult to install correctly. Accuracy issues with the Polar system are not due to bumps in the road, but to an interference signal that occurs with some combinations of gear ratio, power, and cadence. The Polar unit also has many little wires that can easily be broken and wrapped around the drivetrain, as one sensor must be mounted onto the derailleur. Polar has improved its original system, and the W.I.N.D. sensor has been improved to reduce the chance of the fragile wires being cut or broken. However, Polar has not adopted the ANT+ transmission protocol standard (as of late 2009), and this prevents the user from mixing and matching power components.

Polar RS800CX watch

The Polar system does have advantages. One is that the computer portion of the unit can also double as a wrist-mounted heart rate monitor. Polar offers a dedicated bike computer as well, along with many accessories that can be purchased separately and added onto the model, such as a global positioning system (GPS) and a cadence and speed sensor. This makes the Polar unit highly versatile and possibly a good choice for multisport athletes or other cyclists who cross-train in running and swimming. Polar is best known for its heart rate monitors, and these top-of-the-line monitors have so many features that many riders will buy a Polar power meter for these alone. Most owners of the Polar unit were owners of the heart rate monitors first and bought the power option later. The Polar unit is one of the least expensive of the units reviewed here and the most attractive to the triathlon market. A multisport athlete can use the unit for measuring and recording heart rate during a swim, have wattage measurement for cycling, and then use the heart rate data again when running, thereby having a steady supply of data throughout a race or training session and for review afterward. The Polar watch is weatherproof and durable, though unfortunately the power unit has had some problems with these two essential features.

The Polar power meter also contains an altimeter; however, all of the ANT+ power meters on the market also can capture and record altitude, since they can be used with any head unit. Having access to accurate elevation information can be useful, particularly for cyclists living or racing at higher altitudes. Altitude data can help you gain an understanding of how wattage and altitude relate to each other. It's also handy to have altitude readings when reviewing downloaded data because it makes it easier to track where you were in a ride or race when the other data were recorded.

The Polar model measures power at forty samples per second (i.e., it samples vibrational frequency several hundred times per second, chain speed slightly less often, and calculates power values forty times per second) and then averages these measurements over a complete pedal revolution for display to the user. The Polar display is updated every two seconds, with a displayed number captured and stored every second, which is an improvement from earlier models that recorded only at five-second samples.

Although the Polar power meter has some drawbacks, it provides the user with a decent level of power information in a small, lightweight, and relatively inexpensive unit. For those who are interested in power-measuring technology, Polar Electro is definitely a company to watch.

### ergomo

The ergomo was invented by Siegfried Gerlitzki as a way to measure the twisting of any spindle or axle. An avid cyclist, Gerlitzki set out to create the unit when he realized that wattage could easily be measured by a sensor placed on a bicycle's bottom bracket. The ergomo has been in and out of production since 2001 in very limited quantities. The company has had its share of small business start-up difficulties, including a bankruptcy, new owners, and another bankruptcy, but finally has come out of the ashes and is expected to begin production again in early 2010. Ergomo introduced a smaller, lighter computer head in 2006, and that, combined with the fact that the power meter is built into the bottom bracket of the bike frame, has been a plus. Ergomo has many loyal users and continues to sell new systems.

The ergomo measures power differently from the units reviewed above in that it measures the torsion, or twisting, of the bottom-bracket spindle. Every time you pedal, there is a small amount of twisting that occurs on the spindle, similar to the twisting that might occur with a wet towel if you twisted it into a whip. The ergomo contains an optical sensor that allows it to measure the distance the axle twists, and from this distance it calculates the torque and the corresponding watts that are being applied in order to make that caliber of a twist. A small wire coming out of the bottom-bracket shell sends the signal to the handlebar-mounted computer for calculation and display to the rider.

This system allows the rider to use any square taper (ISO), Octalink, or ISIS crank and any wheel set; however, this means it is not compatible with the newer "outboard"-bearing two-piece cranks or with the BB30 standard. The buyer must be willing to use the older three-piece standard cranksets, which are becoming harder to find.

By placing the power-measuring device essentially inside the bicycle frame, the ergomo's designers came up with a way to protect the sensor itself from the elements and simultaneously created the potential for a future mountain-bike unit. This innovation also could very well position ergomo to retrofit the many indoor spin bicycles that exist and enable the company to bring power training to the masses in gyms and fitness clubs.

The ergomo Pro computer, though not ANT+ compatible, allows the user to view the power data in watts per kilogram once his or her weight is entered into the computer. It also enables the rider to see Training Stress Score and Intensity Factor while riding. The Pro computer has coded heart rate capability and an altimeter as well. One feature that will be appreciated by everyone who trains with intervals is the capability of displaying watts in real time and average watts on the same screen while in interval mode.

The most obvious disadvantage of this system is that because the sensor measures power at the bottom-bracket spindle, it measures only the side that twists—the left side. Since the right side of the spindle is attached to the drivetrain, there is no significant twist on the right side. As a result, the ergomo can measure only the rider's left leg power accurately. The computer takes the power out-

ergomo bottom bracket

put from the left leg and doubles it in order to get the wattage. Although initially this may seem to be a problem, in reality it has not proven to be a significant one for the majority of users. Only riders with a large discrepancy in the strength of their legs would have inaccurate readings from the unit. Every rider has a small discrepancy in leg strength, but for the major-ity of people, this discrepancy is less than 5 percent; when on the bicycle, this would result in a difference of less than 10 watts between what an ergomo unit would report and what the SRM or PowerTap would report. If a rider does have a large discrepancy in leg strength—from an injury, for example—then the ergomo can be adjusted to provide the rider with a very accurate picture of his or her wattage.

The ergomo captures from 72 to 144 samples per second and then averages those num-bers before saving the result. The ergomo Pro computer gives a rider the ability to change the recording intervals, which is standard now among all the power-meter computer units, and also can "smooth" the rate of display on the head unit. For example, the rider can choose to record intervals at 1, 2, 5, 10, 15, or 30 seconds. The wattage updates over a rolling aver-age, quickly (one pedal revolution) or slowly (eight pedal revolutions), a feature that is espe-cially helpful when a cyclist is trying to maintain a small range of wattage during training.

Some concerns with the ergomo have been the longevity of the bearings inside the sen-sor, how easily they can be replaced, and the cost of replacement. Ergomo includes a war-ranty on the unit for up to 10,000 miles and states in its literature that the bearings may last longer than 15,000 miles. Whether this will be the case with all owners remains to be seen.

If ergomo can continue to produce a high-quality product and provide good customer ser-vice, then the company should be able to rebound very well from its recent financial difficulties.

## Quarq

Quarq Technology out of Spearfish, South Dakota, has come into the marketplace with a crank-based power meter that is similar to the SRM offerings. With the advent of the ANT+ transmission protocol, Quarq chose to focus on producing the power meters themselves and has so far opted out of the computer-head-unit business. It's the first company in the in-dustry to take this stance; in fact, Quarq does not even produce its own cranks but instead retrofits existing compatible cranks for use with its power meter. Created by Jim Meyer, an engineer with a Ph.D. from the Massachusetts Institute of Technology, Quarq Technology offers its power meter, which is called the CinQo, in both compact and standard bolt patterns, allowing users a choice in chainrings. The CinQo is compatible with many high-end carbon-fiber cranksets, such as Full Speed Ahead (FSA), SRAM, and Specialized, and Quarq continues to build newer models for other cranksets as well. Cyclists who already own compatible cranksets can send them to Quarq for retrofitting. For cyclists with other types of cranksets, this limitation would pretty much preclude using the CinQo until a later time when Quarq expands its capabilities.

Quarq CinQo

Quarq Qollector

Nevertheless, the CinQo does have advantages, including some unique features. The power meter is well designed, with the machined and anodized, highly durable spyder containing the electronics for capturing and transmitting the power-meter data to an ANT+ computer. Battery replacement is simplified by a "Q-pod" that sits on the outside of the spyder in what looks like a single contact lens holder that contains the battery. Untwist the top, replace the battery, and off you go again. This innovative method eliminates frustrating downtime and minimizes loss of precious data. The power meter is very lightweight, adding only about 85 grams to a normal crankset; operates at 60 hertz; is highly weatherproof; and retails for a relatively low price. All of these features, combined with the fact that it's built into essentially the crankset itself, make the CinQo an attractive choice.

Since there is no Quarq computer head unit, the user is free to purchase any ANT+ compatible computer head, the most popular being the Garmin 705 computer. This proves to be both an advantage and a disadvantage for the Quarq company. On the one hand, it means that Quarq's designers can focus all their development efforts on the power meter itself. On the other hand, it limits the product's usefulness because the data available to the user are constrained by the capabilities of the computer head unit itself. Quarq has attempted to get around this problem by introducing a new product called the Qollector.

The Qollector is merely a "black-box" data-recording device, mounted on the backside of the front fork of the bike, that intercepts the ANT+ broadcast transmissions. It records all the data packets without down-sampling any of the data available from the ANT+ sensors, but these data then can be downloaded later via an integrated USB plug. The whole device is basically a USB drive and ANT+ radio hooked together—a very simple and clean concept. It allows the user to record all of the data being transmitted while using a very simple ANT+ bike computer that just reads and displays wattage, which can be of great benefit after a highly intense cycling event where focusing on the terrain ahead is of utmost importance, such as a track race, a mountain-bike race, or even a BMX race.

Quarq Technology came into the power-meter marketplace relatively late, but it turned this new-kid-on-the-block position into an advantage. The company has been able to avoid some of the pitfalls that the other power-meter manufacturers have fallen into while at the same time working closely with the ANT+ protocol developers to ensure perfect compatibility.

### iBike/iAero

When Velocomp introduced the first iBike power-meter computer back in 2006, it was recognized as an ingenious device. It contained a highly calibrated altitude sensor, an accelerometer, and a pitot tube for measuring the opposing air pressure caused by ambient wind and the cyclist's movement down the road.

The critical (and patented) innovation of the iBike is that its sensors measure opposing forces instead of applied forces—the measurement methodology used by all other power meters. The practical implication of this approach is that the iBike's critical sensors are located in its computer head instead of on the wheel, crank, or chain, making the iBike small, lightweight, and relatively inexpensive. The iBike's sensors, combined with a highly sophisticated algorithm that computes opposing forces based on sensor readings, allow the iBike computer to determine wattage in a completely novel manner.

The iBike is really about the measurement of force:

$$\text{Power} = \text{Force} \times \text{Speed}$$

Later chapters will have more to say about this basic equation. Here, suffice it to say that cyclists apply force to their bike pedals in order to overcome the forces of resistance that are opposing their forward motion (hill climbs, wind resistance, rolling resistance, acceleration, and so on). Direct-force power meters measure the forces applied by the cyclist; the iBike is the first power meter to measure the resistive or opposing forces working against the cyclist. According to Newton's Third Law, resistive (opposing) forces must *exactly* equal applied forces. The iBike uses Newton's Third Law by taking sensor readings of opposing forces and combining the resulting data with some key inputs from the user (weight, an aerodynamic coefficient, and a rolling resistance number) to come up with the applied forces that determine the cyclist's power.

It's hard to believe that relatively simple measurements of opposing forces, mathematically processed in a small bike computer, could tell you exactly how hard you are pushing down on the pedals in real time. Surprisingly, however, the iBike does a very good job of it and in most situations produces the same numbers as a direct-force power meter mounted on the same bike on the same ride (more on this below).

As is the case with any successful new technology, the iBike has gone through continuous and rapid improvement. There have been two major revisions of the iBike since its introduction in 2006, and the company has responded very well to consumers' requests. The Generation III iBike series (iSport, iPro, and iAero) was released in late 2008 with excellent improvements. While all three models are ANT+ compatible, only the iAero offers wireless ANT+ capability as a standard feature.

The iAero is Velocomp's top-of-the-line unit. In addition to power measurement, it offers the rider "Snapshot $C_dA$": the ability to see $C_dA$ numbers on-screen whenever the rider coasts for a few seconds. ($C_dA$ is the cyclist's aerodynamic drag.) Also, and somewhat surpris-

iBike/iAero

ingly, the iAero works in tandem with competitors' wireless direct-force power meters to determine what Velocomp calls "Continuous $C_dA$." With a direct-force power meter, $C_dA$ is reported on the iAero's screen continuously, even when the cyclist is pedaling.

A measurement related to Continuous $C_dA$ is something that Velocomp calls "Time Advantage." Time Advantage is the amount of time you "pick up" when you go into a more aerodynamic position than your standard riding position, or the time you "lose" by sitting up and taking a drink of water. This figure is displayed continually on your iAero, and at the end of a ride you might learn, for example, that you "saved" over three minutes because you held yourself in a more aerodynamic position for a certain period of time.

In order for the "Continuous $C_dA$" and "Time Advantage" measurements to work, the iAero must be paired with an ANT+ direct-force power meter. This makes the iAero one of the most sophisticated bicycle computers available to date, as it is able to work with every ANT+ direct-force power meter on the market. It also means, however, that the iAero requires an ANT+ direct-force power meter in order to obtain its real-time measurements. (See sidebar on determining $C_dA$ and Crr using the iAero.) If the iAero is mounted on a bike with an ANT+ Sport direct-force power meter, the power displayed on the iAero's screen comes from the direct-force power meter, and the iAero records power data from both the direct-force power meter and the iAero, along with windspeed and slope

## Determining C$_d$A and Crr Using the iAero

When utilized in conjunction with another power meter, the iAero version of the iBike power meter provides the unique capability of calculating C$_d$A (the product of the dimensionless coefficient of drag, C$_d$, and frontal area, A, measured in square meters, or m$^2$) and Crr (the dimensionless coefficient of rolling resistance) from the power data provided by the other device and the windspeed, acceleration, elevation, and environmental measurements provided by the iAero's sensors. The cyclist simply has to perform an out-and-back ride of at least 2 (and ideally 4 or more) miles on a reasonably straight, low-traffic road. The beauty of this feature is that you don't have to be a math whiz or even a techno geek to make use of it. The C$_d$A and Crr measures simply give you some hard data to refer to when you are experimenting with anything that might change your aerodynamics, such as body position on the bike or different clothing.

The values for C$_d$A and Crr that best match the iAero's calculated power to that measured by the reference power meter are iteratively determined by the iBike software, taking into consideration the mass of the rider and the equipment being used, the assumed efficiency of the drivetrain, and the like. In our experience, the values for C$_d$A and Crr determined in this way are not as precise as those obtained by the use of more formal field-testing procedures (see "Precision in Aerodynamic Testing" in Chapter 12), even when testing is carefully performed on a fairly well-sheltered road under conditions of limited wind. This may be due to the propagation of small errors in the measurement of each of the numerous variables required to perform the calculations. Even so, the convenience of the approach is such that many different aerodynamic positions or pieces of equipment could potentially be compared in a relatively short amount of time. It is also at least theoretically possible that windspeed data and/or elevation data from the iAero could be used to further refine the C$_d$A estimates obtained using formal testing (for example, using the regression approach), or to extend the ability to perform such measurements with reasonable precision under a wider array of conditions and on a wider variety of courses.

In addition to the "calibration ride" procedure described above, when used along with another ANT+ compatible power meter the iAero provides real-time estimates of C$_d$A, when you are either coasting ("Snapshot C$_d$A") or pedaling ("Continuous C$_d$A"). Theoretically, a rider could use this feedback to improve his or her aerodynamic position by making small changes at any point during a ride and observing the result. Unfortunately, the variability of the measurements, combined with the manner in which the data are displayed (in a small font to only two decimal places, with no smoothing options available), makes it difficult to detect the sorts of subtle changes likely to be of interest to an experienced competitor.

information—something that no other power-meter CPU provides. As a result, some iAero users take their direct-force power-meter CPU off their bike and use the iAero as the display and recording device.

For some it's hard to call the iBike's iSport, iPro, and iAero computers "power meters" in the conventional sense of the term. The iBike is not a direct-force power meter, and it can be a bit mind-bending to adjust to the concept and implications of opposing-force measurement. That said, the iBike, when stacked up against a direct-force power meter, reports some very impressive numbers. Indeed, many of the questions that critics of the original, first-generation iBike raised have been addressed through improvements in firmware to handle differences in road surfaces as well as temperature changes and complicated setup requirements.

One thing that seems nearly impossible for the iBike to account for is the fact that a rider never remains in the same position on the bike throughout the ride. The initial calibration for the iBike measures the $C_dA$ of the rider in his or her "usual" ride position and uses that number as part of its opposing-force calculation. Adjustments in one's position can cause the iBike to report wattage differences, however, particularly when the rider deviates substantially from the usual riding position. Wattage readings during these periods can climb 5 to 10 percent higher than other power meters report for the same stretch of the ride.

The iBike is the lightest and least expensive power-measuring device on the market, and based on its popularity it seems clear that it meets wattage-measurement needs. When combined with an ANT+ direct-force power meter, the iPro and iAero become two of the best options for consumers to use as head units. Beginners to power training and pro cyclists in tough racing situations alike can benefit from seeing real-time $C_dA$, as it does increase the rider's awareness of aerodynamic efficiency. Although Velocomp doesn't make a direct-force power meter, it has nevertheless brought the lightest, most technologically advanced power-measuring computer and ANT+ compatible head unit to the market.

### Garmin/MetriGear

In the fall of 2010, Garmin acquired upstart MetriGear in order to make a move into the power-meter market. Their offering is expected to be available in mid-2011 and is a pedal-based power-meter system called Vector. Officially a "force" meter and not a "power" meter, Vector calculates wattage based on the forces created by the rider at the pedals, but in addition to the vertical forces it also captures the lateral forces, which allows the cyclist to see whether the location of applied forces throughout the pedal stroke might make a difference in the wattage output. If extensive field data can be collected across riders, it may be possible to develop a new set of metrics to aid cyclists, coaches, bike fitters, post-injury physical therapists, and others to identify and correct fit issues.

Garmin/MetriGear's approach is to measure the applied forces on both the left and right pedals simultaneously throughout the pedal stroke. With its custom sensor and electronics system embedded in the spindle of the pedals, the Vector's measurement of forces and power calculations are precise. It can easily be moved from bike to bike and is lightweight. Initially, however, the Vector will be compatible only with Speedplay pedals (it is mounted in the hollow center of the pedal itself). The force data will be transmitted on the ANT+ network to an ANT+ computer head, so it can be paired with any of the ANT+ computer heads on the market. The jury is still out on the robustness of the design, the longevity of the sensor, and other performance measures of the device. After its release, look for reviews in cycling magazines and on websites.

## ANT+ COMPATIBLE HEAD UNITS

The independent head units reviewed below are the only ones available as of early 2010. As adoption of the ANT+ protocol continues to grow, we expect there will be more bike computers that read ANT+ power-meter transmissions.

### Garmin

Garmin has been the leader in this area, and rightly so, since it owns the ANT+ wireless protocol and has been successful in getting it universally adopted. As of early 2010, Garmin has three different head units that read ANT+ power meters. The Edge 705 is the flagship of the Garmin line and includes mapping functions (a mapping chip is available as an option), highly customizable screens, and a simple interface with an easy handlebar- or stem-mount setup. The 705 also allows the user to create a "course" and then load it into the 705 for turn-by-turn directions. It has definitely become the most popular ANT+ computer head among power-meter users, and Garmin's sponsorship of a pro cycling team shows that the company is dedicated to expanding its visibility within the cycling world.

Garmin Edge 705

Garmin also has a smaller, less expensive unit, the Edge 500, that does not include mapping functions or the ability to load a course but still has all the other features that make it possible to train properly with a power meter. It attaches to the bike stem or handlebars. Finally, Garmin offers the Forerunner 310XT, a wristband device designed for runners and hikers, which also reads ANT+ enabled power meters.

Although it is not designed specifically for cyclists, the 310XT still has a few cycling-friendly menus to choose from and display. This makes it an excellent option for triathletes, who can use it to track an open-water swim, see their bike wattage, and then measure running pace.

### Specialized

Specialized has dabbled in bike computers off and on over the years and has come back into the market in 2010 with its ANT+ compatible computer, the SpeedZone Digital Pro. This is a simple computer that reads wattage and records data. The nice thing about this computer is that it is simple and easy to use, and sometimes simple is better.

### Trek

When Lance Armstrong asked Trek for a lightweight computer that would read his ANT+ direct-force power meter and also record and store data for his Tour de France comeback, Trek responded, designing the Node computer around these simple requests. Trek also now installs a Duo Trap sensor in the chainstay of the Trek Madrone bike frame (which captures the speed info and sends it to the Node). The company has thus entered the world of bicycle computers in a big way, providing a nice alternative for ANT+ direct-force power-meter users. This device is similar to the Specialized computer in that it is a simple computer and easy to use; however, again you need those data from the download to make the most of power-meter training.

Table 2.1 provides a breakdown and a comparison of power meters on the market today.

### POWER SOFTWARE: HOW A BIKE GEEK'S TOY BECOMES A TOOL

The true usefulness of a power meter comes from post-ride analysis of the data. Understanding the data presented on the display while racing or training certainly has benefits and is worthwhile; however, you will be taking advantage of the power meter's true strength only when you can download the recorded data and sift through the graphs to gain meaningful insights that will help you improve in cycling. Because a power meter records data at sampling rates of possibly many times per second, the sheer volume of information from even a one-hour ride can be overwhelming. The question then becomes: What does it all mean? That's where the software comes in. The software that comes with the product should present the facts in an easily digestible manner that allows even the novice computer user to make decisions about training.

Each power meter comes with its own software, and each type has its own strengths and weaknesses. These pros and cons are outlined in Table 2.1; in later chapters we will look at specific charts and graphs and discuss what they mean.

### SRMWin

SRMWin, the software supplied with every SRM power meter and freely downloadable on the Web, is a well-designed program that allows the user to easily view the downloaded data, create a range around any period of interest, and track fitness changes over time. One of the unique features of the software is that one must know how to use it in order to program the SRM PowerControl and delete old data from it. Although the SRM PowerControl can largely be programmed from the computer head itself, a few functions need to be programmed with the software.

One of the more perplexing graphs provided in the SRM software is found by clicking on the "Analysis" button. Although it looks like something a three-year-old could draw, it is actually a complex graph showing changes in the relationship between heart rate and power throughout any given workout. Once you learn how to use it, however, it can be handy. Another feature not to be overlooked in the software is the "Periodic Chart," which allows the user to track fitness changes over time.

SRMWin's main weaknesses are that it is very "grid-like" in appearance and that it does not allow for the creation of custom charts. It also has a less than satisfactory diary function because it does not provide enough space to write in more than brief comments.

### PowerTap PowerAgent

PowerTap released an updated version of its PowerAgent software in late 2009. The original PowerLink and subsequent PowerAgent software lacked many features that other programs had, such as providing the opportunity to view fitness changes over time, so the new software was created to correct these shortfalls. PowerAgent comes free with the PowerTap computer and allows the user to download data to a computer, configure settings inside the computer head, and update the firmware on the head unit if needed. PowerTap consulted with Dr. Allen Lim in the development of the program, and as a result many aspects of his coaching and scientific philosophies are reflected in the product. The new PowerAgent software contains some charts for historical comparisons and also displays Training Stress Score, Intensity Factor, and Normalized Power.

### Polar Precision Performance

Polar Electro had an advantage in its software development efforts because it is a large enough company to have in-house programmers. This enabled Polar to produce a very polished product. The Precision Performance software has been updated several times and has improved with each new version.

| TABLE 2.1 | | A Comparison of Power Meters | |
|---|---|---|---|
| | | **Specifications** | |
| **ERGOMO PRO** | Measurement location | Bottom bracket (Campagnolo, Shimano OctaLink, ISIS) | |
| | Method | Direct-force power meter: Photointerrupter circuit | |
| | Claimed accuracy | ±1.5% | |
| | Recording interval | 1, 5, 10, or 30 sec. | |
| | Memory capacity | 12–342 hr. | |
| | Calibration | By manufacturer | |
| | Mass (grams) | Bottom bracket with bolts and wires = 304<br>Computer and mount = 100 | |
| | Pedal analysis | No | |
| | MSRP | $1,600 | |
| **POWERTAP COMP, ELITE+, PRO+, SL+, SLC+** | Measurement location | Rear hub | |
| | Method | Direct-force power meter: 4 strain gages | |
| | Claimed accuracy | ± 1.5% | |
| | Recording interval | 1 sec. | |
| | Memory capacity | 7.5–180 hr. | |
| | Calibration | By manufacturer | |
| | Mass (grams) | Hub = 402–624<br>Computer = 39.5–100<br>Mount/wiring = 10–36 | |
| | Pedal analysis | No | |
| | MSRP | $600–$2,100 | |
| **QUARQ CINQO SATURN** | Measurement location | Crankset (SRAM, FSA, Rotor, Cannondale, Specialized, or Lightning) | |
| | Method | Direct-force power meter: 20 strain gages | |
| | Claimed accuracy | ±2% | |
| | Recording interval | 1 sec. (with Garmin Edge unit, sold separately) | |
| | Memory capacity | Dependent on Garmin Edge specs | |
| | Calibration | No | |
| | Mass (grams) | Cranks = 621–815<br>Garmin Edge 57–105 | |
| | Pedal analysis | No | |
| | MSRP | $1,495 (required Garmin not included) | |

| Advantages | Disadvantages | Other |
|---|---|---|
| • Good software (TrainingPeaks WKO+) with many useful analysis tools<br>• Fourth-generation design, major improvements to computer with altitude and coded HR; available in 5 langages<br>• Fully hard-wired system is not affected by electronic or radio interference; allows use of any wheel; up to 30 intervals can be marked<br>• Backlight display for night rides, infrared download along with cable download<br>• Rechargeable battery, with 27 hr. of time, good for 21,000 hr.<br>• Same as Sport; computer can be programmed for multiple bikes<br>• Computer setup can be done from software<br>• Contains TSS/IF/NP inside the computer head; altitude and coded HR<br>• Might be the best solution for MTB | • Large/heavy computer, wired; not ANT+ compatible<br>• Bearings must be factory serviced ($300) every 15,000–20,000 mi.<br>• Not easily moved from bike to bike, only usable by older style 3-piece cranks<br>• Only left leg power is measured due to measurement in the bottom bracket axle<br>• Went out of business in 2008, restarted in 2010; limited production | Major improvements in features, including very robust interval function, and ability to view average and current power in interval mode, along with TSS, IF, NP |
| • Easy to move from one bike to another<br>• Affordable and accurate; upper models have expanded memory (up to 180 hr.); can store only one file but can create unlimited number of intervals<br>• Compact, readable, easy-to-use display; new Joule (2010) computer head has workout summaries and displays TSS, IF, NP<br>• Most hub internals (axle, freehub, and drive side bearings) are user-serviceable without disturbing strain gages and electronics; upper models have beefed-up bearings and large-diameter axles<br>• Wireless feature makes these easy to install; easiest to remove for racing—just swap rear wheels<br>• Measures actual cadence (more accurate than the standard model's "virtual" cadence)<br>• Available in disc wheel, MTB disc, and fixed-gear options<br>• Available in Campy and Shimano freehubs<br>• PowerAgent available in Mac version | • Mediocre software interface<br>• Limits wheel choice<br>• Wheel-based system (not hub itself) is more likely to be damaged in crash<br>• Wired version not ANT+ compatible<br>• Torque must be zeroed regularly<br>• Hub requires modification to be used with fixed gear | Data transmission is through carbon-fiber "windows" in hub shell; electronics are completely contained inside hub; only batteries are accessible from cap |
| • Very durable, completely waterproof (including roof racks and spray washing); 2-yr. warranty<br>• Simple to use; calibrate by pedaling backward<br>• Very cost-effective for lightweight, race-ready system; $1,000 less than comparable SRM systems<br>• User replaceable battery (CR2450)<br>• No limit on wheel choice<br>• ANT+ compatible; allows for any computer head unit; simple to install | • Not made to be moved from one bike to another, but can be done relatively easily with 2-piece cranks<br>• To change cranks and use the same power meter, must be sent back to factory | |

*continued >*

| TABLE 2.1 | A Comparison of Power Meters, continued | |
|---|---|---|
| | | **Specifications** |
| **SRM PROFESSIONAL** | Measurement location | Crankset (SRAM, FSA, Cannondale, Shimano, or Campagnolo) |
| | Method | Direct-force power meter: 4–8 strain gages |
| | Claimed accuracy | ±2.5% |
| | Recording interval | 0.5–30 sec. |
| | Memory capacity | 45 min.–225 hr. |
| | Calibration | By manufacturer |
| | Mass (grams) | 721–1,648<br>Computer = 120<br>Mount/wiring = 30 |
| | Pedal analysis | Extra option |
| | MSRP | $1,945–$4,000 |
| **IBIKE** | Measurement location | Handlebar or stem |
| | Method | Opposing forces: wind, hills, acceleration, friction |
| | Claimed accuracy | ±3% |
| | Recording interval | 1 or 5 sec. |
| | Memory capacity | 13 or 65 hr. |
| | Calibration | Coast down and 2-mile ride |
| | Mass (grams) | Computer = 62<br>Mount/sensors = 30–51 |
| | Pedal analysis | No |
| | MSRP | $199–$799 |
| **POLAR CS/RS 600X** | Measurement location | Chainstay and rear derailleur |
| | Method | Chain speed and vibration frequency |
| | Claimed accuracy | ±5% |
| | Recording interval | 1, 2, 5, 15, or 60 sec. |
| | Memory capacity | 4:57–76:37 hr. |
| | Calibration | No |
| | Mass (grams) | Sensors = 118<br>Computer = 53<br>Mount/wiring = 71 |
| | Pedal analysis | Yes |
| | MSRP | $710 |

| Advantages | Disadvantages | Other |
|---|---|---|
| • Very good software<br>• Time-tested, reliable design; newest PC VII has many updates<br>• Displays rolling average for current wattage<br>• Large memory capacity, can store multiple workouts<br>• No limit on wheel choice<br>• ANT+ compatible; allows for any computer head unit; simple to install<br>• Easy marking of intervals with one push of the "set" button<br>• Also available for MTB, track, and BMX | • Expensive<br>• Not made to be moved from one bike to another, but can be done relatively easily now with 2-piece cranks<br>• Some find display more difficult to read<br>• Daily zero-offset recommended<br>• User serviceable, but factory service recommended every 1,500 hr.; replacement interval for cranks (not including power-measuring unit) is once yearly<br>• SRM crank is slightly more flexible than other models; other cranks are at considerable additional cost; Cannondale and Specialized cranks must come from user<br>• Not useful on tandems<br>• Impacted more by temperature changes than other power meters | Average power display obtained only from pedaling time, but non-zero values (i.e., when coasting) included by SRM software |
| • Very good Mac/PC software; firmware upgradable through software<br>• Third-generation design; accuracy comparable to more expensive brands; ANT+ compatible, so combined with a direct-force power meter it can display aero data<br>• Displays rolling average for current wattage<br>• Large memory capacity; no limitation on number of workouts<br>• No limitations on wheel, crank, bottom bracket choice<br>• Easiest to move from bike to bike<br>• Can measure aerodynamics when paired with direct-force power meter in real time, otherwise available for download<br>• Displays TSS, IF, NP<br>• Displays windspeed, hill slope, elevation | • Requires more calibration steps, including tilt, weight, and coast-down<br>• More difficult to check accuracy<br>• Not accurate during steep turns<br>• Not suitable for MTB and problematic if water gets inside Aero pressure port<br>• Must have "clean" air, so mounting can be an issue for some tri bikes | Least expensive option; regular, free firmware and software updates add features and improvements |
| • If you have the watch already, a cost-effective upgrade<br>• Feature-rich software, and extra hardware features like altitude<br>• Allows use of wheel or crank of your choice<br>• Large memory capacity, stores many workouts<br>• Not affected by temperature<br>• Does not require calibration | • Difficult to move from bike to bike<br>• Small display is hard for some to navigate<br>• Difficult installation (multiple sensors and cables)<br>• Averaged data cannot be viewed during intervals (or "laps"), only at the end of the ride<br>• Accuracy questionable on stationary trainers, possibly from harmonic vibration effects<br>• Not practical on MTB and cannot be used with fixed gear | Display and software give average power for pedaling time only |

Polar's product line emphasizes heart rate data, and this is reflected in its software. Although this is a great strength for athletes who are interested primarily in heart rate, it is a continued weakness in the Polar system for power-meter users, and one that such users will find critical.

The most robust areas of the Precision Performance software are its highly detailed calendar functions and its advanced diary tools. However, for detailed power analysis, the Polar software needs further development.

### TrainingPeaks WKO+

The TrainingPeaks WKO+ Software, formerly called CyclingPeaks, is one of five programs offered as stand-alone, after-market products. The authors developed it in 2002–2003 along with Kevin Williams. The software was renamed WKO+ (for "workout plus") in 2007 and branded under the TrainingPeaks Software product line. Since WKO+ was introduced in 2003, it has set the standard among power-meter users for tracking fitness changes and conducting detailed analyses. (WKO+ Software was used as the basis for most of the art you'll find in this book.)

Along with a variety of charts and graphs, WKO+ offers Quadrant Analysis and scatter graph plots allowing users to understand the neuromuscular demands of cycling as well as their cardiovascular improvements. One of the most popular features of the program is that it allows users to change and create custom charts on the "Athlete Home Page." By doing this, and by tracking fitness progression with the "Mean Maximal Power Periodic Chart," a rider can very quickly decide whether to make changes in his or her training program or continue with a current plan of action. The development of WKO+ also incorporated some new concepts, namely Normalized Power and Training Stress Score, which we will discuss in depth in later chapters.

With the release of version 3.0 in late 2009, WKO+ integrated a feature called "Multi-File/Range Analysis" into the software that allows the user to "create ranges" around important time periods and then overlay those graphs on top of each other for instant comparison. This takes interval analysis to the next level, as it makes it much easier for the user to access information on the positive and negative aspects of each interval, hill repeat, sprint, or repeated climb and then, based on that information, to make decisions about future training sessions. Chapter 6 includes a sample of the Multi-File/Range Analysis used to compare intervals and two performances in the same race. Other examples follow in later chapters.

WKO+ is platform neutral so data from any power meter can be downloaded directly into the software, and it can also import all the file formats produced by the other companies via a simple "drag and drop" onto the open application. As of late 2009, it is compatible with and can directly download data from more than sixty-five devices, including GPS watches and running pods. Thus, old data from a different power-meter software application can be quickly imported. This makes WKO+ a user-friendly and robust system.

There are a few ways that WKO+ falls short. For starters, WKO+ lacks Mac compatibility. However, it is possible to use WKO+ on a Mac even though there is no Mac-specific version. In order to run WKO+ on a Mac, you simply need to utilize a third-party program that allows Windows to run on a Mac. There are many WKO+ users running this setup successfully. (For more information on how to do this, see the FAQs on the TrainingPeaks.com website.)

WKO+ also lacks detailed diary features. This can easily be reconciled through the use of the online service provided at TrainingPeaks.com, as there are many similar features online that allow users to upload and review their power files online. The online interoperability has proven to be very helpful for coaches and athletes, as an athlete can download his or her power file directly into WKO+ and then, with one click, upload the power file from within WKO+ to his or her personal account on TrainingPeaks.com. A coach can then download that athlete's file from within WKO+. Having an interactive component is one of the many strengths of this software: This is one aspect that is currently missing from other programs.

### CyclingPeaks ERG+

Developed in 2004 by Paul Smeulders, ERG+ offers some excellent tools for building ergometer or power versus time training sessions on a CompuTrainer. To do so, the user can draw a series of shapes ("Hat," "Sawtooth," "Sharkfin," or "Wedges") and lines representing the desired target power profile for the workout, using an absolute watts scale, a percentage of threshold power, or any other standard test quantity.

ERG+ can also read on-bike power-meter files to automatically find, measure, and categorize intervals. It then displays the average power, the power trend, and the duration of each "effort" and "rest" phase. This unique feature shows the user whether he or she executed the interval correctly and notes the amount of time spent over or under a targeted goal. This is a useful feature for coach and athlete alike.

The connection between this feature and the creation of a customized workout for a CompuTrainer is where the product really shines. Intellicoach will take your power-meter file from the road and convert it into an erg file, thus easily replicating a favorite ride or race so that it can be practiced indoors. Cyclists can "scale" the workout to be harder as fitness progresses. With the release of version 2.0 of ERG+, CyclingPeaks added the ability to support MultiRider CompuTrainer studio sessions and the ability to build workouts based on specific Training Stress Scores and Intensity Factors that you might want to achieve during a workout.

Since ERG+ was not designed as a complete power-meter analysis tool, it's not fair to compare it with other third-party power-analysis programs. Intellicoach does not provide a way to view fitness changes over time; it also lacks a diary function and some other key ingredients that would make it a complete package. However, it does perfectly what it was designed to do, and for anyone who owns a CompuTrainer, it's an essential piece of software.

### Golden Cheetah

This is a free software package that has been built for Mac OSX and is developed under an open-source license. It depends on work done by power-training programmers in their spare time, and this means that support for the product is minimal and updates are sporadic. Golden Cheetah is compatible with many, but not all, of the power meters and power-meter files, however, and does provide a relatively good set of analysis tools.

### PowerCoach

Unfortunately, the authors were unable to obtain a copy of this program to evaluate it in detail. According to the information presented at the PowerCoach website, however, this program was originally designed for the Mac, and it appears to be quite detailed and graphics oriented. It enables the user to create 3D graphs that can, for example, show cadence in relation to different time periods and wattages.

––––––––

Since we published the first edition of this book, power meters have become increasingly common among cyclists of all abilities. The retail prices are becoming more accessible for cyclists looking to experiment with power. As with any investment in equipment, it's important that you evaluate the features that you are most likely to use to improve your riding. Of course, there are still plenty of us who are bike geeks, pure and simple, and we want to have the best just because it feeds our fascination with cycling.

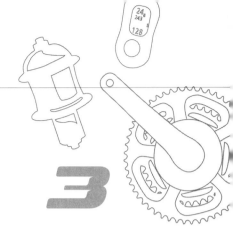

# Power-Based Training: Where to Begin?

***Training with a power meter is not difficult,*** and certainly anyone can install one on a bike. But actually using the equipment, and especially the software, in the way that they were intended to be used will take some work on your part. After purchasing a power meter, one of the most common questions athletes ask is, How do I use this thing? As with any new tool, it will take time for each rider to learn the intricacies of the power meter and to take the steps that are needed to achieve success. Look at it this way: If you were the proud owner of a new Ferrari sports car, would you have to take lessons at the local race car driving school to enjoy it? No, of course not. But doing so would certainly enhance the experience of owning the car. In the same way, you'll get the most out of owning a power meter when you learn how to take advantage of all the features that it offers. By following the first three steps presented in this chapter, you will be able to take the plunge in training with power.

The ultimate reason for having a power meter is to reach your goals and achieve your potential in cycling. Surely, the scientist in all of us wants to experiment with new toys and gear, but that same scientist recognizes that, as cyclists or multisport athletes, using a power meter is quite possibly one of the best ways to get to know ourselves at an even deeper level. The power meter has brought a very complex tool to the layperson, and this complexity has created much confusion and caused many potential users to have reservations about using the technology. Such cutting-edge tools have traditionally been reserved for exercise physiologists in the lab studying the biomechanics of movement and human physiological limits to the *n*th degree. Until now, what they have learned has not been common knowledge. But with power meters becoming more accessible and more popular, all that is changing.

This chapter describes how you can take your first steps in training and racing with a power meter; after reading it you should have a clear understanding of what to do next.

## STEP 1: DATA COLLECTION AND FUNCTIONAL THRESHOLD POWER

The very first thing that you should do, once you have installed the hardware on your bike, is to start riding with your power meter and just downloading the data to get a sense of what, say, 300 watts means in relation to your heart rate, cadence, speed, and so on. You will begin to understand what different wattage numbers mean in the real world, and then associate those numbers with your ride. A downloaded power-meter file is, quite literally, a second-by-second re-creation, or diary, of your ride in graph format. You will begin to see what happened to your power output when you were riding in a crosswind, on a particularly long climb, on a set of short difficult hills, or before and after you stopped for a drink at the convenience store, and all those associations will help you to better understand your cycling. But it is when you go on to the next step that you will be able to get the biggest bang for your training buck, so to speak.

Once you have some rides under your belt, and a sense of how to operate the computer display attached to your handlebar while riding, you should schedule your first testing session. Running the test described below will enable you to begin to determine your training zones and thus allow you to give the correct focus to your efforts. With this first test, you will find out how many watts you can currently produce at your functional threshold power (FTP), establishing a fitness baseline.

It would be a good idea to repeat this threshold test once a month in order to assess your fitness, track performance changes, and decide whether to make changes to your training program based on the results. There are two important things to remember: (1) You should always test on the same stretch of road or on an indoor trainer, and at close to the same time of day and with similar weather conditions; and (2) you should minimize any external influences that would affect your performance, such as stress levels or the amount of sleep you got the night before. This way you can be confident in comparing the results from different tests.

But what is functional threshold power, and why is it important for you to test for it?

### *What Is Functional Threshold Power (FTP)?*

The term "threshold" has become synonymous with the word "confusion" in the minds of many athletes. There are many different words for essentially the same concept: anaerobic threshold (AT), lactate threshold (LT), maximal lactate steady state (MLSS), onset of blood lactate (OBLA), and just plain old "threshold." It seems that there are just as many possible quantitative definitions, with different versions of the concept based on heart rate (HR), blood lactate, wattage, and so on. As a result, even in many scientific articles the authors have to present their own definition to clarify what they are talking about.

For more than thirty years, exercise physiologists have known that the exercise intensity at which lactate begins to accumulate in a person's blood—that is, his or her LT—is a powerful predictor of that person's endurance performance ability. This is because although an individual's cardiovascular fitness—that is, his or her maximal oxygen uptake ($VO_2$max)—sets the upper limit to his or her rate of aerobic energy production, it is the individual's metabolic fitness—that is, LT—that determines the percentage or fraction of this $VO_2$max that he or she can utilize for any given period of time.

The physiological factors determining LT are complex, but essentially blood lactate levels serve as an indirect marker for biochemical events within exercising muscle. More specifically, a person's LT reflects the ability of his or her muscles to match energy supply to energy demand, which in turn determines the fuel "mix" (i.e., carbohydrate versus fat) used and the development of muscle fatigue. Consequently, LT is the single most important physiological determinant of performance in events ranging from something as short as a 3 km pursuit to a stage race lasting as long as three weeks. This is especially true when LT is expressed in terms of power output, which also takes cycling efficiency into account. Because the effort that is experienced by an athlete when exercising at any given intensity is dependent upon his or her power output relative to power at LT, this parameter provides a physiologically sound basis around which to design any power-meter-based training program.

However, few athletes have ready access to lactate testing on a regular basis. What's more, even those who do are still generally dependent on the person performing the test to first design an appropriate protocol, and then to correctly interpret the results. This is actually more difficult than many realize, and the data obtained are rarely more accurate or precise than those obtained using much simpler field tests (since the best predictor of performance is performance itself). Thus, while blood lactate testing does have a role to play in the preparation and training of cyclists, for routine purposes we prefer to rely on a far more pragmatic approach, which is to simply use a power meter to determine a rider's functional threshold power (FTP). FTP is the highest power that a rider can maintain in a quasi–steady state for approximately one hour without fatiguing. When power exceeds FTP, fatigue will occur much sooner, whereas power just below FTP can be maintained considerably longer.

### Determining Functional Threshold Power

So, how do you go about determining your functional threshold power using a power meter? There are a number of different ways to do this, each of which has its advantages and disadvantages, but all of which provide very similar estimates of threshold power. In order of increasing complexity, these are:

1. **Power Frequency Distribution Charts.** A good estimate of your FTP can often be obtained by simply uploading all of your training data into your power-meter software and then examining the power frequency distribution chart (see Figure 3.1). Because exercising above threshold power is quite strenuous and there is a limit to how long you can do so, there will often be a rather noticeable drop-off above this point in the graph. (This same approach works even better for identifying an individual's spontaneously achieved maximal heart rate, thus reducing or even eliminating the need for formal testing.) Of course, this method works best if the time period examined includes some high-intensity training and/or racing, which serves to make the distinction between sub-threshold and supra-threshold efforts more distinct. Also, sometimes the drop-off in time spent above threshold power is more apparent when the width of each power "bin" is reduced from the default of 20 watts to a smaller value, such as 5 or 10 watts.

2. **Routine Steady Power.** Another way to estimate your threshold power without performing any formal testing is to simply evaluate the steady power that you can routinely produce in training during longer hard efforts, such as intervals or repeats

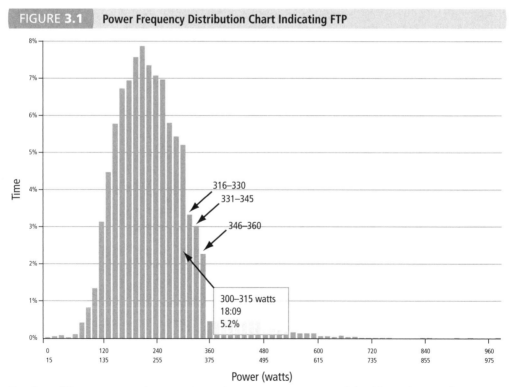

**FIGURE 3.1**     **Power Frequency Distribution Chart Indicating FTP**

*The drop-off in power occurs between 300 and 315 watts, 5.2 percent of the ride, and 316 and 330 watts, where frequency drops to 3.2 percent.*

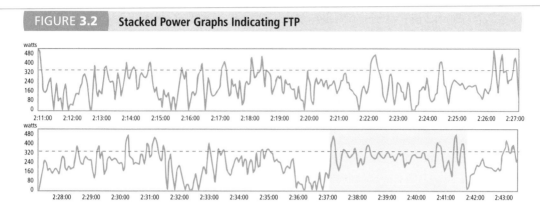

| FIGURE 3.2 | **Stacked Power Graphs Indicating FTP** |

*Placing a "gridline" in an area of the graph where power is relatively constant (see highlight, 2:37–2:41:45) could help you in determining FTP. In this case, FTP is estimated at 325 watts.*

aimed at raising LT, or during longer climbs. In most power-meter software, perhaps the easiest way of doing this is to add a horizontal gridline to a "stacked" graph of an appropriately chosen workout (or race), and then look for places where your power is quasi-constant for some minutes at a time (see Figure 3.2). You can then adjust the gridline up or down as needed to home in on the best estimate of your functional threshold power.

3. **Normalized Power.** Perhaps an even more precise way of determining your threshold power, yet one that still does not require formal testing, is to use power-meter software to examine your Normalized Power (a concept explained in greater detail in Chapter 7) during hard mass-start races of approximately one hour. Since TrainingPeaks WKO+ Software automatically calculates Normalized Power even if you haven't yet entered a value for your threshold power, using the program first to analyze several race files may be the quickest way to derive a good estimate of your threshold power.

4. **One-Hour Time Trial.** Since, by definition, the best measure of performance is performance itself, the most direct estimate of your FTP will be obtained by simply doing a one-hour time trial. By examining the horizontal graph of the data from such a trial in your power-meter software (perhaps with a little smoothing applied), you will be able to quickly tell whether your effort was well paced or whether you started out too hard and then faded. In the latter situation, the data for average power will somewhat underestimate your true threshold power.

5. **Critical Power.** Finally, those who are more mathematically inclined may wish to perform formal testing to determine their "critical power" as described in the scientific literature. Briefly, this approach consists of plotting the total work performed (in

joules) during a series of relatively short (i.e., between 3 and 30 minutes), all-out efforts against their duration (in seconds), then fitting a straight line to the data points. The slope of this line is critical power, which corresponds quite closely with FTP as determined by using any of the previously described methods. See the sidebar on "Critical Power" for more detail.

With all these different ways to test your FTP, you may wonder which one to start with. We believe that the best way to begin is to just go out and do a ride specifically designed to find your threshold, such as the one described in the next section. This is without a doubt the first big step in your new adventure in training with power.

## Critical Power

A number of equations have been presented in the scientific literature describing human power output as a function of time, some derived from modeling based on the underlying physiology, and some simply derived empirically. One of the simplest and most robust, though, is the original "critical power" concept first proposed by H. Monod around 1960. Various formulations of this idea have been presented, but the original equation is a hyperbolic of the form

$$t = AWC/(P - CP)$$

where t is time to exhaustion, P is current power, CP is work rate (i.e., power) asymptote, and AWC is degree of curvature of the relationship.

In this form, time to exhaustion is the dependent variable and is determined by power output (P) in relation to the individual's critical power (CP). In other words, how long you can go is determined by how hard you are exercising relative to your own ability. Although this is logical, actually fitting data to such a curvilinear relationship isn't especially convenient. Hence, it is common to rearrange this equation to yield a linear equivalent. That is:

$$Wlim = AWC + (CP \times t)$$

In this expression, Wlim is the total amount of work that can be accomplished during a maximal exercise bout continued to fatigue and is the product of power and time (since power = work ÷ time, work = power × time), plus a fixed contribution from anaerobic work capacity, that is, AWC.

The above equation is of the form y = mx + b, where the slope of the line represents a rider's "critical power." Conceptually, CP is a power that can be sustained "for a very long time without fatigue," and is "an inherent characteristic of the aerobic energy supply system." On a practical basis, CP has been shown to be closely correlated with (albeit somewhat higher than) power at lactate threshold. On the other hand, the y-intercept of this relationship, AWC, represents a fixed amount of work that can be accomplished during an exercise task to fatigue but is nonrenewable.

Conceptually, this parameter reflects anaerobic capacity (not power)—that is, the total amount of energy that can be liberated from nonaerobic energy sources, or the breakdown of high-energy phosphate stores (adenosine triphosphate [ATP] and phosphate creatine [PCr]), and via production and accumulation of lactate. Support for this interpretation comes from experiments showing a close correlation between AWC and total work performed during an all-out 30-second exercise test (that is, a Wingate test) or, even more convincingly, between AWC and maximal accumulated $O_2$ deficit. Moreover, CP may be influenced by interventions that would be expected to affect aerobic energy production, such as hypoxia, whereas AWC is not. Conversely, interventions expected to influence anaerobic capacity, such as creatine loading or resistance training (in untrained persons), have been shown to alter AWC without changing CP.

The critical power concept is not without limitations. In particular, it tends to greatly overestimate the maximal power that can be generated for only a few seconds, and predicts that there should be a power output below which fatigue will never occur. In addition, the exact values obtained for AWC and CP depend in part on the testing protocol—for example, the exact combination of powers and durations used to define the curve, how fatigue is defined, and the like. Nonetheless, despite its simplicity, this equation describes the power-versus-duration curve quite well over a fairly wide range of exercise intensities and durations, from efforts lasting for just a couple of minutes to efforts of a couple of hours (although again, since the relationship between work and time isn't truly linear, extrapolating beyond the range upon which the calculations are based will result in overestimation).

Understanding the original critical power concept can be very helpful if you own a power meter because it provides a means of quantifying changes in fitness beyond just "I was able to sustain *x* watts for *y* seconds!" Specifically, the critical power paradigm allows you to determine whether changes in anaerobic or aerobic function (or both) are responsible for any such improvements in performance, and thus to plan future training based on this insight. Furthermore, if you know your CP and AWC, it is possible to predict your maximal power at intermediate, unmeasured durations with considerable accuracy—which can be quite useful, for example, when preparing for a time trial contested over

*continued >*

***Critical Power,*** *continued*

a distance and duration that you have not raced before (or recently). Finally, because CP corresponds very closely to functional threshold power, determining your CP provides yet another means of determining this parameter.

If you decide to pursue this approach, there are two ways of obtaining the necessary data points: (1) by conducting specific, formal tests to determine the maximal power that you can sustain for various periods of time (or the maximal time that you can maintain a certain power), or (2) by using a software program such as WKO+ or SRM to cherry pick your best performances for those same periods out of, for example, race files. In either case, it is important that the data you use in the analysis truly represent your best effort, or your CP and/or AWC may be significantly under- or overestimated. Also, you should avoid using data from efforts that are so short (e.g., less than 3 minutes) that full utilization of AWC may not be ensured, or so long (e.g., more than 20 minutes) that the assumption of linearity of the work-time relationship is seriously violated.

Finally, it is important to realize that, as with any regression analysis, the slope (i.e., CP) is estimated with greater certainty than the intercept (i.e., AWC). In other words, whereas the value derived for CP using this method is generally capable of being repeated and is relatively unaffected by the particular combination of data points used, the value obtained for AWC will tend to be more variable. You should therefore be more cautious when interpreting changes in AWC and attempting to make adjustments in your training. You can more reliably adjust training upon noting measured changes in your CP.

## Testing Protocol

### Functional Threshold Power

The purpose of this initial test is to do a ride where you can average the highest watts possible for a substantial period of time. Be sure to do the same warm-up, and to use the same intensity in your warm-up, each time you do the test. The warm-up and recovery intervals throughout the test should be at about 65 percent of your functional threshold power, which would be Endurance pace. After the three fast pedaling intervals, the true warm-up begins.

When you begin the 5-minute all-out effort, punch it and hold it! Start at a high pace, but not so high that you die at the end. You should have a little in reserve to kick it to the finish line in the last minute. The goal of this first part is twofold: first, to "open" up the legs for the rest of the effort, and second, to capture your ability to produce watts in what is called VO$_2$max power, or Level 5 (discussed later in this chapter). Your next effort is more likely to be truly representative of your FTP.

For the 20-minute time trial, ride on a road that is fairly flat, allowing a strong, steady effort for the entire 20 minutes. Do not start out too hard! Get up to speed and then try to hold that speed. If you have never done one of these efforts before, try this on a steady climb or into a slight headwind, where you are forced to ride at a maximum effort for the entire 20 minutes. Your goal is to produce the highest average wattage over the entire period. If you suddenly run out of energy, you will not be able to produce your true maximal steady-state power. It is always better to be a little under what you believe to be your FTP for the first 2 minutes, build speed, and then ride at your maximum level in the last 3 minutes.

Finish the ride at an easy pace.

| TEST | **Functional Threshold Power** | | | |
|---|---|---|---|---|
| | **Time** | **Description** | **% of FTP** | **% of FTHR** |
| | 20 min. | Endurance pace | 65 | 70 |
| Warm-up | 3 × 1 min. (1 min. RI) | Fast pedaling, 100 rpm | N/A | N/A |
| | 5 min. | Easy riding | 65 | <70 |
| | 5 min. | All-out effort | max | >106 |
| Main set | 10 min. | Easy riding | 65 | <70 |
| | 20 min. | Time trial | max | 99–105 |
| Cooldown | 10–15 min. | Easy riding | 65 | <70 |

**Note:** *FTP = Functional Threshold Power. FTHR = Functional Threshold Heart Rate. N/A = Not Applicable*

Once this test is over and you have downloaded the data, you will need to figure out what your average power was for the entire 20-minute effort. Then you will take this number and subtract 5 percent from it. The number that results will be your functional threshold wattage value. (Hold on to this number, as we will come back to it later in this chapter.) So, for example, if you average 305 watts for the 20-minute time trial, you would calculate that $305 \times 0.05 = 15.25$, and $305 - 15.25 = 290$. Thus, your functional threshold power is 290 watts.

The reason for subtracting 5 percent of the watts from your 20-minute test is that FTP is defined as the highest average wattage or power that you can maintain for 60 minutes. Because some athletes have a hard time focusing for 60 minutes on a maximal effort, and those who can learn very quickly that a 60-minute time trial is not that much fun, we have found that 20 minutes is more realistic in terms of getting athletes to do more regular and higher-quality tests. Since 20 minutes is a shorter time period, it incorporates more of the athlete's anaerobic capacity, however, and this skews the wattage data by about 5 percent over a 60-minute effort. By subtracting that 5 percent, you will come up with a wattage number that would be very close to your 60-minute power measure.

One goal of any training program is to increase power at threshold (FTP), and how often threshold power changes significantly depends in part on an individual's training history and habits. For example, someone who is just beginning to cycle or returning to cycling after a long break may see large and rapid changes in threshold power at first, whereas an experienced rider who has been training for many years, or an athlete who maintains a high level of conditioning year-round, will probably experience much less variation. In general, assessing FTP four to six times a year (e.g., in the middle of winter training, near the start of serious outdoor training as a baseline, partway through the pre-competition period to track improvement, a couple of times during the season to determine peak fitness, and finally, after your peak fitness is over for the season, to determine how far you have "fallen") is probably sufficient.

## STEP 2: POWER-BASED TRAINING LEVELS

With more and more cyclists using power meters, the need has clearly arisen for power-based training programs akin to those used with heart rate monitors. To help meet this demand, Andrew Coggan, coauthor of this book, developed a series of power-based training levels, or zones. In doing so he drew upon fundamental principles of exercise physiology as well as approximately two decades of experience with power-based training in both laboratory and field settings.

| TABLE **3.1** | Power-Based Training Levels | | | | | |
|---|---|---|---|---|---|---|
| Level | Description | % of FTP* | % of FTHR* | RPE** | Typical Duration of Continuous Ride | Typical Duration of Interval Effort |
| 1 | Active Recovery | <55 | <68 | <2 | 30–90 min. | N/A |
| 2 | Endurance | 56–75 | 69–83 | 2–3 | 60–300 min. | N/A |
| 3 | Tempo | 76–90 | 84–94 | 3–4 | 60–180 min. | N/A |
| 4 | Lactate Threshold | 91–105 | 95–105 | 4–5 | N/A | 8–30 min. |
| 5 | VO$_2$max | 106–120 | >106 | 6–7 | N/A | 3–8 min. |
| 6 | Anaerobic Capacity | 121–150 | N/A | >7 | N/A | 30 sec.–3 min. |
| 7 | Neuromuscular Power | N/A | N/A | Maximal | N/A | <30 sec. |

*Percentage of average power and average HR are at functional threshold.
**RPE uses 10-point Borg Scale (see Table 3.3).

The seven levels are categorized in Table 3.1, and other aspects of the levels are noted in Table 3.2. We will explore the factors that were taken into consideration in developing the power-based levels. At the end of the chapter you will see an example of how to determine training levels and use that knowledge in developing a training program.

### The Basis for the System

Power at lactate threshold is the most important physiological determinant of endurance cycling performance because it integrates VO$_2$max, the percentage of VO$_2$max that can be sustained for a given duration, and cycling efficiency. As such, it is more logical to define

| TABLE **3.2** | Expected Physiological and Performance Adaptations for Levels 1–7 | | | | | | |
|---|---|---|---|---|---|---|---|
| **Adaptation** | **1** Active Recovery | **2** Endurance | **3** Tempo | **4** Lactate Threshold | **5** VO$_2$max | **6** Anaerobic Capacity | **7** Neuro-muscular Power |
| Increased plasma volume | | + | ++ | +++ | ++++ | + | |
| Increased muscle mitochondrial enzymes | | ++ | +++ | ++++ | ++ | + | |
| Increased lactate threshold | | ++ | +++ | ++++ | ++ | + | |
| Increased muscle glycogen storage | | ++ | ++++ | +++ | ++ | + | |
| Hypertrophy of slow-twitch muscle fibers | | + | ++ | ++ | +++ | + | |
| Increased muscle capillarization | | + | ++ | ++ | +++ | + | |
| Interconversion of fast-twitch muscle fibers (Type IIx → Type IIa) | | ++ | +++ | +++ | ++ | + | |
| Increased stroke volume/maximal cardiac output | | + | ++ | +++ | ++++ | + | |
| Increased VO$_2$max | | + | ++ | +++ | ++++ | + | |
| Increased muscle high-energy phosphate (ATP/PCr) stores | | | | | | + | ++ |
| Increased anaerobic capacity ("lactate tolerance") | | | | | + | +++ | + |
| Hypertrophy of fast-twitch fibers | | | | | | + | ++ |
| Increased neuromuscular power | | | | | | + | +++ |

*Note: The plus signs represent the magnitude of adaptation for a given "dose" of training. The more plus signs, the greater the adaptation.*

training levels relative to an athlete's threshold power than it is to, for example, define them vis-à-vis power at VO$_2$max (just as it is more logical to define HR-based training levels relative to threshold HR than to use maximal HR). Determining the appropriate number of levels, however, is somewhat tricky; the number is bound to be arbitrary because the physiological responses to exercise really fall on a continuum, with one intensity domain simply blending into the next.

A compromise must therefore be made between defining more levels, thus better reflecting the continuum that exists in reality, and defining fewer levels, for the sake of simplicity. Andrew felt seven levels were the minimum needed to represent the full range of physiological responses and to adequately describe the different types of training required and used to meet the demands of competitive cycling. Table 3.2 lists the primary physiological adaptations expected to result from training at each level, although these will obviously be influenced by factors such as the initial fitness of the individual, the duration of each workout, the time taken between interval efforts, and other factors.

### Heart Rate Guidelines

Relating the specified power levels to corresponding heart rate ranges or zones is somewhat difficult to do owing to the inherent variability of heart rate as well as individual differences in the power–heart rate relationship (even when referenced to threshold power). Nonetheless, approximate heart rate guidelines have been provided in Table 3.1 so that they can be used along with power to help guide training, if desired.

### Perceived Exertion Guidelines

The values used in Table 3.1 for perceived exertion are from Gunnar Borg's ten-point category-ratio scale (see Table 3.3), not the original twenty-point scale that is more commonly used. We use this scale because it explicitly recognizes the nonlinear response of many physiological variables (e.g., blood and muscle lactate) and thus provides a better indicator of overall effort. Since perceived exertion increases over time even at a constant exercise intensity (power), the suggested values or ranges refer to perceived effort as determined relatively early in a training session or series of intervals.

| TABLE **3.3** | Perceived Exertion Scale |
|---|---|
| **Rating** | **Description** |
| 0 | Nothing at all |
| 0.5 | Extremely weak |
| 1 | Very weak |
| 2 | Weak (light) |
| 3 | Moderate |
| 4 | Somewhat strong |
| 5 | Strong (heavy) |
| 6<br>7 | Very strong |
| 8<br>9<br>10 | Extremely strong |
| • | Maximal |

### Other Issues

Although this method of determining an individual's power level is based on the average power that an individual produces during a workout or interval effort, consideration must also be given to the distribution of power. For example, average power during mass-start races typically falls within Level 3, but racing at Level 3 is often more stressful than training at Level 3 because in racing there is greater variability (and therefore higher peaks) in power. Similarly, because of soft-pedaling and coasting, the average power achieved during a hilly ride or group training session is not equivalent to the same average power achieved during a completely flat ride or solo workout.

In part, this variability in power is already taken into account in the definitions of the various levels, especially Levels 2 and 3 (training at the higher levels will tend to be much more structured than training at the lower levels, thus limiting variations in power). Furthermore, there is obviously an inverse relationship between power output and the duration that this power can be sustained. Obviously, power during shorter training sessions or efforts will fall toward the higher end of a given range, whereas power during longer sessions or efforts will fall toward the lower end of a given range. Nonetheless, a workout consisting of 30 minutes of cycling at Level 1 (a warm-up, for example), 60 minutes of cycling at Level 3, and then another 30 minutes of cycling at Level 1 (a cooldown) would best be described as a Tempo training session, even though the overall average power might fall within Level 2.

### How to Determine Your Training Levels

If you performed the functional threshold power test described in Step 1, you have defined your power at 20 minutes and derived your 60-minute power from that. Now you can take this value and plug it into the percentages for each level to obtain your wattage range at each level.

Let's look at a hypothetical example to see exactly how this works. Joe Athlete has a threshold of 290 watts. His training levels are defined in Table 3.4.

Because 55 percent of 290 is 159.5 (290 × 0.55 = 159.5), we can say that at Level 1, Joe's wattage range will be from 1 to 160. At Level 2, his wattage range will be from 161 to 218 (because 161 is about 56 percent of 290, and 218 is about 75 percent of 290). Calculating the other percentages, it turns out that Joe's range will be from 219 to 261 watts at Level 3, from 262 to 305 at Level 4,

| TABLE **3.4** | Calculating Power Levels Based on FTP of 290 W | |
|---|---|---|
| Level | % of FTP | Power (W) |
| 1 Active Recovery | <55 | 1–160 |
| 2 Endurance | 56–75 | 161–218 |
| 3 Tempo | 76–90 | 219–261 |
| 4 Lactate Threshold | 91–105 | 262–305 |
| 5 VO₂max | 106–120 | 306–348 |
| 6 Anaerobic Capacity | 121–150 | 349–435 |
| 7 Neuromuscular Power | N/A | N/A |

and so on. To come up with your own ranges, you can do the same calculations using your own threshold figure instead of Joe's 290.

Once you've constructed your own table, what do you do with it? Again, let's look at what our hypothetical Joe Athlete could do. Now that he knows his training levels, he can begin to train with a specific wattage range in mind as a goal. This will allow him to improve in the specific areas that need work. If Joe needs help on his VO₂max power, then he can begin to specifically address that "hole" in his fitness by working in the 306–348 watt range. Joe also knows that if he is to go on a recovery ride, then he must stay below 160 watts in order to really help his body to recover. Otherwise, he would risk riding too hard and not getting sufficient recovery.

Since Joe has used a heart rate monitor before, he can also begin to understand the relationship between his heart rate zones and his new wattage levels. For Level 3 (Tempo) riding using wattage, Joe will see watts between 219 and 261. He may find that his heart rate fluctuates all the way from his Level 2 (Endurance) heart rate zone to his Level 4 (Lactate Threshold) heart rate zone, while his power is still at the Tempo level. Joe can now see how fatigue, dehydration, and low blood sugar might impact his wattage dramatically even when it does not impact his heart rate, or vice versa. Each individual is different, and knowing the different training levels will allow Joe to train effectively. He may find that he was not training as hard as he could have in the past, and he can make sure his wattage does not drop below the training level he is targeting. Joe can now begin to make the shift from his previous heart rate–based training into a power-based training scheme.

## STEP 3: COLLECT MORE DATA

We'll address specific workouts in Chapter 5, but at least for now, you have taken the first two steps in training with a power meter. Step 3 is the fun part of training with a power meter: All you have to do is go out, ride and stomp on the pedals, and see what you can do. It will bring new meaning to training rides and training loops that you have done hundreds of times. Meanwhile, you'll be learning how many watts it takes to get up your local hill or how hard you have to go during the Tuesday-night world championships in order to win the sprint coming back into town.

You can also begin to learn which roads in your area are the best stretches to do specific intervals that require you to hold a small wattage range. If you are doing a threshold workout (Level 4), you may find that you can easily hold your watts steady on a long, gradual climb, for example, and that might be your best place to do this type of a workout. By collecting all these data, you will begin to understand your strengths and weaknesses as a cyclist, which gives you a head start on the next step in your training.

# Determining Your Strengths and Weaknesses

**Athletes are always sizing themselves up**, and cyclists are no exception. On rides you may have heard other cyclists saying, "Oh, I am a bad climber" or "I have no snap or sprint." You may have said these types of things yourself. And maybe there have been times when you correctly assessed your relative weaknesses, or when those other cyclists were able to pinpoint exactly what was holding them back. But oftentimes, such guesses are just not on target. By using the power-meter data that you collect in races, in training rides, and in tests, it is possible to create a "Power Profile" of your strengths and weaknesses. We have developed a method of doing just that, and in this chapter you will learn how to use this method—which incorporates power-meter technology, of course—to create a profile of your own strengths and weaknesses as a cyclist—based on the facts, rather than your subjective opinion.

## THE POWER PROFILE

When we first began collecting data on various riders, it was because we simply wanted to get a clearer picture of the power that different types of cyclists could produce. What levels could be attained by elite pro riders? What could masters riders do? What about beginners? From these datasets, we were able to create the Power Profile chart (see Table 4.1). Our original intention was to compile enough information that we would be able to see whether the athletes we were coaching were on track with their training. However, when we started to plot riders' profiles, we were determined to find that this way of looking at things gave us clues to the relative strengths and weaknesses of individual riders and their physiological systems.

| TABLE **4.1** | Power Profile Chart | | | | | | | |
|---|---|---|---|---|---|---|---|---|
| | **MAXIMAL POWER OUTPUT (W/kg)** | | | | | | | |
| | **Men** | | | | **Women** | | | |
| | 5 sec. | 1 min. | 5 min. | FTP | 5 sec. | 1 min. | 5 min. | FTP |
| | 25.18 | 11.50 | 7.60 | 6.40 | 19.42 | 9.29 | 6.74 | 5.69 |
| | 24.88 | 11.39 | 7.50 | 6.31 | 19.20 | 9.20 | 6.64 | 5.61 |
| | 24.59 | 11.27 | 7.39 | 6.22 | 18.99 | 9.11 | 6.55 | 5.53 |
| | 24.29 | 11.16 | 7.29 | 6.13 | 18.77 | 9.02 | 6.45 | 5.44 |
| World class (e.g., international pro) | 24.00 | 11.04 | 7.19 | 6.04 | 18.56 | 8.93 | 6.36 | 5.36 |
| | 23.70 | 10.93 | 7.08 | 5.96 | 18.34 | 8.84 | 6.26 | 5.28 |
| | 23.40 | 10.81 | 6.98 | 5.87 | 18.13 | 8.75 | 6.17 | 5.20 |
| | 23.11 | 10.70 | 6.88 | 5.78 | 17.91 | 8.66 | 6.07 | 5.12 |
| | 22.81 | 10.58 | 6.77 | 5.69 | 17.70 | 8.56 | 5.98 | 5.03 |
| | 22.51 | 10.47 | 6.67 | 5.60 | 17.48 | 8.47 | 5.88 | 4.95 |
| Exceptional (e.g., domestic pro) | 22.22 | 10.35 | 6.57 | 5.51 | 17.26 | 8.38 | 5.79 | 4.87 |
| | 21.92 | 10.24 | 6.46 | 5.42 | 17.05 | 8.29 | 5.69 | 4.79 |
| | 21.63 | 10.12 | 6.36 | 5.33 | 16.83 | 8.20 | 5.60 | 4.70 |
| | 21.33 | 10.01 | 6.26 | 5.24 | 16.62 | 8.11 | 5.50 | 4.62 |
| | 21.03 | 9.89 | 6.15 | 5.15 | 16.40 | 8.02 | 5.41 | 4.54 |
| | 20.74 | 9.78 | 6.05 | 5.07 | 16.19 | 7.93 | 5.31 | 4.46 |
| Excellent (e.g., Cat. I) | 20.44 | 9.66 | 5.95 | 4.98 | 15.97 | 7.84 | 5.21 | 4.38 |
| | 20.15 | 9.55 | 5.84 | 4.89 | 15.76 | 7.75 | 5.12 | 4.29 |
| | 19.85 | 9.43 | 5.74 | 4.80 | 15.54 | 7.66 | 5.02 | 4.21 |
| | 19.55 | 9.32 | 5.64 | 4.71 | 15.32 | 7.57 | 4.93 | 4.13 |
| | 19.26 | 9.20 | 5.53 | 4.62 | 15.11 | 7.48 | 4.83 | 4.05 |
| | 18.96 | 9.09 | 5.43 | 4.53 | 14.89 | 7.39 | 4.74 | 3.97 |
| Very good (e.g., Cat. II) | 18.66 | 8.97 | 5.33 | 4.44 | 14.68 | 7.30 | 4.64 | 3.88 |
| | 18.37 | 8.86 | 5.22 | 4.35 | 14.46 | 7.21 | 4.55 | 3.80 |
| | 18.07 | 8.74 | 5.12 | 4.27 | 14.25 | 7.11 | 4.45 | 3.72 |
| | 17.78 | 8.63 | 5.01 | 4.18 | 14.03 | 7.02 | 4.36 | 3.64 |
| | 17.48 | 8.51 | 4.91 | 4.09 | 13.82 | 6.93 | 4.26 | 3.55 |
| | 17.18 | 8.40 | 4.81 | 4.00 | 13.60 | 6.84 | 4.17 | 3.47 |
| | 16.89 | 8.28 | 4.70 | 3.91 | 13.39 | 6.75 | 4.07 | 3.39 |
| Good (e.g., Cat. III) | 16.59 | 8.17 | 4.60 | 3.82 | 13.17 | 6.66 | 3.98 | 3.31 |
| | 16.29 | 8.05 | 4.50 | 3.73 | 12.95 | 6.57 | 3.88 | 3.23 |
| | 16.00 | 7.94 | 4.39 | 3.64 | 12.74 | 6.48 | 3.79 | 3.14 |
| | 15.70 | 7.82 | 4.29 | 3.55 | 12.52 | 6.39 | 3.69 | 3.06 |
| | 15.41 | 7.71 | 4.19 | 3.47 | 12.31 | 6.30 | 3.59 | 2.98 |
| | 15.11 | 7.59 | 4.08 | 3.38 | 12.09 | 6.21 | 3.50 | 2.90 |
| Moderate (e.g., Cat. IV) | 14.81 | 7.48 | 3.98 | 3.29 | 11.88 | 6.12 | 3.40 | 2.82 |
| | 14.52 | 7.36 | 3.88 | 3.20 | 11.66 | 6.03 | 3.31 | 2.73 |
| | 14.22 | 7.25 | 3.77 | 3.11 | 11.45 | 5.94 | 3.21 | 2.65 |
| | 13.93 | 7.13 | 3.67 | 3.02 | 11.23 | 5.85 | 3.12 | 2.57 |
| | 13.63 | 7.02 | 3.57 | 2.93 | 11.01 | 5.76 | 3.02 | 2.49 |
| | 13.33 | 6.90 | 3.46 | 2.84 | 10.80 | 5.66 | 2.93 | 2.40 |
| Fair (e.g., Cat. V) | 13.04 | 6.79 | 3.36 | 2.75 | 10.58 | 5.57 | 2.83 | 2.32 |
| | 12.74 | 6.67 | 3.26 | 2.66 | 10.37 | 5.48 | 2.74 | 2.24 |
| | 12.44 | 6.56 | 3.15 | 2.58 | 10.15 | 5.39 | 2.64 | 2.16 |
| | 12.15 | 6.44 | 3.05 | 2.49 | 9.94 | 5.30 | 2.55 | 2.08 |
| | 11.85 | 6.33 | 2.95 | 2.40 | 9.72 | 5.21 | 2.45 | 1.99 |
| | 11.56 | 6.21 | 2.84 | 2.31 | 9.51 | 5.12 | 2.36 | 1.91 |
| Untrained (nonracer) | 11.26 | 6.10 | 2.74 | 2.22 | 9.29 | 5.03 | 2.26 | 1.83 |
| | 10.96 | 5.99 | 2.64 | 2.13 | 9.07 | 4.94 | 2.16 | 1.75 |
| | 10.67 | 5.87 | 2.53 | 2.04 | 8.86 | 4.85 | 2.07 | 1.67 |
| | 10.37 | 5.76 | 2.43 | 1.95 | 8.64 | 4.76 | 1.97 | 1.58 |
| | 10.08 | 5.64 | 2.33 | 1.86 | 8.43 | 4.67 | 1.88 | 1.50 |

If a rider had a strong anaerobic capacity as compared with his or her lactate threshold, for example, then we could see this easily in his or her profile. If a rider was talented neuromuscularly but challenged cardiovascularly, this, too, was easy to quantify in the Power Profile. What started out as a way to compare an individual's performance against others turned out to be one of the most effective ways to quantify the relative strengths and weaknesses of each rider.

There have been other attempts to generate guidelines or benchmarks for power output. These have usually been based on racer category (i.e., Cat. I, Cat. II, etc.). Aside from satisfying people's natural curiosity, though, such category-based values are of limited practical use—after all, the best measure of a racer's competitive ability relative to others is found in actual race performance, not power output. If, however, valid standards were available for power across different durations that represented different physiological characteristics or abilities rather than simply racing categories, then it would be possible, we reasoned, to identify a particular individual's relative strengths and weaknesses. In other words, we would be able to see how a cyclist was doing in one area compared with how he or she was doing in other areas, rather than how he or she was doing in comparison with others. This is where the true value of Power Profiling comes in. When you know your relative strengths and weaknesses, you can develop a program to improve in the weak areas, and that is when you will see real progress. And it may even be possible to identify events where you could be expected to achieve the greatest success, and thereby build on your strengths. Our goal was to develop rational guidelines that could be used for these purposes.

### The Approach

In theory, tables of standards for power output for different durations could be generated by simply collecting data on a large number of cyclists of widely varying ability. However, it is highly unlikely that any coach or researcher would have access to a sufficiently large database for this approach to be very accurate. As an alternative, estimates of power output for riders of differing abilities could be derived from actual performance—for example, in time trials. This approach, however, would require one to make somewhat tenuous assumptions regarding body mass, aerodynamic drag, and so on, and such a method would become particularly complex when applied to shorter-duration, non-steady-state events (e.g., 1 km on the track).

Therefore, we decided to "anchor" the upper and lower ends of each range based on the known performance abilities of world champion athletes and untrained persons, respectively. For example, a world-class match sprinter can produce over 23 watts per kilogram (W/kg) in a 5-second sprint, whereas an untrained beginner might produce only 10 to 12.5 W/kg. We assigned ranges in between these extremes to six other divisions (exceptional, excellent, very good, good, moderate, and fair), found in Table 4.1. In addition, we used our own data on the wide variety of athletes with whom we worked to provide confirmation of these figures. The advantage of this approach is that it enhances the validity of comparisons across event durations—for example, a "world-class" power output should be equivalent regardless of whether the duration over which it is measured is 5 seconds or 1 hour.

### Choice of Target Durations

We chose index efforts of 5 seconds, 1 minute, and 5 minutes and a fourth measure at functional threshold power because we believed they would best reflect neuromuscular power, anaerobic capacity, maximal oxygen uptake ($VO_2$max), and lactate threshold (LT), respectively. This does not imply that a 1-minute all-out effort is completely anaerobic (in fact, roughly 40–45 percent of the energy expended during such exercise is derived aerobically), or that it fully utilizes anaerobic capacity (which generally requires 1.5–2.5 minutes to deplete). Nor does it mean that a 5-minute all-out effort entails exercising at precisely 100 percent of $VO_2$max (most athletes can sustain a power that would elicit 105–110 percent of their $VO_2$max for this duration). However, power output over these target durations would be expected to correlate well with more direct measurements of these different physiological abilities. The durations of these index efforts were also chosen in an attempt to increase the reproducibility of the data, as well as for convenience in gathering the data.

## Testing Protocol

### Power Profile

To create a Power Profile of your own strengths and weaknesses in cycling, you will need to complete the Power Profile Test described below. You have already gathered one figure for your Power Profile: You'll use the result from the Functional Threshold Power Test described in Chapter 3 for the FTP column of the profile. To do the test described below, it is again important to find a section of road where you will not be interrupted by stop signs or intersections, and again, it should be a place that you can return to periodically for retesting. The wind conditions should be similar every time you conduct the test, and you should be at a similar place in your training block. It is also a good idea to do the test right after a "rest week" so that you will be fresh and also relatively fit. Be sure to always perform the same warm-up routine on the way to your "testing grounds."

The majority of your warm-up should be in Levels 2 and 3 (Endurance and Tempo from the categories listed in Table 3.1). Make sure you have at least 10 minutes of easy pedaling before the first effort. When you begin your test efforts, do not worry about cadence, heart rate, or anything besides the stop clock, and make sure you drive it to the end of each timed effort. In other words, just do the work, and what happens, happens. Record your efforts as intervals on your power meter, if possible.

| TEST | **Power Profile** | | | |
|---|---|---|---|---|
| | **Time** | **Description** | **% of FTP** | **% of FTHR** |
| Warm-up | ~45 min. | Easy riding | 65 | <70 |
| | 3 × 1 min. (1 min. RI) | Fast pedaling, 110 rpm | 80–90 | 80-90 |
| Main set | 5 min. (3–5 min. RI) | FTP effort | 100 | >106 |
| | 1 min. (3–5 min. RI) | All-out effort | >150 | >106 |
| | 10 min. | Easy riding | 70–80 | <68 |
| | 5 min. (10 min. RI) | Out of the saddle, all-out effort from 20 mph Hammer in final 45 sec. | >115–120 | >106 |
| | 1 min. (5 min. RI) | Out of the saddle, all-out effort from 20 mph Be seated to drive to the finish | >150 | >106 |
| | 1 min. (5 min. RI) | All-out effort | >150 | >106 |
| | 2 × 15 sec. (2 min. RI) | Out of the saddle, hard sprint from 15 mph | max | N/A |
| Cooldown | 15 min. | Easy riding | 60–70 | <68 |

**Note:** For recovery intervals (RI) keep power at 60–70% of Functional Threshold Power (FTP).

That's it. Go for a short cooldown ride to get in at least 300–500 kilojoules more at Level 2 to call it a good training ride.

Now, download your data and pick out the best watts for each time period.

### Power-to-Weight Ratio

Since weight influences how many watts you can produce, it is important to find out your power-to-weight ratio. How many watts per kilogram can you produce? A rider who weighs 200 pounds and produces 350 watts up a hill, for example, will be able to ride side by side with another rider who weighs 125 pounds but is producing only 218 watts. Why? Because for each of these riders, the power-to-weight ratio is the same, at 3.85 watts per kilogram.

The power-to-weight ratio is very important in cycling. The higher your power-to-weight ratio, the stronger you are as a cyclist. That is why in cycling, it can be said that one of the main goals is to be as light as possible in weight, but to produce the highest possible watts. The trick is figuring out at what weight you produce the most watts.

In order to find out your ratio, you will first need to know how much you weigh in kilograms. To do this, divide your weight in pounds by 2.2. For example, if you weigh 165 pounds, you would divide 165 by 2.2 to discover that you weigh 75 kilograms. Now, take your wattage numbers at each time period and divide them by your weight in kilograms. If you held 423 watts for 5 minutes (and you weighed 75 kilograms), for example, you would divide 423 by 75. In this case, you would get 5.64, which would mean that you produced 5.64 watts per kilogram. The Power Profile chart is stated in watts per kilogram because it is the standard scientific power-to-weight ratio measurement used around the world.

### Application and Interpretation

To use the Power Profile tables that follow, first find the profile best suited to your riding. Then, simply locate the peak or maximum power that you can generate for 5 seconds, 1 minute, and 5 minutes and at functional threshold power, and find corresponding values in the rows of the table. You can also print out extra copies of the table from the TrainingPeaks website or make a copy of the table from this book, and circle or highlight where your performance falls in the list of ranges. If your performance falls between two values, which will often be the case, assign the nearest ranking. It is critical that the values used in this analysis be truly reflective of your very best effort over that duration; otherwise, the resultant profile may be distorted, leading to inappropriate conclusions and decisions about training.

What emerges as you highlight your results will be a unique pattern that shows your relative strengths and weaknesses in cycling. You may find that you are at a higher level in sprinting, for example, than in efforts requiring endurance, or vice versa. The pattern may change slightly over time as you train and work on the weak areas. Although every Power Profile is unique, there are some typical patterns. These patterns are explained below. However, in considering these examples, keep in mind that performance at each duration is being evaluated in light of the world's best cycling performances. Thus, road cyclists will tend to appear relatively weak in 5-second sprints in comparison with match sprinters, and nonendurance track racers will likely have relatively low 5-minute and FTP levels relative to their abilities at the shorter durations.

Also keep in mind that, based on physiological considerations, an inverse relationship might be expected to occur between anaerobic and aerobic efforts—that is, someone who is great in aerobic forms of exercise, such as the Tour de France, may not be as strong in anaerobic forms, such as the match-sprint event on the track. At the same time, however, a positive association might be expected between pairs. (Although the scientific literature is in fact split on whether there actually is an inverse relationship between short-term and long-term power, there is clearly a positive association within each category.)

### Examples of Power Profiles
### All-Rounder

The cyclist who is an all-rounder will have a generally horizontal plot across all the categories (see Table 4.1A). That is, all four values will fall at about the same point in that individual's range. The all-rounder does not necessarily excel at any one thing but is likely competitive in his or her category across a broad range of events.

| TABLE 4.1A | All-Rounder | | |
|---|---|---|---|
| MAXIMAL POWER OUTPUT (W/kg) | | | |
| 5 sec. | 1 min. | 5 min. | FTP |
| 18.07 | 8.74 | 5.12 | 4.27 |
| 17.78 | 8.63 | 5.01 | 4.18 |
| 17.48 | 8.51 | 4.91 | 4.09 |
| 17.18 | 8.40 | 4.81 | 4.00 |

Given the fact that only specialists will likely truly excel at the extreme durations, very few individuals will show this pattern and still fall at the upper end of each range. Instead, the vast majority of nonelite athletes will likely show a generally horizontal Power Profile because they have not yet developed specific strengths. This is a very common profile for beginning racers; as a racer or other rider trains more and more, those areas of strength will begin to reveal themselves.

## Sprinter

A good sprinter will typically have a distinctly downsloping plot (especially between the 1-minute and 5-minute categories) (see Table 4.1B). This pattern is characteristic of an athlete whose natural abilities are skewed toward success in short-duration, high-power events. Since aerobic ability is quite trainable, such an individual may be able to become more of an all-rounder through focused training; however, if the individual is a sprinter who has already been training hard for many years, he or she may always still be better at anaerobic efforts than at aerobic ones. If so, focusing on events that favor these abilities, such as track racing and criterium, may result in the most success.

## Time Trialist, Climber, or Excellent Steady-State Rider

A distinctly upsloping plot (again, especially between the columns for 1 minute and 5 minutes, but also between 5 minutes and FTP) is typical for the classical time trialist (see Table 4.1C). This is because most time trialists are weak in neuromuscular power and anaerobic capacity, but have relatively high aerobic power and an especially high lactate threshold. Though such athletes may be able to improve their performance by spending lots of time practicing sprints, this may not be the case if the training results in a decline in their strength, which

| TABLE 4.1B | Sprinter | | |
| --- | --- | --- | --- |
| MAXIMAL POWER OUTPUT (W/kg) | | | |
| 5 sec. | 1 min. | 5 min. | FTP |
| 21.63 | 10.12 | 6.36 | 5.33 |
| 21.33 | 10.01 | 6.26 | 5.24 |
| 21.03 | 9.89 | 6.15 | 5.15 |
| 20.74 | 9.78 | 6.05 | 5.07 |
| 20.44 | 9.66 | 5.95 | 4.98 |
| 20.15 | 9.55 | 5.84 | 4.89 |
| 19.85 | 9.43 | 5.74 | 4.80 |
| 19.55 | 9.32 | 5.64 | 4.71 |
| 19.26 | 9.20 | 5.53 | 4.62 |
| 18.96 | 9.09 | 5.43 | 4.53 |
| 18.66 | 8.97 | 5.33 | 4.44 |
| 18.37 | 8.86 | 5.22 | 4.35 |
| 18.07 | 8.74 | 5.12 | 4.27 |
| 17.78 | 8.63 | 5.01 | 4.18 |
| 17.48 | 8.51 | 4.91 | 4.09 |
| 17.18 | 8.40 | 4.81 | 4.00 |
| 16.89 | 8.28 | 4.70 | 3.91 |

| TABLE 4.1C | Time Trialist, Climber, Steady-State Rider | | |
| --- | --- | --- | --- |
| MAXIMAL POWER OUTPUT (W/kg) | | | |
| 5 sec. | 1 min. | 5 min. | FTP |
| 19.85 | 9.43 | 5.74 | 4.80 |
| 19.55 | 9.32 | 5.64 | 4.71 |
| 19.26 | 9.20 | 5.53 | 4.62 |
| 18.96 | 9.09 | 5.43 | 4.53 |
| 18.66 | 8.97 | 5.33 | 4.44 |
| 18.37 | 8.86 | 5.22 | 4.35 |
| 18.07 | 8.74 | 5.12 | 4.27 |
| 17.78 | 8.63 | 5.01 | 4.18 |
| 17.48 | 8.51 | 4.91 | 4.09 |
| 17.18 | 8.40 | 4.81 | 4.00 |
| 16.89 | 8.28 | 4.70 | 3.91 |
| 16.59 | 8.17 | 4.60 | 3.82 |
| 16.29 | 8.05 | 4.50 | 3.73 |
| 16.00 | 7.94 | 4.39 | 3.64 |
| 15.70 | 7.82 | 4.29 | 3.55 |

is sustainable power. A time trialist could indeed improve his or her sprint, but the small improvements in the sprint may not result in more race wins; meanwhile, the time spent working on sprints would mean less time spent on improving FTP—therefore, by practicing sprints, the time trialist could lose fitness and perform worse in time trial races.

## Pursuiter

A sharply inverted V pattern represents an athlete who has both relatively high anaerobic capacity and high aerobic ability, and who is thus well suited for events such as the pursuit (see Table 4.1D). Alternatively, a potential all-rounder who simply hasn't focused on raising his or her lactate threshold to its highest possible level may exhibit this same pattern.

On the other hand, the sharp V pattern is a relatively unlikely combination, given the expected inverse relationship between neuromuscular power and lactate threshold and the positive relationship expected between VO$_2$max and lactate threshold. Should such a pattern be observed, care should be taken to ensure that the values being used are truly representative of the athlete's abilities.

| TABLE **4.1D** | Pursuiter | | |
|---|---|---|---|
| **MAXIMAL POWER OUTPUT (W/kg)** | | | |
| **5 sec.** | **1 min.** | **5 min.** | **FTP** |
| 19.55 | 9.32 | 5.64 | 4.71 |
| 19.26 | 9.20 | 5.53 | 4.62 |
| 18.96 | 9.09 | 5.43 | 4.53 |
| 18.66 | 8.97 | 5.33 | 4.44 |
| 18.37 | 8.86 | 5.22 | 4.35 |
| 18.07 | 8.74 | 5.12 | 4.27 |
| 17.78 | 8.63 | 5.01 | 4.18 |
| 17.48 | 8.51 | 4.91 | 4.09 |
| 17.18 | 8.40 | 4.81 | 4.00 |
| 16.89 | 8.28 | 4.70 | 3.91 |
| 16.59 | 8.17 | 4.60 | 3.82 |
| 16.29 | 8.05 | 4.50 | 3.73 |
| 16.00 | 7.94 | 4.39 | 3.64 |
| 15.70 | 7.82 | 4.29 | 3.55 |
| 15.41 | 7.71 | 4.19 | 3.47 |
| 15.11 | 7.59 | 4.08 | 3.38 |
| 14.81 | 7.48 | 3.98 | 3.29 |

### Limitations and Caveats

The Power Profile standards are based on the performance capacities of young adults and thus do not account for the effects of aging (or development). We considered developing age-specific standards, but rejected this idea because it would be difficult to collect sufficient data. Attempting corrections based on known physiological changes would also be difficult.

For example, starting around age 30, VO$_2$max declines a little each year. In men it declines annually by about 0.5 mL/kg/min. (that is, milliliters per kilogram per minute, the standard measure used for VO$_2$max); in women, it declines at a slightly slower rate, about 0.35 ml/kg/min. a year. Muscle strength and power, in contrast, can generally be well maintained, with training, until around age 50, but they begin to decline somewhat more rapidly thereafter. Therefore, for maximum accuracy, different age-based correction factors might need to be applied to the different columns. It is unlikely, however, that these differential changes with age are sufficient to significantly alter a rider's own profile, and we suggest that Table 4.1 simply be applied as is, regardless of a rider's age.

## THE FATIGUE PROFILE

While knowing your Power Profile is very useful, it doesn't quite tell you the whole story. What you now have is an awareness of your gross strengths and weaknesses, which is certainly helpful for the purpose of designing a training program. But if you are a sprinter, what kind of sprinter are you? Are you a sprinter who has such a blisteringly fast snap that no one can beat you in the final 100-meter dash to the finish line? Or are you a sprinter who can go from 350 meters out and then go so fast that no one can even come close to catching you? Or what if your strength is $VO_2$max and your 5-minute power is good, but your 3-minute power is way above and beyond your category? Or maybe your power at 5 minutes is okay but your power doesn't really drop off much when you get all the way out to 8 minutes? Figuring out your strengths at this level might have a profound impact on your training plan and could also affect your racing strategy and tactics. In an effort to further drill down into the data, we developed the Fatigue Profile, which will help you to pinpoint your strengths and weaknesses with greater precision and make the most of them in your racing season.

To start with, we defined each physiological training area in a broader way, so that at Level 7, or Neuromuscular Power, we mean not just the best 5 seconds, but the best 10 seconds and 20 seconds as well. For Level 6, Anaerobic Capacity, it made sense to look at power at 30 seconds, 1 minute, and 2 minutes, so that we could more fully understand whether a rider has above-average fatigue resistance or below-average resistance. For Level 5, $VO_2$max, we expanded the range as well, incorporating efforts from 3 minutes in duration up to 8 minutes in duration. At 3 minutes, your $VO_2$max is certainly being taxed, but even at 8 minutes the majority of your energy is being produced via the $VO_2$max system. Finally, at Level 4, Lactate Threshold, we took the 20-minute FTP test and expanded it to include tests for 60 and 90 minutes of Normalized Power, so that we could learn about the point at which a rider's muscles fatigued and the role that played in overall fitness and training.

Now what do all these revelations mean to you? Unfortunately, you have to collect even more data (unless you already have adequate data from training with a power meter), but the knowledge you gain from it will likely prove to be well worth the effort. The testing protocols that follow will help you define your Power Profile. We recommend that you test two specific systems on one day and then, depending on your fitness, you either rest for at least two days before testing the next two systems, or do the next test the very next day. Start out with Levels 6 and 7 first so that you can get in the harder, shorter, more intense efforts when you are freshest.

Since the Level 4 testing includes 60- and 90-minute Normalized Power along with 20-minute average power, we recommend that you cherry-pick your best 60- and 90-minute Normalized Power results from previous data. Of course, if you wish, you may go out and test these time periods, doing your best for each of them. But these data might be easier to obtain from race data or from a hard group ride. The 20-minute test should be done regularly, however, so that you will know how your FTP changes and how it fits in with your Fatigue Profile.

## Testing Protocol

### Fatigue Profile: Levels 6 and 7 (Anaerobic Capacity and Neuromuscular Power)

This test actually tests Level 7 first, and then Level 6. For the small-ring sprints, ride a flat to very gently upward-sloping road (3 percent grade or less). Your gearing should be near 39:16. There are no shifting restrictions, but try to wind out each gear before shifting to the next harder one.

| TEST | Neuromuscular Power, Level 7 | | | |
|---|---|---|---|---|
| | Time/Distance | Description | % of FTP | % of FTHR |
| Warm-up | 20 min. | Easy riding | 65 | <70 |
| Main set | 3 × 50–75 m (2–3 min. RI) | Small-ring sprints from 8–10 mph | max | N/A |
| | 150 m (5 min. RI) | Big-ring sprints (53:17) from 18 mph (50:16 for compact) | max | N/A |
| | 250 m (5 min. RI) | Big-ring sprints (53:15) from 18 mph (50:14 for compact) | max | N/A |
| | 300–350 m (5 min. RI) | Big-ring sprints (53:13) from 24 mph (50:13 for compact) | max | N/A |
| | 15 min. | Easy riding | 60–70 | <68 |

The efforts for Level 6, described below, can be done on a hill for extra resistance. Each effort needs a recovery time of at least 4 minutes, and even if you need more, that's fine. There are no gearing restrictions, but do put out your absolute best power for each time period—so don't start your 30-second test with a gear of 53:13! Power will likely start out high and quickly drop off (especially in the first big effort). Here are the guidelines:

| TEST | Anaerobic Capacity, Level 6 | | | |
|---|---|---|---|---|
| | Time | Description | % of FTP | % of FTHR |
| Main set, continued from above | 30 sec. (4 min. RI) | All-out effort | >200 | N/A |
| | 1 min. (4 min. RI) | All-out effort | >150 | N/A |
| | 2 min. (4 min. RI) | All-out effort | >140 | >106 |
| Cooldown | 30 min. | Easy riding | 56–75 | 69–83 |

*Note: For recovery intervals (RI) for both Level 7 and Level 6, keep power at Level 2, 56–75% of Functional Threshold Power (FTP).*

## Testing Protocol

### Fatigue Profile: Level 5 (VO₂max)

Warm up well and give each of these time periods your best! Your goal in these tests is to produce the very best power you can for each effort, so if you need a little more recovery time between them, then you should take it.

| TEST | VO₂max, Level 5 | | | |
|------|------|------|------|------|
| | Time | Description | % of FTP | % of FTHR |
| Warm-up | 20 min. | Easy riding | <75 | <80 |
| Main set | 3 min. (5 min. RI) | All-out effort | avg. >118 | >106 |
| | 5 min. (5 min. RI) | All-out effort | avg. >113 | >106 |
| | 8 min. | All-out effort | avg. >108 | >106 |
| | 30 min. | Easy riding | <75–80 | 85–90 |
| | 20 min. | Threshold effort | 100 | 99–105 |
| Cooldown | 30 min. | Easy riding | <75–80 | 85–90 |

*Note: For recovery intervals (RI), keep power at Level 2, 56–75% of Functional Threshold Power (FTP).*

### *Defining Your Fatigue Resistance*

Once you have done the two Fatigue Profile tests, we recommend setting up your charts based on the different energy systems that you have tested. Using the WKO+ software, you can make the charts shown in Figures 4.1 through 4.4, which will enable you to create your Fatigue Profile. The Fatigue Profile includes categories that relate to your fatigue resistance: well below average, below average, average, above average, and well above average.

If you have been training with a power meter for awhile, you might not need to complete all the testing protocols in this chapter to define your Fatigue Profile. The charts you created from the WKO+ software (see Figures 4.1–4.4) will give you insight into how you might use existing data to show your bests (mean maximal power) for the four key energy systems—Levels 4–7. As you accumulate more and more rides in your data set, your charts will build over several months, showing how your mean maximal power fluctuated over the season.

Each energy system includes three common intervals. For Level 7, you will be looking at peak power for 5 seconds, 10 seconds, and 20 seconds. There will be telltale drop-offs or rises in the power generated. You might notice that your peak power for 5 and 10 seconds is proportional, but there is a greater gap between peak power at 10 seconds and 20 seconds, as shown in Figure 4.1. This is a helpful clue to understanding your personal Fatigue Profile.

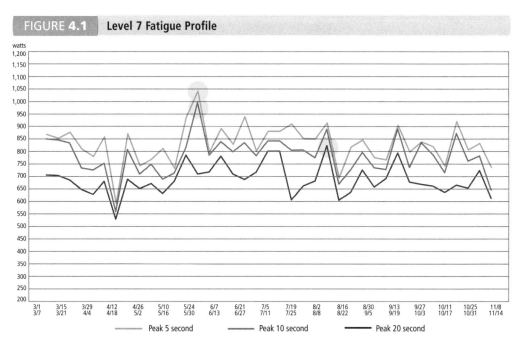

**FIGURE 4.1** Level 7 Fatigue Profile

*By cherry-picking this athlete's best data, we see that he has a best 5 second of 1,044 W, a best 10 second of 996 W, and a best 20 second of 823 W. Notice how the 20-second line is visually farther away from the 5-second and 10-second lines. This is a clue that fatigue resistance could be below average.*

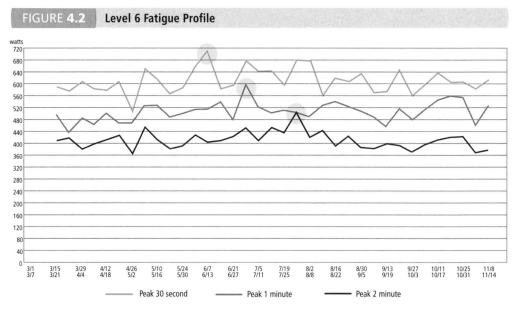

**FIGURE 4.2** Level 6 Fatigue Profile

*Again, taking the best values for 30 second, 1 minute, and 2 minute, we can learn more about the strengths and weaknesses of the rider within the individual energy system. In this case, the rider has a best 30 second of 710 W, a best 1 minute of 598 W, and a best 2 minute of 503 W. Notice how evenly spaced the lines are. This is a classic example of average fatigue resistance.*

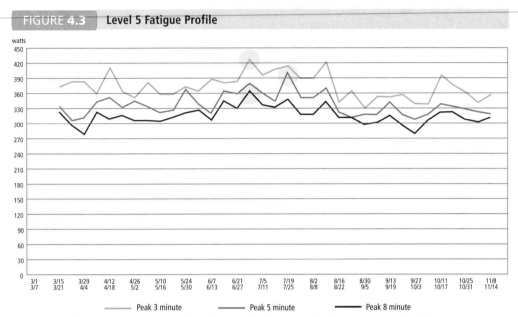

FIGURE **4.3**     **Level 5 Fatigue Profile**

Peak 3 minute ——— Peak 5 minute ——— Peak 8 minute

*For Level 5, VO$_2$max power, cherry-picking the best 3 minute at 428 W, 5 minute at 401 W, and 8 minute at 364 W will give us the needed information to determine if this rider has strong power and average or strong endurance within the VO$_2$max system. Notice there is a greater distance from 3 to 5 minute than from 5 to 8 minute This is most likely an example of average to above-average fatigue resistance.*

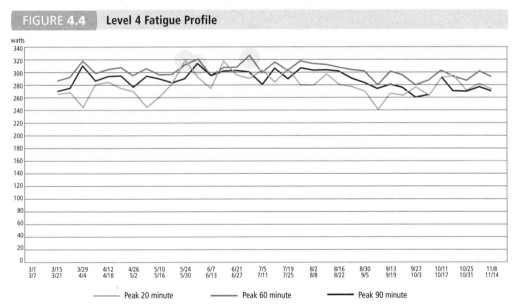

FIGURE **4.4**     **Level 4 Fatigue Profile**

Peak 20 minute ——— Peak 60 minute ——— Peak 90 minute

*For the Threshold power profile, notice the 20-minute average power is actually lower than the 60-minute Normalized Power (NP), which most likely reflects that this athlete has a strong anaerobic capacity and therefore does very intense efforts above his threshold and returns to it quickly, creating a higher NP. The rider has a best 20 minute of 320 W, a best 60 minute of 326 W, and a best 90 minute of 314 W. Notice that the lines are very close to each other. This is a perfect example of above-average fatigue resistance.*

**TABLE 4.2    Fatigue Profile Guidelines**

| Fatigue Resistance | LEVEL 7, NEUROMUSCULAR POWER | | | LEVEL 6, ANAEROBIC CAPACITY | | |
|---|---|---|---|---|---|---|
| | 5 sec. | 10 sec. | 20 sec. | 30 sec. | 1 min. | 2 min. |
| Well below average | 100% | 41–55% | 61–75% | 100% | 31–45% | 50–70% |
| Below average | 100% | 31–40% | 47–60% | 100% | 25–30% | 36–50% |
| Average | 100% | 22–30% | 35–46% | 100% | 21–24% | 23–35% |
| Above average | 100% | 15–21% | 20–34% | 100% | 10–20% | 15–22% |
| Well above average | 100% | 5–14% | 8–19% | 100% | 5–9% | 8–14% |

Note: AP = Average Power; NP = Normalized Power

**TABLE 4.3    Fatigue Profile Examples**

| Fatigue Resistance | LEVEL 7, NEUROMUSCULAR POWER (W) | | | | LEVEL 6, ANAEROBIC CAPACITY (W) | | | |
|---|---|---|---|---|---|---|---|---|
| | Description | 5 sec. | 10 sec. | 20 sec. | Description | 30 sec. | 1 min. | 2 min. |
| Well below average | Very high explosiveness | 1,800 | 1,000 | 500 | Very strong initial effort | 850 | 500 | 300 |
| Below average | High explosiveness | 1,400 | 910 | 588 | Strong initial effort | 700 | 511 | 385 |
| Average | | 1,200 | 900 | 696 | | 600 | 450 | 402 |
| Above average | Strong endurance | 1,100 | 902 | 803 | Strong endurance | 600 | 510 | 420 |
| Well above average | Tremendous endurance | 1,000 | 880 | 850 | Tremendous endurance | 550 | 530 | 500 |

When you see this larger gap between the lines charted, then you know that your 20-second power drops off much more quickly than the drop from 5 to 10 seconds, and your fatigue resistance could be below average. In Figure 4.2, notice how even the spacing is between the lines—this is indicative of average fatigue resistance because the drop-off from one interval to the next appears to be similar. This is just the first point of triangulation in determining your Fatigue Profile. By creating these Fatigue Profile charts to review over time, you can refine your training and racing.

Table 4.2 shows the Fatigue Profile Guidelines you will use to create your personal profile. We will need to calculate the percentage of fatigue resistance, so let's take a closer look at the math involved. Joe Athlete completed his testing protocols or reviewed his existing power data and deduced that his peak power for Level 7 is as follows:

| | |
|---|---|
| 5 sec. | 1,550 watts |
| 10 sec. | 900 watts |
| 20 sec. | 500 watts |

The relationship between these numbers, namely the drop-off that we see between each output, will tell Joe exactly what his Fatigue Profile looks like. To quantify this relationship,

| LEVEL 5, VO$_2$MAX | | | LEVEL 4, LACTATE THRESHOLD | | |
|---|---|---|---|---|---|
| 3 min. | 5 min. | 8 min. | 20 min. (AP) | 60 min. (NP) | 90 min. (NP) |
| 100% | 15–20% | 24–30% | 100% | 7–11% | 15–25% |
| 100% | 8–14% | 18–23% | 100% | 4–6 % | 8–14% |
| 100% | 4–7 % | 10–17% | 100% | 2–4 % | 5–7% |

| LEVEL 5, VO$_2$MAX (W) | | | | LEVEL 4, LACTATE THRESHOLD (W) | | | |
|---|---|---|---|---|---|---|---|
| Description | 3 min. | 5 min. | 8 min. | Description | 20 min. (AP) | 60 min. (NP) | 90 min. (NP) |
| Strong initial effort | 340 | 320 | 299 | Strong endurance | 300 | 291 | 282 |
| | 340 | 306 | 272 | | 300 | 285 | 270 |
| Strong endurance | 400 | 332 | 292 | Strong 20 min. effort | 350 | 315 | 280 |

he will take both his 10-second peak power and his 20-second peak power as a percentage of wattage produced at 5 seconds. We do this by taking the difference between the two outputs (1,550 – 900 = 650 watts) and dividing by the power generated at 5 seconds (650 ÷ 1,500 = 43%). So, Joe finds out that from 5 to 10 seconds he experiences a 43 percent reduction in power. When he repeats this process to find his fatigue resistance at 20 seconds, he finds that his power at 20 seconds marks a 68 percent reduction in power as compared to his initial 5-second peak power (1,550 – 500 = 1,050, 1,050 ÷ 1,550 = 68%).

From these calculations, we can finish our triangulation of Joe's Fatigue Profile for Level 7. Joe's fatigue resistance for this energy system is well below average. Even though Joe has incredibly explosive power at 5 seconds, his wattages degrade quickly. You can follow this logic in Table 4.3. The same calculations are repeated for Levels 4, 5, and 6, according to Table 4.2. You will confirm your own triangulation when comparing these calculations with your mean maximal power charts and the examples and descriptions in Table 4.3.

Your Fatigue Profile reveals exactly what kind of a sprinter you are (Level 7), whether you should only race in criteriums (Level 6, above average fatigue), or if you should habitually attack from the start of the race (Level 4, above average fatigue resistance). Let's explore the different categories that relate to your fatigue resistance in more detail.

### Categories of Fatigue Resistance

#### Below-Average or Well-Below-Average Fatigue Resistance

If you are in either the "below average" or "well below average" category, this doesn't mean that all hope is lost and you should take up bowling. It simply means that although you do have below-average fatigue resistance, your abilities favor producing power at the shorter durations within each category. In other words, you have a very high wattage in the shortest time periods in each level tested, but a quick and dramatic drop-off of wattage in the longest time periods in the ranges.

For example, if you were a sprinter like Robbie McEwen, then you would be able to create a very high peak 5-second wattage, perhaps 1,800 watts, but then, by the time the 20-second drill came up, your power might be down at the 700-watt range, which would be a 63 percent degradation in power. These explosive sprinters have incredible "snaps," or the ability to accelerate very quickly, but they cannot maintain them for very long. Hence they have below-average fatigue resistance at the 20-second mark.

The difference between "well below average" and just "below average" *could* be a reason for you to question your training emphasis or your racing tactics. Those in the "well below average" category may need to accept that they are natural-born sprinters, for example, and that no amount of training will change that. Proper selection of races—and the tactics employed in those races—is critical for success. However, although someone with below-average fatigue resistance obviously has a tendency toward the shorter durations within the energy system tested, he or she may also be able to significantly increase fatigue resistance and change that category through careful training. Only Levels 6 and 7 get the distinction of having five categories, as the wattage differences in these levels are more significant than at longer durations and the differences between individuals in their fatigue resistance are more marked.

#### Average Fatigue Resistance

In the third category, the rider's power declines steadily from the first time period tested to the longest time period tested. So, for example, let's say that in testing your Anaerobic Capacity, you did 550 watts for 30 seconds and then 400 watts for 1 minute, but by 2 minutes you could average only 300 watts. For each time period there was a similar percentage decrease in wattage, and this puts you in the average power category for this level.

#### Above-Average and Well-Above-Average Fatigue Resistance

The fourth and fifth categories, above average and well above average (or good endurance), define the rider whose watts do not degrade very much over the entire range of time periods in the test. He or she may not have the highest wattages in the shortest time periods, however. For example, a rider with above-average fatigue resistance at $VO_2max$ could have a 3-minute wattage of 270, a 5-minute wattage of 250, and an 8-minute wattage of 240. This very low rate of wattage drop-off shows that this rider has above-average fatigue resistance within this given energy system. A well-above-average rider is at the extreme in this category and, just like the well-below-average rider, probably won't be able to change his or her natural genetic limits; therefore, this rider should make an effort to choose racing tactics and races that suit his or her strengths.

### Interpreting Fatigue Resistance

By discovering whether you have well-below-average, below-average, average, above-average, or well-above-average fatigue resistance within each range, you can go on to determine which races or terrain might be best suited for you as well as the specific time periods that you might need to focus on improving. For example, you could have a very high wattage number for your 30-second test in Anaerobic Capacity, but also below-average fatigue resistance in Anaerobic Capacity. This would be an advantage in races requiring high wattages for up to 30 seconds, but what if your upcoming race has three hills per lap and each hill is 2 minutes long? Although you might be able to attack at the bottom and beat everyone up the first bit of the hill, the last part of the hill will be troublesome for you. On the other hand, as Sam Krieg, one of the Peaks Coaching Group coaches, says, "It's the shorter durations that win the bike races. It's the guys who can outsnap you right near the finish or just have that perfect 3-minute burst of maximum power timed to perfection that win races. Fatigue resistance is super-important as well, but big wattage numbers in the shorter durations might be more important." Understanding where you are within each category helps to refine your training, which in turn enhances your racing.

Another example of this principle can be found in the sprint. Let's say that your Power Profile is that of a sprinter (downward-sloping to the right), but every time you initiate the sprint from 300 meters out, you get beaten on the line, with riders slowly closing the distance as you fatigue within the last 50 meters. A sprinter with plenty of explosiveness has an incredible "snap" and has a good chance of winning a short 100-meter sprint, but may be lacking in endurance when it comes to a longer sprint. It might be possible to overcome this limitation in training, or it might not, but one thing is certain: A sprinter with below-average fatigue resistance needs to be sure to wait until the last 100 meters before hitting the front if he or she is going to win the race. This is exactly the type of sprinter that Robbie McEwen is, and just about every time there has been a long sprint and he has had to "drag-race" a sprinter with above-average fatigue resistance, such as Alessandro Petacchi, he has lost. Robbie won when he was able to pop out of the line with 100 meters to go and then unleash his incredible 5-second burst of power.

### Caveats for the Fatigue Profile

You might find that you don't fit perfectly in one category or another. Use your best judgment in each case. If your power output is a little closer to one category, then assume that's most likely correct.

Another caveat you must consider when creating your Fatigue Profile is that it's possible you don't have enough power data to get a good representative sample size for each time period. This is why it's critical that you test each time period and be certain that you have more than one data sample in each of the time periods. Otherwise, the data are skewed and the resulting Fatigue Profile will be inaccurate.

## POWER PROFILING VERSUS FATIGUE PROFILING

With Power Profiling, you compare power *across* durations taken to be representative of Neuromuscular Power, Anaerobic Capacity, VO$_2$max, and Lactate Threshold so as to gain insight into your relative strengths and weaknesses, that is, to find out how much power you can actually produce. With Fatigue Profiling, you compare power *within* ranges of durations taken to be representative of the same physiological abilities, again to gain insight into your relative strengths and weaknesses. But in this case, you are interested in how well you can resist different forms of fatigue.

Since there is no duration at which performance is dependent upon one, and only one, ability, there is some overlap between these approaches. For example, someone with especially high anaerobic capacity and hence 1-minute power will tend to have a higher 5-minute power and will also tend to have less drop-off in power over the 3- to 8-minute duration. Still, breaking it down into Power Profiling and Fatigue Profiling does help put it all into perspective. We'll provide real-life examples of Fatigue Profiling in Chapter 9, "Developing a Power-Based Training Plan." There is also an online widget to create your Fatigue Profile on the Peaks Coaching Group website in the "Training and Racing with a Power Meter" journal section.

---

Now that you have created your own Power Profile and Fatigue Profile, you can easily see the areas in your own cycling that need to be addressed. Use these tables to motivate yourself to make improvements and also to race or ride to your strengths. If you are a world-class sprinter, it might be futile to try to break the Mt. Evans hill-climb record. You may even have limitations in certain areas because there is a genetic basis to your strengths and weaknesses. But in most cases, it is possible to focus your training and make strides toward specific goals. It's also important that you revise your chart on a regular basis (such as once every four to six weeks) in order to note any improvements from your previous training block. This is an excellent way to make sure all your hard work is going in the right places.

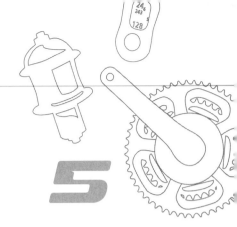

# Using Power for Optimal Workouts

**Now that you know your functional threshold power and power levels,** and have determined your strengths and weaknesses as a cyclist by constructing a Power Profile, you can begin to change your training to better address your unique situation. You can improve in the weak areas, and you can track your fitness increases. By developing specific workouts based on wattage, you will be able to monitor your efforts in training more accurately. You will be able to make better decisions about when to stop an interval, when to take a rest day, and when to tackle greater challenges. The tips presented in this chapter are not meant to last for only a season, nor do we present a "one size fits all" workout plan that every cyclist can follow. Rather, our goal is to help you to discover how to develop your own training program to meet your unique set of objectives, and how to reevaluate and revise that program as you make progress.

## TRAINING OPPORTUNITIES

Simply said, you can use your power meter on every ride, but some rides are more useful than others for optimizing the technology as a tool in achieving your peak performance. Specifically, you should use your power meter:

*On an indoor trainer.* On a trainer, it is easy to regulate your wattage, as there are no external influences, such as wind or traffic, to interfere, and you can easily hold to a specific wattage range.

*On flat roads.* This is also an excellent place in which to utilize a specific wattage protocol, as the terrain allows for a steady power output.

*In time trials.* Using your power meter to help maintain your pace right at lactate threshold is one of the greatest ways to incorporate it into racing. You can stick to your power goal like glue and also select the best cadence. Use your power meter to follow the cardinal rule of time trialing: Don't start too hard, don't start too hard, don't start too hard!

*In hill climbs.* When climbing a gradual grade, you can stay within a small range of power and use watts to maintain an optimal pace. You can determine your optimal climbing cadence by doing multiple repeats on a climb, selecting different cadences each time, and seeing which cadence produces the most watts.

*While doing specific intervals and training protocols.* Using your power meter to do, for example, a 5-minute interval at 295–305 watts is a perfect example of being able to really dial in your training. Using heart rate as a guide for doing the same 5-minute interval could cause you to go too hard in the beginning, thus reaching a higher power level than you wanted and overshooting your goal for the effort.

*While doing "race-winning intervals" and other wattage-based workouts.* You will begin to put together your own favorite workouts using wattage, and that will help motivate you to achieve even more success. By using the "interval" or "set" function to mark an interval, you can watch your average wattage while executing the interval, and this can become a great "carrot" for you to push harder than before.

## THE "STOCHASTIC" NATURE OF CYCLING

One of the first things you may notice when you begin riding with a power meter is the highly variable nature of your wattage. One second it's 500 watts, the next second it's 0 watts, and the next it's 220 watts. Although your power seems "stochastic," or random, it is actually just highly variable because of the nature of the terrain, the wind, the riders around and in front of you, and so on. This seeming randomness makes it very hard to maintain your watts in a narrow range. Only on the flattest of roads, with little to no wind, or on an indoor trainer is it possible to adhere strictly to a small range of wattage.

Because of this inherently stochastic nature of cycling, it is important not to become discouraged if you are unable to hold a perfect 300 watts while doing, for example, a lactate threshold interval. Rather than trying to hit a specific wattage target, you should attempt to stay within a particular range. Avoid overdoing the maximum watts for a particular effort. For example, if your goal is to work the lactate system but not go too hard, you might focus on producing at least 300 watts, but not exceeding 320 watts, while holding a 90 rpm cadence. The importance of correctly pacing your efforts during a specific interval will become very evident, because it is pacing that will allow you to successfully complete the interval correctly.

As you read through the workout suggestions that follow and begin to incorporate them into your training, make sure that you also choose the correct terrain for each type of ef-fort. In this way, you will activate the appropriate physiological systems. If you are trying to improve your anaerobic system with 1-minute efforts at 475–500 watts, for example, then make sure you are attacking a slight uphill for that minute or a flat road without any downhills. If you are focusing on a 60-minute effort in your Tempo level, then make sure that you keep your watts in this range 90 percent of the time. There may be times when you have to go up a hill and your watts will be over your Tempo range, and this is fine; just make sure that you apply steady power and come back to the Tempo range when you crest the hill. The same applies on the downhills, where it's nearly impossible to push hard enough on the pedals to create a high wattage number, and that's okay; just make sure you are on the gas as much as possible and back to your Tempo range soon.

If you live in an area that offers only one type of terrain, then you will have to make adjustments in your training to overcome this. For example, if all the roads available to you are flat, you could use the wind to your advantage in generating more resistance to push against. Rolling hills present the greatest challenge to holding a smooth and steady power output. If you live in an area with only rolling hills, focus on staying within your target wattage range on the uphills. It would be difficult, in any case, to make rolling terrain into a Tempo ride: If you wanted to end your ride with your average watts in the Tempo level, then you would have to hammer up every hill, because your watts would go down on every downhill run. Unfortunately, this would not be a Tempo workout! It would be a hill-repeat workout, and most likely you would be working on your VO$_2$max or your anaerobic capacity system. The nature of hilly terrain also makes it very tough to do easy recovery rides and endurance rides without having to put your power in the upper training levels. If you live in such an area and you need a rest, then ride on an indoor trainer so you can more easily adhere to the recovery wattage guidelines.

## GUIDELINES FOR OPTIMAL INTERVALS

When should you stop doing repeats? Is there a point at which doing just one more interval is actually not helping you anymore? Can you do too many intervals? And at what point do you experience diminishing marginal returns? These questions have probably been asked by every cyclist and coach a thousand times over, and they have been the source of many an argument between sports scientists. But there is an easy answer to all of them: It depends!

It depends on your goal for that particular workout, your current level of fitness, the big picture of how that session fits into the goals you have for your training, and your own ability to dig deep and put out a 110 percent effort. Since there are so many factors involved in making a decision about when to end an interval session, it is difficult to provide precise guidelines, and any guidelines put forth will likely not address all the issues. Nevertheless, we have presented a way to determine the optimum number of repeats in Table 5.1. These

| TABLE 5.1 | When to Stop Intervals |
|-----------|------------------------|
| **Intervals** | **Average Drop in Power** |
| 20 min. | 3–5% |
| 10 min. | 4–6% |
| 5 min. | 5–7% |
| 3 min. | 8–9% |
| 2 min. | 10–12% |
| 1 min. | 10–12% |
| 30 sec. | 12–15% |
| 15 sec. | Peak power drops by 15–20%; average power for interval drops by 10–15% |

*Note: The percentage drop in average watts is based on the number of watts achieved in the third effort. For example, when doing 5-minute intervals, a rider is ready for a rest when his or her average watts for an interval are 5–7 percent lower than they were for the third effort.*

numbers are based on our review of more than 3,000 power-meter files and our experience of working with more than 1,000 athletes in training with power. We produced this table for the first edition, but it has now been validated again and again in our work with hundreds of additional athletes over the past few years. In fact, it has proven to be so useful that we would like to expand on this concept and argue that this is one of the key reasons to use your power meter in every training session.

All serious cyclists strive for optimal training, but in the past, without a way to quantitatively measure (and record) the true work done in training workouts, we have only been able to guess at the optimal number of intervals to be carried out in order for an athlete to gain the most benefit. When Joe Friel wrote the first edition of *The Cyclist's Training Bible* and explained his personal coaching and training philosophy, he said: "An athlete should do the least amount of the most specific training that brings continual improvement." When we first read that, it made sense to us immediately, but at the same time we scratched our heads and asked, "How do I know it's the right amount, though? What determines 'the least amount'?" Being the overachievers and hypercompetitors that we were, it didn't jibe with our own training philosophy, which was that the person who trains the hardest and the most will be the most successful. If your competitor is out doing ten hill repeats, then shouldn't you be out doing fifteen, just so you are stronger than he or she?

The problem was that there was no way to accurately quantify diminishing marginal returns when doing intervals. The question, How many intervals is enough? just couldn't be answered. Now, with your power meter and the information in Table 5.1, an answer is possible: You can do "intervals to exhaustion," or accurately determine the correct number of intervals to do in each session, without going too far over the hump in the diminishing marginal returns curve. It is still with some hesitation that we provide these guidelines. Being able to quantify a rider's percentage wattage reduction after each interval by using a power meter has opened up the possibility of truly narrowing the factors that determine when interval sessions should be stopped; however, continued research needs to be done in this area. Therefore, keep in mind that the guidelines presented in Table 5.1 should be adjusted according to your own situation, fitness level, and goals. In the table, we have based the percentage drop-off on the third interval that you complete because typically, the effort that a rider can put forth in his or her first two intervals will be much higher than what that rider could actually repeat multiple times. Since we assume you are "fresh" when you begin your interval session, we throw out those first two efforts for the purpose of determining when to stop a workout. Obviously, if you are doing longer intervals in which you might complete only two intervals total, then this rule does not apply.

Let's look at an example. Let's say that an athlete wants to work on his VO₂max power to prepare for a race with eight 5-minute climbs. From Chapter 3, we know that his VO₂max is stressed when he is riding at between 106 and 120 percent of his functional threshold power. The intensity must be in the correct training range in order to place enough stress on that energy system, in this case the VO₂max, to stimulate improvement. At the same time, the duration of the effort must be long enough to stress that energy system. If the athlete rode at 120 percent of FTP for only 30 seconds, that would not be long enough to actually cause an adaptation to occur. For the VO₂max system to adapt to a training stimulus, a minimal effort of 3 minutes is necessary, with the maximum duration being about 8 minutes. After 8 minutes, it's very difficult, if not impossible, for most people to maintain 106–120 percent of FTP.

Understanding this relationship between time and intensity will allow him to set some guidelines about the optimal number of intervals to do in his workouts. For instance, since he is trying to improve his VO₂max system, and wants to prepare for the race with eight 5-minute climbs, then he should do eight 5-minute intervals at 106 to 120 percent of FTP (let's use an FTP of 300 watts in this example). The first interval could be at 360 watts, the second at 350, and the third at 340. This third interval is what we call the "repeatable" interval. The watts that he does in that interval are the watts that he can repeat multiple times. The first two efforts are the "fresh" efforts when he has plenty of glycogen in his muscles and a lot of anaerobic work capacity available to produce big wattage; once that anaerobic work capacity is used up, he is left with just the right amount of energy to produce an effort that can be repeated.

The reason this is so important is that we must take the wattage in the third effort and subtract 5 percent from it (in this case, 340 × 0.05 = 17, and 340 – 17 = 323 watts) to determine when to stop the repeats. When this athlete cannot average at least this many watts (323) for his interval, he is going to stop, as he would now not be training intensely enough to elicit enough stress to cause a training improvement or adaptation. Let's say that in the sixth interval he produces 320 watts, and because he is an overachiever (like many serious cyclists) and he wants to make absolutely certain that he has done as much as possible, he does one more interval. But then, let's suppose that by the time he is in the second minute of the interval, he sees that he cannot even maintain 310 watts, much less 320 or more. This immediately lets him know that he is now working below the intensity needed to stimulate the VO₂max system. He cannot maintain the wattage over time needed to create enough stimulus for improvement.

These intervals-to-exhaustion guidelines can help you to understand exactly when to stop doing interval repeats. It's all based on that telling third effort. Of course, it requires a bit of mental math out on the training ride, but as long as you know the percentage drop-off to look for in each time period, then you should be able to quickly and easily figure out how many intervals are optimal for each workout.

In the next example, shown in Figure 5.1, we see a case where the athlete could have done more intervals to gain even more training adaptation. This athlete's watts didn't drop at all from the first interval to the third interval; instead they actually went up. The athlete's third interval averaged 320 watts. A 5 percent drop-off would be 304 watts, which would suggest that the athlete should do just one last interval before stopping. Unfortunately, he stopped after the fifth interval when he could have easily done another, if not two or more, because the fourth interval was still less than a 5 percent drop-off in power.

We are all limited by the time we have to train, and we all want to train in the most efficient way possible. Using your power meter to figure out the optimal number of training intervals for each workout makes sense. It allows you to put Joe Friel's philosophy into practice: "Train just enough for success." With a power meter, you can quantify your optimal training load in the grand scheme and truly optimize your training each day. As a result, you can improve at the highest rate that you are capable of. And when you can train at an optimal level, you'll be assured of success.

**FIGURE 5.1**    **Power Graph Showing Insufficient Intervals**

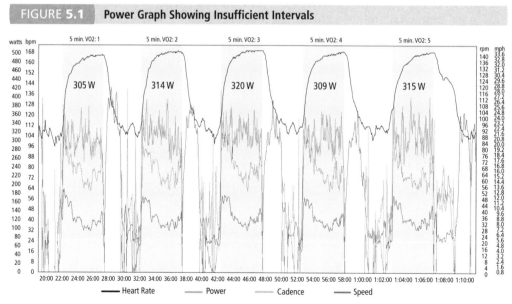

*In this scenario, the athlete "underachieved." The athlete's third interval averaged 320 W. 5 percent off of this number would be 304 W. However, the athlete's last interval was at 315 W, so he could have done at least one more effort if not a couple more.*

## WORKOUTS FOR POWER-BASED TRAINING

Below, we describe sample workouts that correspond to different cycling goals. Here, we use the fictitious "Joe Athlete" once again, to give you some ideas about how to train at the specific training levels that you learned about in Chapter 3 (see Table 3.1). By reading the following workouts and charting the best routes for them where you live, you'll be better prepared to adhere to the intended philosophy of each workout. Be sure to always be safe and careful in your workouts and think about the big picture: Don't just focus on the numbers. You will find a complete Workout Guide in Appendix B.

Our hypothetical Joe Athlete is a Category III racer, and his functional threshold power wattage is 290. His heart rate at this level is 175 bpm, and his max heart rate is 200. Joe weighs in at 160 pounds, and his ratio of watts per kilogram at threshold is about 4. He is a very good sprinter and has very good anaerobic capacity as well. His Power Profile is downward-sloping to the right (the typical "sprinter" described in Chapter 4).

In these workouts, we are assuming the best of conditions, from weather to road surface to a strong and healthy Joe. Joe also pedals at his normal "self-selected" cadence, unless the workout description says otherwise. To find the correct number of watts for your workouts, you will have to calculate the percentages from your own functional threshold power using the instructions presented in Chapter 3. In some cases, when specifying power for Joe Athlete at different training levels, we've rounded the range to the nearest increment of 5 watts to make it easier to apply on the training ride.

### Level 1: Active Recovery

Joe Athlete does his Active Recovery (Level 1) workout when he needs to recover from a hard workout the day before or cool down at the end of a hard workout.

| WORKOUT | Level 1, Spin | | | |
|---|---|---|---|---|
| | Time | Description | % of FTP | % of FTHR |
| Warm-up | 15 min. | Easy riding | 48–51 | 65 |
| Main set | 1 hr. | Spin, 90–95 rpm | 55 | <68 |
| Cooldown | 15 min. | Easy riding | <48 | 65 |

There are two options that Joe might choose for a Level 1 ride. The first one lasts for about 1.5 hours. Joe warms up for 15 minutes, holding his watts under 148 (that is, staying within 48–51 percent of his threshold power of 290 watts). Then he rides for the next hour with his watts under 160 (55 percent), keeping his cadence nice and smooth at 90–95 rpm. He cools down for 15 minutes, maintaining his wattage below 140 (48 percent).

For the second option, Joe rides for a total of 1 hour, warming up for 10 minutes, with his watts under 140 (a range of 45–48 percent), then keeps his cadence about 5–8 rpm higher than his normal, self-selected cadence for the next 40 minutes, maintaining his watts at 145–160 (50–55 percent). He cools down at his normal cadence, with watts under 140 (48 percent).

| WORKOUT | | Level 1, 1 Hour | | |
|---|---|---|---|---|
| | Time | Description | % of FTP | % of FTHR |
| Warm-up | 10 min. | Easy riding | 45–48 | 65 |
| Main set | 40 min. | Spin, +5–8 rpm | 50–55 | <68 |
| Cooldown | 10 min. | Easy riding | <48 | 65 |

This is an embarrassingly slow pace, and that is why too many elite racers do not do enough riding at this level. When you are going out for a recovery ride, it should really be slow and all about recovery. If you go above the upper limit of the wattage range for this level, then you are riding too hard to recover properly, but not hard enough to train. It is very important physically to do Active Recovery rides because they help to flush your system of built-up waste products, keep your body in a rhythm of riding, and maintain suppleness in your muscles.

Reminder: It is okay if your watts go above the 55 percent level a few times during the ride. When you get back from your ride and download the data, however, the average power should be under the 55 percent level.

## Level 2: Endurance

When Joe wants to build a base of endurance and enhance his aerobic fitness, he emphasizes Endurance rides (Level 2). Over time, training in this range will lead to the development of a stronger heart muscle, increase mitochondrial levels in the cells, develop more capillarization in his muscles, and result in an overall increase in his stamina.

| WORKOUT | | Level 2, 2.5 Hours | | |
|---|---|---|---|---|
| | Time | Description | % of FTP | % of FTHR |
| Warm-up | 15 min. | Easy riding | <56 | 65 |
| Main set | 2 hr. | Endurance | 69–75 | 69–83 |
| Cooldown | 15 min. | Easy riding | <56 | 65 |

| WORKOUT | | Level 2, 3.5 Hours | | |
|---|---|---|---|---|
| | Time | Description | % of FTP | % of FTHR |
| Warm-up | 15 min. | Easy riding | <65 | 68 |
| Main set | 3 hr. | Endurance with 8-sec. bursts every 10 min. | 69–75 | 69–83 |
| | 8 sec. | Bursts, 120 rpm | 103 | 104–105 |
| Cooldown | 15 min. | Easy riding | <55 | 65 |

For this workout, Joe may take a 2.5-hour ride, starting with a warm-up of 15 minutes with his output in watts at less than 162 (less than 56 percent of FTP, or Active Recovery pace). He then rides at a level of 200–220 watts (69–75 percent) for 2 hours. His cadence is self-selected. He cools down for 15 minutes, with his watts under 162 (56 percent).

Alternatively, he may ride for 3.5 hours total, warming up for 15 minutes while keeping his watts under 190 (65 percent). He then rides with his watts at 200–220 (69–75 percent) for 3 hours, but includes some bursts of faster riding once every 10 minutes (8 seconds, seated, taking rpm to 130 and watts to 300, or 103 percent). The rest of the ride is at a normal, self-selected cadence, and he cools down for 15 minutes, keeping his watts under 150.

It is very important that you do enough of these longer rides to prepare your body for harder levels of riding. The longer you can ride, the better. The workouts described below for Levels 3–7 are on the short side; therefore, to receive the benefits of riding at an Endurance level, long Level 2 rides are the best.

### Level 3: Tempo

The Tempo level is the "meat and potatoes" of every cyclist, and it is probably the level that cyclists ride in more than any other. A Tempo ride should be done at a pace that feels fast and also takes some work.

Do not underestimate the amount of work that training in this level requires. However, this level of training is also one of the most beneficial for most cyclists. Riding in Level 3 causes some of the greatest adaptations in your training stress. It's the best bang for the buck, so to speak. There are a variety of ways to effectively train in Level 3, and two of these are described below. But remember to keep the big picture in mind. Do not worry, for example, if your watts go above 90 percent of your threshold (the upper limit of Level 3) on a few hills or in a short headwind section. That's okay: It's the average watts (or normalized watts—discussed in more detail in Chapter 7) that are important.

Many a coach has referred to this level as a cyclist's "no-man's-land," and it's true that training in this level will not make you either a better sprinter or a better hill climber. If you spend too much time here, you just get very good at riding at Level 3 and not much else. It is wise not to get caught in the trap of constantly spending valuable training time in this level. If you want to improve your power at $VO_2max$, then you will have to train at $VO_2max$ power: Tempo power just won't be sufficient.

If you have limited time, however, or if you are trying to increase your muscular endurance, then this level is just what the doctor called for. If all you have is 3 hours a week to ride, then drill it in the upper range of Level 3 and get in a great workout; or, if you are getting prepped for a long 100-mile race, then being able to ride in this zone for 2.5–3 hours will pay off with a possible podium finish.

Here are two 2.5-hour rides for our fictitious Joe Athlete, with more options found in Appendix B. For the first ride, he warms up for 15 minutes, keeping his watts under 200, or 68 percent, which is

| WORKOUT | Level 3, 2.5 Hours | | | |
|---|---|---|---|---|
| | Time | Description | % of FTP | % of FTHR |
| Warm-up | 15 min. | Easy riding | <68 | <70 |
| Main set | 2 hr. | Tempo | 76–90 | 84–94 |
| Cooldown | 15 min. | Easy riding | <55 | <68 |

a good intensity to begin warming up the muscles. It's not as easy as recovery pace, but it's not so hard that it will undermine the entire workout. Joe then rides at Tempo pace, between 76 and 90 percent of his threshold (220–260 watts). He tries his best to hold this

| WORKOUT | | Level 3, Cadence Work | | |
|---|---|---|---|---|
| | Time | Description | % of FTP | % of FTHR |
| Warm-up | 15 min. | Easy riding | <68 | <70 |
| Main set | 40 min. | Tempo | 76–90 | 84–94 |
| | 20 min. | Cadence work, −15 rpm | 76–90 | 84–94 |
| | 40 min. | Tempo | 76–90 | 84–94 |
| | 20 min. | Cadence work, +15 rpm | 76–90 | 84–94 |
| Cooldown | 15 min. | Easy riding | <55 | <68 |

range over hills, on flats, and even on downhill runs. The emphasis is on spending as much time as possible in the 240–260 (82–90 percent) range. He keeps his cadence at his self-selected level, metering his efforts on hills. He may go over 260, and that's fine, but he does not sprint up hills.

For the other option, Joe warms up with his watts under 200 (68 percent), then rides at between 76 and 90 percent of his threshold, 220–260 watts. However, this time he does two 20-minute segments of specific cadence work. The first one is at a cadence 15 rpm lower than his self-selected cadence to emphasize strength endurance; the second is at a cadence 15 rpm higher than his self-selected cadence, emphasizing leg speed and muscular endurance. Again, he goes steady and smooth, metering his effort on hills.

An alternative approach to Tempo workouts is to treat the Level 3 ride as a fartlek workout. That is, deliberately vary the power to try to replicate the "stochasticity" of mass-start racing. In other words, as you ride at Tempo pace, randomly accelerate and vary your power within that Tempo wattage to better simulate the demands of racing. Although this may or may not necessarily be better than following the option described above, training in this manner will tend to be highly specific to the demands of racing. Since mass-start racing is not limited to a specific level of training, applying a fartlek-type philosophy will definitely help foster improvement. If you take this approach, your rides should be shorter, however, since you will be creating more training stress than in just a nice, solid, steady Tempo ride.

### Lower Level 4: Sub-Threshold, or the "Sweet Spot"

The lower part of Level 4 is what we call the Sub-Threshold level, or the "sweet spot." This sweet spot occurs at about 88–94 percent of your functional threshold power. That means that it is on the cusp of both the Tempo level and the Lactate Threshold level. Although this is not exactly an official level of its own, it is an excellent place to begin building your FTP and pushing it higher.

In our coaching, we encourage the athletes we work with to train heavily in this area at the beginning of the racing season, before moving into training right at their FTP (91–105 percent). This intensity level is also great to revisit right around the middle of June in order to achieve a second peak in the fall. Even if an athlete is not trying to achieve a second peak, we incorporate this sweet spot training into his or her schedule at least once or twice every fourteen days. Figure 5.2 highlights this important training zone.

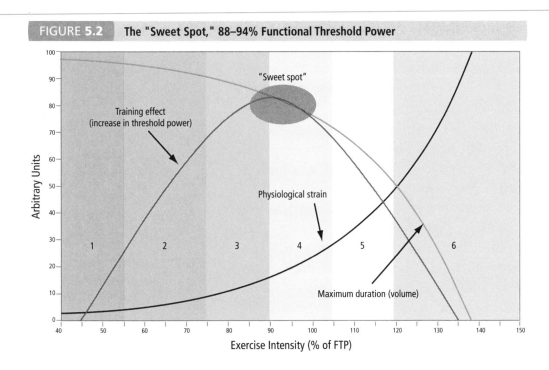

| FIGURE **5.2** | The "Sweet Spot," 88–94% Functional Threshold Power |

Riding in this range certainly does not help significantly with your sprint, your power at VO₂max, or your anaerobic capacity. Nor is it going to make you the best criterium racer. But at the same time, if all your training were in this area, at least you probably wouldn't get dropped. All in all, it's one of the most beneficial places to spend your training time. Just make sure that you are training the other systems as well.

### WORKOUT — Level 4, Sub-Threshold

| | Time | Description | % of FTP | % of FTHR |
|---|---|---|---|---|
| Warm-up | 15 min. | Easy riding | <68 | <70 |
| Main set | 5 min. | All-out effort | 100 | >106 |
| | 2 × 20 min. (15 min. RI) | Sub-threshold with high cadence | 88–94 | 95–98 |
| | 8–10 × 1 min. (2 min. RI) | Fast pedaling, +105 rpm | 85–95 | 90–98 |
| Cooldown | 15 min. | Easy riding | <55 | <68 |

To train at this level, Joe Athlete would ride for 2–2.5 hours, warming up well for 15 minutes at below 200 watts (68 percent), then do one 5-minute effort at 290 watts, or 100 percent of threshold power. This is to get his body ready for some solid work. He would then do two efforts of 20 minutes each with his watts at a range of 255–272 (88–94 percent of threshold power). It is critical for him to stay in this range as best he can. He would rest for 15 minutes between efforts. He uses a gear that allows him to keep his cadence in his self-selected range, or challenges himself to pedal just a touch faster than he normally would. He finishes the workout with several (eight or ten) 1-minute intervals of fast pedaling with a high cadence (over 105 rpm), holding his watts under 280 (85–95 percent range), and resting for 2 minutes between efforts. The goal is not to go super-hard, but to spin a high cadence at Sub-Threshold power. Then, he goes into his cooldown.

There are other options to Joe's workout at this level. Depending on his fitness level, the time of year, and his experience in cycling, it might be better for him to start out with a shorter time period and build up as he gains more fitness. For example, for the main part of the workout, he could start with three 12-minute efforts and build up to four 12-minute efforts, then start over at three 15-minute efforts, build to four 15-minute efforts, and then move to two 20-minute efforts. A Category III racer like Joe Athlete should not need to do more than two 20-minute efforts, but cyclists rated in higher categories should strive to build to four 20-minute segments.

In any case, he should do at least six to eight of these workouts before moving to specific threshold work. This type of workout is a good base upon which to build threshold work, so he should be sure to make it a base that is wide and strong. If he moves to upper Level 4 work and above too soon, he could compromise the solidity of this foundation.

Remember: When you are working at this level, don't hammer over hills; instead, keep your pedaling pressure steady up to the crest of the hill.

### *Typical Level 4: Threshold*

Threshold-level workouts are meant to focus directly on improving your FTP, and they are done right at FTP. They are strenuous and require a solid recovery between efforts and also between workouts. Otherwise, they are very similar to the previous level, Sub-Threshold. The only difference is that the intensity is increased a notch to hold you right on your "edge." These are important workouts to perform, not only so you can increase your ability to handle the level of intensity needed to maintain this type of effort, but also so that you can continually improve your threshold power.

| WORKOUT | Level 4, Traditional Threshold | | | |
|---|---|---|---|---|
| | Time | Description | % of FTP | % of FTHR |
| Warm-up | 15 min. | Easy riding | <68 | <70 |
| Main set | 5 min. | All-out effort | 100 | >106 |
| | 5 min. | Easy riding | <68 | <70 |
| | 2 × 20 min. (10–15 min. RI) | Threshold | 96–105 | 98–106 |
| Cooldown | 15 min. | Easy riding | <76 | <75 |

Joe Athlete will ride for 2–2.5 hours to train at this level, with a 15-minute warm-up in which he holds his watts under 200 (68 percent). He then gets in one "blowout" effort with watts at 290 (100 percent), followed by 5 minutes at an easy pace—that is, less than 200 watts (68 percent). After that, he does two 20-minute efforts at 288–305 watts (96–105 percent), with 10–15 minutes of resting in between. After the second effort, he cruises for 15 minutes with his watts below 220 (76 percent).

Joe could have used other options that parallel those under the previous level for building up to the 20-minute efforts. If he chose to do so, he would have simply followed those plans, but at FTP wattage instead of just below that level.

If your goal is to become a strong Category III racer, we suggest building up to riding for at least 1 hour at this power level.

### Nontypical Level 4 Workouts

There are some other ways to train at Level 4 that are not so typical. These workouts might give you a different way to think about training at this important level.

For a 2-hour ride, warm up for 15 minutes at 68 percent of your FTP (for Joe Athlete, that would be less than 200 watts). Then do one strong 5-minute effort at 100 percent of threshold watts. For the main part of the ride, do a 10-minute effort at 100–107 percent, and then bring up the intensity by 10 watts in each successive minute until you reach your limit. See if you can increase the number of minutes you last, as well as your ability to hold a constant load and pace. Follow up with a cooldown.

Another 2-hour ride would also start with the 15-minute warm-up, with watts under 68 percent of FTP and the 5-minute effort at 100 percent. Next, however, you would cruise for an easy 5 minutes, then begin a 15-minute effort with specific wattage goals: Begin strong, at 110 percent of your FTP, and hold this for 2 minutes; drop the wattage

| WORKOUT | | Level 4, Ramp from Threshold | | |
|---|---|---|---|---|
| | **Time** | **Description** | **% of FTP** | **% of FTHR** |
| Warm-up | 15 min. | Easy riding | 68 | <70 |
| | 5 min. | All-out effort | 100 | >106 |
| Main set | 10 min. | Threshold | 100–107 | >106 |
| | | *Increase 10 watts each min. until you reach limit* | *+10 watts* | *>100* |
| Cooldown | 15 min. | Easy riding | <76 | <75 |

| WORKOUT | | Level 4, Crisscross | | |
|---|---|---|---|---|
| | **Time** | **Description** | **% of FTP** | **% of FTHR** |
| Warm-up | 15 min. | Easy riding | <68 | <70 |
| | 5 min. | Blowout effort | 100 | >106 |
| | 5 min. | Recover | <70 | <75 |
| | 2–3 × | Drill | | |
| Main set | *2 min.* | *Ride at threshold level* | *110* | *>106* |
| | *4 min.* | *Back off 10 watts each min.* | *−10 watts* | |
| | *2 min.* | *Build 10 watts each min.* | *+10 watts* | |
| | *7 min.* | *Hold power steady* | *95–105* | *>106* |
| | | *Repeat drill 2–3 times, with recovery between each effort* | | |
| Cooldown | 15 min. | Easy riding | <68 | <70 |

down by about 10 watts each minute for 4 minutes; bring the watts back up by 10 watts each minute for 2 minutes; and hold it here for the remaining 7 minutes (try to pick it up to 110 percent in the last 45–60 seconds if you can). Repeat this drill two or three times and allow for good recovery between efforts.

The goal of this exercise is to start out hard in order to load up the system with lactate, demand a steady output for a short period of time, scale back to prevent exhaustion, and then force yourself to hold just at your threshold power or a touch above. In the end, you ramp back up in order to make a final push.

Another nontypical ride at this level could be called the "Hour of Power." It could equally be called the "Hour of Pain." This is a particularly hard workout that has been popularized by Bill Black, an elite masters athlete. He created it to combat the boredom of indoor training during a long Maine winter. Give it your best shot!

| WORKOUT | Level 4, Hour of Power | | | |
|---|---|---|---|---|
| | **Time** | **Description** | **% of FTP** | **% of FTHR** |
| Warm-up | 15 min. | Easy riding | <68 | <70 |
| Main set | 20 min. | Ramp up to Threshold | 91–105 | 95–105 |
| | 1 hr. | Steady Threshold effort with 10-sec. bursts every 2 min. | 100 | >100 |
| | 10 sec. | *Burst, out of the saddle*<br>*Shift down, drop or raise cadence 20 rpm* | 105 | >100 |
| Cooldown | 15 min. | Easy riding | <68 | <70 |

**FIGURE 5.3    Bill Black's Hour of Power**

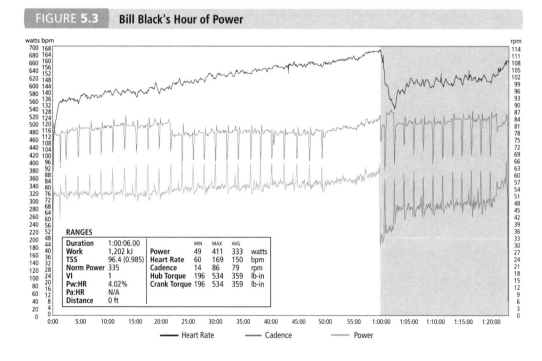

Begin this 1.5-hour workout by ramping up to your threshold power level (100 percent of FTP), reaching it by the 20-minute mark. If you want to work on muscle tension, then do 80 rpm; otherwise, pedal at a self-selected cadence. Now hold this wattage for the rest of the hour, as you are now training correctly to enhance your FTP. Every 2 minutes, get out of the saddle for 10 seconds, shift down a gear, and drop or raise the cadence by 20 rpm. Then cool down at the end of the hour.

Figure 5.3 shows a graph of Bill Black's "Hour of Power." In this screen shot, you can see how he gradually builds up to his FTP, incorporating small bursts during this time. Note how his heart rate gradually increases throughout the workout, showing the effects of possible overheating and/or dehydration.

### Level 5: VO$_2$max

Designed to elicit improvements in your VO$_2$max, or the maximal volume of oxygen uptake, workouts for Level 5 range from 3 to 8 minutes, with the majority of work typically done in the lower end of this range of time.

Joe Athlete, for example, out on a 2-hour ride, may want to work at this level to boost his VO$_2$max. If so, he would begin with a 15-minute warm-up, keeping his wattage at less than 200 (that is, less than 68 percent of FTP). Then he would do one 5-minute interval at 290 watts (100 percent), followed by 5 minutes at an easy pace. The main part of the workout would then begin. He would do six 3-minute efforts, trying for an average of 340 watts (117 percent of FTP or greater) in each effort. He would rest for 3 minutes between efforts. Following the sixth one, he would cruise easy for 10 minutes, and then do four 2-minute efforts with 4 minutes of rest between them. In these four efforts, he would try to average between 330 and 350 watts (113–120 percent). Finally, he would cool down.

Another 2-hour ride at this level would start out the same way—the same 15-minute warm-up, the same 5-minute interval at 100 percent of FTP, and the same easy 5 minutes. The main part of the workout, however, would be different. Joe would start out with five efforts in which he pushed his level of watts to 330 (113 percent), and in each successive

| WORKOUT | Level 5, VO$_2$max Intervals | | | |
|---|---|---|---|---|
| | Time | Description | % of FTP | % of FTHR |
| Warm-up | 15 min. | Easy riding | <68 | <70 |
| | 5 min. | All-out effort | 100 | >106 |
| | 5 min. | Easy riding | 68 | <70 |
| Main set | 6 × 3 min. (3 min. RI) | VO$_2$max | 117 | >106 |
| | 10 min. | Easy riding | 68 | <70 |
| | 4 × 2 min. (4 min. RI) | VO$_2$max | 113–120 | >106 |
| Cooldown | 15 min. | Easy riding | 68 | <70 |

| WORKOUT | | Level 5, VO$_2$max Build | | |
|---|---|---|---|---|
| | **Time** | **Description** | **% of FTP** | **% of FTHR** |
| Warm-up | 15 min. | Easy riding | <68 | <70 |
| Main set | 5 min. | All-out effort | 100 | >106 |
| | 5 min. | Easy riding | 68 | <70 |
| | 5 × Build (5 min. RI) | VO$_2$max efforts, adding 30 seconds with successive intervals (5.0 min., 5.5 min., 6.0 min., 6.5 min., 7.0 min.) | 113 | >106 |
| | 2 × 3 min. (5 min. RI) | All-out effort | >100 | >106 |
| Cooldown | 15 min. | Easy riding | 68 | <70 |

effort, he would try to extend the time by 30 seconds. The first effort would last 5 minutes, the second would last 5½ minutes, the third would be 6 minutes, and so on.

Be sure to apply the intervals-to-exhaustion concept and Table 5.1 to all of these workouts. If you try this workout and cannot extend the efforts by an additional 30 seconds each, then try reducing the intensity by 10–15 watts (3–5 percent) so that you can do them for the full recommended times. Do not reduce the intensity below 106 percent, however. Instead, go ahead and start with shorter periods of time, but work toward extending the duration. Do 5–8 minutes of Recovery-level riding between efforts. Finish the workout with two hard, all-out 3-minute efforts reaching 100 percent or greater of FTP, and rest for 5 minutes between efforts.

VO$_2$max is an important factor in racing, and therefore, training at this level is essential for cyclists who race. This fact became obvious when Hunter started to examine the downloaded power-meter files of the athletes with whom he worked who had won races. He began to see a pattern, and once he noticed it, he realized that it was appearing again and again. In these files, the race-winning move always contained an initial attack to create separation from the field—that is, a breakaway—then a continued high effort to establish the separation, followed by a relative settling in at threshold power and a finish with a short burst of speed. This type of race-winning effort is considered a VO$_2$max effort because of the short amount of time available to complete the effort and the average power that the breakaway move elicits. Practicing this exact pattern is the perfect race-winning simulation. It is a series of moves that plays out just as easily in a criterium as it does in a road race or even a track points race. Because the power-meter data reveal how they work, it is possible to put these efforts inside a solid, Endurance-pace workout to increase your chance of winning and create a super workout.

In Figure 5.4, it is easy to see the initial explosive effort that was needed to create a separation from other racers. At the same time, the upper line, which represents heart rate, climbs to respond to this quick burst of power. As the effort continues, the watts come down to hug the threshold power line (bottom dashed line), and then the effort ends with a short

| FIGURE **5.4** | **Race-Winning Effort** |
|---|---|

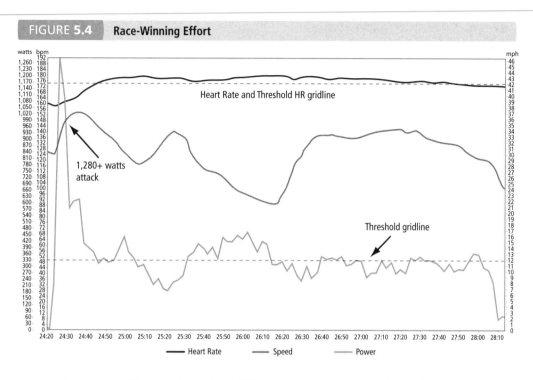

increase in wattage. The speed line (middle) provides a perspective about the terrain. Notice that as the speed goes down right in the middle of the graph, the power goes up dramatically, indicating that the rider is going up a hill.

A workout that duplicates these race-winning efforts includes five to eight efforts, following a sensible warm-up. Each effort begins with a 30-second sprint (15 seconds out of the saddle), and you must average approximately 200 percent of your threshold power in these, peaking at around 300 percent (for Joe Athlete, this would be a 600-watt average and a peak of 850–950). Then you would ride for 3 minutes at 100–104 percent of your FTP (290–300 watts for Joe) and finish with a 10-second burst, trying to reach 200–250 percent of FTP. Rest for 5–6 minutes, then cool down for 15 minutes at Level 2.

| WORKOUT | **Level 5, Race-Winning Effort** | | | |
|---|---|---|---|---|
| | **Time** | **Description** | **% of FTP** | **% of FTHR** |
| Warm-up | 15 min. | Easy riding | <68 | <70 |
| Main set | 5–8 × | Drill | | |
| | 30 sec. | Sprint, first 15 sec. out of the saddle | avg. 200 | N/A |
| | 3 min. | Long, intense riding | 100–104 | >106 |
| | 10 sec. | All-out effort | 200–250 | N/A |
| | 5–6 min. | Recovery | 68 | <70 |
| Cooldown | 15 min. | Easy riding | 56–75 | 69–83 |

### Level 6: Anaerobic Capacity

Anaerobic Capacity (AC) efforts are usually completed in time intervals of 2 minutes or less. These are very intense, short, hard efforts, and they are difficult to do correctly without the use of a power meter. The intensity of these efforts is far beyond what can be maintained aerobically. It is a supra-maximal intensity—that is, it requires more than 100 percent of your VO$_2$max.

Level 6 efforts are much higher in intensity than Level 5 efforts, and they are carried out long enough to stress the anaerobic capacity system, which means they hurt! Training at this level includes the greatest variety of efforts, however. There is a huge difference between a 30-second effort and a 2-minute effort, although both train the AC system. This variety makes it exciting to create lots of different intervals and workouts. The key is to reach the required intensity; the duration of the effort can change somewhat. These Level 6 exercises should be performed when you are relatively "fresh" in your training week.

| WORKOUT | Level 6, Optimal Intervals | | | |
|---|---|---|---|---|
| | Time | Description | % of FTP | % of FTHR |
| Warm-up | 15 min. | Easy riding | 56–75 | 69–83 |
| Main set | 8 × 2 min. (2–3 min. RI) | Hard as you can<br>*Stop intervals when power is <120–122%* | avg. 135 | >106 |
| | 8 × 1 min. (3 min. RI) | All-out effort<br>*Stop intervals when power is <128–131%* | avg. 145 | >106 |
| Cooldown | 15 min. | Easy riding | 56–75 | 69–83 |

To add some Anaerobic Capacity work to your training diet in a 2-hour ride, start with a standard warm-up, then set your power meter to show average watts in "interval" mode. Then do about eight 2-minute efforts pedaling as hard as you can, using average watts as a "carrot" to push all the way to the end. The goal? Average 135 percent of FTP (390 watts, for example, for Joe Athlete). Reach for that, and stop when you can no longer reach 120–122 percent of FTP, which would be a 10–12 percent drop in power, in your average. Joe Athlete, for example, would stop when he could no longer reach an average of 348–355 watts. Recover for at least 2–3 minutes, more if needed, then finish with eight 1-minute efforts, trying to average at least 145 percent of FTP (420 watts, for Joe), with 3-minute rest periods between efforts. Do all of these efforts unless you are unable to reach 128–131 percent, which would represent a 10–12 percent drop in power (370–380 watts in our hypothetical example). This guideline goes along with the intervals-to-exhaustion idea.

Another 2-hour ride includes hill repeats. Get in a 20-minute warm-up, and then do eight to ten hard hills. Each should be between 45 seconds and 1.5 minutes long. Try to average around 140 percent of FTP for each effort, and sprint in the last 25 meters or so

| WORKOUT | Level 6, Hills | | | |
|---|---|---|---|---|
| | **Time** | **Description** | **% of FTP** | **% of FTHR** |
| Warm-up | 20 min. | Easy riding | <68 | <70 |
| Main set | 8–10 × hills (4–5 min. RI) | Hard hills (45 sec.–1.5 min.), sprinting final 25 meters *Stop after 10% drop in power* | avg. 140 | >106 |
| Cooldown | 20–30 min. | Easy riding | 56–75 | 69–83 |

to explode at the top of each hill. Rest for 4–5 minutes between attempts. Stop the efforts when you experience a 10 percent drop in power from your performance in the second or third interval. Finish with a 20- to 30-minute cooldown at Endurance pace.

In Appendix B there are more Level 6 rides that develop Anaerobic Capacity, specifically working intervals of 2 minutes, 1 minute, and 30 seconds. See Anaerobic Capacity Workouts 6 and 7 for descriptions of these workouts.

### Level 7: Neuromuscular Power

Level 7 exercises are super-short, high-intensity efforts usually lasting less than 10 seconds each. They place a larger load on the musculoskeletal system than on the metabolic systems. In these short efforts, it would be difficult to use power as a guide for training, since the efforts themselves are so explosive and short that you would have to focus more on handling the bike than on reading your power meter.

Quite literally, there are hundreds of ways to do these workouts. Anytime you do a sprint workout, you are Neuromuscular Power training, and you will want to perform these workouts when you are the most "fresh" during the week, as the intensity of the workout is very high and you will need to be highly energized for them.

When you do these efforts, do not concern yourself with looking at your power meter. You can review the data later, while you are cooling down between sprints. The most important thing is to get all the sprints done and continue to add more repetitions as you get stronger.

Appendix B includes several good "peak sprint" workouts (see Neuromuscular Power Workouts 5 and 6). The sprints done in the small chainring typically do not involve gear changes. The objective is to wind the gear out and increase cadence to 120 rpm by the end of the interval.

The sprints in the big chainring include one or two gear changes, with an emphasis on a hard jump at the start of the interval, winding out the gear at a high cadence (110–120 rpm) before shifting.

One of the goals of this workout is to show that you do not need to "dump" the chain into the hardest gear for a sprint. Sprinting starts out with a hard jump in a gear that you can turn over. Then, as you wind out each gear, you shift down one. It's just like driving a car with a stick shift: You work down the gears when the rpms reach the correct range.

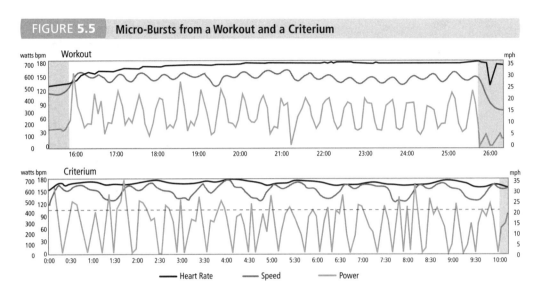

**FIGURE 5.5**    **Micro-Bursts from a Workout and a Criterium**

Another Level 7 workout that has become very popular is called the "micro-burst work-out." It is an excellent exercise to do on the indoor trainer, and it really focuses on improving your neuromuscular power. Since the efforts are 15 seconds each, using an indoor trainer makes them highly controllable. You can easily use your power meter for pacing. The micro-burst workout is designed to improve your ability to produce the explosive power that is needed for the initial "snap" in a sprint, for the jump out of the saddle in a criterium, or for the standing start in a track event. When you view data from this workout and compare them to data from a criterium, you can easily see that the downloaded files are very similar in nature. This shows the importance of specificity in training (see Figure 5.5).

For a typical 2-hour micro-burst workout, do a standard warm-up and then do two sets of micro-bursts lasting 10 minutes each. A micro-burst effort is 15 seconds "on" and 15 seconds "off," repeated continually for the 10 minutes. For the "on" segment, go to 150 percent of FTP (for our fictitious Joe Athlete, that would be 435 watts), and draw back to 50 percent of FTP (145 watts) for the 15-second "off" segment. Follow this up with 20 minutes of easy spinning, and then begin your next block. This block includes ten 10-second sprints out of the saddle, with at least 2 minutes of easy pedaling between efforts. Try to reach 300–350 percent of threshold power as your max wattage. Then cool down for 15 minutes.

A slight variation of this workout that still attacks the neuromuscular power system is also a good exercise. Again, it is a 2-hour ride that begins with a standard warm-up. Then, set a pace at the lower end of Level 3—approximately 76–80 percent of FTP, and hold this pace for the next hour. Within this hour, do a 10-second, out-of-the-saddle burst every 3 minutes, trying to reach 150 percent of FTP, and hold it there for the 10 seconds. Make sure your cadence stays high. You should have no more than one or two gear changes, if any. Cruise for the rest of the ride at below 80 percent of FTP, and then cool down.

---

In summary, all the training levels are continuous: There is no definitive starting or stopping point for any of them. You do not just go from training your aerobic capacity while you are riding in Level 3 (76–90 percent of FTP) to magically training your threshold at 91 percent of FTP in Level 4. The physiological systems in the human body that you are training meld into one another; if you are training in Level 3, you are using a larger percentage of that particular system than you are using for other systems at that intensity. It does not mean that the other systems are unaffected, however. It's important to remain aware of the big picture, or the philosophy of the workout, and not to get too caught up in becoming a slave to the numbers.

These workouts should help you to begin using your power meter in training. They are by no means the only workouts you can do, however. There are hundreds of ways to design a workout using wattage, and we encourage you to create others that will help you to achieve your goals. You can also make use of more than 65 workouts in Appendix B. When you begin to design your own workouts, just make sure that you are aware of the different training levels that you will be addressing and the impact these factors will have on your goals for the given workout. Intervals are one of the most important things you can do in order to improve, and doing the optimal number of them in each training ride is key. Remember to utilize Table 5.1 and the rules for optimizing your efforts. With your power meter you can now rest assured that you are training all of your systems optimally.

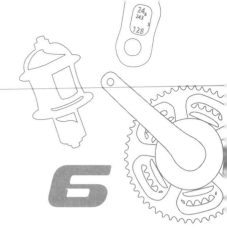

# 6

# *Interpreting the Data*

***Up to this point, you have been getting familiar*** with your new power meter, and if you have followed some of the steps presented in previous chapters, you have learned a lot about how to train with it. You know your training levels and your functional threshold power, you have evaluated your cycling skills using the Power Profile, and you know how to create workouts with wattage. The next step in conquering this learning curve is to understand what the downloaded data mean.

Once you begin to download your power meter data and view the graphs, you will no doubt have many questions, such as:

- What should I do now that I have all these great data?
- How can I use this information to plan for tomorrow and next week?
- How do I pick out what is important?

The rest of this chapter is devoted to answering these questions. Your power meter will give you a quantitative summary of your ride and periods of significant effort, showing your maximum wattage and average wattage, heart rate, cadence, and kilojoules of energy burned. You can pinpoint significant fluctuations in power during the workout (see "What Is a 'Match'?" later in this chapter). You can review your cadence, which is especially helpful over periods of high power output. You can review the relationship between total work done and time spent at varying levels of intensity. Understanding all of these data will make your approach to training more sophisticated.

Interpretation of the data is the key to understanding your current level of fitness, how it has changed over time, and how you might need to adapt your training to make progress in your cycling. Every chart and graph has meaning, just as every ride has meaning in your overall training program. Your rest days are just as important as your hard training days, and it is the same with your power-meter data: All your data are significant. Record every ride, every race, every time you get on the bike, and make sure to download that file. It's remarkable how many cyclists there are who profess to be "training with power," but then confess that they've never even downloaded their power-meter data! Download your data. It's important. Race with your power meter. That is important, too. Your best data will come from your races, and you'll learn the most from those files.

Try to pinpoint areas of a race that may be significant and determine the exact power demands of those areas, and then compare them with your training data. You can determine what level of power would have been needed to stay with the front group when the winning split occurred. You can evaluate your power output when you got dropped to see what happened: Your cadence might have been too low or maybe your pedaling stroke became sloppy due to fatigue, and your torque was too high compared with your power output. You can compare this race with others or similar rides. All of this analysis will help you to gain insight into how you can become a stronger cyclist.

We will mainly use TrainingPeaks WKO+ Software in this analysis, partly because it provides the greatest ability to "drill down" into the data. If you are using other software, it is important that you work with it and take the time to analyze the information fully. Only by downloading and correctly interpreting your own data will you be able to utilize your power meter to the utmost extent. By taking these steps, you will discover a whole new world of possibilities in training and racing.

## ADJUSTING YOUR CALIBRATIONS AND SETTINGS

First, let's do some housekeeping in order to make your data the best they can be. Make sure to set your power meter on the smallest sampling interval you can do in order to get the greatest accuracy in recording your ride. For some power meters, this limits the total time that it can record your ride, so set the recording rate higher if you are doing a longer ride. When you have your wheel circumference measured (and make sure to measure it precisely, with your weight on the bike and correct pressure in the tire), you are ready to go for a training ride. Make sure that you zero the power meter before you begin. There is nothing more frustrating than coming home from a ride only to see that your zero-offset point was not at zero when you started and your data are essentially worthless. Finally, make sure that your power meter is calibrated. With an SRM, you can do a calibration process that is on the SRM website; with PowerTap, you can use the "stomp" test, which is on the FAQ for Power-Based Training website, referenced in Appendix A of this book.

Later, when you are viewing the graph of your data, either look at the data without any "smoothing" or with just five-second smoothing. There are some inherent issues in how power meters measure power, as discussed in Chapter 2, so smoothing the data in your software application might be the best way to get rid of any "noise" that may be misleading.

The problem is that, though smoothing gets rid of some of the jaggedness in the data, many times it obfuscates the true peaks and valleys in the data. In five-second smoothing, the data are smoothed over five-second time periods. This is short enough that you lose little of the meaning contained in the data, and it is easier on the eye to comprehend than if you do not smooth the data at all; thus, five-second smoothing might be best in all but a few cases.

We'll start by looking at each individual file; later, we'll come back to the larger perspective of managing your training over time using the "Athlete Home Page."

## POWER DISTRIBUTION
### *Time Spent Pedaling (and Not Pedaling)*

Let's open a workout file and begin to look at the "Journal" page of your workout. The first task is to view your power distribution chart. If it is from a race, then check out how much time you spent *not* pedaling. That is an interesting fact to know because you may have even spent too much time pedaling in a race. The name of the game is saving energy. Most winning road racers do not pedal at least 15 percent of the time. If you are pedaling more than 85 percent of the time in a race, then you need to think about where you are sitting in the peloton. The downloaded power distribution charts of road-race winners usually look like the one shown in Figure 6.1.

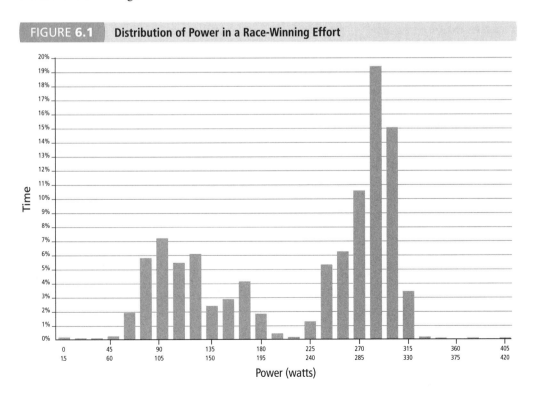

FIGURE **6.1**　　**Distribution of Power in a Race-Winning Effort**

In this chart, you can see that the cyclist spent lots of time at under 60 percent of his or her FTP (that is, saving energy and resting) and then lots of time at FTP. For this rider, this translates into lots of time under 180 watts and lots of time over 285 watts. That means the winners usually pedal the least, but when they do pedal, they pedal the hardest. This is imperative to remember.

On a normal training ride, the time spent not pedaling is not that important. Instead, what is important is how much time you spend in your power zones. Therefore, you should also begin to look for the time drop-off around your functional threshold power level. Notice that in Figure 6.1 there is a huge drop-off in the amount of time that this rider spent at 315– 330 watts compared with the amount of time that he or she spent at 300–315 watts. Based on this information, one could make a ballpark guess that this rider's FTP is somewhere on the upper end of the 300–315 bar; it is unlikely to be over 315 watts. How do we know this? Since we know that, by definition, you can ride right up to your FTP, but not much over it, we should expect to see a larger percentage of time in the "bin" that most closely represents that FTP edge. (See "Determining Functional Threshold Power" in Chapter 3 to review this and other methods of identifying FTP.) Winning racers will spend lots of time just at FTP, but not much above it, because they know how to pace themselves well. Similar trends may show up in your power-meter download.

### Time in Power Levels

The next thing to consider in looking at the power distribution chart is whether you spent enough time in the level that you were interested in. If you were trying to make strides in an area in which you are weak, did you ride at that level long enough to achieve your overall goal? Examine your power distribution chart by levels. This will enable you to make sure you trained in the correct level to maximize your training time. It is important to set up your training levels correctly first, in regard to your FTP, in order to make sure that the calculations will be correct.

Since your fitness changes over time, and your power levels are calculated on the threshold value, these absolute numbers will change throughout the year. For example, say that in January your FTP was 200 watts. This would mean that your Tempo level (Level 3, 76–90 percent of FTP) would be between 152 and 180 watts. Anytime you are riding within this range, you will be accumulating time in Level 3, and you will see this in the corresponding bar in the power distribution chart. By June, however, you may have raised your FTP to 260 watts. Your corresponding Level 3 watts will now be 197–234. Because your fitness has increased so dramatically, 152–180 watts is now in your Level 2, or Endurance level. This

## One Caveat to Reviewing Time in Power Levels

There is one issue that you should be aware of when looking at your power levels. Consider, for example, that if you alternated between pedaling for 15 seconds at 400 watts and pedaling for 15 seconds at 100 watts, and kept this up for an entire hour, you would end up spending 30 minutes pedaling at 400 watts, which is a power that you might be able to maintain for only about 4 minutes if you were pedaling at this level continuously. Obviously, there's something going on that is not evident when you look at just "time in level," and that is the impact of how long each "foray" into a particular power level actually lasts. This is not an issue when using heart rate, because (1) heart rate lags behind changes in power—that is, it is automatically smoothed by your physiology so that very short forays get averaged into the mix; and (2) you can use heart rate only for levels requiring less intensity than maximum heart rate or $VO_2$max. In other words, "time in level" is much more meaningful when applied to heart rate than when applied to power.

is great news. But you will have to adjust your settings, and your training, to make further progress. Remember to update these associations as your fitness changes.

### HEART RATE DISTRIBUTION

Once you have determined your power output in relation to your ride, the next thing to look at is your heart rate distribution chart. This graph reveals how much time you spent in your heart rate zones. In the heart rate distribution chart, just as in the power distribution chart, if you look at a large enough dataset that includes time spent at and above FTP, you can see where the heart rate threshold would be. Make sure that you have the data range set at three to five heartbeats per minute to more easily see where this step-down occurs. In Figure 6.2, it is easy to see the sharp decline from 160–165 bpm to 165–170 bpm.

### CADENCE DISTRIBUTION

By examining the cadence chart, you can start to see how much time you typically spend in different cadence ranges (see Figure 6.3). This can be informative if you are actively trying to increase or decrease your cadence for a specific workout or for overall physiological change. It also tells you something about yourself and may provide a clue to the percentages of fast-twitch and slow-twitch muscle fibers in your body.

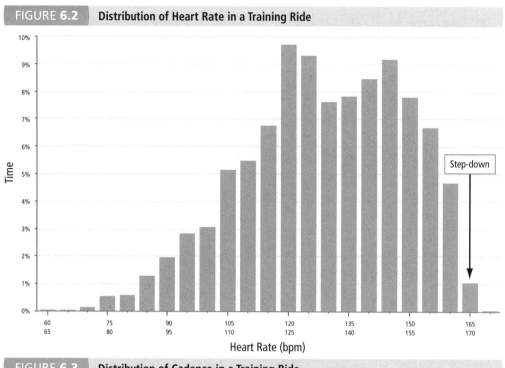

FIGURE **6.2**    **Distribution of Heart Rate in a Training Ride**

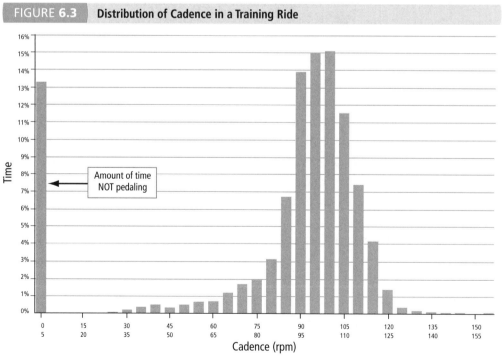

FIGURE **6.3**    **Distribution of Cadence in a Training Ride**

*This rider spends a large percentage of time over 90 rpm, with an even larger percentage over 100 rpm, thus giving us a clue to his muscle type.*

This chart also provides further information about how much time you spend not pedaling. The power distribution chart will show you this as well, but the cadence chart is more accurate, and here's why. Since the data ranges are smaller in the cadence chart than in the power distribution chart (you should view this chart in increments of 5 rpm), you will see, for example, the time you spent pedaling at between 1 and 5 rpm, between 6 and 10 rpm, and so on, which is more precise than the 0–20 watt bin in the power distribution chart.

## MEAN MAXIMAL POWER, OR CRITICAL POWER

Now that you have examined the overall ride, you should narrow the perspective to look at your peak power for the ride. By plotting your peak power over small slices of time, you can view a telling graph of your mean maximal power, or "critical power," as some coaches call it. This is quite literally a plot of your best average power for each second of the ride. (See sidebar, "What Are CP Values?") This is quite literally a plot of your best average power for each second of the ride.

The Mean Maximal Power (MMP) Curve is revealing for a variety of reasons. One is that it gives you the ability to confirm that you are working in the correct training level when working out. In an intense race file, the chart helps you to pinpoint weaknesses and strengths. When you examine maximal power for a relatively large set of data (six months or greater), the shape of the curve will be based on your personal set of abilities. Distinctive changes in the slope of the curve may reveal how much you rely on different physiological systems.

For example, the slope of your Mean Maximal Power Curve might be very consistent from 20 seconds out to 2.5 minutes but run at a lower angle from 2.5 minutes out to 25 minutes. This might tell you that at 2.5 minutes your body shifts emphasis from the anaerobic capacity system to the $VO_2$max and lactate systems. Each rider is different, and this is one reason why it is important to read and interpret this graph regularly. If you see a distinct hump in the curve at around 3–6 minutes, that is, a very high output of power in that section in relation to the rest of the curve, this indicates your strength at $VO_2$max power. Or, if you see a plateau in the curve, you may have a weakness in your ability to produce power in the time period where the plateau occurs.

It is important to compare similar time periods from workout to workout. If you did a workout with 5-minute efforts, and then looked at the watts you produced at 6 minutes, the data may not be indicative of your overall ability. To obtain valid data, you would need to do specific 6-minute efforts. Also, if you did not do sprints or lactate threshold intervals, then your max power on the chart would not be representative of your true max when you do sprints, and your lactate threshold would not be representative of your true FTP. If you are looking to see the big picture from this curve, then create the MMP Curve over a larger period of time—maybe even looking at an entire year's worth of data in order to get the true

## What Are CP Values?

"Critical power" as defined by exercise scientists refers to the power in watts that you could maintain indefinitely. This means in theory, of course, as ultimately there isn't any level of power you would be able to maintain indefinitely; eventually you would fall off your bike in extreme fatigue! However, world-renowned author and coach Joe Friel has popularized a different meaning for the term "critical power" (CP) among cyclists and coaches using power meters. Joe defines it as the best average power that you can maintain for a given amount of time. Another term with the same meaning is "mean maximal power." Joe described the critical power principle in his booklet *Training with Power* (2001). For the description below, we have borrowed heavily from this booklet with his permission.

To further understand this concept, let's look at an example. Say that you did an Olympic-distance triathlon with a 40 km bike leg. In that leg, you averaged 300 watts over exactly 60 minutes. We might conclude that your FTP is 300 watts. But would you be able to average a higher wattage if you were riding for only half that time? Most likely, the answer would be yes, because you would have energy in reserve at 30 minutes. Therefore, the best average power output (300 watts) in the 40 km race was "critical" to the time duration of 60 minutes. In the same way, you would have best average power outputs that would be critical to 30 minutes, 12 minutes, 1 minute, and so on. Your critical power would be different for each time period.

Training at each critical power level produces physiological adaptations and fitness results specific to that workload. When you know your critical power at 6 minutes (CP6), for example, you can train very precisely by using your power meter to optimally stress the physiological systems that limit the VO$_2$max system. Joe suggests critical power zones for 12 seconds (CP0.2), 1 minute (CP1), 6 minutes (CP6), 12 minutes (CP12), 30 minutes (CP30), 60 minutes (CP60), 90 minutes (CP90), and 180 minutes (CP180). To determine your critical power for these times, you simply do time trials at those durations and then create a zone around them by adding and subtracting 2.5 percent of the average power. For example, if your CP6 is 390 watts, then your CP6 zone would be 380–400 watts.

You can also simply view the "Mean Maximal Power Curve" in Training Peaks WKO+ software. As long as you have a large enough sample of files to pull from, you will be able to easily pick out these durations and their corresponding critical power. CP values may be applied to heart rate zones during training, a principle that is described in Joe's books, which include *The Cyclist's Training Bible*, *The Mountain Biker's Training Bible*, and *The Triathlete's Training Bible*.

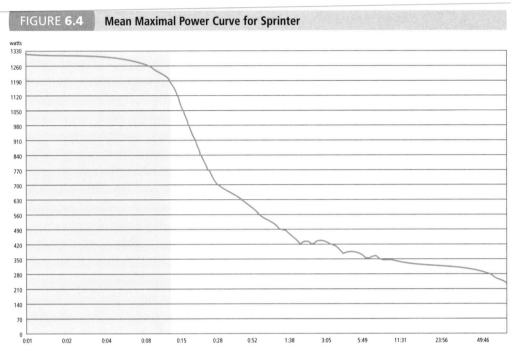

FIGURE **6.4**     **Mean Maximal Power Curve for Sprinter**

*Example of a pure sprinter. Note how long this athlete is able to produce a very high amount of power and the time associated with the "break" point of sprint or neuromuscular power decline.*

picture. Figure 6.4 shows a classic example of an MMP Curve for a sprinter. Note the relatively long period of time at a very high power output. In this example, the rider weighed only 153 pounds, so based on her Power Profile, she is considered a world-class sprinter. We'll examine these charts in more detail in Chapter 9.

## INTERPRETING POWER GRAPHS

There are many ways to view your ride in the power-meter software, and each can reveal more information about you as a rider and about the workouts you complete. The graph of your ride tells the story of your ride second by second. Examining these graphs, which at first may look like a bunch of squiggly lines, and discerning their story are what this section is all about.

### Stacked and Horizontal Views

Each type of software represents the data a little differently in graph mode, and each type has its advantages and disadvantages. When we were creating TrainingPeaks WKO+ Software, we faced a dilemma about how to show the graph. A stacked view would present raw data that had not been interpolated, smoothed, or "smashed together." However, there are times

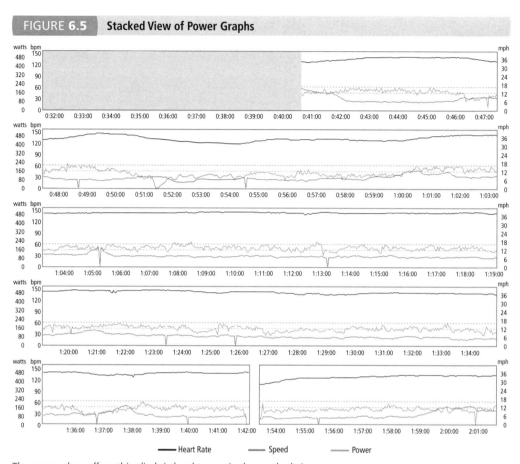

**FIGURE 6.5    Stacked View of Power Graphs**

——— Heart Rate    ——— Speed    ——— Power

*The power drop-off on this climb is hard to see in the stacked view.*

when it is also useful to view the data all on one screen, or horizontally. When viewing the stacked graphs, it may be difficult, for example, to see a small decrease in power over a period of 60 minutes or longer. A horizontal view is better for this type of analysis. Therefore, we decided to include both options in the WKO+ Software. In Figures 6.5 and 6.6, you can see that the stacked view makes it difficult to find the decrease in power right at the end of the climb, whereas the horizontal view makes this easy to locate and analyze.

We recommend that you begin with the horizontal view with no smoothing or with five-second smoothing, as this will enable you to see your ride from a broad perspective. From this view you can easily determine the segments of the effort that you want to examine in more detail. Many times we begin to mark up the file in this view and then switch over to the stacked view in order to better define the exact start and finish of each period of work. If it is a road ride, then we view the watts, heart rate, and speed lines. Viewing speed allows you to determine whether the work was being done on an uphill or on the flats. If

| FIGURE **6.6** | **Horizontal View of Power Graphs** |

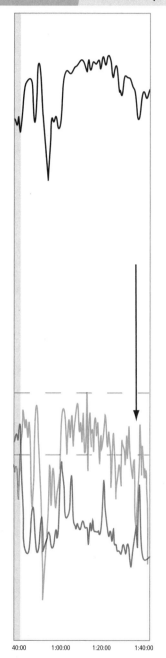

40:00    1:00:00    1:20:00    1:40:00

*Decrease in power at the end of a long climb is much easier to see in a horizontal view.*

the workout was aimed at specific cadence goals, we take out speed and add in cadence in order to better understand the power-to-cadence relationship. If it is a trainer ride, then we view watts, heart rate, and cadence, as speed is largely irrelevant on a trainer.

### Areas of Interest

Begin analyzing your data by scanning through your ride and finding areas of interest. You can create a range around a specific area of interest (that is, mark an interval) to gain further insight into the numbers. You can also mark intervals while you are on your bike so they will be easy to find and view later. However, if you did not mark a particular effort—maybe it was an intense mountain-bike race, for example, and you couldn't afford to take your hands off the handlebars to mark it—then you can find that area later. For example, let's say you went over a 25-minute climb in your mountain-bike race. This should be easy to view, as your heart rate will be high, your speed low, and your power fairly constant. The graph of this portion of your ride might look something like the one presented in Figure 6.7.

Notice that when the climb begins, the power line becomes smoother, the speed line is lower, and the heart rate line climbs rapidly. Even though this is a mountain-bike file, the power is relatively smooth despite undulations in the trail.

### Interval Shape and Meaning

The line for each interval that you do will have a slightly different shape, and this shape means something about how you paced yourself in the interval, how relatively fresh or tired you were, and whether you gave it your all or didn't quite get the job done. By comparing the different shapes of the interval lines with each other, you can learn much about

**FIGURE 6.7**     **Creating a Range in a Power Graph**

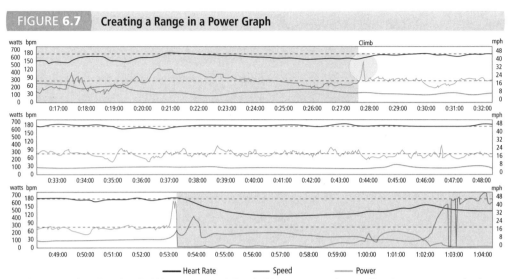

Gridlines are placed at threshold heart rate and threshold watts. Note the small spike in power at the beginning of this 25-minute mountain bike climb, which makes it possible to find this segment of the ride easily.

**FIGURE 6.8**     **Interpreting the Shape of Intervals**

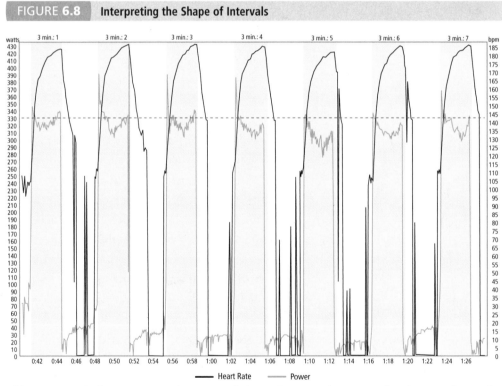

*This power graph shows seven 3-minute Intervals in a VO₂max workout. Interval 1 shows perfect pacing, Interval 2 was too hard, and Intervals 3–6 were dialed in. Also see Figures 6.9–6.12. Judging from the power generated in Interval 7, this athlete could have done more efforts.*

your efforts, and this will help you to determine a better pacing strategy, set a bigger wattage goal, or plan the number of intervals to do.

Let's look at the various shapes of the intervals and what they mean. Figure 6.8 shows 3-minute intervals done by an elite track racer in her preparation for the Canadian Track Nationals. In this example, the graph is in the horizontal view so that we can see all the intervals at one time. We have created a range around each interval in order to pull out the data for just that interval. One of the first things you may notice is the shape of the power lines. Notice that there is a general trend that each one follows. Each interval starts with a hard effort; the power drops down about 1 minute into the effort, however, and then the wattage rises again at the end of the interval. We might call this pattern a "twin peak interval."

Humans adapt easily to stress, and good athletes quickly learn pacing after they have done only a few intervals. But this pacing may be arbitrary instead of deliberate, and analyzing the files may enable you to make better pacing decisions. That is the case here: A closer look at the files provides interesting clues to how this track racer could improve.

To be fair to this athlete, even though she is an elite-level Canadian track racer, this is the very first time she had ever tried this specific workout, and so she was learning just how hard she could go for each interval. The goal in this workout was to do seven 3-minute repeats as hard as she could, with 3 minutes of easy pedaling between efforts. We estimated that she would be able to hold $VO_2$max power (for her, 315–325 watts), as this 3-minute time period is perfectly within the $VO_2$max power level. We told her to just go as hard as she could and didn't give her a specific wattage goal. Since this was her first workout for this time period, we did not want to color her results with some wattage number that might or might not be right for her. We also wanted to see how well and how quickly she would adapt to the effort so that we could uncover any weaknesses that she might have at this level. The workout was performed on an indoor trainer.

In Interval 1, notice how there is a peak at the beginning and end, with a little valley in the middle (see Figure 6.9). This is perfect pacing, and it's her first interval. She's very "fresh," and as a result she does very well. This shape also indicates that she was a little conservative, so as not to "blow up," and then she realized that she had more to give and throttled it at the end. So, in terms of going all-out, she didn't, but in terms of giving it her best time and watts, she was dead on. This is a textbook example of creating your best average watts in an interval.

In Interval 2, our Canadian cyclist went too hard (see Figure 6.10). The power drops off very quickly, and she has no power in the end. In the first interval she was a little worried about going too hard, so she held back, and at the end of the interval she realized she could have gone harder. In the second interval, she drills it from the start, but "blows up." At this point, she must have realized that she started the interval pedaling too hard.

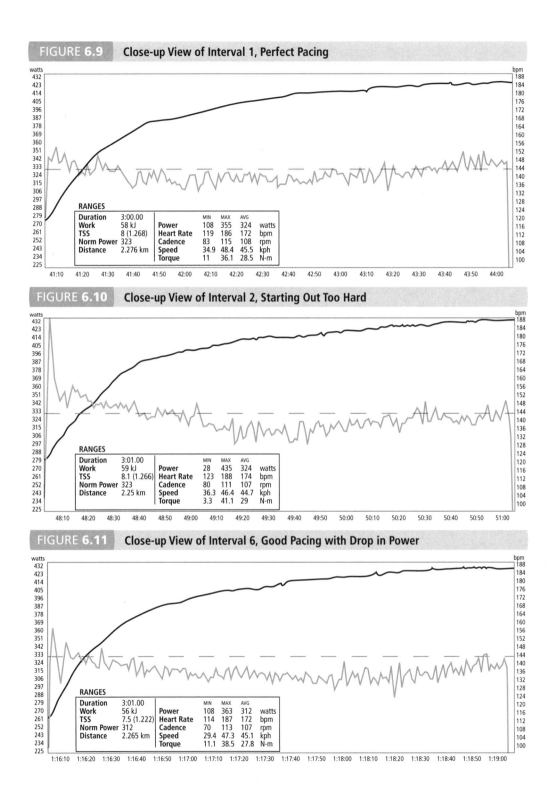

FIGURE **6.9**    **Close-up View of Interval 1, Perfect Pacing**

RANGES

| | | | MIN | MAX | AVG | |
|---|---|---|---|---|---|---|
| Duration | 3:00.00 | | | | | |
| Work | 58 kJ | Power | 108 | 355 | 324 | watts |
| TSS | 8 (1.268) | Heart Rate | 119 | 186 | 172 | bpm |
| Norm Power | 323 | Cadence | 83 | 115 | 108 | rpm |
| Distance | 2.276 km | Speed | 34.9 | 48.4 | 45.5 | kph |
| | | Torque | 11 | 36.1 | 28.5 | N-m |

FIGURE **6.10**    **Close-up View of Interval 2, Starting Out Too Hard**

RANGES

| | | | MIN | MAX | AVG | |
|---|---|---|---|---|---|---|
| Duration | 3:01.00 | | | | | |
| Work | 59 kJ | Power | 28 | 435 | 324 | watts |
| TSS | 8.1 (1.266) | Heart Rate | 123 | 188 | 174 | bpm |
| Norm Power | 323 | Cadence | 80 | 111 | 107 | rpm |
| Distance | 2.25 km | Speed | 36.3 | 46.4 | 44.7 | kph |
| | | Torque | 3.3 | 41.1 | 29 | N-m |

FIGURE **6.11**    **Close-up View of Interval 6, Good Pacing with Drop in Power**

RANGES

| | | | MIN | MAX | AVG | |
|---|---|---|---|---|---|---|
| Duration | 3:01.00 | | | | | |
| Work | 56 kJ | Power | 108 | 363 | 312 | watts |
| TSS | 7.5 (1.222) | Heart Rate | 114 | 187 | 172 | bpm |
| Norm Power | 312 | Cadence | 70 | 113 | 107 | rpm |
| Distance | 2.265 km | Speed | 29.4 | 47.3 | 45.1 | kph |
| | | Torque | 11.1 | 38.5 | 27.8 | N-m |

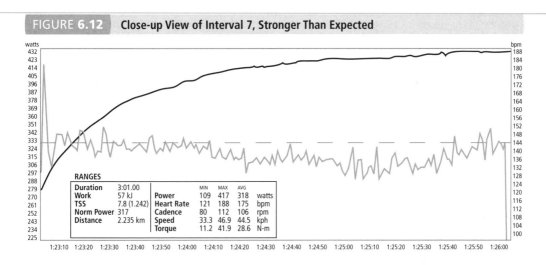

| FIGURE **6.12** | Close-up View of Interval 7, Stronger Than Expected |
| --- | --- |

**RANGES**

| Duration | 3:01.00 | | MIN | MAX | AVG | |
| --- | --- | --- | --- | --- | --- | --- |
| Work | 57 kJ | Power | 109 | 417 | 318 | watts |
| TSS | 7.8 (1.242) | Heart Rate | 121 | 188 | 175 | bpm |
| Norm Power | 317 | Cadence | 80 | 112 | 106 | rpm |
| Distance | 2.235 km | Speed | 33.3 | 46.9 | 44.5 | kph |
| | | Torque | 11.2 | 41.9 | 28.6 | N-m |

By the time she does Intervals 3, 4, 5, and 6, she has this figured out (see Figure 6.11). Perfect! This is as hard as she could go; she has these intervals nailed. However, we are starting to see an intriguing pattern: Note how each effort has a little power "hole" after the first minute (see 1:17:05–1:17:25 in Figure 6.11). This tells us that our track racer is having a hard time transitioning from her purely anaerobic capacity, which requires fast-twitch muscles, to using a larger percentage of her slow-twitch muscles every time she hits a certain point in the interval. It's as if her "depth" of anaerobic capacity is not "deep" enough. We should be seeing that drop-off occur closer to the 2:30 mark (1:18:30 in Figure 6.11).

But this is exactly why we did not give her a wattage goal in the beginning of the workout, and the strategy worked. Now we can see that she might have a weakness in this transition period, and we can determine how to address this issue. To do that, it helps to look at Interval 7 (see Figure 6.12). In this last interval, she held back and did not push it hard enough. At this point, if she was at her limit and feeling fatigued, we would have seen a quicker drop-off in power from the start to the finish. In addition, she would not have been able to bring up the power at the end of the final effort. Instead, Interval 7 presents a profile that is very similar to the profile for Interval 1; however, since it is not the first effort but the last one, we need a different interpretation. That interpretation is this: Ultimately, she could have done a few more of these efforts before reaching a point of diminishing marginal returns or using the intervals-to-exhaustion concept.

We can conclude that this rider has good average pursuit power and good cruising power in pursuit. Her repeatability is good, as evidenced by the relatively low drop-off in power from Interval 2 and Interval 3 to Interval 7. (When looking for "repeatability," always compare the second and third intervals with the last one to really see the drop-off in power, because the first interval always takes place when the athlete is "fresh," and the wattage is therefore not one that can be repeated multiple times.)

From this analysis, we can suggest areas for improvement. Because this athlete seems to fade too fast if the initial effort is too high, practicing her pacing from the start would be important. By holding back a hair more on the start, and then consciously focusing on that time period from minute 1 to minute 2, she could begin to eliminate the quick drop in power during that time period. If she can boost her ability to keep the pressure on throughout that period and then dig deep for the last minute, she will really reduce her time.

## ANALYZING AND COMPARING YOUR EFFORTS
### Multi-File/Range Analysis

TrainingPeaks WKO+ Software features Multi-File/Range Analysis (MFRA), which allows you to overlay ranges within a given workout or from different workouts and thus compare intervals or complete workouts. Figure 6.13 is an example of an MFRA. This tool also makes it easy to sort intervals according to different criteria. When comparing one ride (or race) with another, you can see exactly where the power was created, which could give you a clearer understanding of your ride/race. Below is a table from an MFRA graph, which compares a series of twelve hill repeats done by one rider. Each repeat was about 1 minute long.

Although it can be hard to pick out individual intervals when there are so many, it's easy to see which was the strongest and which was the weakest. With the ride downloaded onto his computer, this rider would simply click on the "Average Power" column to sort the

| TABLE 6.1 | Multi-File/Range Analysis: Comparing Hill Repeats | | | | | | | | | | | |
|---|---|---|---|---|---|---|---|---|---|---|---|---|
| **HILL REPEATS SORTED** | | | | | | | | | | | | |
| Interval | Duration | Work (kJ) | TSS (IF) | Min Pwr | Max Pwr | Avg Pwr | Min Cad | Max Cad | Avg Cad | Min Spd | Max Spd | Avg Spd |
| 1 | 01:04.0 | 29 | 3.1 (1.318) | 246 | 603 | 459 | 70 | 81 | 76 | 15.5 | 17.4 | 16.6 |
| 4 | 01:06.0 | 26 | 2.4 (1.15) | 163 | 565 | 404 | 42 | 102 | 72 | 8 | 17.3 | 15.1 |
| 5 | 01:10.0 | 28 | 2.6 (1.163) | 212 | 504 | 403 | 61 | 110 | 78 | 10.2 | 16 | 14.6 |
| 6 | 01:10.0 | 28 | 2.5 (1.144) | 154 | 516 | 403 | 50 | 90 | 79 | 9.8 | 16.7 | 15 |
| 7 | 01:19.0 | 30 | 2.9 (1.15) | 76 | 555 | 392 | 48 | 134 | 70 | 10.2 | 16.8 | 14.4 |
| 3 | 01:13.0 | 28 | 2.5 (1.101) | 144 | 560 | 390 | 57 | 87 | 77 | 9.6 | 15.8 | 14.4 |
| 9 | 01:14.0 | 28 | 2.5 (1.095) | 130 | 476 | 389 | 35 | 67 | 57 | 9.4 | 15.7 | 14.1 |
| 12 | 01:14.0 | 28 | 2.4 (1.087) | 149 | 529 | 382 | 32 | 50 | 46 | 10.1 | 16.2 | 14.8 |
| 2 | 01:13.0 | 27 | 2.4 (1.08) | 153 | 520 | 377 | 55 | 170 | 89 | 9.3 | 15.5 | 14.6 |
| 10 | 01:17.0 | 28 | 2.4 (1.051) | 138 | 456 | 369 | 36 | 63 | 55 | 8.1 | 15 | 13.6 |
| 8 | 01:21.0 | 28 | 2.4 (1.026) | 105 | 467 | 356 | 37 | 95 | 67 | 6.5 | 15.8 | 13.5 |
| 11 | 01:18.0 | 27 | 2.1 (0.988) | 78 | 471 | 347 | 35 | 52 | 49 | 8.8 | 14.9 | 13.4 |

*This cyclist's fifth interval was an average power of 403 W, and then his eleventh one (at the bottom of the column) was 347 W. On his final effort, he dug deep and cracked out 382 W. This is good application of the intervals to exhaustion principle.*

intervals (as shown in Table 6.1). Once he has done so, he can see how closely he followed the intervals-to-exhaustion principle explained in Chapter 5. In this case, he did well. Note that his fifth interval was 403 watts. A 10 percent decrease would be close to 360 watts. His eleventh interval was 347 watts, and he did one more, with his twelfth interval being 382 watts. He knew that he was seriously struggling in his eleventh interval, so he went all-out for the twelfth and then headed home.

When you want to compare a race across different years, the Multi-File tool makes this possible. Make certain that you select exactly the same range of data so you can compare apples with apples. Figure 6.13 illustrates a race that the athlete did in two consecutive years. He placed second in year 1. In year 2 he won, with a solo breakaway after an attack 45 minutes into the race. It is possible to see when the breakaway started on the graph because his heart rate climbed suddenly at that point. It's interesting that the winning power file shows a reduction in cadence from the previous year. A likely explanation is that in year 1, he was in a breakaway with three other riders; his cadence was probably higher because he was rid-

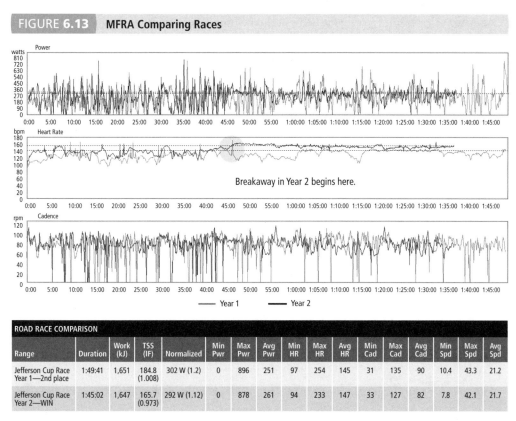

**FIGURE 6.13** **MFRA Comparing Races**

| Range | Duration | Work (kJ) | TSS (IF) | Normalized | Min Pwr | Max Pwr | Avg Pwr | Min HR | Max HR | Avg HR | Min Cad | Max Cad | Avg Cad | Min Spd | Max Spd | Avg Spd |
|---|---|---|---|---|---|---|---|---|---|---|---|---|---|---|---|---|
| **ROAD RACE COMPARISON** |||||||||||||||||
| Jefferson Cup Race Year 1—2nd place | 1:49:41 | 1,651 | 184.8 (1.008) | 302 W (1.2) | 0 | 896 | 251 | 97 | 254 | 145 | 31 | 135 | 90 | 10.4 | 43.3 | 21.2 |
| Jefferson Cup Race Year 2—WIN | 1:45:02 | 1,647 | 165.7 (0.973) | 292 W (1.12) | 0 | 878 | 261 | 94 | 233 | 147 | 33 | 127 | 82 | 7.8 | 42.1 | 21.7 |

*Note the differences in heart rate, power, and cadence from one year to the next. In Year 2 the heart rate was higher, the cadence was lower, and the power production was smoother than in Year 1.*

ing with other cyclists and matching surges in between pulls at the front. The lower cadence in the solo breakaway file might indicate that this rider prefers to produce a higher force on the pedals with lower cadence when riding by himself at FTP. We will use this same file in Chapter 7 to illustrate a principle about the force-cadence relationship.

### Scatterplots

When you want to compare different data channels—heart rate versus power, speed versus distance, or power versus cadence—you might want to use a scatterplot. A scatterplot can give you a good sense of how the different data channels relate to each other. When you plot distance on the Y-axis of the graph and power on the X-axis, it becomes easy to see at which distances you had the highest power outputs. Figure 6.14 illustrates this comparison. You can also see when the athlete hits the hill in each lap of the race.

Let's consider another example of how the scatterplot can help you in your training. With the cadence on the Y-axis and power on the X-axis, the scatterplot allows you to identify what cadence you prefer when doing intense $VO_2$max intervals. In Figure 6.15, we see a screen shot of a workout in which the rider did a series of race-winning intervals. The lighter color is the plot of the race-winning intervals and the darker color is the rest of the workout. In the plot below, it is apparent that this athlete typically pedals at a cadence of 90–94 rpm

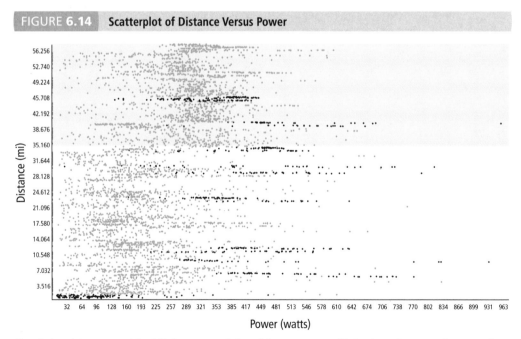

FIGURE 6.14    **Scatterplot of Distance Versus Power**

*The darker dots represent the hill done on each lap of the racecourse. Notice how the power increases from mile 35 to the finish. This was when the racer went into a breakaway.*

when doing hard intervals. Even though his wattage ranges from 200 to 900, he still maintains this cadence. While this might seem all too obvious, it does give us some additional insight into this rider and where he self-selects his cadence. This can be helpful for future workouts when he works on making sure his race-winning attack is truly enough to win the race he has in mind.

Finally, in our last example we will again plot cadence on the Y-axis and speed on the X-axis, but this time we will consider a cyclocross race. Looking at Figure 6.16, you can see a strong correlation between how fast the rider is pedaling and how fast his bike is going. At a certain cadence, about 100–105 rpm, as you can see from the plot, he shifts to a harder gear in order to continue increasing his speed. This could indicate a need for improvement in pedaling speed, or it could mean that more muscular strength is needed when he shifts into the harder gear. The relationship between cadence and speed is an interesting one, similar to the relationship between cadence and power.

Cyclists can learn a lot by taking a closer look at these data streams. In cycling, besides making yourself more aerodynamic, there are only two variables involved in going faster:

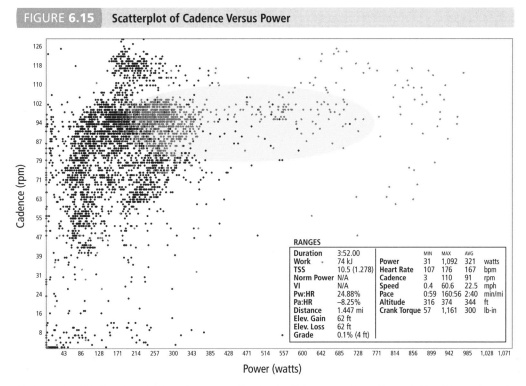

**FIGURE 6.15**     **Scatterplot of Cadence Versus Power**

| RANGES | | | | MIN | MAX | AVG | |
|---|---|---|---|---|---|---|---|
| Duration | 3:52.00 | | | | | | |
| Work | 74 kJ | Power | | 31 | 1,092 | 321 | watts |
| TSS | 10.5 (1.278) | Heart Rate | | 107 | 176 | 167 | bpm |
| Norm Power | N/A | Cadence | | 3 | 110 | 91 | rpm |
| VI | N/A | Speed | | 0.4 | 60.6 | 22.5 | mph |
| Pw:HR | 24.88% | Pace | | 0:59 | 160:56 | 2:40 | min/mi |
| Pa:HR | –8.25% | Altitude | | 316 | 374 | 344 | ft |
| Distance | 1.447 mi | Crank Torque | | 57 | 1,161 | 300 | lb-in |
| Elev. Gain | 62 ft | | | | | | |
| Elev. Loss | 62 ft | | | | | | |
| Grade | 0.1% (4 ft) | | | | | | |

*Cadence is plotted on the Y-axis and power on the X-axis. This shows where the majority of the cadence is for this athlete's race-winning intervals and how different the power can be within each interval. Meanwhile, cadence stays in a narrow range.*

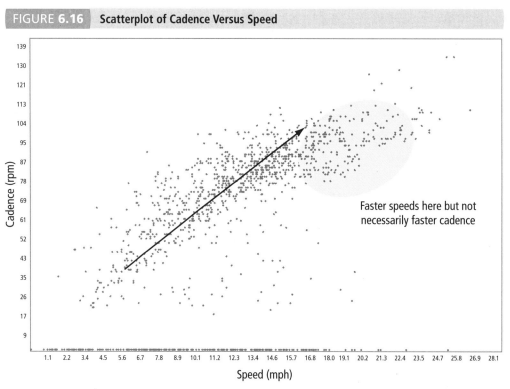

**FIGURE 6.16    Scatterplot of Cadence Versus Speed**

Faster speeds here but not necessarily faster cadence

*Note the linear relationship between speed and cadence up to about 104 rpm, at which point the athlete isn't able to increase his speed by pedaling faster. This indicates a need for improvement in pedaling speed and a possible need for muscular strength in order to use a bigger gear at higher speeds.*

You can pedal harder and you can pedal faster. The scatterplot can help you to understand which one of these options (or combination of them) might be more beneficial for you to set goals in as you train.

### "Fast Find"

Another way to make comparisons is to look deeper into a specific effort—to examine your cadence, for example. Training specifically for your discipline is very important. If you always train on the flats, but most of your races are in the mountains, then you are not training for the specific demands of the races in which you are competing.

The "Fast Find" feature, which currently is exclusive to TrainingPeaks WKO+ Software, also aids in making comparisons. Let's say you did several 3-minute efforts, then some 30-second efforts, a 10-minute effort, and a few 1-minute fast pedaling efforts. You can easily find these efforts by defining them based on the length of the interval and the wattage that was held during that time. The "Fast Find" feature can help you to find these efforts quickly.

## What Is a "Match"?

"Match" is an elusive term used by riders and coaches in the bike-racing world. When you "burn a match," you have done a hard effort. It's an effort in which you had to dig deep or really push yourself. Any bike racer knows what it feels like to have burned a match, but until now, no one has really tried to quantify exactly what a match is.

Why do you need to know what a match is? Think of it this way: As a rider, you start out the day with a full set of matches in your matchbook, but every time you go hard, do an attack, or hammer over a hill, you burn one of your matches. The size of the matchbook is different from one cyclist to the next, but nobody has an infinite number, so it is important to burn your matches at the right time, whether you are competing in a race or just training. Otherwise, you may be left with an empty matchbook when you still might need to use some matches to finish well, and your chances of performing at your best may have been drastically reduced. If you burn all your matches before the end of the race, it's doubtful you will win. Indeed, if your matches are burned prematurely, it's certain that you won't win.

So, with regard to matches, your goals are fourfold: (1) figure out exactly what a match is for you; (2) figure out the size of your matchbook; (3) try to increase the number of matches you have; and (4) burn your matches at the right time in the race in order to optimize your chances for success.

For most riders and racers, a match can be defined as an effort in which one goes over threshold power by at least 20 percent and holds it there for at least 1 minute. Of course, burning the proverbial match could involve an effort longer than 1 minute, but as the time period gets longer, the percentage above threshold power would be lower. Table 6.1 estimates the power required to burn a match for different time periods for a rider with an FTP of 330 watts. Remember, however, that there is no exact definition of "match," and these numbers would be different for every individual. You may be able to use the power-meter software to determine exactly when and how you burn your own set of matches. It may be illuminating to make a chart for yourself like the one presented in Table 6.2, where you attempt to quantify your own matches.

| TABLE **6.2** | Power Required to "Burn a Match" | |
|---|---|---|
| Time | % of FTP | Power |
| 1 min. | 120+ | 396 |
| 5 min. | 114–120 | 376–396 |
| 10 min. | 108–114 | 356–376 |
| 20 min. | 100–108 | 330–356 |

*Note: In this example, the athlete's FTP is 330 watts.*

Now that you have a general idea of what a match is, you need to figure out how many matches you have at your disposal. There are only two ways to do this: You could do a super-hard training ride in which you have planned out the matches that you are going to burn, or you could do a tough race that requires a lot of match burning. The great thing is that you now know, based on your rate of perceived exertion and rate of exhaustion, when you have burned a match and when you are out of matches. Listen to your body as you ride, and then go back through your downloaded data to find your matches.

If you are using the "Fast Find" feature, under the Edit button, in the TrainingPeaks WKO+ Software, you can enter some parameters that will help you find those matches. For example, let's assume that your threshold power is 330 watts. Take 120 percent of 330 watts, which is 396 watts, and enter that into the "Leading Edge." Then take 330 watts and enter that as your "Trailing Edge," since you are still going hard at that point. Select 1 minute as the minimum duration, and 5 minutes as the maximum duration.

The "Fast Find" feature will highlight all of your matches. You can then review the graph of your ride and type notes in the text area that provide some description of that match—for example, "Hard attack on hill" or "Prime sprint." Or you could simply label each "Find" a match and then use the Linking button to link them all together. It might look like the screen shot shown in Figure 6.17.

This screen shot shows another way of viewing a match. We placed a gridline at 330 watts (this rider's threshold power), and then another gridline at 396 watts (120 percent of his FTP) so we could visually scan the graph and look at any area above the 396-watt gridline. These are definite matches. The space under the power line (watts), but above the 330-

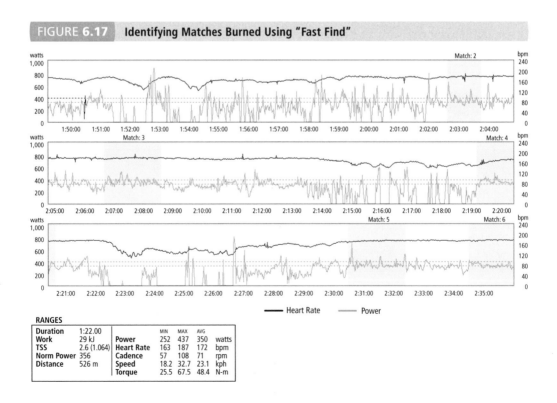

FIGURE 6.17    Identifying Matches Burned Using "Fast Find"

| RANGES | | | | | | |
|---|---|---|---|---|---|---|
| | | | MIN | MAX | AVG | |
| Duration | 1:22.00 | | | | | |
| Work | 29 kJ | Power | 252 | 437 | 350 | watts |
| TSS | 2.6 (1.064) | Heart Rate | 163 | 187 | 172 | bpm |
| Norm Power | 356 | Cadence | 57 | 108 | 71 | rpm |
| Distance | 526 m | Speed | 18.2 | 32.7 | 23.1 | kph |
| | | Torque | 25.5 | 67.5 | 48.4 | N-m |

watt line, is the time spent burning a match. Any significant time spent above 396 watts is like sending up a "flare"!

When you have more insight into when your matches occur and how many you have before you are "cooked," you can make changes in your training that will increase both the size of your matchbook and the intensity of the flame from each match. At the same time, by using a power meter in a race, you can review the data post mortem and determine whether you spent too many matches in the beginning of the race or spent them at the correct times to optimize your chances for success. This is one of the great benefits of racing with a power meter. It allows you to see your performance objectively and determine whether you are using the right tactics. At the same time, you can begin to develop a better training plan based around your weaknesses in order to better "toast" your competition.

## OTHER WAYS TO ANALYZE THE DATA

In race files, you can use the power data in the following ways:
- Use "Fast Find" to count the number of laps that you did in a race, define them, and then overlay those laps using a Multi-File/Range Analysis to understand the difference between them.
- Look for your "peaks" and determine where they are in the file. This will help you to gain insight into the hardest parts of your race.
- If you got dropped, see what types of efforts you had to do, the number of watts for these efforts, and where the breaking point was. You can use this information to tailor your training plan.

In training files, you can do the following:
- See how many kilojoules of energy you used during your ride and determine whether you refueled enough to supply the energy you needed.
- View your Quadrant Analysis for each training ride and compare that with the Quadrant Analysis of your races to make sure you are training specifically for your races. We will take a closer look at this in the next chapter.
- Determine when your wattage began to decrease during the ride. How many kilojoules of energy had you expended up to this point?
- Compare your intervals with one another using a Multi-File/Range Analysis. How many repetitions were you able to do before there was a major drop-off in power? Did you do enough intervals? Or did you do too many?

These suggestions should help to get you started looking at your data in a more productive manner. Every time you ride, your data will teach you something new about yourself and also enable you to further define your abilities as a cyclist. You do not need to do a full markup on every file, but it will still be important to review each ride and make notes about that ride and how it fits into the big picture of your fitness and racing goals. The downloaded data from your races will provide important information about the specific demands of the event, and when you understand these demands, you will be able to create a training program that addresses issues specific to your needs and the requirements of the next race. The data that you capture are priceless for helping you to become even more successful and reach your athletic potential. In the next chapter, we'll build on what we've learned here to ultimately prepare you for more productive training and dynamic analysis.

# Beyond Average Power

## It's not about average power . . .

One of the first things that catches the attention of all beginning power-meter users is how variable, or "jumpy," their power output tends to be. This is largely due to the constantly changing levels of resistance that must be overcome when cycling outdoors. The resistance may come from small changes in elevation, gusts of wind, and other external factors. Because of this variability, training with a power meter is not directly comparable to training with a heart rate monitor. In particular, it is very difficult (as well as often counterproductive) to try to keep power constantly within a certain range or zone during a training session.

Just as important, this variability means that the overall average power for a ride or part of a ride is often a poor indicator of the actual intensity of the effort. For example, you could go out and do two 20-minute intervals at your FTP, and your average power for those 20-minute segments might be 300 watts, but since you rode easily before and after the intervals, the average power for the entire ride might be only 180 watts. Does this mean that this workout would have the same effect on your body as an easy recovery ride in which you averaged 180 watts for 2 hours? Obviously not: Both rides may have had the same average power, but they were entirely different in terms of the physiological systems that they called upon and the overall training stress they required.

This limitation to using average power as a measure of intensity is even more apparent in racing because power can vary dramatically from one moment to the next in a race. Most good racers try to conserve energy and then attack, and these extremes skew the averages. For example, after the hardest road race of the year in which you hung on for dear life, you might download your power-meter data and find that you averaged only 200 watts for the entire 4 hours of racing. Since you know that this was the hardest race of the year, obviously there must be something more going on that simply is not reflected in your average power.

## PERIODIZATION OF TRAINING USING POWER-METER DATA

*And it's not about total work.*

In early 2002, we began to explore the possibility of developing an athlete's entire annual training plan based on some measurement that quantified overall training load. Many cyclists plan their training around an arbitrary number of hours based on their category or classification. We felt that there had to be a better alternative. If we could come up with a score for each ride that took proper account of both duration and intensity, it seemed logical that we would be able to look at an athlete's past data, correlate those with successes and failures, and draw some conclusions about whether training had been appropriately structured.

Ultimately, it was our desire to be able to predict when an athlete would achieve a "peak" of fitness, which would make it possible to design the ideal individualized training program. In essence, we hoped to obtain the "Holy Grail" of periodization—that is, to apply the appropriate amount of training stress at the appropriate times, such that an athlete would peak for his or her most important competition(s). For a long time, coaches and athletes have relied on intuition and trial and error to determine how to do this. However, now that we had the capability to precisely measure what a rider was doing during each and every training ride, we believed that it would be possible to make these decisions far more accurately and confidently. The inspiration for this idea came from a number of scientific studies showing that it was possible to accurately model, or predict, training-induced improvements in performance using Dr. Eric Banister's heart rate–based "training impulse" (TRIMP) score to quantify the overall training load.

We briefly considered using the total work performed (in kilojoules, or kJ), since this is a function of both volume (i.e., frequency and duration) and intensity (i.e., average power). However, we recognized immediately that this idea was fundamentally flawed, because (1) it did not account for the limitations of average power, as previously discussed; and (2) it did not account for the nonlinear relationship between many physiological responses and exercise intensity. For example, you might go out and ride for 3.5 hours and in the process perform 2,000 kJ of work, which would require pedaling at an average power of 159 watts. For the average serious rider, this would be a "garden-variety" Level 2 Endurance workout. It probably would not result in undue fatigue on the following day.

On the other hand, you could go out and perform that same 2,000 kJ of work during a ride that lasted only 2 hours by sustaining an average of 278 watts. For all but the most talented athletes, this would be a much more difficult workout, most likely falling into Level 3 or Level 4, and would probably leave them rather tired for one or more days afterward. Two very different workouts may thus require the same amount of total work, but the impact they would have on your body would be completely different.

With the above in mind, we developed a number of unique analytical tools designed to provide greater insight into the true demands of training and racing a bicycle. The first three—Normalized Power™ (NP), Intensity Factor™ (IF), and Training Stress Score™ (TSS)—are interrelated, and we developed them in an attempt to quantify the metabolic demands and overall training load more accurately than would be possible using average power and total work. Normalized Power is integral to the calculation of IF and TSS and serves as a means of accounting for the variability in power during a ride. IF is an athlete's Normalized Power expressed as a fraction of his or her functional threshold power, and as such it is designed to aid in comparisons across individuals. Finally, TSS quantifies the overall training load, similar to the way that Banister's training impulse method quantifies training based on heart rate data. Once these three concepts were developed and integrated into TrainingPeaks WKO+ Software, it became possible to capture a considerable amount of information regarding the demands of a workout based on just these three metrics. A fourth tool, Quadrant Analysis, is also described later in the chapter. Let's look at Normalized Power first, and then we'll introduce the rest of the concepts that will take your power analysis beyond average power.

Some of the reasoning behind these concepts draws on advanced research in exercise physiology and requires some math knowledge to really understand. If you'd rather skip the technical details, you can still get a general idea of how to use these tools by reading through this chapter. But we did not want to leave out the nitty-gritty. If you are the type of cyclist or coach who wants to be thoroughly informed, you will not be disappointed: You are about to get a crash course in some very useful concepts.

## Normalized Power

As stated before, the act of riding, training, and racing a bicycle is a highly variable, or "stochastic," exercise. There are many factors that affect every ride you take: wind, uphills, downhills, quick accelerations, long steady grinding, and so on. Because of this variability, average power is just not a sufficient indicator of the true metabolic demands of your ride. To account for this variability, we developed a special algorithm to calculate an adjusted (or "normalized") power for each ride or segment of a ride (longer than 30 seconds) that you may want to analyze.

The algorithm is somewhat complicated but incorporates two key pieces of information: (1) Physiological responses to rapid changes in exercise intensity are not instantaneous but follow a predictable time course; and (2) many critical physiological responses (e.g., glycogen utilization, lactate production, stress hormone levels, and the like) are curvilinearly, rather than linearly, related to exercise intensity. We calculate Normalized Power by:

1. Starting at the beginning of the data and calculating a 30-second rolling average for power;
2. Raising the values obtained in step 1 to the fourth power;
3. Taking the average of all the values obtained in step 2; and
4. Taking the fourth root of the number obtained in step 3.

This is Normalized Power. TrainingPeaks WKO+ Software will calculate Normalized Power for you. Basically, it's the wattage you would have averaged if you had pedaled smoothly for the entire effort—the power that your body "thought" it was doing, though in reality the effort could have been a very sporadic "on/off" race. In other words, it is an estimate of the power that you could have maintained for the same physiological "cost" if your power output had been perfectly constant (such as on a stationary cycle ergometer), rather than variable. Because of the factors it takes into account, Normalized Power provides a better measure of the true physiological demands of a given training session than reflected by just the average power.

Keeping track of Normalized Power is therefore a more accurate way of quantifying the actual intensity of training sessions and races. For example, it is common for average power to be lower during criteriums than during equally difficult road races, simply because of the time spent soft-pedaling or coasting through sharp turns during a criterium. The Normalized Power values for a criterium and a road race of about the same duration, however, will generally be very similar, reflecting their equivalent intensity. In fact, during a hard criterium or road race of about 1 hour in duration, Normalized Power will often be similar to what a rider can average when pedaling continuously for a flat 40 km time trial. The Normalized Power from mass-start races can therefore often be used to provide an initial estimate of a rider's threshold power.

Figure 7.1 shows the difference between average power and Normalized Power in a road race. In this figure, the power line is very jagged and constantly fluctuating, indicating that this section of the race contained times of high wattage and times of low wattage. This is typical of road races, where the range of power that cyclists produce is very wide and constantly changing. Since these changes from high power to low power occur so quickly, the body does not have enough time between them to fully recover. Thus, although the muscles get very short breaks, the body experiences the same amount of stress that it would if you did one hard constant effort.

Note that in Figure 7.1 the Normalized Power is 357 watts, whereas the average power is 319 watts. In this case, the stress, or physiological "cost," to the body was equivalent to what it would experience at 357 watts. The greater the difference, the more variable and less continuously aerobic the effort was. Charles Howe, editor and author of "FAQ for Power-Based Training" (http://midweekclub.ca/powerFAQ.htm), coined the term "Variability Index." To obtain the Variability Index, simply take the Normalized Power number and divide it by

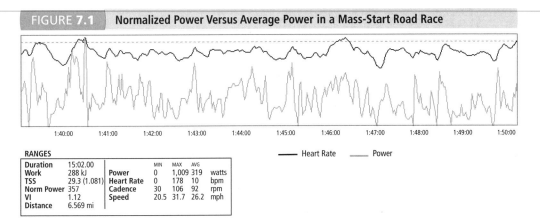

| FIGURE **7.1** | Normalized Power Versus Average Power in a Mass-Start Road Race |

1:40:00  1:41:00  1:42:00  1:43:00  1:44:00  1:45:00  1:46:00  1:47:00  1:48:00  1:49:00  1:50:00

—— Heart Rate    —— Power

**RANGES**

| | | | MIN | MAX | AVG | |
|---|---|---|---|---|---|---|
| **Duration** | 15:02.00 | | | | | |
| **Work** | 288 kJ | **Power** | 0 | 1,009 | 319 | watts |
| **TSS** | 29.3 (1.081) | **Heart Rate** | 0 | 178 | 10 | bpm |
| **Norm Power** | 357 | **Cadence** | 30 | 106 | 92 | rpm |
| **VI** | 1.12 | **Speed** | 20.5 | 31.7 | 26.2 | mph |
| **Distance** | 6.569 mi | | | | | |

the average power number. The more variable your ride (after the 30-second smoothing has been applied), the higher the Variability Index.

The reason all of this is important is that, used correctly, Normalized Power can help you to better define the demands of your event. Table 7.1 shows typical Variability Index values for some common types of cycling events. However, the table is just a rough guideline for helping you to think more critically about variability in cycling. Knowing the demands

| TABLE **7.1** | Variability Indexes for Common Rides |
|---|---|
| **Type of Ride** | **Variability Index** |
| Steady isopower workout | 1.00–1.02 |
| Flat road race | 1.00–1.06 |
| Flat time trial | 1.00–1.04 |
| Hill-climb time trial | 1.00–1.06 |
| Flat criterium | 1.06–1.35 |
| Hilly criterium | 1.13–1.50 |
| Hilly road race | 1.20–1.35 |
| Mountain-bike race | 1.13–1.50 |

of your event is one of the factors key to training specifically for that event. If you are a mountain biker and you are training only on the road, then most likely you will not be ready to handle the constant change in power, cadence, and speed that you will encounter in your next mountain-bike race. You'll learn more about this variability in the section on "Quadrant Analysis" later in this chapter.

Figure 7.2 shows Normalized Power and average power on a steady, relatively constant-gradient climb. It is clear that this type of climb has a much smaller effect on the variability of a rider's power output than the mass-start road race shown in Figure 7.1 did. The wattage line shows how much smoother and more stable the power output was in this effort. The Normalized Power for this section of the ride was 304 watts; the average power, at 300 watts, was only 4 watts lower. Therefore, the Variability Index for the ride depicted in Figure 7.2 is very different from the Variability Index for the ride shown in Figure 7.1 (1.01 for Figure 7.2 versus 1.12 for Figure 7.1). Although these two very different efforts might have a similar physiological cost, their Normalized Power and average power values are very different.

**FIGURE 7.2**    **Normalized Power Versus Average Power on a Steady Climb**

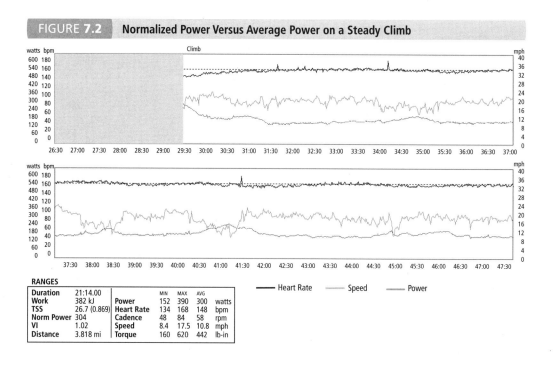

| RANGES | | | MIN | MAX | AVG | |
|---|---|---|---|---|---|---|
| Duration | 21:14.00 | | | | | |
| Work | 382 kJ | **Power** | 152 | 390 | 300 | watts |
| TSS | 26.7 (0.869) | **Heart Rate** | 134 | 168 | 148 | bpm |
| Norm Power | 304 | **Cadence** | 48 | 84 | 58 | rpm |
| VI | 1.02 | **Speed** | 8.4 | 17.5 | 10.8 | mph |
| Distance | 3.818 mi | **Torque** | 160 | 620 | 442 | lb-in |

―― Heart Rate    ········ Speed    ―― Power

## Intensity Factor

Although Normalized Power is a better measure of training intensity than average power, it does not take into account changes in fitness in an individual over time or differences between individuals. It is also important to be able to quantify the intensity of your effort relative to your own abilities, as this plays a key role in the adaptations to training that occur as a result. That is where IF comes in.

IF is simply the ratio of your Normalized Power to your functional threshold power—that is, the fraction of your functional threshold power that you maintained for that workout or part of a workout (i.e., IF = NP/FTP). So, for example, if the Normalized Power for a long training ride that you performed early in the year was 210 watts, and your threshold

**TABLE 7.2**    **Typical Intensity Factor Values in Training and Racing**

| Exertion | IF Value | Notes |
|---|---|---|
| Level 1, Active Recovery | <0.75 | |
| Level 2, Endurance | 0.75–0.85 | |
| Level 3, Tempo | 0.85–0.95 | Also includes road races lasting less than roughly 2.5 hr. |
| Level 4, Lactate Threshold | 0.95–1.05 | Also includes road races lasting less than roughly 2.5 hr, criteriums, circuit races, and longer time trials |
| Level 5 and higher | 1.05–1.15 | Shorter time trials |
| | >1.15 | Prologue time trial, track pursuit, track miss-and-out |

## Using Intensity Factor to Recognize Changes in Fitness

One particularly useful application of IF is to check for changes in functional threshold power. Specifically, an IF of more than 1.05 for a race that is approximately 1 hour in duration is often a sign that the rider's threshold power is actually greater than that presently entered into the TrainingPeaks WKO+ Software program or a spreadsheet program. Thus, by simply examining a rider's IF for various events during the course of a season, you can often recognize increases or decreases in threshold power without formal testing.

For example, let's say that Joe Athlete has set his threshold power at 290 watts and has been training hard for the past eight weeks. However, he hasn't done any formal testing or races lately. Joe heads out to his local district criterium race and gets in a breakaway for about an hour. He comes home and downloads his power-meter data. Looking at his graph, he creates a range around his time "spent off the front," and he sees that his TSS is 114 and his IF is 1.07, with his normalized watts at 310.

Joe knows that this can't be right because, by definition, an hour at threshold should equal 100 TSS points and an IF of 1.0. Joe adjusts his threshold value up to 310, lets the software recalculate his TSS and IF, and sees that the TSS is now 100 and the IF is now 1.0, as expected. That tells Joe that his functional threshold power has almost certainly increased. However, since Joe knows that a 20-watt increase in FTP (i.e., from 290 to 310 watts) in just eight weeks is a relatively large jump, he should probably raise his FTP setting in the software to only 300 watts, and confirm this number through formal testing as soon as possible.

power at the time was 280 watts, then the Intensity Factor for that workout would be 210 divided by 280, or 0.75. However, if you did that same exact ride later in the year, when you were fitter, and by then your threshold power had risen to 300 watts, then the IF would be lower—0.70. IF therefore provides a valid and convenient way of comparing the relative intensity of a training session or race either over time for one rider or from one rider to the next, taking into account changes or differences in threshold power. Table 7.2 shows typical IF values for various training sessions or races.

### Training Stress Score

Although exercise intensity is clearly an important factor in determining the type and magnitude of physiological adaptations to training, exercise frequency and duration—which together determine the overall training volume—are important as well. However, there is obviously an interaction between training intensity and volume—that is, at some point, as your intensity goes up, your volume must come down, and vice versa, or you will become overtrained. To quantify the overall training load and help to prevent such a situation, we developed Training Stress Score.

TSS can be calculated for every workout, and you can view a graphic summary of your recent TSS in a spreadsheet program or in TrainingPeaks WKO+. The PowerTap Joule computer also has the ability to calculate and display TSS as you ride, which is a big help to serious cyclists in modeling performance. TSS takes into account both the intensity (i.e., Intensity Factor) and the duration of each training session, and might best be viewed as a predictor of the amount of glycogen utilized in each workout. If you know the TSS from a certain workout, you can make decisions about how to proceed in your training. A very high TSS resulting from a single race or training session, for example, would indicate that one or more days of rest should be scheduled. The formula for TSS is

$$\text{TSS} = \Big[(s \times W \times IF) \div (FTP \times 3{,}600)\Big] \times 100$$

where s is duration in seconds, W is Normalized Power in watts, IF is Intensity Factor, FTP is functional threshold power, and 3,600 is number of seconds in 1 hour.

The Training Stress Score is based on a 1-hour time trial at your threshold. An athlete riding for 1 hour at FTP would score 100 TSS points, and the IF from this ride would be 1.0. Most serious cyclists know what it feels like to do a time trial for 1 hour and also how much it takes to recover from this effort. There are many 40 km time trials in the United States, and riding 40 km in under 1 hour is and has been the goal of many an aspiring cyclist. More importantly, performance in a 40 km time trial is highly correlated with an individual's power at lactate threshold. With this effort in mind, just about any rider can understand that a 200 TSS ride would represent a "dose" of training equivalent to two 40 km time trials. In contrast, a 100 TSS ride could be a longer 2-hour ride at a lower IF (0.71), which at least in theory would still represent the same physiological cost as a 40 km time trial at an IF of 1.0.

One of the exciting things about TSS, since it is calculated based on functional threshold power, is that beginning riders can work at a level that is right for them to optimize their own training. Although a 300 TSS ride for a beginning rider will be very different, in terms of distance and duration, from a 300 TSS ride for Lance Armstrong, it will put the same degree of stress on the beginner's physiological system and produce an equivalent positive impact. As long as we know the FTP of the athlete, we can easily understand the amount of stress created by his or her efforts, no matter what the category of the rider. The amount of training load that individuals can tolerate, however, will differ. Lance Armstrong might be able to do 300–400 TSS at an IF of 0.85 for 21 days in a row and continue to get stronger, whereas a beginning cyclist may find that just 2 days of training at that level severely "over-reaches" his or her abilities. Because of this difference, we created a scale that can be used as an approximate guide to training (see Table 7.3).

Once you are able to associate your different rides with TSS and IF scores, you will be able to understand the type of ride that someone else did just by hearing what the TSS and Intensity Factor scores were for that ride. Table 7.4 lists some different types of rides and their corresponding scores.

| TABLE 7.3 | Impact of Training Stress on Fatigue | |
|---|---|---|
| **TSS** | **Intensity** | **Recovery Status** |
| <150 | Low | Recovery is generally complete by following day. |
| 150–300 | Moderate | Some residual fatigue may be present the next day, but recovery is generally complete by the second day. |
| 300–450 | High | Some residual fatigue may be present even after 2 days. |
| >450 | Very high | Residual fatigue lasting for several days is likely. |

| TABLE 7.4 | Training Stress Score (TSS) and Intensity Factor (IF) for Different Rides | | |
|---|---|---|---|
| **Event Description** | **Duration (hr.: min.)** | **TSS** | **IF** |
| Easy Level 1 Recovery ride, flat terrain, male Cat. III rider | 1:00 | 12 | 0.37 |
| Easy Level 2 Endurance ride, rolling terrain, male Cat. II rider | 2:30 | 60 | 0.49 |
| C-X race, female masters 40–45 age group | 0:45 | 61 | 0.92 |
| Division 1 pro in an American pro 1/2 criterium | 1:00 | 73 | 0.86 |
| Women's pro criterium | 0:45 | 80 | 1.06 |
| 40 km TT, male Cat. II rider | 0:53 | 89 | 1.02 |
| Typical SuperWeek Cat. III criterium | 1:57 | 109 | 0.75 |
| Typical SuperWeek pro 1/2 criterium (same race as above) | 2:35 | 118 | 0.67 |
| 2005 Mount Evans hill climb, Cat. I | 2:02 | 126 | 0.79 |
| Masters National Road Race, 2005, 55–59 age group | 2:29 | 136 | 0.76 |
| 2005 SuperWeek, Schlitz Park Criterium, Cat. I (same race as above) | 2:28 | 166 | 0.82 |
| Cat. IV road race, rolling terrain, in one small break, rest of time in field | 2:50 | 185 | 0.81 |
| Level 2/3, with 1 hour of threshold climbing | 2:50 | 241 | 0.92 |
| Cat. II dead-flat road race | 3:35 | 246 | 0.83 |
| 2005 SuperWeek, Holy Hill Road Race, Cat. I, small chase group | 4:55 | 266 | 0.74 |
| 2005 US Elite National Championships Cat. I | 5:22 | 272 | 0.71 |
| 2003 Redlands: Oak Glen Stage, Cat. I | 4:55 | 292 | 0.78 |
| Cat. II hilly road race | 4:16 | 305 | 0.85 |
| 2005 Philadelphia USPRO Championship | 5:41 | 307 | 0.74 |
| 2005 Tour de Georgia stage 1, Division 3, USPRO, easy day | 6:00 | 317 | 0.72 |
| 2004 San Francisco Grand Prix | 4:20 | 327 | 0.87 |
| 2005 Lake Placid Ironman, fast female age grouper (fell apart on run) | 5:30 | 330 | 0.73 |
| 2004 Tour de France stage 14, flat 192.5 km (119.6 mi.) | 6:24 | 464 | 0.85 |
| 24-hour MTB race, elite masters male | 24:0 | 1,058 | 0.74 |
| 1,000 km Brevet, done over 3 days, only 5 hours' sleep total, female, age 40 | 42:0 | 1,610 | 0.62 |

By tracking Normalized Power, Intensity Factor, and TSS for each workout and over time, individual athletes and coaches will gain a powerful tool for analyzing the enormous amount of data gathered by training with a power meter. The results of such analyses can then serve as the springboard for improvements in training and, ultimately, race performance.

## QUADRANT ANALYSIS

In order to be successful at racing, you must train in ways that are highly specific to the events in which you compete. That is why it is important to consider the moment-by-moment power fluctuations that occur in cycling using Normalized Power. But power fluctuation is also related to an athlete's neuromuscular power—and that is the issue that we wanted to address when we developed the concept of Quadrant Analysis.

By now you know that when you ride with a power meter, the power fluctuates dramatically. One moment you may be producing 500 watts, the next moment 50 watts, then 250 watts, and so on. These fluctuations are all due to changes in speed, wind, road or trail gradient, and the like. And this can happen in just a few seconds of your ride! Think about these power fluctuations compounded over the entire ride, and then over multiple days of riding. Then consider the power differences between different events within the sport, which arise not because of wind or road conditions but because of the nature and duration of the event. The highly variable nature of cycling power has significant physiological implications, not only in terms of the acute responses to a single ride, but also in terms of the chronic adaptations to repeated training sessions.

Tools such as Normalized Power, IF, and TSS explicitly recognize the seemingly stochastic nature of cycling power output and help coaches and athletes better understand the actual physiological demands of a given race or workout. Even so, to completely understand the physiological consequences of large variations in power, one must also understand how they impact neuromuscular function—that is, the actual forces and velocities that the leg muscles must generate to produce a given power output. Such effects are recognized by the algorithm used to calculate Normalized Power, but only to the extent that they influence metabolism (e.g., via altering fiber-type recruitment patterns). Although strength (or maximal force) per se is rarely a limiting factor in cycling, neuromuscular factors nonetheless can still sometimes play an important role in determining performance. Thus, we realized that it would be useful to be able to analyze power-meter data in a manner that captures this important information and yet could readily be grasped even by nonexperts.

### *Measuring Neuromuscular Power*

"Neuromuscular what?" you may ask. "Neuromuscular function" may sound complicated, but it simply means how fast you can contract a muscle, how strongly you can contract it,

| FIGURE **7.3** | Cadence Distribution Chart |

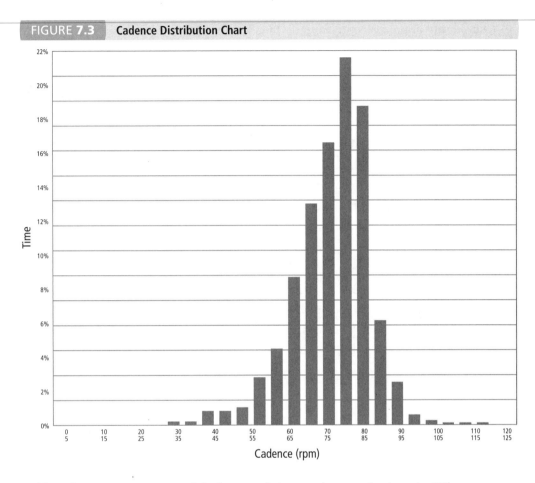

and how long you can contract it before you fatigue and must relax it again. When someone learns a new movement pattern—it could be anything from learning how to type on the keyboard to pedaling a bicycle—those movement patterns are governed by that individual's ability to transfer the information from his or her brain to the muscles that are involved. We all take this for granted, and when it comes to cycling we just pedal, but in reality each of us is different in our ability to make these contractions occur. With your power meter, you can begin to understand your neuromuscular ability, determine whether you are training correctly for cycling success, and then begin to improve your neuromuscular power.

Some information about the neuromuscular demands of a given workout or race can be obtained by examining a frequency distribution histogram of the rider's cadence. Such plots are automatically prepared by most, if not all, power-meter software programs, and thus provide a convenient means of data analysis. Figure 7.3 shows how the cadence from a workout is distributed. In this particular workout, the rider spent a large percentage of her time in the 80–90 rpm range, which would most likely indicate a Level 2 (Endurance) ride.

The velocity of muscle contraction (as indicated by cadence) is only one of two determinants of power, with the other, of course, being force. Unfortunately, at present no power meter on the market directly measures the force applied to the pedal. However, it is possible to derive the average (i.e., over 360 degrees) effective (i.e., tangential to the crank) pedal force (both legs combined) from power and cadence data. The equation looks like this:

$$AEPF = (P \times 60) \div (C \times 2 \times \pi \times CL)$$

where AEPF is average effective pedal force (in newtons, or N); P is power (in watts); C is cadence (in rpm); CL is crank length (in meters); and the constants 60, 2, and $\pi$ serve to convert cadence to angular velocity (in radians/seconds). Additional insight into the neuromuscular demands of a race or training session can then be obtained by preparing a frequency distribution histogram for AEPF that is similar to the one for cadence, as shown in Figure 7.3. (Note that, as with all such plots, graphs like this one do not take continuous efforts into consideration. Each range reflects a compilation of efforts over the course of the ride. This is not an issue, however, because unlike heart rate, for example, neuromuscular responses and demands are essentially instantaneous. Indeed, it is the generation of specific velocities and forces via muscle contraction that essentially drives all other physiological responses.)

**FIGURE 7.4    Scatterplot of Force Versus Velocity**

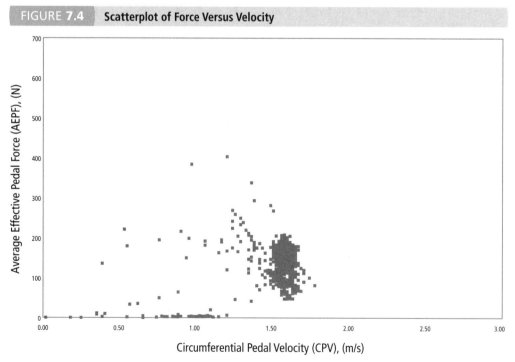

*This figure illustrates force versus velocity for the ride shown in Figure 7.3.*

Although simply examining the frequency distributions of AEPF and cadence provides insight, it does not reveal the relationship between these two variables. This relationship can be quantified only by plotting force versus velocity. Muscle physiologists have used such force-velocity diagrams to describe the contractile properties or characteristics of muscle ever since the early 1920s. Figure 7.4 provides an example of a force-velocity (that is, AEPF, or average effective pedal force) scatterplot. This is the same training session that was used to generate Figure 7.3.

Circumferential pedal velocity—that is, how fast the pedal moves around the circle it makes while pedaling—is derived from cadence as follows:

$$CPV = (C \times CL \times 2 \times \pi) \div 60$$

where CPV is circumferential pedal velocity (in meters/second); C is cadence (in rpm); CL is crank length (in meters); and the constants 2, $\pi$, and 60 serve to convert the data to the proper units. Technically, muscle-shortening velocity, or at least joint angular velocity, should be used instead of circumferential pedal velocity, but CPV has proven to be an excellent predictor of both of these. Because crank length is generally constant, especially for a given individual, one could just as well use cadence instead of circumferential pedal velocity. We have used the latter to be consistent with scientific convention and to emphasize the relationship of cycling-specific plots to the more general force-velocity curve of muscle. A scatterplot of force and velocity, such as that shown in Figure 7.4, presents information that cannot be obtained from simple frequency distribution plots of AEPF and CPV.

However, it can be difficult to detect subtle and sometimes even not-so-subtle differences between roughly similar rides based on such "shotgun blast" patterns, especially if the scaling of the X and Y axes is allowed to vary. Furthermore, without additional information, such force-velocity scatterplots are entirely relative in nature because there are no fixed anchor points or values that can be used as a frame of reference. It is the latter issue that Quadrant Analysis was specifically developed to address.

Quadrant Analysis has been incorporated into version 3.0 of the WKO+ TrainingPeaks Software. We did not include it in earlier versions because we assumed that Quadrant Analysis would be something that most riders would perform only occasionally. This type of analysis has proven to be so helpful, however, that we have added this capability. Whereas many times we look at the common or normal parts of a power file or race, with Quadrant Analysis it is about looking for the "outliers"—the points on the periphery. Quadrant Analysis highlights the outliers in your power file and calls attention to them, and as you learn to interpret them, you will be able to make even more improvements in your training and racing.

Once again, threshold power (and the associated cadence) provides a useful basis for comparison, and in particular for separating relatively low-force from relatively high-force pedaling efforts. (It cannot be overemphasized that the absolute forces generated while cycling are usually quite low, and consequently strength is rarely considered a limiting factor to performance. Later in this chapter we will use Quadrant Analysis to demonstrate this point.)

One factor contributing to the curvilinear relationship between exercise intensity and various metabolic responses (e.g., glycogen utilization, blood lactate concentration) is the recruitment of Type II, or fast-twitch, muscle fibers. Specifically, when you are pedaling at a typical cadence and power output is well below lactate threshold, there is little engagement or utilization of fast-twitch fibers, but with progressive increases in power output, a greater fraction of the total motor unit pool will be recruited to generate the required force. For example, while riding at Level 2 (Endurance), you could be using 90 percent slow-twitch, or Type I, muscle fibers, and only 10 percent fast-twitch, or Type II, muscle fibers. When you pick up the intensity to Level 4, you will continue to use those slow-twitch fibers, but you will begin to recruit significant numbers of fast-twitch fibers as well. In other words, the more intense the effort, the greater your reliance on fast-twitch muscle fibers.

Figure 7.5 shows how the different fiber types are recruited in relation to the intensity of the effort. The Type I fibers are maximally recruited even at a relatively low exercise intensity (i.e., 40 percent of $VO_2$max), whereas the Type IIa and especially Type IIx fibers are recruited only at much higher exercise intensities.

**FIGURE 7.5    Fiber Type Recruitment as a Function of Intensity**

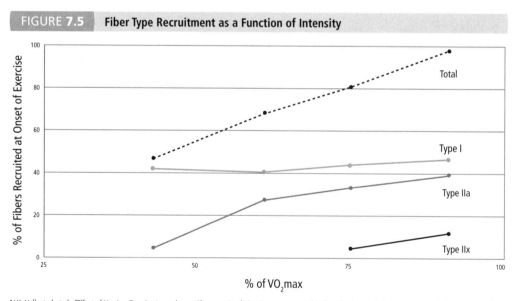

N.K. Vollestad et al., "Effect of Varying Exercise Intensity on Glycogen Depletion in Human Muscle Fibers," *Acta Physiologica Scandinavica* 125 (1985): 395.

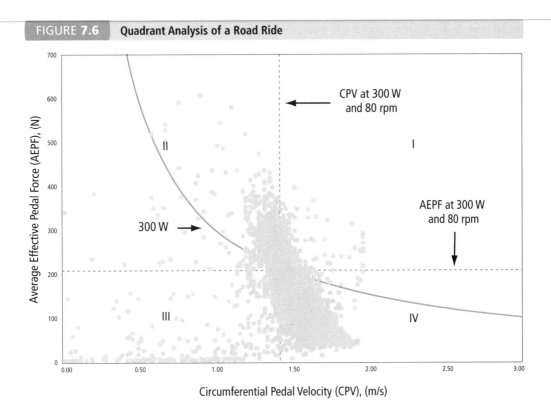

**FIGURE 7.6    Quadrant Analysis of a Road Ride**

Scientific studies using a wide variety of techniques (e.g., electromyography spectral analysis, muscle biopsies) suggest that threshold power represents not only a threshold in terms of the power that an athlete can sustain, but also somewhat of a threshold in terms of fast-twitch fiber recruitment. To state it another way: When pedaling at a typical self-selected cadence, functional threshold power appears to occur at the power (and thus force) at which significant fast-twitch fiber recruitment first begins. Thus, AEPF and CPV at an individual's threshold power can be used to divide the force-velocity scatterplot from any ride into four quadrants, as shown in Figure 7.6.

This division is somewhat arbitrary, in part because of the gradation in force, and thus motor unit recruitment, that occurs when cycling. Also, exercise duration plays an important role in fiber type recruitment, but this is not considered in the figure (to do so would require a three-dimensional plot of AEPF, CPV, and time, which is too complex for routine use). Furthermore, the threshold relationship for fast-twitch fiber recruitment is not really a horizontal line as shown, but more of a curve that falls from left to right. Nevertheless, data points that fall into these four quadrants can be interpreted as follows.

**Quadrant I: high force and high velocity (upper right).** At the extreme, this would be represented by sprinting, but it also includes almost any extended supra-threshold effort on flat ground (e.g., an attack or bridge attempt during a race). Perhaps not surprisingly, mass-start racing on the track (e.g., a points race) invariably entails a significant amount of high-force, high-velocity pedaling due to the typically aggressive nature of this kind of racing and the use of a fixed gear.

**Quadrant II: high force but low velocity (upper left).** Typically, Quadrant II pedaling occurs when climbing or accelerating, especially from a low speed. Indeed, a standing start, in which the initial CPV is zero, is the one situation in cycling where strength is truly limiting. Only when CPV is zero will AEPF be maximal. Racing off-road (e.g., cyclocross or mountain-bike racing) also often involves a significant amount of high-force, low-velocity pedaling. Even a race held on pavement may require a large percentage of such pedaling if the climbs are steep and/or the rider is overgeared. Because AEPF is sufficiently high, pedaling in both Quadrant I and Quadrant II would be expected to entail significant recruitment of fast-twitch fibers.

**Quadrant III: low force and low velocity (lower left).** Rides that entail a very large percentage of pedaling that falls into Quadrant III would typically be focused on recovery or social purposes (e.g., coffee shop rides), not on actual training. However, a mass-start race in which power is highly variable may also involve a good deal of low-force, low-velocity pedaling—for example, when recovering from harder efforts when there is little possibility of an attack, or when soft-pedaling in a large bunch.

**Quadrant IV: low force but high velocity (lower right).** Perhaps the most obvious example of Quadrant IV pedaling would be the use of a low fixed gear or rollers in an attempt to improve pedaling smoothness. Racing may also involve a significant amount of low-force, high-velocity pedaling, especially during events requiring frequent and rapid accelerations (e.g., criteriums).

To further illustrate the applications of the Quadrant Analysis method and the insights it may provide, examples from different types of workouts and races are provided (Figures 7.7–7.12). These examples were specifically chosen because, except for the 40 km time trial provided earlier as a reference, the average (not normalized) power in each case is close to 250 watts. As can be seen, however, the combination and distribution of pedaling forces and velocities accounting for this power output differ significantly. In particular, note the different patterns evident in the plots of the constant-power and micro-burst ergometer training sessions.

FIGURE **7.7**   Quadrant Analysis of a Flat 40 km Time Trial

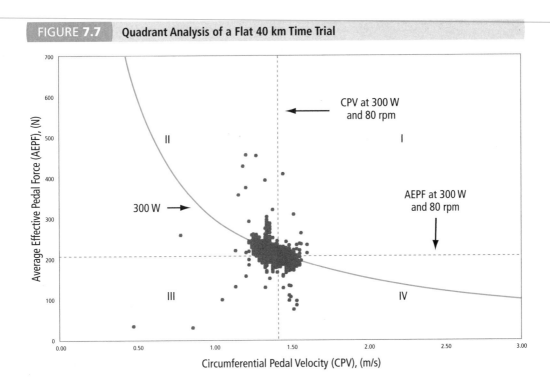

FIGURE **7.8**   Quadrant Analysis of a Constant-Power Ergometer Workout

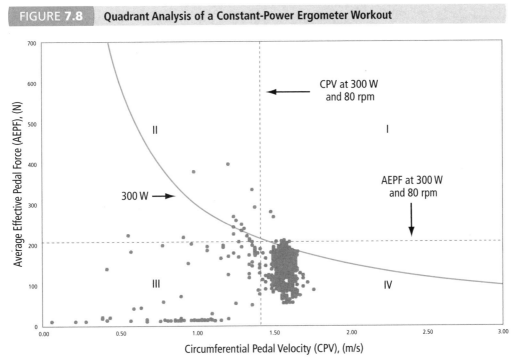

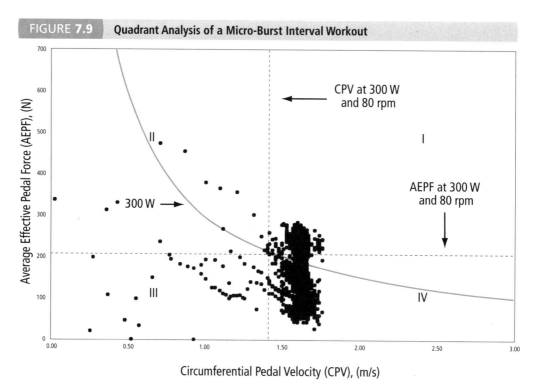

**FIGURE 7.9**    **Quadrant Analysis of a Micro-Burst Interval Workout**

*This workout was done on an ergometer. The micro-burst interval was 15 sec. on, 15 sec. off.*

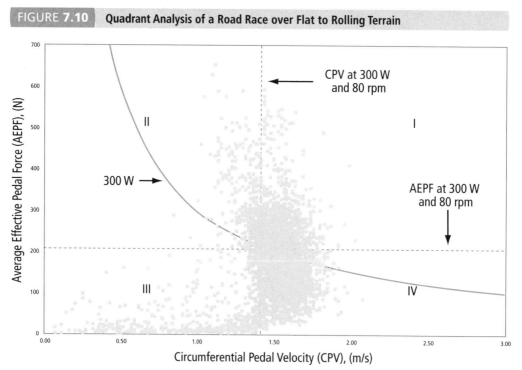

**FIGURE 7.10**    **Quadrant Analysis of a Road Race over Flat to Rolling Terrain**

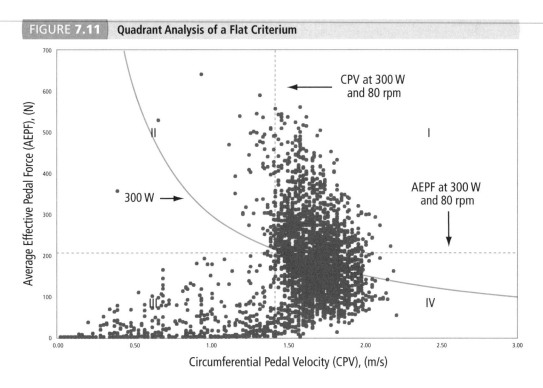

**FIGURE 7.11**    Quadrant Analysis of a Flat Criterium

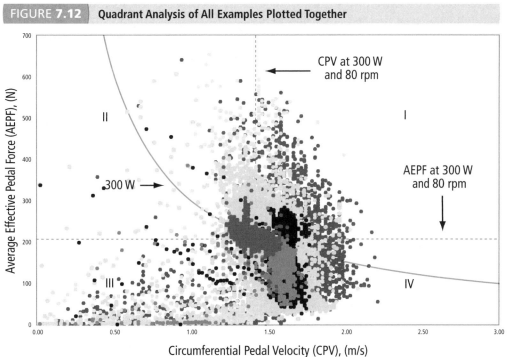

**FIGURE 7.12**    Quadrant Analysis of All Examples Plotted Together

The utility of preparing a force-velocity scatterplot is especially evident in this case, as it reveals an important difference between the two workouts that cannot really be discerned based on average power, Normalized Power, average cadence, and other analyses.

## Quadrant Analysis and Performance

Quadrant Analysis, or at least the calculation of average effective pedal force and circumferential pedal velocity, can also be used to address other specific issues related to cycling performance. What if this method could help you determine the role of strength in generating power and the effectiveness of training for increasing "strength endurance," as it has come to be known? Let's examine it further.

## Strength Versus Power

By definition, strength refers to the maximal force-generating capacity of a muscle or muscle group. Since the force that a muscle can produce inevitably decreases with any increase in its speed of contraction, the strength of a muscle can technically be measured only at zero velocity—that is, during an isometric contraction. (Muscles can actually generate even more force when being slowly lengthened [i.e., during an eccentric contraction], but this fact is generally ignored in discussions where strength is being defined.) Power, by contrast, is defined as the rate at which work is being done and is a function of the force that is produced, the distance over which it is produced, and especially the speed of movement. Unfortunately, many people confuse these two interrelated but nevertheless distinct properties and mistakenly conclude that muscular strength plays an important role in cycling performance.

The fact is that strength, per se, rarely limits an individual's power output. This fact can readily be demonstrated by comparing an athlete's average effective pedal force during training or competition with the maximal force that is being applied to the cranks of a bicycle, taking into consideration the joint angles and other factors involved. Although maximal force can be measured in other ways, for a power-meter user the best way is to simply perform a series of brief, maximal efforts while recording power and cadence at a high frequency (at least once per second). These efforts can be performed either seated or standing, depending on which position is considered most relevant to the question at hand, but each effort should be sufficiently short (for example, less than 10 seconds) such that fatigue does not limit power output. (Note that due to the minimal sampling interval, as well as the aliasing of the PowerTap, the PowerTap power meter may not produce data with sufficient accuracy to be useful in this type of testing and analysis.)

Average effective pedal force (AEPF) and circumferential pedal velocity (CPV) can be calculated from the combined data from these multiple efforts, which, when plotted against one another, should form an essentially straight line that slopes down from left to right.

Extension of this line to the Y-intercept would give us an estimate of the cyclist's maximal AEPF at zero CPV (i.e., his or her strength when pedaling against an infinitely high resistance). Conversely, if we were to extend the line to the X-intercept, we could get at least a theoretical value for maximal CPV at zero AEPF (i.e., the athlete's maximal speed of movement while pedaling without external resistance).

An example of the data resulting from this sort of testing is shown in Figure 7.13, where the data from ten maximal standing-start efforts are plotted along with the AEPF and CPV data from Figures 7.7 to 7.12. As can be seen in Figure 7.13, the maximum force that this individual could produce when pedaling was just over 1,100 newtons (N), or just over 110 kilograms of force (approximately 166 percent of the athlete's body mass). But the highest force the athlete ever generated (had to generate) when racing (e.g., when sprinting) was only about 600 N (i.e., only about 55 percent of maximal force), and during the vast majority of the time the athlete was applying less than 400 N (i.e., only about 35 percent of maximal force). Indeed, even time trialing at FTP required that the athlete repeatedly press on the pedals with only about 25 percent of the maximal force he or she could produce. This was true even though this athlete was a poor sprinter but an excellent time trialist who preferred a relatively low cadence (i.e., less than 80 rpm during the time trial shown in the

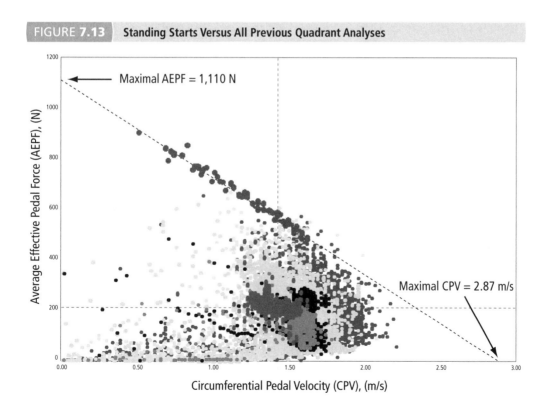

**FIGURE 7.13**  **Standing Starts Versus All Previous Quadrant Analyses**

example), which would require him or her to utilize a higher percentage of his or her strength than is usually the case during a time trial.

From the above analysis, it should be readily apparent that a person's strength rarely limits his or her cycling performance (although the standing starts performed by BMX racers and some track cyclists are a notable exception). The issue, instead, is how much power one can produce, not only throughout a race (i.e., on average) but at key moments during a race (e.g., when attacking or following an attack, during the final sprint, and so on).

Even so, as shown in Figure 7.13, it is actually rather unusual for a rider to generate 100 percent of his or her maximal power during an endurance event such as a road race or criterium. This is evident from the fact that only a relatively small number of points (collected, in this case, at 1-second intervals) lie close to, or even slightly above, the rider's maximal AEPF-CPV line (which coincides with the maximal power the rider can generate at any given CPV). In other words, even though a rider might be pedaling as hard as he or she can at certain times during such a race, the power produced is usually lower than the maximum produced at that CPV (or cadence). The discrepancy is due to short- or long-term fatigue. That is why it is so important to work on enhancing the ability of your muscles to produce adenosine triphosphate by training the anaerobic and aerobic pathways. Even sprinters, who depend on short-term speed, can train their muscles to resist fatigue.

This analysis implies that training strictly to increase strength (e.g., by lifting heavy weights at a slow speed) would have a limited effect, at best, on the maximal power output of a trained cyclist. Indeed, a number of scientific studies have now demonstrated this to be the case, even when the test employed (such as a maximal 30-second effort at only 50 rpm) has favored the likelihood of finding a positive effect. This outcome has to do with the specificity principle: Resistance training performed at slower speeds primarily increases the force that can be generated at such speeds and has little or no impact on the force that can be generated at higher speeds (i.e., at speeds closer to the speed at which power is maximal).

Indeed, when carried to an extreme, training with weights may actually result in a reduction in the maximal shortening velocity of muscle, and hence an impairment of maximal power, at least at high contraction velocities. In terms of Figure 7.13, this would correspond to a steepening of the AEPF-CPV line (i.e., the Y-intercept would be higher, meaning that strength has increased, but the X-intercept would be farther to the left, meaning that maximal pedaling speed has declined). Although there may be ways to mitigate such effects (for example, by doing more "explosive" movements, such as those used in plyometrics), our point here is that cyclists who ride with a power meter don't need to rely on guesswork or anecdotal reports by coaches or other cyclists to figure out whether any off-the-bike training they choose to do beneficially impacts their performance. Instead, using tools such as Quadrant Analysis, they can determine the answers to such questions for themselves.

### Strength Endurance Training

Some coaches over the past twenty years or so have advocated strength endurance intervals as part of a well-rounded training program for cyclists. Although the precise format of these intervals varies, in general they consist of pedaling for extended periods (e.g., 5–20 minutes) at a moderate to high intensity but at an abnormally low cadence (e.g., 45–75 rpm). More recently, this form of training seems to have gained popularity among triathletes under the rubric of "big-gear" training. Based on anecdotal evidence, the proponents of this form of training claim that it improves performance, although there seems to be no consensus on the particular aspect of performance that it is thought to benefit.

Strength, per se, plays a very small role in determining power output. The growing realization that more traditional forms of resistance training, such as weight lifting, provide little or no benefit to cyclists is possibly contributing to the increasing popularity of strength endurance training. Coaches who employ these workouts are attempting to provide a more specific form of on-the-bike resistance training that will enable a cyclist to make gains applicable to racing. However, it appears that few, if any, of the people who recommend strength endurance training have actually considered whether the forces generated during these sessions are in fact sufficient to cause beneficial adaptations to occur. Instead, most seem to have simply assumed that just because the cadence is lower than usual, and hence the pedaling forces higher, there will be an increase in muscular size and strength, and hence in maximal power. In fact, the average effective pedal force during strength endurance intervals is generally too low to represent a significant overload. A laboratory study performed in New Zealand in 2005 found that such training does not increase either the size (estimated using anthropometry) or the maximal force production (determined using isokinetic dynamometry) of the leg extensor muscles.

Figure 7.14 compares the AEPF produced during two typical strength endurance sessions performed by the same athlete who did the rides analyzed in Figure 7.7 to 7.12. These sessions consisted of pedaling either for two 20-minute efforts at 250 watts or for five 5-minute efforts at 300 watts, both at 45 rpm. A "no-gripping" rule was applied, as advocated by some coaches, to minimize the recruitment of upper-body musculature. To mimic the inertial load a cyclist encounters while climbing a moderate grade, the efforts were performed on a Velodyne trainer operating in ergometer mode while using a 53:12 gear combination. The selected power outputs represented only 90 percent of that which the individual would normally be able to maintain for these durations, but they were in fact nearly maximal in light of the markedly suboptimal cadence.

Pedaling at 45 rpm during the strength endurance workouts resulted in an AEPF approximately twice that required to pedal at the same power(s) but at a more normal cadence of 85–90 rpm (results not shown). Nevertheless, the AEPF produced during the two

FIGURE **7.14**    **AEPF and CPV During Strength Endurance Intervals**

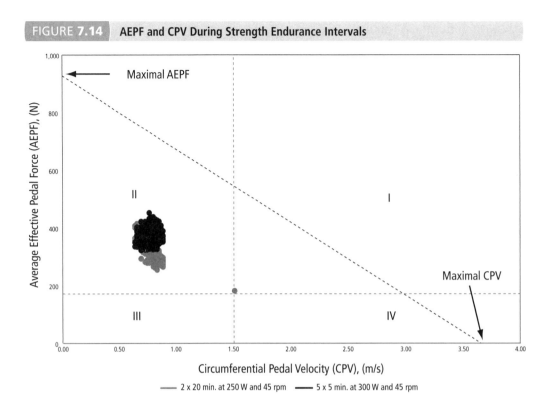

2 x 20 min. at 250 W and 45 rpm    5 x 5 min. at 300 W and 45 rpm

strength endurance sessions still required less than 50 percent of the athlete's strength, an amount equivalent to that produced during weight training at only 50 percent of one repetition maximum (1 RM). Indeed, even accounting for the decline in muscle force with increasing cadence, the AEPF during the strength endurance workouts was still lower than two-thirds of the individual's velocity-specific maximum force.

This result may at first seem surprising, especially to anyone who has performed such training and has felt that he or she was pushing very hard on the pedals. However, the finding is consistent with the fact that the test subject was able to perform 1,125–1,800 "reps" (i.e., five 5-minute segments or two 20-minute segments at 45 rpm) with this load. Furthermore, when  it is taken into account that peak force on the pedals was roughly twice the average force (i.e., AEPF), then one can determine that the athlete was not pushing any harder with his leg extensors than he would when, for example, performing step-ups with only body mass for resistance (i.e., 68 kg × 9.81 N/kg = 667 N). The strength endurance sessions were therefore actually much more like climbing many flights of stairs than traditional weight training. Consequently, these sessions would be unlikely to result in any significant hypertrophy and/or strength gains, at least in an athlete performing other forms of training.

Proponents of strength endurance training have also proposed that such workouts improve performance via enhanced recruitment of Type II (fast-twitch) muscle fibers. This, it is argued, produces greater physiological adaptations in these fibers than training at a normal cadence, and hence leads to greater improvements in performance. However, the basic premise that strength endurance training results in markedly greater utilization of Type II fibers may not be correct.

Again, consider the Quadrant Analysis plot of the two strength endurance training sessions presented in Figure 7.14. When the athlete was performing strength endurance training, AEPF and CPV clearly fell well into Quadrant II, in which there is relatively low velocity and relatively high force. Since the AEPF during these efforts was greater than that resulting from pedaling at functional threshold power and a self-selected cadence, it would at first glance seem that significant recruitment of Type II muscle fibers must have occurred. As previously discussed, however, the AEPF during the strength endurance workouts was still well below the individual's velocity-specific maxima, which presumably reflects maximal recruitment of all fibers—that is, both Type I and Type II. Therefore, either a significant percentage of Type II muscle fibers was not recruited by the strength endurance training, or they were not recruited as frequently as they are during very short efforts.

The AEPF associated with pedaling at functional threshold power and a self-selected cadence represents the approximate force at which significant Type II fiber recruitment appears to begin. But, as you may recall, the exact force at which this occurs varies in a velocity- and time-dependent manner (i.e., it is higher at a lower CPV and lower at a higher CPV). Or, to state it another way, the AEPF threshold for Type II muscle fiber recruitment is better represented by a line that slopes downward from left to right, approximately parallel to the maximal force-velocity line, than as a strictly horizontal "cutoff." (Again, the separation of Quadrants I and II from III and IV using a strictly horizontal line is really just a matter of convenience, since no "anchor point" other than functional threshold power and self-selected cadence is usually available.) From this perspective, it seems much less clear that strength endurance training results in significantly greater recruitment of Type II muscle fibers. The AEPF during these two workouts is nearly as far below the maximal AEPF at that CPV as it is when a rider is pedaling at a more typical cadence.

Even if strength endurance training does enhance Type II muscle fiber recruitment, it is unclear why this would be necessary or desirable. When endurance athletes do not perform strength endurance training, Type II fibers can still be sufficiently recruited, and hence trained, to cause the almost complete replacement of Type IIx by Type IIa fibers and to result in an aerobic ability of Type II fibers equal to that of the same athlete's Type I fibers.

———————

The concepts presented in this chapter are advanced, but they are important, and it is very useful to understand them when training with power. Associating your rides with how many TSS points you accumulated, and figuring out how that will impact your recovery, can be a profound learning process. Knowing that an hour of work at your FTP equals 100 TSS points with an Intensity Factor of 1.0 will help you to better associate levels of training load with your rides. You will begin to understand the levels of training load that would be provided in a ride with your local Tuesday night group, the ride you do on your mountain-climbing day, the workout you do to reach Level 3 (Tempo), and so on, and from this knowledge you can use TSS and IF on a daily basis to design a more complete training plan. This is one of the greatest uses you will discover with your power meter. Never before have we been able to so closely and accurately quantify training load for each individual cyclist and for his or her unique individual and cumulative workouts over entire years of time. With these tools, the power meter allows you to see how your training load will impact you after your ride, two days later, one week later, and even a month later.

Quadrant Analysis provides another level of understanding about the specificity of your workout. If you are a triathlete and all you are doing are mass-start road races, it is very likely that you would not be ready for your upcoming triathlon, "neuromuscularly" speaking. By learning how your events fall into the four quadrants, you can determine whether your training is specific to that quadrant. Don't expect to be a successful criterium racer if you spend a majority of your time in Quadrant III riding back and forth to the coffee shop. But make sure that you are in Quadrant III when you are doing your recovery rides. Using Quadrant Analysis on selected rides and races will help to confirm that you are training properly and to achieve peak performance at cycling events.

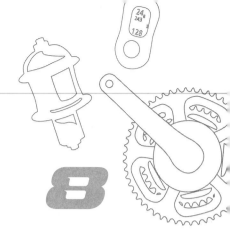

# Using Power to
# Manage Performance

*Pro cyclists talk a lot about "form."* When they are "on form," they feel unbeatable. But what is form? We all know it when we feel it, but we can never really describe it. Where does it come from and how can one acquire it?

Coaches are responsible for creating form in their athletes. Not only do coaches want to make sure their athletes have it; they want to make sure athletes have it on race day. And herein lies the challenge: How can you achieve form exactly on the day when you want to have it? How will you know that the training you are doing now will give you the necessary peak when you want it? Are you training too hard? Are you training hard enough? What about the type of training? Are you training in the proper training zones, and is there enough variety in your training to make sure each physiological system is improving? Every cyclist and coach is looking for answers to these questions.

Any good coach or smart training program can increase your fitness or make you faster; however, the true challenge is not just to be faster. It's to be fitter and faster than before at the exact time that you want to be. Fortunately, power data enable us to better predict performance, using an approach we have termed the "Performance Manager." It's important for you to understand how the Performance Manager works, even if it takes a little time to sort out the technical details. In this chapter, we will explain an alternative model that has often been used in research studies, along with the limitations of that model, and then explain how our Performance Manager works. Finally, we will explain how to apply the Performance Manager to create your own fitness peaks at the right times.

## BANISTER'S IMPULSE-RESPONSE MODEL

When attempting to design the optimal training program, most coaches and athletes rely upon some combination of tradition, trial and error, and basic training principles (for example, the overload principle). A number of scientific studies, however, have investigated the relationship between the volume and intensity of training and the resulting improvements in performance in a more direct, quantitative manner. These studies have used a wide variety of mathematical approaches, but the vast majority have employed what is typically referred to as the "impulse-response model," first proposed by Dr. Eric Banister in 1975.

In the impulse-response approach, the effects of training on performance are modeled as a transfer function with "inputs" and "outputs." The inputs are the daily "doses" of training, which are a combination of volume and intensity, and the outputs are the results of the training, the individual's predicted performance. Training is said to exert two opposing effects: (1) positive adaptations to training that result in improved performance, which are longer-lasting, or "chronic," and (2) negative consequences of recent exercise bouts, such as residual fatigue, which are shorter in duration, or "acute." These acute, negative effects can obscure the chronic, positive effects, but only for a period of time.

The impulse-response model has been successfully applied to a number of different sports, including weight lifting, hammer throwing, running, swimming, cycling, and triathlon. The factors it takes into account have been shown to account for more than 70 percent, and often more than 90 percent, of the day-to-day variation in performance. Moreover, the model has been shown to accurately predict changes in performance-related parameters considered indicative of training (over)load and/or adaptation, such as serum hormone levels (for example, of testosterone), enzyme levels (for example, of creatine kinase), and psychological measures of anxiety or perceived fatigue.

The model has therefore been used to optimize training and tapering regimens, to evaluate the impact of training in one sport on performance in another (such as the impact of training in running on performance in cycling), and so on. In most of these studies, the metric used to track training load has been Banister's heart rate–based "training impulse" (TRIMP) score, but other ways of quantifying training have also been used (especially in studies of nonendurance sports, but also in, for example, swimming). Roughly speaking, the model appears to work equally well regardless of precisely how training has been quantified.

The impulse-response model would therefore appear to be a highly useful tool for coaches and athletes wishing to maximize their probability of success in competition, and in fact some prominent national team programs in cycling have attempted to exploit this approach. There are, however, a number of significant limitations to the impulse-response model, some of which may be purely academic, but others that clearly limit its usefulness in a practical sense.

## Banister's Impulse-Response Model

We can express these changes in an individual's performance over time as a mathematical equation:

$$p_t = p_0 + k_a \sum_{s=0}^{t-1} e^{-(t-s)/\tau_a} w_s - k_f \sum_{s=0}^{t-1} e^{-(t-s)/\tau_f} w_s$$

where $p_t$ is the performance at any time t, $p_0$ is the initial performance, $k_a$ and $k_f$ are gain or multiplier terms relating to the magnitudes of the positive adaptive and negative fatigue effects (and also help in converting the units that are used to quantify training to the units that are used to quantify performance), $\tau_a$ and $\tau_f$ are time constants describing the rate of decay of the positive adaptive and negative fatigue effects, and $w_s$ is the daily training dose.

The impulse-response model therefore has four adjustable parameters, $k_a$, $k_f$, $\tau_a$, and $\tau_f$, which are constrained such that $k_a$ is less than $k_f$, and $\tau_a$ is less than $\tau_f$. The best-fit solution to the model is determined iteratively, that is, by repeatedly measuring both the daily dose of training and the resulting performance, and then adjusting the values of these parameters to result in the closest correspondence between the model that was predicted and actual performances. Figure 8.1 illustrates the effects of a single bout of training on performance resulting in a TSS of 100, as predicted by this model. Performance (the difference between the two terms of the equation above) is initially predicted to

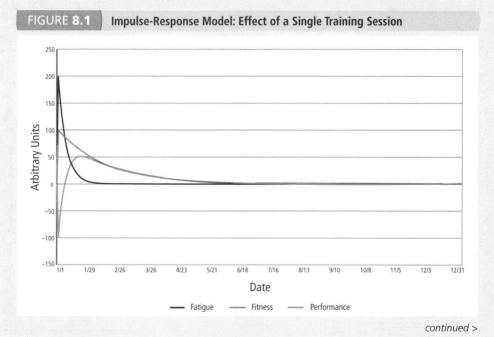

FIGURE **8.1**     Impulse-Response Model: Effect of a Single Training Session

*continued >*

*Banister's Impulse-Response Model, continued*

be diminished or degraded because of the acute, negative influence of training. As this effect passes, however, the positive adaptations to training begin to dominate, such that performance is eventually improved.

The impact of repeated bouts of training on performance is thus the summation of individual impulses, with the ultimate effect (that is, when, or even whether, training results in an increase or decrease in performance, and the extent to which this is true) depending on the magnitude and timing of each "dose" of training. This principle is illustrated in Figure 8.2, which depicts the response to a sustained increase in daily training to 100 TSS per day.

**FIGURE 8.2**    **Impulse-Response Model: Adaptation to Sustained Training**

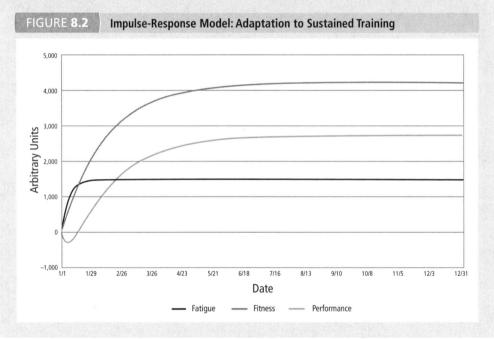

## LIMITATIONS OF THE IMPULSE-RESPONSE MODEL

First, although the impulse-response model can be used to accurately describe changes in performance over time, it has not been possible to link the mathematical structure of the model to specific, training-induced, physiological events relevant to fatigue and adaptation, such as glycogen resynthesis or mitochondrial biogenesis. In this regard the model is purely descriptive in nature, like a black box into which it is not possible to see. Although this by no means invalidates the approach, being able to connect the model parameters (in particular, the time constants $\tau_a$ and $\tau_f$ ; see sidebar, "Banister's Impulse-Response Model," for definition of variables) to known physiological mechanisms would allow the model to be applied with greater confidence and precision.

Second, the impulse-response model assumes that there is no upper limit to performance. Instead, it assumes that a greater amount of training *always* leads to a higher level of performance, at least once the fatigue resulting from recent training has dissipated. In reality, plateaus happen. Like it or not, there will always be some point at which further training will not result in a further increase in performance. Even if you can avoid illness, injury, overtraining, or just mental burnout, this holds true.

Third, to obtain a statistically valid fit of the model parameters to the actual data, it is necessary to have multiple, direct, quantitative measurements of performance over a duration that is comparable to that of the goal event. The exact number depends in part on the particular situation, but from a purely statistical perspective it would take somewhere between 5 and 50 measurements per adjustable parameter. Since the model has four adjustable parameters ($\tau_a$, $\tau_f$, $k_a$, and $k_f$), performance would have to be directly measured between 20 and 200 times in total. Furthermore, since the model parameters can change over time (with training), these measurements should all be obtained in a fairly short period of time. Indeed, Banister himself suggested revisiting the fit of the model to the data every 60 to 90 days, which would mean directly measuring an athlete's maximal performance ability at least every fourth day, if not several times per day. This is obviously unrealistic, especially outside the setting of a laboratory research study.

Fourth, even when an adequate number of performance measurements are available, the fit of the model to the previously collected data may not be accurate enough for the results to be truly helpful in projecting future performance (which is obviously necessary to be able to use the impulse-response model to plan a training program). This is especially true when you consider that, in keeping with the saying "The best predictor of performance is performance itself," the bar is already set quite high through knowledge of your current performance ability. For example, in most cases even the best taper regimen will only improve performance less than 5 percent, and usually by less than 2 percent. Consequently, the impulse-response model would need to be able to predict performance on race day with at least this degree of accuracy to be of great practical use. This is generally not the case.

Finally, while values reported in the scientific literature for the time constants for fitness and fatigue ($\tau_a$ and $\tau_f$) are generally pretty consistent in most scientific studies, there is considerable variability among individuals and studies in the gain factors (i.e., $k_a$ and $k_f$). In part, this is because these values serve not only to "balance" the two integrals in the equation but also to quantitatively relate the training load to performance in an absolute sense. In other words, for the exact same set of data for the same individual, the values for $k_a$

and $k_f$ would be different if power were expressed in terms of horsepower instead of watts. However, this is not the only explanation for the variation in $k_a$ and $k_f$ between studies, as even their ratio varies significantly across studies, with this variation seemingly unrelated to factors such as the overall training load. Because of this variability, it is difficult, if not impossible, to rely on generic values for $k_a$ and $k_f$ from the literature to overcome the limitations caused by performance plateaus and accurate testing of performance. This is especially true given the fact that the impulse-response model is more sensitive to variations in these gain factors than it is to variation in the time constants, especially $\tau_a$ (for example, increasing or decreasing $\tau_a$ by 10 percent changes the output of the model by less than 5 percent).

## THE PERFORMANCE MANAGER CONCEPT

The relative complexity of the impulse-response model and its limitations led us to search for a more practical way of analyzing data obtained using a power meter. We wanted our model to work in a manner that was consistent with the results of previous scientific research yet still simple enough to be used and applied outside of a laboratory setting. The starting point for this search was recognition of the simple fact that performance is typically greatest when training is first progressively increased to a very high level to build fitness, after which the athlete reduces his or her training load—that is, tapers—to eliminate residual fatigue. Or, to put it more simply, "form equals fitness plus freshness."

With this perspective in mind, we recognized that eliminating the gain factors ($k_a$ and $k_f$) from the impulse-response model solved two problems: (1) It removed any uncertainty regarding the precision with which they can be estimated (with the price being that interpreting the results of the calculations becomes as much a matter of art as of science); and (2) it allowed for substitution of simpler, exponentially weighted moving averages for the more complex integral terms in the original equation (because, at least qualitatively, they behave the same way). Based on this logic, the components of the Performance Manager were then defined.

**Chronic Training Load (CTL).** Taking into consideration both volume and intensity, CTL provides a measure of how much an athlete has been training historically, or chronically. It is calculated as an exponentially weighted moving average of daily TSS (or TRIMP) values, with the default time constant set to 42 days. (In effect, what this means is that your CTL is primarily a function of the training that you have done in the past three months.) CTL can therefore be viewed as analogous to the positive effect of training on performance in the impulse-response model—that is, the first integral term in the equation given earlier—with the caveat that CTL is a *relative* indicator of changes in performance ability due to changes in fitness, not an absolute predictor (since the gain factor, $k_a$, has been eliminated).

**Acute Training Load (ATL).** Again, taking into consideration both volume and intensity, ATL provides a measure of how much an athlete has been training recently, or acutely. It is calculated as an exponentially weighted moving average of daily TSS values, with the default time constant set to 7 days. (In effect, what this means is that your ATL is primarily a function of the training that you have done in the past two weeks.) ATL can therefore be viewed as analogous to the negative effect of training on performance in the impulse-response model—that is, the second integral term in the equation—with the caveat that ATL is a *relative* indicator of changes in performance ability due to fatigue, not an absolute predictor (since the gain factor, $k_f$, has been eliminated).

**Training Stress Balance (TSB).** As the name suggests, Training Stress Balance (a term coined by cycling coach Dave Harris) is the difference between chronic and acute training loads: TSB = CTL − ATL. TSB provides a measure of how much an athlete has been training recently, or acutely, compared with how much he or she has trained historically, or chronically. Although it is tempting to consider TSB as analogous to the output of the impulse-response model—that is, as a predictor of actual performance ability—the elimination of the gain factors $k_a$ and $k_f$ means that it is really better viewed as an indicator of how fully adapted an individual is to his or her recent training load—how "fresh" the athlete is likely to be.

In a moment we will explore these concepts in more detail as we begin to quantify form, but you can see that performance depends not only on TSB but also on CTL. This is in keeping with saying that "form equals fitness plus freshness." The "art" in applying the Performance Manager lies in determining the precise combination of TSB and CTL that results in maximum performance. To put it another way: In the Performance Manager concept, an individual's CTL (and the "composition" of the training resulting in that CTL) determines his or her performance potential (at least within limits). The individual's TSB influences his or her ability to fully express that potential. Actual performance at any point in time will therefore depend on both CTL and TSB, but determining how much emphasis to accord to each is now a matter of trial and error—that is, experience—not science.

To help illustrate these conceptual differences between the impulse-response model and the Performance Manager, consider Figure 8.3, which shows the effects on CTL, ATL, and TSB of a "square-wave" increase in daily training load from 0 TSS per day to 100 TSS per day as of January 1: The situation being modeled is therefore identical to that shown in Figure 8.2; the only difference is that the lines on the graph have been generated using the Performance Manager approach instead of the impulse-response model.

As shown in the figure, both CTL and ATL respond to this sudden increase in training in an exponential fashion, just like the fitness and fatigue components of the impulse-response model, and with identical time courses (since the time constants are the same). TSB shows an initial reduction followed by an exponential rise, which is qualitatively similar to

**FIGURE 8.3** | **Performance Manager: Adaptation to Sustained Training**

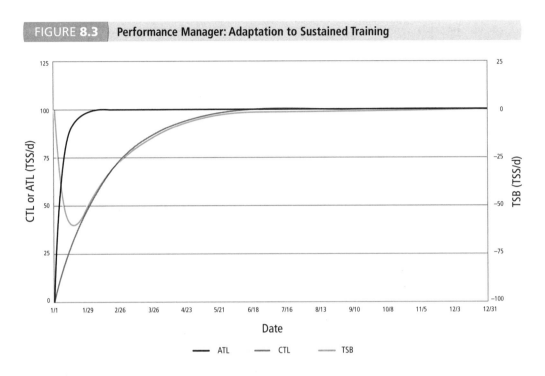

— ATL    — CTL    — TSB

the time course of performance as predicted by the impulse-response model. However, the minimum in TSB occurs later than the reduction in performance would be predicted to occur by the impulse-response model when using the same time constants (42 days and 7 days for $\tau_a$ and $\tau_f$, respectively). Moreover, unlike performance as predicted using the impulse-response model, TSB never exceeds its initial level but instead rises mono-exponentially to eventually equal CTL (and ATL). This differing behavior is a consequence of the elimination of the gain factors $k_a$ and $k_f$ from the impulse-response model, as well as the substitution of exponentially weighted moving averages for the integral sums.

## PEAKING WITH POWER

Now that we have explained how and why we came up with the Performance Manager concept, let's get back to that nebulous idea of being "on form" on the right day of the season: race day. A quick reminder that

Form = Fitness + Freshness

A rider can be fit at the end of the Tour de France, but he will be very tired, and not on form. On the other side of the coin, if he has not ridden a bike for two months, he will be very "fresh" and rested, but not very "fit," and therefore not on form either. Sitting on the couch and channel surfing for the two months before the race (so that he is fresh) will cause him to lose that precious fitness he'll need to compete. And if he trains very hard to become super fit, but does not rest and taper before the race, then he will be fit, but unable to apply that fitness because he is fatigued. Only the correct balance of fitness and freshness will create form.

What exactly is "fitness," then? Basically, it's a response to training stress. A dose of training is given to the athlete, and then the athlete adapts and responds positively to that dose, which then creates improvements and efficiencies in the body. These improvements accumulate to make the athlete fitter and faster. So, fitness is created from training stress, or training load. The training load has to continually increase in intensity and/or volume in order to create a greater adaptation.

Training load can increase in many ways, but with a power meter it is easy to define an exact training load. By quantifying your training using TSS, you can better understand how the cumulative effects of training load are influencing your body, then use that knowledge to determine when to rest and when to continue to push yourself further with your training. The complex ways in which different types of training stress affect overall fitness and fatigue levels are an area currently under study; in fact, theories about training load are on the cutting edge of exercise physiology theory, and the jury is still out on how it all works.

### Managing Fitness and Fatigue (CTL and ATL)

We've touched upon the concept of Chronic Training Load, the cumulative effect that builds up over a long period of time. The basic idea behind all the research is that an ideal level of CTL is beneficial because it causes your body to undergo positive fitness adaptations. But the period of time involved in getting those adaptations to happen (again, through hard training) can be anywhere from 3 weeks to 6 weeks, 6 months, or 2 years. All "old school" cycling coaches will say that you "just need another 20,000 kilometers in your legs" and you'll be at the top.

In many ways, these coaches are correct, as it takes years to fully develop the physiological systems needed for racing at the highest levels. The more kilometers you have in your legs, the more training stress you'll be able to handle and the faster you'll become. Your current fitness depends not only on what you did in training a week ago, but also on what you did in training 6 weeks ago. The span of time that matters for CTL may be shorter or longer than 6 weeks ago—that is up for debate; however, the workouts you did 6 weeks ago are without a doubt impacting your performance today. The workouts you did 3 weeks ago are impacting you even more. The thing to remember is that CTL refers to the long-term effects resulting primarily from the workouts you have done in the past 3 months.

Acute Training Load, on the other hand, is accumulated over a shorter period of time—using the default time constant, primarily in the past two weeks. Since CTL is more closely related to "fitness," and ATL is more closely related to your "fatigue," then the workouts done during a weekend are very much going to impact your ability to do some hard work during the week. Therein lies another challenge: If you rest too much, you will start to lose fitness (CTL will fall), but if you train before you are properly rested, then you will fail to get the greatest bang for your training buck. Since your ATL "drives" your CTL, if you stop training in the short term, then this will impact your long-term fitness.

This principle is very similar to the ones you use to manage your own budget at home. You have a certain amount of income coming in each month, you have fixed expenses that must be paid each month, and you have some variable expenses that occur each month (such as that stellar deal the bike shop just offered you on a sweet new set of carbon wheels!). If you buy those wheels, in the short term you may be very happy (whoever said money can't buy happiness hasn't bought a set of really fast wheels!), and you may win some races. But if you can't pay some of your fixed expenses because of the purchase of the wheels, you are going to have to spend some extra hours at the office to compensate for your lack of long-term budgeting. Similarly, if you train too hard in a block of training, you'll overtrain (over-spend), and it could take you months to recover from that training block. The opposite scenario applies as well. If you get too much rest, then your long-term fitness will deteriorate. You might come onto form too soon or lose watts at your functional threshold.

Accumulated ATL is what forces you to rest after a hard week of training, and it is what builds your CTL. Without those hard, intense training blocks, you would never achieve a high enough CTL to create meaningful, long-term fitness adaptations. On the one hand, it is important that you naturally build your CTL; on the other, it is the rest periods that enable your body to adapt to the ATL. ATL and CTL go hand in hand, and trying to manage these two essential components of your training program can be one of the toughest things to master. And yet, it can have a more profound impact on your overall fitness than any other aspect of training.

### Managing Form (Training Stress Balance)

To review our main points: Form is the proper balance of fitness and freshness. Fitness is based on training stress or training load. So, to take our thinking one step further:

1. Form = Fitness + Freshness.
2. Fitness is the result of training stress.
3. Freshness is the result of rest.
4. Therefore, form comes from the combination of training stress and rest.
5. "Form" can be renamed "Training Stress Balance."

TSB thus represents how well you have been juggling your training load and your rest periods. If you want to create form, you must have the proper balance of the two. If your TSB is a positive number, this indicates more freshness. You would have a good chance of

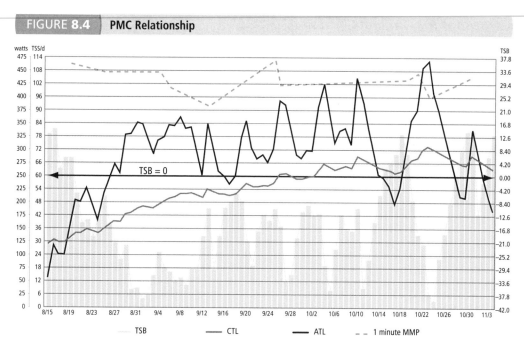

| FIGURE 8.4 | **PMC Relationship** |

*Acute Training Load (ATL) "drives" the Chronic Training Load (CTL). As harder workouts are completed in the short term, they build the fitness in the long term. The orange bars represent your Training Stress Balance (TSB), or your "freshness." When they go above "0," you are coming into form. The dashed line represents peak wattages created by the athlete.*

riding well during those "positive" days; you are both fit and fresh. When your TSB is a negative number, this indicates more fatigue. You are most likely tired from a high training load, which could mean that both your CTL and your ATL are too high. In the TrainingPeaks WKO+ Software, the Performance Manager Chart puts these concepts into a visual format that can help you to balance your training stress (see Figure 8.4).

As we begin to understand that ATL drives CTL, and that CTL is closely related to your level of fitness, then the questions become: How hard can I train, and is there an optimal training load? How much should I ride? How hard should I ride? Should I ride when I'm tired? How tired *is* too tired to train? When will I be recovered enough to train hard again? Joe Friel may have said it best in *The Cyclist's Training Bible* when he wrote, "An athlete should do the least amount of the most specific training that brings continual improvement." If you can win the race with ten $VO_2$max intervals, then why do twelve or fifteen? But how can a rider know how much is enough? The answer to that question lies in the power meter and the software you use with it. By using your power meter and the Performance Manager Chart, you can begin to determine your personal optimal training load. It is possible to mathematically quantify "when enough is enough."

### Guidelines for Optimal CTL and ATL

Although most of a racer's attention is likely to be focused on using the approach to manage the peaking process, other benefits clearly exist and should not be overlooked. In our experience, across a wide variety of athletes and disciplines (for example, elite amateur track cyclists, masters-age marathon mountain-bike racers, and professional road racers), the "optimal" training load seems to lie at a CTL between 100 and 150 TSS per day. Individuals whose CTL is less than 100 TSS per day usually feel that they are undertraining: They recognize that they could tolerate a heavier training load if only they had more time to train, or if other stresses in life (such as job and family responsibilities) were minimized. (This does not necessarily mean that their performance would improve as a result, which is why the word "optimal" in the sentence above is in quotation marks.) On the other hand, few, if any, athletes seem to be able to sustain a long-term average of more than 150 TSS per day.

Indeed, analysis of power-meter data from riders in the 2006 Tour de France and other hors catégorie international stage races indicates that the hardest stages of such races typically generate a TSS of 200–300. This illustrates how heavy a long-term training load of more than 150 TSS per day would be (since the average daily TSS of the Tour de France is reduced by the inclusion of rest days and shorter stages, such as individual time trials). It is generally considered quite difficult to maintain such an effort for three weeks, much less for the three months or more that it would take for CTL to fully "catch up."

In addition to the absolute magnitude of CTL, we can learn a lot about an athlete's training (and/or mistakes in training) by examining the pattern of change in CTL over time. Specifically, a 4- to 6-week plateau in CTL during a time when the focus of training has not changed and performance is constant is generally evidence of "training stagnation." Athletes in this situation might feel they are training well by being very consistent and repeatedly performing the same workouts, but in fact this is not training at all. It is simply maintaining, because the overload principle is not being applied. We'll look at patterns of change in CTL more closely in the first of two case studies presented later in this chapter.

In contrast, attempting to increase CTL too rapidly is often a recipe for disaster and frequently leads to illness or other symptoms of overreaching or overtraining. Of course, since changes in CTL are driven by changes in ATL, any sudden increase in the training load (due, for example, to a training camp or a stage race) must be followed by an appropriate period of reduced training or recovery. To state this idea yet another way: Failure to periodically "come up for air" by allowing TSB to rise toward, if not all the way to, neutrality may lead to problems. If ATL is greater than CTL for too long, you will become overtrained. Ultimately, overtraining can lead to burnout.

We have found that most cyclists can increase their CTL at a rate of 3–7 TSS per day per week. When you increase your CTL at a rate greater than 7 TSS per day per week for more than 4 weeks in a row, then the level of intense weekly training could be too much and send you into an overtraining downward spiral. It's fine to increase TSS at a rate of more than 7 per day for 1 week, and possibly even for 2 weeks, but longer periods can lead you into a chronically overreached state.

Weekly totals also need to be considered to keep the Acute Training Load at an appropriate level. Apply caution when increasing ATL more than an average of 70 TSS per day within a 7-day time period. That's a lot of hard training in a short period of time and can also trigger an overtraining situation. By examining the Performance Manager Chart, and hovering just over the ATL line from the start of a 7-day period to the end, it can be easy to track whether you are increasing your short-term training load too quickly. Everyone handles a training load differently, however, and a twenty-two-year-old pro can certainly manage a quicker rate of increase for ATL and CTL than a fifty-five-year-old masters rider. Although an increase of 70 TSS per day in 7 days might be fine for some people, it could put others over the edge.

### Guidelines for Optimal TSB for Racing

To be fresh on race day, watch your Training Stress Balance each day. When you reach a "zero balance" in your TSB, you are neither fresh (which requires a positive TSB) nor fatigued (which requires a negative TSB). If you have a negative TSB that is rising, you are recovering from the deep hole of training that you have been in; that doesn't mean that you cannot have a good performance, however (see Figure 8.5). Precise values for TSB will depend on the individual and the time constants used to calculate CTL and ATL (if you rely on the default time constants, CTL and ATL are 42 and 7 days, respectively), so don't apply these guidelines too literally. If you review your training and find that you need to increase the time constant, the TSB at which you are most fresh will be lower. This is especially true with ATL.

So what is the ideal TSB for race day? In other words, how much freshness is enough? We surveyed about 200 athletes in our quest to answer this question, asking them what their TSB was when they created a "Personal Best for Power" across any time range. This meant that whether it was for 1 minute, 1 minute and 23 seconds, or 3 hours and 10 seconds, we wanted to know what their TSB was when their best wattage for that time period occurred. This gave us enough information to create a set of charts that has been very effective in showing how much freshness is just right for different types of events.

Figure 8.6 shows that personal bests for power in all time periods have occurred at a wide range of TSBs, from –30 to +30, with many of them occurring in the mid-range that we call neutral (–10 to +10). The majority of personal bests occurred with TSBs between –5 and +15. In other words, the athletes we queried did very well when they allowed their TSBs to become positive, but not overly so. When we examined this chart, it caused us to think a

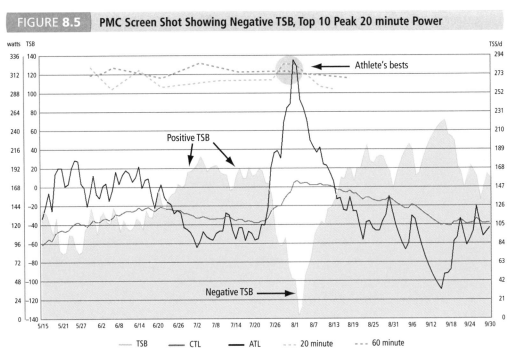

**FIGURE 8.5** | **PMC Screen Shot Showing Negative TSB, Top 10 Peak 20 minute Power**

*A positive Training Stress Balance is not always necessary in order to have one of your best rides. In this example, note that four of the athlete's bests occurred at a time when his TSB was −62 to −130! Also note that before these bests he had a positive TSB for nearly 3 weeks.*

**FIGURE 8.6** | **TSB Prior to Personal Best for Power, All Time Ranges**

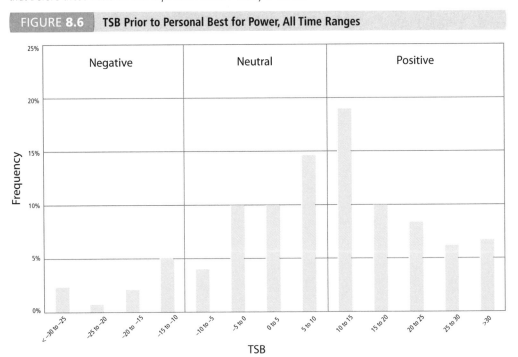

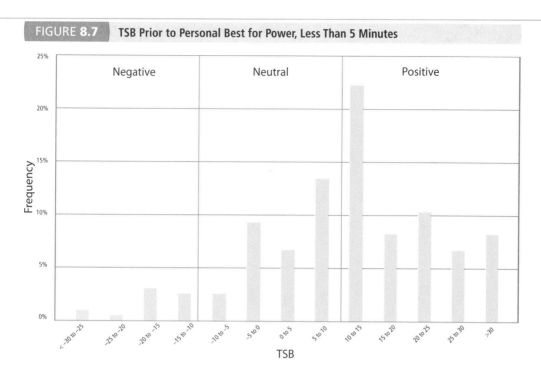

FIGURE 8.7     **TSB Prior to Personal Best for Power, Less Than 5 Minutes**

bit more about this issue and then separate out the data for two different time periods. We wanted to see if there might be a difference in the TSB values for personal bests if the effort lasted less than 5 minutes or more than 5 minutes. What we found was that personal bests for time periods of less than 5 minutes occurred when the TSB was even more on the positive side of the scale (see Figure 8.7).

This makes sense from a physiological standpoint, as shorter efforts (that is, efforts of less than 5 minutes, for the purposes of our study) require more neuromuscular power and anaerobic capacity than long efforts, and these will be at their highest when the athlete is well rested. One of the obvious conclusions that can be drawn from this chart is that in short, heavily anaerobic events (track, BMX, short hill climbs), it is best to be very well rested. In the personal bests from time periods of 5 minutes or more, there is a swing back to the center. This also makes sense, as longer time periods are more aerobic in nature and therefore require more fitness and less freshness. In Figure 8.8, there is a nice bell curve distribution for TSBs from –10 to +25. This shows that athletes are as likely to have a personal best with a –10 TSB as they are with a +25 TSB. If an athlete's TSB is –10, this most likely means that he or she is recovering from a negative number further to the left on the graph, rather than getting more and more fatigued. Likewise, if a personal best occurs on a day when an athlete's TSB is +10, it was probably not the first day that the athlete had a positive TSB; he or she probably crept up to that number to produce the big wattage on that

**FIGURE 8.8**    **TSB Prior to Personal Best for Power, Greater Than 5 Minutes**

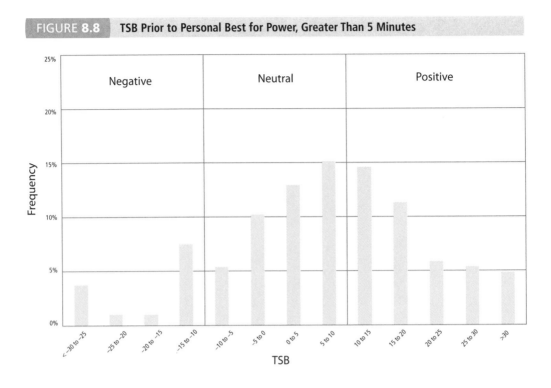

particular day. Figure 8.8 also demonstrates that an athlete who is competing in a longer event, such as a road race, a mountain-bike race, or a stage race, should not taper or rest too much beforehand, as this could mean missing that peak window.

In conclusion, the more anaerobic the event, the more important it is to be fresh, and the more aerobic the event, the more important it is to be fit. To create form, determine the balance of fitness and freshness you want for the event you have in mind, and make a plan to have your TSB reach that optimal point at the right time. The Performance Manager is equally valuable as a lens through which to view previous attempts at peaking. With the knowledge you gain, you can modify or replicate past performances with a greater degree of confidence.

## CASE STUDIES

One of the best ways for any cyclist to learn how to use the Performance Manager Chart is by looking at other cyclists' charts, learning the story behind each one, and then taking the lessons that can be learned from them to heart. The Performance Manager can be used for every discipline in cycling in which it is possible to use a power meter to track training stress—so road racers, mountain-bike racers, cyclocrossers, and track racers can all benefit from examining this type of information. As you review the case studies presented below, think about how these lessons could apply to your own situation. It is important just to collect data from every ride, no matter how easy or intense it is, so that you can conduct this same sort of analysis to chart your own progress.

### Timing TSB for Multiple Peaks in a Season

Matt is a thirty-year-old Category I racer. His Power Profile is upward-sloping to the right, and his FTP is 5.2 watts per kilogram. He started out the fall season with some serious cyclocross races and did eleven races throughout the winter, achieving a nice top-ten placing at CX Nationals. While training and focusing on cyclocross, he worked at a high level of intensity on the trainer, as he lives in a relatively cold climate and cannot train outside in the winter. With the volume low but the intensity high, his CTL was not very high in the fall.

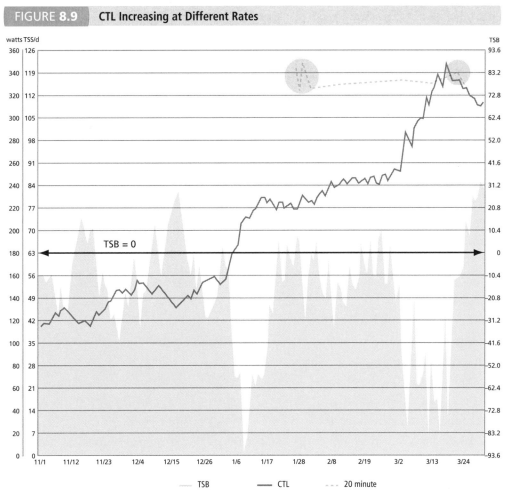

**FIGURE 8.9    CTL Increasing at Different Rates**

*Four of the rider's bests occurred after a taper and a positive TSB of as little as +8. The third best occurred after a short rest from a large increase in CTL.*

As Figure 8.9 shows, Matt's CTL increased at different rates during this time period as he completed each mesocycle of training and started a new one. Matt has employed the concept of having a progressive rise in CTL, so he quickly brings his CTL up during certain periods, then allows that new CTL level to stabilize and grow slowly and steadily. When he is ready for the next big ATL "shock," he "doses" himself with a big week of training stress, which has the effect of increasing his CTL quickly again.

As his CTL rises, his TSB drops. Moreover, even a small decrease in the CTL ramp rate can result in a positive TSB, which could be a good predictor of a good performance. Figure 8.9 shows how a small decrease in CTL can create a positive TSB. Also, take note of the 20-minute mean maximal line, which shows the ten best 20-minute wattages for this time period. Note that four of Matt's best 20-minute wattages occurred at the end of January after a taper, which was preceded by a large increase in CTL. Matt's third best 20-minute wattage occurred at the end of March, immediately after another steep increase in CTL at a ramp rate of 12 TSS per day for 2 weeks. Although the TSB was still negative at this point, it was clearly climbing positively. It is important to recognize that TSB does not necessarily need to be a positive number in order to create a peak performance; it just needs to be climbing to a positive number.

Now that we have looked at some specific aspects of Matt's Performance Manager Chart, let's take a look at the overall chart (see Figure 8.10). By doing so, we can see whether the training plan he followed did the job and allowed him to peak when he wanted to peak. We are also looking for clues about this season's performance and use that information to determine how he can improve on it for next year. Matt had two major objectives for the year, top performances at the Tour of Gila in early April and at the Masters Nationals in mid-July.

In his Performance Manager Chart, we see that his highest wattage numbers occurred in January, coming off an intense cyclocross season and his first solid Build cycle. This was unplanned. It occurred at an early-season stage race in which he placed third overall. But it wasn't until we looked back at the season later that we realized these were his peak wattage numbers for the year. The chart also reflects the two times that he got sick during the year. Both times, his TSB became very positive from the lack of riding.

Unfortunately, the first bout of illness occurred right after his second main Build phase in March. This leads us to ask whether the increase in CTL was too rapid, with the stress of the training load contributing to the illness. During the Build phase, his CTL increased at a relatively quick rate (12 TSS per day), so he was under a high load of training stress. But the illness also occurred the week after a very hard race. It had rained and snowed during the race, and Matt had become slightly hypothermic. So we can conclude with a fairly high degree of certainty that the stress of the race, coupled with the high rate of increase in his CTL, compromised his body's immune system and caused him to pick up a cold. Of course,

| FIGURE **8.10** | **PMC for Entire Year** |

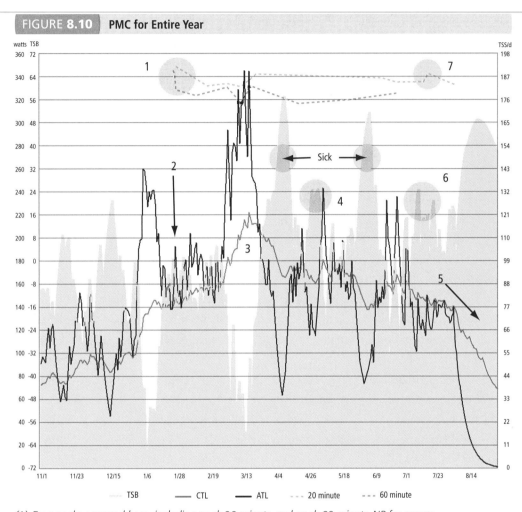

*(1) Four peaks occurred here, including peak 20-minute and peak 60-minute NP for season.*
*(2) Top 3—LV stage race.*
*(3) Question of the season: Was this increase too rapid and one of the causes of the illness afterward?*
*(4) "Ebay guy" at Gila. Underperformed at goal race for season, due to previous illness and toll it took on fitness.*
*(5) CTL is dropping rapidly, now showing signs of a decrease in FTP and overall fitness.*
*(6) Longest period of positive TSB.*
*(7) Masters Nationals, 2nd in RR, 6th in TT, 3rd best 20-minute power for season.*

this was poor timing to have him "on form" for the Tour of Gila. Another thing to notice is the dramatic slip in Matt's CTL from 122 TSS points to 90 TSS points while he was sick.

As we examine the chart further, we see that Matt achieved his third highest wattage for the season at the Masters Nationals. This came during his longest period of time with a positive TSB. He performed very well at the Masters Nationals, coming very close to a national championship, with a second-place finish in the road race. Finally, we can see his CTL gradually slipping at the end of the racing season as he backed off his training and started to ride just for pleasure and fitness maintenance.

Matt's Performance Manager Chart shows not only how a small drop in CTL can create a good performance, but also how a period of illness can impact training load and how tough it can be to stay on that fine line between too much training stress and not enough. Matt's form could really shine in mid-July after his longest period of positive TSB. Planning training loads for an athlete who has multiple goals for the season, especially at different times during the season, is more complicated than planning for a simple, straightforward season with a single race as the main objective—but it's another great reason to utilize the Performance Manager Chart to its fullest extent. That means knowing how to interpret and analyze the chart. Knowing the "story" behind the chart is critical to interpretation, however, and the art of coaching is therefore still very much a part of the process.

### Timing TSB for a Single Peak

Dave is a Category II masters time trialist over fifty-five years old. His FTP is 5.2 watts per kilogram. After two years without a "stars and stripes" at Masters Nationals, he decided to put all of his eggs in one basket and do everything right in order to win a national championship. From a coaching perspective, planning for this kind of season is both easy (because there is just one main peak to achieve) and scary (because something could go wrong and that all-important goal could be missed).

Dave had a solid off-season and put in some good workouts on the trainer and in the gym, and he came into the season fit and ready to perform well. As his coach, Hunter was trying to bring his CTL gradually up to 100 points at the peak of his training, while at the same time not digging a big hole with his TSB from which it would be hard for him to recover. The goal when increasing CTL was to help Dave get even stronger. He had one smaller intermediate goal in mid-May that he wanted to be sure to win as well, which fit nicely with the plan of having him rested before his final buildup to Nationals.

Figure 8.11 shows a steady buildup of CTL throughout the season. During May, Dave's CTL stabilized somewhat, as he wanted to be fresh for the weekend races. Then, in late May, his CTL started climbing, as he was putting in the workouts required to be on form for July Nationals. It is interesting to note that even while Dave had a negative TSB, he was still winning races (March through June). His level of fitness was already that much higher than that of his peers; even when he was tired, he could still easily win.

At Masters Nationals, he achieved his best 20-minute and 60-minute Normalized Power for the season. Though his TSB for much of this time period was +25, he was clearly riding well, and his fitness was at an all-time high (with an FTP of 5.2 W/kg, not too bad for a fifty-five-year-old!).

| FIGURE **8.11** | **Dave Johnson's Entire Season** |

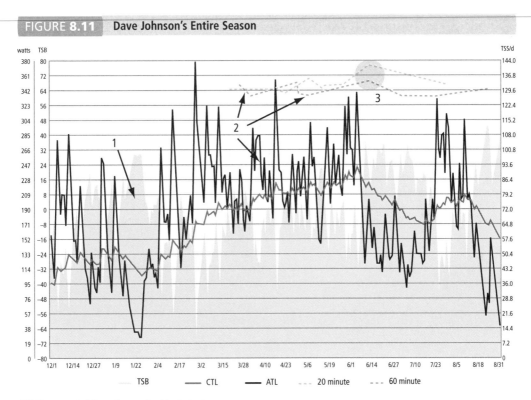

*(1) Dave got sick and wasn't able to train.*
*(2) Note the short positive TSB weekends and corresponding personal bests. These short periods of recovery were done in order for Dave to be fresh for early-season key races.*
*(3) Best 20-minute and 60-minute NP for the year on the day he wanted it. Results: Masters Nationals, 2nd in TT, 1st in Crit, 4th in RR.*

After his success at Masters Nationals, Dave decided to go to Masters Worlds and try for a rainbow jersey. Figure 8.12 shows that Dave's CTL took a dramatic slide downward during and after Masters Nationals. This was planned, as Dave had originally decided to call it a season after that event; it wasn't until later that he made the decision to race for the rainbow jersey. Once this decision was made, he amped up his ATL in order to rebuild some lost fitness. As the ATL went up, the CTL rose to about 80 TSS points, which was close to Dave's "normal" sustainable training load.

When Masters Worlds approached, it was time to taper off the training and hope for the best. Dave went into the time trial with a TSB of +35, which netted him a solid top-ten placing in the TT. However, his form was clearly not the same as it was in mid-June, as he was only able to ride at 4.9 watts per kilogram for the time trial. The Performance Manager Chart allowed Hunter to rebuild Dave's CTL at the appropriate rate and to a level that could be sustained for a couple of weeks before tapering. This guaranteed that Dave's fitness would

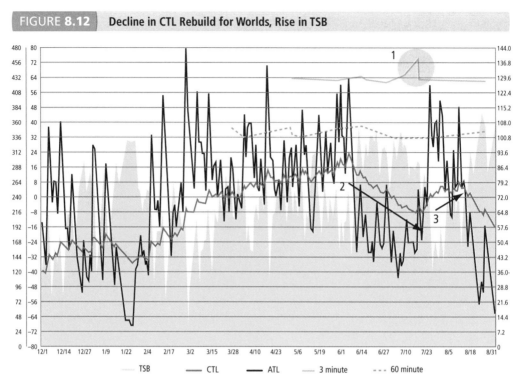

**FIGURE 8.12** Decline in CTL Rebuild for Worlds, Rise in TSB

*(1) The result of nearly 6 weeks of positive TSB, or freshness. A huge 3-minute personal best of 462 watts, 6 percent higher than any previous 3-minute best for the year.*
*(2) Note the decline in CTL before the decision to attend Masters Worlds, which gives Dave nearly 6 weeks of positive TSB.*
*(3) Rebuild for Masters Worlds. A short 2 weeks, but large ATL dose.*

increase without overdoing it. In this way we protected his immune system and were able to give him time to recover before Worlds.

Dave performed at his best right on time, just as predicted by the Performance Manager Chart. His CTL climbed at a steady rate, and his TSB was generally negative for most of the season as he built for his peak at Masters Nationals. Even though his TSB was negative, he still performed well against his peers, as he was fitter than them even when tired. It was no surprise that he performed well at Masters Nationals, as he had performed well nearly all season with a negative TSB. In hindsight, had Hunter known that Dave was going to Masters Worlds, he would not have let Dave's CTL drop so much after Nationals. But since that was a relatively late decision, Hunter did the best he could to get Dave's CTL back to a sustainable level without causing his ATL to skyrocket. In terms of managing training loads, this is a perfect example of how powerful the PMC can be when an athlete has very focused goals based around a specific time period.

## APPLYING THE PERFORMANCE MANAGER CONCEPT

Successfully using the Performance Manager entails some degree of "art," and you may need some time to become a good "artist." The following hints, tips, caveats, and limitations are offered in hopes of speeding up this process.

### Strive for Accuracy

The concepts embodied in the Performance Manager apply regardless of how the training load is quantified. You can use this approach to evaluate and manage your training whether you are using TRIMP scores, RPE, or TSS. If you decide to quantify your training with TSS, it is important that your values be based upon valid, up-to-date estimates of FTP because the TSS calculated for a particular workout varies as a function of the square of the Intensity Factor (IF) (that is, TSS = duration [hours] $\times$ IF$^2$ $\times$ 100). Digging a little deeper, TSS is the inverse square of your estimated functional threshold power (because IF = Normalized Power (NP) $\div$ FTP). In other words, if you decrease your FTP by 4 percent (for example, using 240 watts instead of 250 watts), your TSS for a particular workout will be 8 percent higher. Your higher TSS will then affect CTL, ATL, and TSB. An inaccurate functional threshold power will magnify errors in your data and ultimately manifest as mistakes in your training. Interestingly enough, it is sometimes possible to identify periods of consistent over- or under-estimation of functional threshold power if your response to training deviates significantly from what was anticipated based on the Performance Manager approach.

### Use Power with Consistency

The Performance Manager approach is predicated on the assumption that you will use your power meter during every workout and race, producing a value for TSS in order to maintain consistent data. This consistency will make the data more reliable. However, it is not at all uncommon for individuals to choose to race without the power meter, for data files to be corrupted during collection (for example, if the memory of the power meter is exceeded) or lost during downloading, for the power meter to stop working entirely, and so forth. When these lapses occur, you need to estimate any missing TSS, or the Performance Manager data will be distorted. Missing values for TSS can be estimated a number of different ways:

1. From a "library" of comparable workouts performed previously.
2. From heart rate data, which can be used to estimate Normalized Power, allowing TSS to be calculated manually (TSS = duration [hours] $\times$ IF$^2$ $\times$ 100, where IF = NP $\div$ FTP ).
3. By simply estimating the Intensity Factor and then calculating TSS using the above formula. (When using this approach, it is useful to recall the typical Intensity Factor associated with different types of training sessions and races; see Table 7.2.)

You might assume the second approach would be best since it is based on actual data, but in reality there is little reason for us to recommend it over the other two approaches. It is often possible for experienced power-meter users to estimate their TSS just as accurately, if not more accurately, without heart rate data as with the data. Any error introduced as a result of poorly estimating the true TSS for one or two missing workouts is likely to be minimal. However, if you were missing a large amount of data (for example, more than 10 percent of all files for a particular block of time), then the output of the Performance Manager calculations during and after that period should be interpreted with considerable caution. This emphasizes the importance of racing with a power meter, since athletes often incorporate frequent racing into their training program when attempting to peak.

### Start with Educated Assumptions
Because Chronic Training Load depends on the accumulation of fatigue and positive adaptations over a longer period of time, you will need to collect data for a fairly long period of time before the Performance Manager calculations can be considered accurate (see the build-up of CTL in Figure 8.3). Obviously, if you are a new power-meter user you will not have a large database of files that can be analyzed to determine your starting point. Similarly, a longtime power-meter user may not have reliable data, whether as a result of failing to track changes in functional threshold power or training without a power meter for a lengthy period of time (for example, while it is being repaired). In such cases, it may be necessary to "seed" the model with initial values for CTL and ATL.

To calculate appropriate values, start by identifying how you typically train. Most athletes train at an intensity resulting in 50–75 TSS per hour (with an average weekly Intensity Factor of between about 0.70 and 0.85). If you train more, mostly or entirely outdoors, or in a less structured fashion, your score probably falls toward the lower end of this range, whereas if you train less, frequently indoors, or in a more structured fashion, your score will tend to fall toward the upper end of this range. Unless there is a specific reason to do otherwise (for example, transitioning from using a spreadsheet to track TSS to using the Performance Manager within WKO+), assign the same value to both CTL and ATL (with TSB assumed to be zero). Over time your CTL will become evident, in which case you may want or need to go back and revise these initial estimates. Of course, the calculated values for CTL, ATL, and TSB should be interpreted cautiously following such a "seeding" until you accumulate sufficient data.

### Build Precision with Experience
The default time constants of the Performance Manager—that is, 6 weeks for CTL and 7 days for ATL—were chosen as nominal values based on the scientific literature. As with the

fitness component of the impulse-response model, the precise time constant used to calculate CTL in the Performance Manager has a limited impact. While some users may still wish to experiment with changing this value, there seems little to be gained. However, the calculations in the Performance Manager are sensitive to the time constant used to calculate ATL, and hence TSB (since TSB = CTL – ATL).

Part of the art of using the Performance Manager consists of learning what time constant for ATL provides the greatest correspondence between how you actually feel or perform on a particular day and how you might be expected to feel or perform based on CTL, ATL, and TSB. Younger individuals, those with a relatively low training load, and those preparing for events that place a greater premium on sustained power output (such as longer time trials, 24-hour mountain-bike races, or long-distance triathlons) often find better results using a somewhat shorter time constant—for example, 4–5 days instead of 7 days. Conversely, masters-age athletes, those with a relatively high training load, and those preparing for events that place a greater premium on nonsustainable power output (shorter time trials, criteriums) may obtain better results using a somewhat longer time constant than the default value—for example, 10–12 days instead of 7 days. (Of course, since athletes preparing for longer events often, but not always, carry higher overall training loads, this tends to constrain the optimal time constant more than would otherwise be the case.)

### Maintain Your Perspective

Although the Performance Manager is an extremely valuable tool for analyzing training on a macro scale, it is important to also consider things on a micro scale, such as the nature and demands of the individual training sessions that produce the daily TSS values. The composition of your training is just as important as the overall dose, and the usefulness and predictive ability of the Performance Manager depends on the individual workouts being chosen and executed in light of your competition goals. Suppose an elite pursuiter builds her CTL up to the same high level during both a road-focused, intense period of training at Levels 2, 3, and 4 early in the season and a track-focused, intense period of training at Levels 5, 6, and 7 immediately before the national championships. Even after a comparable period of tapering (to achieve the same positive TSB and gain the same amount of freshness), she would still not be expected to perform as well in an actual pursuit early in the season as she would later in the season. Conversely, she would probably perform better in a road time trial early in the season than later in the season because the training she was performing at that time would have been more appropriate, or more specific, for the time trial event. In both cases, however, CTL, ATL, and TSB would be good indicators of training load and adaptation.

When you are in the midst of training hard, it can be difficult to see the forest for the trees. The Performance Manager gives you that 10,000-foot view of the forest, but don't lose sight of the individual workouts. It is important to note that the impulse-response model has the same limitation. The specificity principle always applies.

---

The principles for coaching, training, and the periodization of training really haven't changed much in decades. The principles that Dr. Tudor Bompa put forth back in 1968 still apply today: You still have to build, taper, and rest in order to create an overload and then allow for an adaptation to that new level of stress. Dr. Eric Banister's ideas from the 1970s are still useful. The art of coaching is very much alive as well, and cycling coaches still have to rely on all their years of personal experience—from racing, from working with athletes at all levels of skill and ability, and from those "gut instincts" that also become more accurate over time. What has changed is our ability to accurately quantify training dose and response with the use of a power meter. The power meter is truly revolutionizing the way athletes and coaches look at training. With the addition of the Performance Manager Chart in the TrainingPeaks WKO+ Software, we are now learning how to better predict peaks of fitness, determine when an athlete needs to rest in order to prevent overtraining, and plan a season so that the athlete has a much better chance of being on form at the right time.

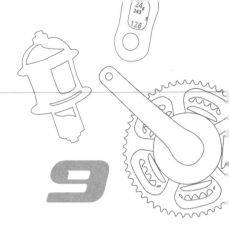

# Developing a Power-Based Training Plan

*Sometimes in cycling, it's hard to know* whether you are indeed improving or everyone else is just going slower. Now that you have some tools, tips, and tricks for training with power, you can begin to track your improvement; seeing your wattage improve, in turn, can be quite a motivator for continued hard work. In this chapter you will learn how to develop a training plan based on wattage that will take you to the next level of fitness.

Rather than looking at methods and theories about training itself—other complete training books are available to cover those issues—we will focus specifically on how to integrate wattage into your training plan. This is a chance to put into practice what we have learned about training with a power meter—Fatigue Profiling, Quadrant Analysis, and more detailed explanations of power training principles. To do this, we will look at two case studies in developing a training plan. First of all, you must start with the things you know, such as weekly training time constraints, strengths and weaknesses, and goals. From these known items, you can begin to fill in the blanks of your training plan—for example, how hard to train, which roads to train on, and whether to do sprints, endurance rides, or hill climbs. You'll end up with a finished product that is your "blueprint" to success.

## SAMPLE TRAINING PLANS

Our first fictitious cyclist, Bob Rider, is a fast, masters-age cyclist (age 42) with good bike-handling skills who is already doing well in the local club rides. The second is Jill Racer (age 32), who is in the last eight weeks before her peak event, the state championship criterium. The menu of workouts found in Appendix B complements the case studies in this chapter, and you might find them useful in your own training as well. By the end of the chapter you will be ready to use power to shape your own training plan.

### Bob's 16-Week Threshold Improvement Plan

Bob is ambitious and excited about cycling. He has decided to begin racing this season and compete in ten events. He really wants to do well in a two-day stage race in late May that has a 10-mile time trial and a 25-mile criterium on Saturday, and then a 50-mile road race on Sunday that has a 5-mile climb on the course.

Bob only recently began going on weekly "racing" group rides, and he has eight to twelve hours a week to train, including weekends. He is a decent climber, but his skills are lacking in time trialing and sprinting as compared with other local racers. Bob weighs 155 pounds (70.5 kg), and his current FTP is 250 watts, or 3.55 watts per kilogram (W/kg). His peak 5 seconds is 845 watts (11.99 W/kg), his peak 1 minute is 480 watts (6.81 W/kg), and

| TABLE 9.1 | Power Profile of Bob Rider | | | | |
|---|---|---|---|---|---|
| | | AVERAGE POWER OUTPUT (W/kg) | | | |
| Level | Category | 5 sec. | 1 min. | 5 min. | FTP |
| World record | | 25.18 | 11.50 | 7.60 | 6.40 |
| World class | Int. Pro | 24.00 | 11.21 | 7.34 | 6.17 |
| Exceptional | Dom. Pro | 22.22 | 10.48 | 6.68 | 5.61 |
| Excellent | Cat. I | 20.44 | 9.75 | 6.02 | 5.04 |
| Very good | Cat. II | 18.66 | 9.02 | 5.37 | 4.48 |
| Good | Cat. III | 16.59 | 8.29 | 4.55 | 3.91 |
| Moderate | Cat. IV | 14.81 | 7.56 | 4.05 | 3.55 |
| Fair | Cat. V | 13.04 | 6.83 | 3.40 | 2.78 |
| Untrained | | 12.01 | 6.10 | 2.74 | 2.22 |
| Bob's Test Results (watts) | | 845 | 480 | 320 | 250 |
| | W/kg | 11.99 | 6.81 | 4.54 | 3.55 |

**Note:** Bob Rider weighs 70.5 kg. Average Power Output data can be reviewed in more detail in Table 4.1.

| TABLE 9.2 | Fatigue Profile of Bob Rider | | | | | |
|---|---|---|---|---|---|---|
| | LEVEL 7, NEUROMUSCULAR POWER | | | LEVEL 6, ANAEROBIC CAPACITY | | |
| Fatigue Resistance | 5 sec. | 10 sec. | 20 sec. | 30 sec. | 1 min. | 2 min. |
| Well below average | 100% | 41–55% | 61–75% | 100% | 31–45% | 50–70% |
| Below average | 100% | 31–40% | 47–60% | 100% | 25–30% | 36–50% |
| Average | 100% | 22–30% | 35–46% | 100% | 21–24% | 23–35% |
| Above average | 100% | 15–21% | 20–34% | 100% | 10–20% | 15–22% |
| Well above average | 100% | 5–14% | 8–19% | 100% | 5–9% | 8–14% |
| Bob's Test Results (watts) | 845 | 808 | 786 | 480 | 450 | 380 |
| W/kg | 100% | 4.4% | 7.0% | 100% | 14.6% | 20.8% |

his peak 5 minutes is 320 watts (4.54 W/kg). His Power Profile (Table 9.1) slopes upward to the right, with a slight peak at his 5-minute (or VO₂max) power. He is a good climber and has a good power-to-weight ratio, but as he is a relatively poor time trialist and sprinter, we know he is lacking in absolute power.

These observations are reflected in his Power Profile by his higher-than-normal 5-minute power and the fact that he does not do as well as others in shorter, hard efforts. Of the three main body types, Bob could be characterized as an "ectomorph," which means that he has a thin build with relatively small muscles, or a larger percentage of slow-twitch muscle fibers (the other types are mesomorph, for someone with a medium build and a relatively even distribution of fast-twitch and slow-twitch muscle fibers, and endomorph, someone with a heavier build, a greater percentage of body fat, and mostly fast-twitch muscle fibers). Taking Bob's test data and putting them into the Fatigue Profile (Table 9.2) gives us further insight into Bob's capabilities. His fatigue resistance in Level 7 is well above average, which means he can maintain his power all the way out to 20 seconds. However, his peak power at 5 seconds is weak. The power he would need for an explosive "snap" just isn't there.

Bob's fatigue resistance for Level 6 is also above average. His 2-minute power is not much higher than his 30-second power, which means, again, that he doesn't have a lot of strength at anaerobic capacity. Bob's Level 5 Fatigue Profile is a bit of an enigma. He crosses over into below-average fatigue resistance, which is surprising, because his 5-minute power is good and is even considered a strength in the normal Power Profile. But his 3-minute power is quite a bit higher than his 5-minute power, and then at 8 minutes his power drops off like a stone. This is a significant departure from his normally high fatigue resistance. We see the same pattern emerging in Bob's Level 4 Fatigue Profile, however, and now the light-bulb starts to come on, showing what could be a real weakness for him.

Bob's 20-minute average power is in the average range, but his 60-minute and 90-minute Normalized Power also drop off steeply. Along with below-average fatigue resistance

| | LEVEL 5, VO₂MAX | | LEVEL 4, LACTATE THRESHOLD | | |
|---|---|---|---|---|---|
| 3 min. | 5 min. | 8 min. | 20 min. (AP) | 60 min. (NP) | 90 min. (NP) |
| 100% | 15–20% | 24–30% | 100% | 7–11% | 15–25% |
| 100% | 8–14% | 18–23% | 100% | 4–6 % | 8–14% |
| 100% | 4–7 % | 10–17% | 100% | 2–4 % | 5–7% |
| 320 | 262 | 240 | 250 | 223 | 190 |
| 100% | 18.1% | 25.0% | 100% | 10.8% | 24.0% |

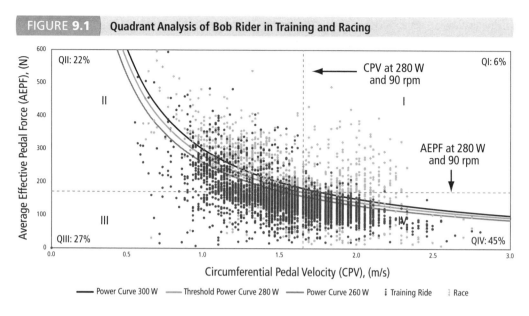

FIGURE **9.1**    **Quadrant Analysis of Bob Rider in Training and Racing**

in Levels 4 and 5, and the fact that he is a poor time trialist, these key indicators confirm that lack of metabolic fitness could be an issue for Bob. In other words, his muscles just are not trained well enough to handle sustained power efforts. It's highly possible that Bob isn't training long and hard enough for his fatigue resistance to be above average in Level 4. Unfortunately, training time could be the limiting factor for him. And only highly focused training at Tempo (the sweet spot) for long enough periods of time will provide the muscular stress he needs to improve that fatigue resistance.

To get a feel for Bob's pedaling style, we can use Quadrant Analysis. Since Bob has an ectomorph body type, he is not a big and bulky guy. This, along with his poor fatigue resistance at Level 5, leads us to suspect that he has to spend most of his time in Quadrant IV (high cadence, low force) in order to produce enough watts to compete. In the Multi-File Quadrant Analysis shown in Figure 9.1, we see a race file (lighter color) and a training ride (darker color) from Bob. Note that in both cases the largest percentage of his time was spent in Quadrant IV, which is just as we had predicted. Bob just does not have the muscular power he would need to spend a significant percentage of his time in Quadrants I and II.

Now let's summarize Bob's strengths and weaknesses.

**Strengths**

Above-average fatigue resistance in
  Levels 6 and 7
Good FTP for his category
Good hill climber

**Weaknesses**

Below-average explosive power in Level 7
Below-average short-term anaerobic power in
  Level 6
Below-average fatigue resistance in Levels 4 and 5

| **Strengths, cont.** | **Weaknesses, cont.** |
|---|---|
| Good 5-minute VO$_2$max effort | Below-average muscular strength |
| | Below-average muscular endurance at 60-minute |
| | average power and 90-minute Normalized Power |

This summary, along with our understanding of Bob's goals for the season as stated above, will help us to determine a plan of attack for Bob to optimize his training time.

First, to address Bob's weakness in muscular endurance at 60 minutes and 90 minutes, and in order to help him improve his fatigue resistance at Levels 4 and 5, we will make him do some rides on the weekends that are longer than the durations that are in his comfort zone. We will also make them tough, with plenty of sweet-spot work and sustained power-output efforts near his FTP. Second, to improve Bob's ability to create more force so that he can improve both his explosive sprints and his time trialing, we will use big-gear power efforts and have him climb some steep hills using a harder gear than he normally would choose. We will also make sure he gets plenty of practice on his time trial bike mashing a big gear for short periods. Finally, to make sure his FTP continues to improve, we'll have him do plenty of 10-, 15-, and 20-minute efforts at FTP.

We'll have Bob begin his plan in early February and take it through his peak event, giving him a complete 16-week program. The plan, described in Table 9.3, has a general pattern. Bob will have a complete rest day every Monday. His Tuesday, Wednesday, and Thursday workouts will constitute the "meat" of the program, and Friday will generally be for Active Recovery (Level 1), although sometimes Bob will do specific workouts on Friday in order to build three strong workouts on consecutive days. The weekend will include a long group ride (or race) on Saturday, and a medium-length ride (or race) on Sunday. We'll build up his fitness in the classic "three weeks on, one week off" periodization model and monitor it along the way with his downloads in case a change in direction is needed. All of his workouts will be based around wattage and can be found in Appendix B using the codes from Table 9.3.

## Weeks 1–4

The first part of Bob's training program is designed to introduce him to speed changes and also to work at threshold. Because Bob has a weakness in his short efforts, we will begin to work on his ability to change speeds. We'll work on his threshold as well throughout the 16 weeks, and on the weekend, even though his FTP is already decent.

Bob will also start addressing his limiter of muscular power by incorporating some big-gear work. Let's take a look at a specific workout and find out how having a power meter will help him to complete his workout correctly (see Workout 9.A/TEMP-W8).

| TABLE 9.3 | | Training Plan: 16-Week Threshold Improvement | | | | | |
|---|---|---|---|---|---|---|---|
| Week | Mon. | Tues. | Wed. | Thurs. | Fri. | Sat. | Sun. |
| 1 | AR-W1 | NP-W3 | END-W1, 1.25 hr. | LT-W1 | AR-W1 | TEMP-W2, 2–2.5 hr. | END-W1, 1.5–2 hr. |
| 2 | Rest day | SubLT-W1 | NP-W3 | AR-W1 | TEMP-W8 | TEMP-W2, 3 hr. | END-2 hr. |
| 3 | Rest day | AR-W1 | SubLT-W1 | TEMP-W4 | AR-W1 | END-W4 | END-W2 |
| 4 | Rest day | AR-W1 | AR-W1 | AR-W1 | Rest day | TEMP-W2, 2 hr. | Rest day |
| 5 | AC-W4 | LT-W2, 1.25 hr. | AR-W1 | NP-W3 | AR-W1 | TEMP-W9 | END-W2 |
| 6 | Rest day | TEMP-W3 | NP-W5 | VO2-W1 | Rest day | END-W7, 4 hr. | END-W4, 2.25 hr. |
| 7 | Rest day | LT-W2, 1.5 hr. | TEMP-W3 | AR-W1 | NP-W3 | TEMP-W7 | END-W4, 2.5 hr. |
| 8 | Rest day | AR-W1 | Rest day | AR-W1 | Rest day | TEMP-W2, 2–2.5 hr. | Rest day |
| 9 | TEST | AC-W3 | TEMP-W8 | END-W1, <68% FTP | RACE-W2 | Race or LT-W8 | END-W4, 2.5 hr. |
| 10 | Rest day | Rest day | NP-W5 | AC-W6 | AR-W1 | Race or WATTS-W1 | END-W3, 3–4 hr. |
| 11 | Rest day | NP-W4 | VO2-W5 | AR-W1 | RACE-W2 | Race or LT-W8 | END-W4, 2.5 hr. |
| 12 | Rest day | AR-W1, 1.25 hr. | AR-W1, 1.25 hr. | AR-W1, 1.25 hr. | Rest day | TEMP-W2, 2 hr. | Rest day |
| 13 | AC-W2 | NP-W3 | LT-W5 | END-W1, 1.5 hr. | AR-W1 | RACE-W1 | TEMP-W6 |
| 14 | Rest day | LT-W4 | AC-W7 | AR-W1, 1.25 hr. | AR-W1 or RACE-W2 | END-W8 | Race or TEMP-W6 |
| 15 | Rest day | LT-W5 | AC-W2 | AR-W1, 1.25 hr. | AR-W1 | Race | Race |
| 16 | Rest day | AR-W1, 1.25 hr. | AR-W1, 1.25 hr. | AR-W1, 1.25 hr. | RACE-W2 | Race | Race |

| WORKOUT 9.A | | Tempo with Big Gear (TEMP-W8) | | |
|---|---|---|---|---|
| | Time | Description | % of FTP | % of FTHR |
| Warm-up | 15 min. | Fast pedaling, 90–100 rpm | <75 | <83 |
| Main set | 5 min. | Hard effort, burst in last 30 sec. | 100–110 | N/A |
| | 5 min. | Recover | <68 | <75 |
| | 1 hr. | Tempo with 20-sec. sprints every 5 min. | 68–80 | 80–90 |
| | *20 sec.* | *Seated big-ring sprint* | *160–200* | *N/A* |
| Cooldown | 10–20 min. | Spinning in small ring | <55 | <68 |

On Friday of Week 2, Bob will begin his workout with 15 minutes of pedaling at 100 rpm, keeping his power at the bottom of Level 2 (Endurance). This will give him three consecutive days of training for 2 weeks in a row in order to create a stronger "overload" of work. After he warms up, he'll get his legs ready for some work by doing a hard effort requiring him to hammer out one 5-minute effort right at his threshold power. He'll up the intensity in the last 30 seconds to 270 watts to push himself over the edge, then recover with 5 minutes of easy pedaling, with his watts under 150.

Then, every 5 minutes for the next 60 minutes, Bob will do an effort in the 53:13 gear for 20 seconds, trying to hold 400–500 watts and pushing this big gear. Staying seated the entire effort, he'll try to jump hard into it and get it going as fast as he can in 20 seconds. This effort is aimed at developing neuromuscular power. Bob's cadence will be low in the beginning and get faster with each second, so he should focus on pushing hard on the pedals and being as smooth as possible. Between efforts, he'll ride for 5 minutes easy, with his cadence in the 90–100 rpm range, and his wattage should be around 150–200. Then he'll cool down for 10–20 minutes with small-ring spinning (cadence 95–100 rpm, but watts below 140).

As you can see, having the ability to regulate his effort specifically with watts in mind will allow Bob to get the most out of this workout and also keep him from overdoing the efforts and undermining his upcoming workouts.

The weekends are critical for training because they allow Bob to get in a longer ride and improve his overall aerobic fitness. Although Bob isn't a weekend warrior, he also has to take advantage of the additional time in order to build more stamina in his legs. At the end of the cycle, he will be in need of a rest week to recharge and allow his body to adapt. Then he can come back stronger than ever for the next 4-week block.

## Weeks 5–8

Bob starts off this block with some intensity to work on his anaerobic capacity and increase the length of his threshold power intervals. By Week 6, Bob is ready for a sprint workout and also a time trial workout to focus on improving his "snap" and his power at VO₂max.

Thursday workouts are unique in that they are dependent on what happens on Tuesday and Wednesday as well as what is going to happen on Saturday. In general, there is no set pattern to Thursdays. Some days Bob will be resting in order to recover from his Tuesday and Wednesday workouts and also to get ready for Saturday. On other Thursdays, he'll get in a strong workout, either because he had an easier day on Wednesday or because we are creating a nice three-day block of training.

Let's take a look at his time trial workout on Thursday of Week 6, a ride that will take 1.5 hours (see Workout 9.B/VO2-W1). He'll begin the workout with 15 minutes at Level 2 (Endurance) pace, with his watts at 140–190, pedaling smoothly at a self-selected cadence. After the warm-up, he'll complete six mock time trials. Each will be 6 minutes long but will reach only 96–102 percent of his FTP. This should be around 240–255 watts. He'll try to start out strong, but not too fast, as he'll need to pace himself in these efforts, and then hold like glue to his wattage goal. These trials will help him to learn pacing, enable him to get

| WORKOUT 9.B | VO₂max Efforts (VO2-W1) | | | |
|---|---|---|---|---|
| | **Time** | **Description** | **% of FTP** | **% of FTHR** |
| Warm-up | 15 min. | Endurance pace | 56–75 | 69–83 |
| Main set | 6 × 6 min. (6–8 min. RI) | VO₂max TT, fast | 96–102 | 100–105 |
| Cooldown | 15 min. | Easy riding | 56–75 | 69–83 |

in some solid work at threshold power, and also give him enough time while at threshold power to develop a solid, powerful rhythm. These intervals are about going fast, but not hammering at max pace. He'll rest for at least 6–8 minutes between efforts with his watts below 120. Bob will then cool down for 15 minutes, holding his watts below 190.

The weekend rides should get progressively longer each week, bringing Bob's endurance up gently and only when he's ready. Bob will do some focused threshold work in Week 7 on Tuesday and Wednesday by getting in multiple intervals at his FTP, and by the end of the week he should be ready for his Week 8 rest week.

## Weeks 9–12

Week 9 starts off with a monthly testing protocol to see how much Bob's threshold has improved. It may be time to increase his threshold power number in the software and adjust his workouts accordingly. He should test his threshold when he's still fresh from his rest week; he also still has 8 weeks to go before his big event, so knowing threshold power now is critical. The "monthly" power test does not have to be done monthly; however, it is important to do this test at least once every 8 weeks.

The testing protocol does not just look at threshold power. It is important also to test the four Power Profile time periods and update the Power Profile chart accordingly. The testing protocol is a great workout in and of itself, so Bob will not be losing anything by completing it.

| WORKOUT 9.C | Monthly Testing Protocol (TEST) | | | |
|---|---|---|---|---|
| | **Time** | **Description** | **% of FTP** | **% of FTHR** |
| Warm-up | 15 min. | Easy riding | 56–75 | 69–83 |
| | 3 × 1 min. (1 min. RI) | Fast pedaling, 100+ rpm | <80 | <90 |
| | 3 min. | Easy riding | <68 | <75 |
| Main set | 5 min. | All-out | max | >105 |
| | 10 min. | Endurance | 68–75 | 69–83 |
| | 2 × 1 min. (5 min. RI) | Anaerobic capacity | 125–150 | >105 |
| | 5 min. | Recovery | <68 | <75 |
| | 3 × 20 sec. (3 min. RI) | Super jumps | max | N/A |
| | 10 min. | Easy riding | 56–75 | 69–83 |
| | 20 min. | TT Test | 100 | 99–103 |
| Cooldown | 15 min. | Easy riding | 56–75 | 69–83 |

To begin the testing protocol (see Workout 9.C/TEST), Bob starts with a 15-minute warm-up. Then he'll do three fast pedaling efforts at 100 rpm for 1 minute each, with 1 minute between efforts. These are to help open up the legs and finish warming up the muscles. After the fast pedaling, he'll ride for 3 minutes easy with his watts at less than 170. Then he'll go for it—doing one 5-minute all-out effort. He'll punch it as hard as he can and hold the highest watts he can for the 5 minutes. He should not start too hard, though. Then he'll ride for 10 minutes easy at less than 190 watts. The next efforts are a test of his anaerobic capacity: He'll do two 1-minute efforts, with 5 minutes between efforts. He should be out of the saddle and accelerating hard up to speed, and then really pushing until the end of the minute. After the second effort, he'll do 5 minutes easy at watts less than 170.

Bob will then finish off the short tests with a test of his neuromuscular power, or sprinting ability, doing three 20-second "super jumps." For these, he should jump as hard as he can out of the saddle and then sprint, as if he were about to win a race, for 20 seconds. We just will take the best 5 seconds to look at, but to get that segment he needs to do the full 20 seconds of effort and make sure he gives it his all. He should rest for 3 minutes between efforts with very easy pedaling, with watts less than 120, then ride easy for 10 minutes or so with his watts at 150–190, and finally complete a 20-minute time trial. At this point, he should try to produce the best average watts he can for the entire 20 minutes. If he starts out too hard, he'll blow up in the first 5 minutes, but it's important for him to give it his all, focus, and push hard. After this, he should cool down for 15–30 minutes of easy pedaling with his watts around 150.

Bob should also start to race on the weekends and to work on more race-specific efforts. Threshold power work will continue on the weekends, both in long training rides and in races. This block is the most important segment for building muscular endurance and overall aerobic endurance; therefore, the weekend rides, if not races, are much longer and intense than before. Bob should be very ready for a rest week in Week 12, as his chronic training load is really starting to build up now.

## Weeks 13–16

This is the final block leading up to Bob's goal—racing weekend. Week 13 starts out with three hard days in a row to take advantage of being fresh and to get in some high-quality work. At the end of Week 13, Bob is going to do a practice 20 km time trial in order to get all his gear and his position dialed in, and so that he can experience the sheer intensity of a 20 km flat-out time trial effort. This will be an important test for Bob, as up to this point he hasn't done any threshold work over 20 minutes, and he hasn't done such work in his time trial position, either.

| WORKOUT **9.D** | | Race Preparation: Classic Tune-up (RACE-W2) | | |
|---|---|---|---|---|
| | **Time** | **Description** | **% of FTP** | **% of FTHR** |
| Warm-up | 15 min. | Easy riding | 56–75 | 69–83 |
| Main set | 1.5 hr. | Endurance with 2 sets of intervals throughout ride | 65–75 | 75–83 |
| | *3 × 1 min. (5 min. RI)* | *Anaerobic Capacity* | >150 | >105 |
| | *3 × 30 sec. (5 min. RI)* | *All-out* | max | N/A |
| Cooldown | 15 min. | Easy riding | 56–75 | 69–83 |

Week 14 is another tough training and racing week. Bob should do a hard Anaerobic Capacity workout on Wednesday, and either two days of racing that weekend or two hard days of training. The week preceding Bob's key event is a rest week that allows him to rebuild his muscle glycogen stores, rid his body of any residual muscle soreness, and make sure that he comes into his big weekend with plenty of enthusiasm for the event. It's absolutely essential that Bob not overdo it in this week. If he does, he may compromise his finishing position in his key event.

The beginning of this final week is a great time for Bob to get any work done on his bicycle if it needs maintenance. It's a sure sign of a beginner to wait until two days before the event to try to change old, worn-out parts. Bob should take care of any mechanical issues on the Monday of Week 16. After a few days of rest, Bob should shake out the "cobwebs," getting in a solid race tune-up (that is, for his body, not his bike) on the day before his event. This is a critical workout and will help to prepare his muscular and cardiovascular systems for some intense work the next day.

The tune-up is a simple yet very effective workout (see Workout 9.D/RACE-W2). Bob will ride 1.5 hours at upper Level 2 (Endurance) pace, 160–190 watts, and within this 1.5 hours he will do three hard efforts of 1 minute each, with at least 5 minutes of easy riding between them. These are random efforts and can be done toward the beginning, middle, or end of the ride. They can also be done on hills or on a flat road. The key is to really push hard on these in order to prepare the legs for the next day's event. It is also critical that Bob do three hard 30-second sprints on this ride, starting out of the saddle and sprinting for at least 15 seconds, and then settling back into the saddle and driving the bike to the line for the full 30 seconds. A long rest is required between these efforts as well in order to completely recover and to be able to reproduce a maximal effort for the next one. Therefore, he should rest, with easy pedaling, at Endurance pace for 5 minutes between the sprints. As with the 1-minute intervals, these can be done at any time during the ride, as long as he groups them together. It is important that he leave at least 15 minutes of easy recovery riding before finishing for the day.

By the end of this training period, Bob should have improved his muscular power and endurance so that when it comes time to hit Level 4 and 5 efforts, he can maintain it for a longer period of time. Along with increasing his FTP, Bob has become a more complete cyclist and should easily be able to handle any racing situation.

### Jill's 8-Week Peak Performance Plan

Now we'll look at Jill, who has been racing for five years and has had close misses at winning the state championship criterium every year. This year she is determined to win.

In the past Jill was in breakaways at the finish, but she lost out to her archrival in the final sprint each time. Jill has about the same amount of time as Bob to train—eight to twelve hours a week—and has excellent bike-handling skills. She weighs 130 pounds (59.1 kg), and her current FTP is 220 watts, or 3.72 watts per kilogram. Her best 5 seconds is 956 watts, her best 1 minute is 452 watts, and her best 5 minutes is 260 watts, which makes Jill's Power Profile (Table 9.4) nearly flat across all four durations. In other words, she's a solid all-rounder.

| TABLE **9.4** | Power Profile of Jill Racer | | | | |
|---|---|---|---|---|---|
| | | AVERAGE POWER OUTPUT (W/kg) | | | |
| Level | Category | 5 sec. | 1 min. | 5 min. | FTP |
| World record | | 19.42 | 9.29 | 6.74 | 5.69 |
| World class | Int. Pro | 18.87 | 9.06 | 6.36 | 5.36 |
| Exceptional | Dom. Pro | 17.50 | 8.48 | 5.79 | 4.87 |
| Excellent | Cat. I | 16.13 | 7.91 | 5.21 | 4.38 |
| Very good | Cat. II | 14.77 | 7.33 | 4.64 | 3.88 |
| Good | Cat. III | 13.40 | 6.76 | 3.98 | 3.21 |
| Moderate | Cat. IV | 12.03 | 6.18 | 3.44 | 2.82 |
| Fair | Cat. V | 10.66 | 5.61 | 2.83 | 2.32 |
| Untrained | | 9.29 | 5.03 | 2.26 | 1.83 |
| Jill's Test Results (watts) | | 956 | 452 | 260 | 220 |
| | W/kg | 16.18 | 7.65 | 4.40 | 3.72 |

**Note:** Jill Racer weighs 59.1 kg. Average Power Output data can be reviewed in more detail in Table 4.1.

Let's take a look at Jill's Fatigue Profile (Table 9.5) as well to see what we can learn from it that could be used to help her change her training for the better. Jill's fatigue resistance is average in Level 7 (Neuromuscular Power), and that means she can stand to improve in both her explosiveness and her fatigue resistance at 20 seconds. Since she has lost in the final sprint in previous years, it will be helpful to examine the actual race files, which fortunately are available. In this way, we can determine whether she lacked snap in a short sprint or lacked fatigue resistance in a long sprint. Or perhaps she was hanging on for dear life in the breakaway and was just too fatigued in the final sprint to really contend.

| TABLE 9.5 | Fatigue Profile of Jill Racer | | | | | |
|---|---|---|---|---|---|---|
| | **LEVEL 7, NEUROMUSCULAR POWER** | | | **LEVEL 6, ANAEROBIC CAPACITY** | | |
| **Fatigue Resistance** | **5 sec.** | **10 sec.** | **20 sec.** | **30 sec.** | **1 min.** | **2 min.** |
| Well below average | 100% | 41–55% | 61–75% | 100% | 31–45% | 50–70% |
| Below average | 100% | 31–40% | 47–60% | 100% | 25–30% | 36–50% |
| Average | 100% | 22–30% | 35–46% | 100% | 21–24% | 23–35% |
| Above average | 100% | 15–21% | 20–34% | 100% | 10–20% | 15–22% |
| Well above average | 100% | 5–14% | 8–19% | 100% | 5–9% | 8–14% |
| Jill's Test Results (watts) | 956 | 717 | 573 | 502 | 452 | 263 |
| W/kg | 100% | 25.0% | 40.0% | 100% | 10.0% | 47.6% |

Jill's Level 6 Fatigue Profile shows that she has below-average fatigue resistance, and her power at 2 minutes really drops off. Although her 30-second power is impressive, she cannot maintain it and struggles at 2 minutes. All of this, combined with what we know about her Level 7 fatigue resistance, seems inconsistent: If she has just an average fatigue resistance at 20 seconds, why is it that she puts out such big numbers at 30 seconds? It's a good question, but to find the answer, we must keep digging.

Jill's Fatigue Profile shows a fatigue resistance that is just average or perhaps a little above average at Level 5, as her 8-minute watts are still fairly good. This could indicate that she knows exactly how to pace her power production at $VO_2max$. However, it doesn't give us any new insights into her impressive 30-second number and poor 2-minute watts. As we examine her power at Level 4, we see that she has average fatigue resistance here as well. Her watts drop off at a normal and predictable level from 20 minutes to 90 minutes. Jill is still

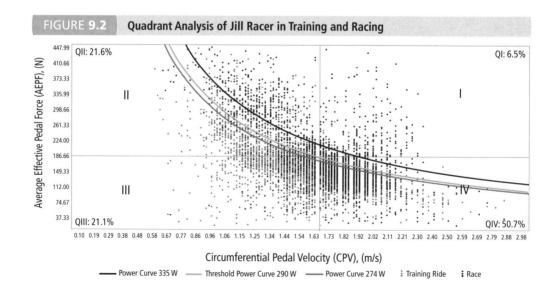

FIGURE 9.2   Quadrant Analysis of Jill Racer in Training and Racing

| | LEVEL 5, VO$_2$MAX | | | LEVEL 4, LACTATE THRESHOLD | | |
|---|---|---|---|---|---|---|
| 3 min. | 5 min. | 8 min. | 20 min. (AP) | 60 min. (NP) | 90 min. (NP) |
| 100% | 15–20% | 24–30% | 100% | 7–11% | 15–25% |
| 100% | 8–14% | 18–23% | 100% | 4–6 % | 8–14% |
| 100% | 4–7 % | 10–17% | 100% | 2–4 % | 5–7% |
| 282 | 260 | 248 | 250 | 238 | 225 |
| 100% | 7.8% | 12.1% | 100% | 4.8% | 10.0% |

a bit of an enigma, so we will need to dig into her Quadrant Analysis for even more detective work.

Since we are trying to get a better understanding of Jill's anaerobic capacity, we'll examine her power file from an Anaerobic Capacity workout and compare that with a criterium race file. Figure 9.2 is a Quadrant Analysis of these two rides. In the criterium, Jill spent most of her time in Quadrant IV, but in the training ride she spent most of her time in Quadrants II and III. These two rides represent distinctly different ways to create wattage. It's clear that Jill is not mimicking the demands of racing when she trains. This could be why her Level 6 power drops off so abruptly at 2 minutes.

When we consider these plots along with the Fatigue Profiling for Level 6, the only explanation that fits is that Jill's fast-twitch muscle fibers fatigue quickly. When extending an effort out to 1 minute or more, she has to increase her cadence in order to maintain a high wattage (and the wattage still drops off dramatically).

When this happens, we have discovered, two principles apply: (1) From an exercise physiological standpoint, the athlete needs to train the ability to pedal at 105 rpm for the 1 to 2 minutes and/or improve in neuromuscular power, so that he or she does not experience excessive fatigue after 30 seconds; and (2) it can be hard for an athlete to pace himself or herself correctly in a race situation, since it is a "make-or-break" effort, so it is important to train one's pacing skills. If Jill learns to pace herself, she could get a side benefit: improving her power at the 1- to 2-minute time period. She could do Level 6, Workout 2, in Appendix B to achieve this, as it challenges her to reduce her overall output while maintaining a high wattage for as long as she can at less than 90 rpm. When she can't maintain this, then she stops the effort, recovers, and goes again.

We would also want to investigate Jill's gear selection, particularly while sprinting, and possibly her sprinting technique as well. Since she has an impressive 30-second power, one would think that her 20-second power would also be impressive, but as mentioned above, this is not the case. This inconsistency leads us to believe that either her gear selection isn't correct for her sprinting (starting out in too easy a gear) or her sprinting technique is just not as effective as it could be.

**Strengths**

Average fatigue resistance at Levels 4, 5, and 7

Excellent breakaways with short, hard pulls

Good FTP for her category

Good steady-state riding (time trialing could be a strength with more training)

Excellent bike-handling skills

**Weaknesses**

Below-average fatigue resistance in Level 6

Below-average short-term anaerobic power in Level 6

Extreme fatigability in shorter efforts

Poor explosiveness in initial sprint

Possible technique issues with sprinting

As Jill's coaches and advisers, we need to figure out a plan of attack. Since her main goal of the year is to win the state criterium championship, and she has come close so many times but lost in the final sprint, we are going to have a three-pronged plan. First, we'll find ways to improve Jill's neuromuscular power so that she can have a more explosive sprint initially and also be able to hold it for a little longer. This will involve doing sprint workouts and big-gear intervals at least two times a week.

Second, we'll work on improving Jill's anaerobic capacity to eliminate some of the excessive fatigability she has in Level 6. She will do at least one workout each week that will focus on increasing her overall wattages at Level 6 while continuing to improve her "repeatability."

Third, we'll work on improving Jill's FTP to see if we can eliminate the need to sprint in the finish. It would be great if she could just ride away and win the race solo! This will require at least two workouts a week (one could be a race on the weekend) that emphasize both sweet-spot and threshold intervals from 10 to 20 minutes long.

We'll have Jill begin her plan in early April and take it through her peak event, which is the first weekend in June, giving her a complete 8-week peaking program. The plan, described in Table 9.6, has a general pattern that is similar to the one used for Bob's plan. Jill will have a complete rest day every Monday. Her Tuesday, Wednesday, and Thursday workouts will constitute the "meat" of the program, and Friday will generally be for Active Recovery (Level 1), although sometimes Jill will do specific workouts on Friday in order to build three strong workouts on consecutive days. The weekend will include a long group ride (or race) on Saturday and a medium-length ride (or race) on Sunday. We'll build up her fitness to a crescendo with 3 hard weeks, then 1 rest week followed by 2 final hard weeks, and a final 2-week taper period. All of her workouts will be based around wattage and can be found in Appendix B using the codes from Table 9.6.

| TABLE **9.6** | Training Plan: 8-Week Peak Performance | | | | | | |
|---|---|---|---|---|---|---|---|
| Week | Mon. | Tues. | Wed. | Thurs. | Fri. | Sat. | Sun. |
| 1 | LT-W10 | LT-W9 | NP-W2 | AR-W1 | SUBLT-W4 | END-W8 | END-W4, 2.5 hr. |
| 2 | Rest day | AR-W1 | NP-W5 | AC-W3 | VO2-W6 | END-W8 | END-W4, 2.5 hr. |
| 3 | Rest day | AC-W3 | VO2-W6 | AR-W1 | RACE-W2 | RACE-W3 | TEMP-W10, 3 hr. |
| 4 | Rest day | AR-W1 | AR-W1 | AR-W1 | Rest day | TEMP-W1, 1.5 hr. | Rest day |
| 5 | Rest day | AM: NP-W5 PM: AC-W7 | VO2-W2 | LT-W4 | Rest day | VO2-W2 | END-W9, 5 hr. |
| 6 | Rest day | AR-W1 | VO2-W3 | VO2-W2 | LT-W3 | WATTS-W5 | SubLT-W3 |
| 7 | Rest day | AR-W1 | Rest day | AR-W1 | AR-W1 | END-W4, 2.5 hr. | VO2-W5 |
| 8 | AR-W1 | AC-W6 | VO2-W6, 5 × 5 min. | AR-W1 | AR-W1 | Road Race/ Crit. RACE-W3 | END-W8, 3–4 × 3 min. |

| WORKOUT **9.E** | Lactate Threshold Crisscross Interval | | | |
|---|---|---|---|---|
| | Time | Description | % of FTP | % of FTHR |
| Warm-up | 15 min. | Easy riding | 56–75 | 69–83 |
| | 3 × 1 min. (1 min. RI) | Fast pedaling, >110 rpm | <80 | <90 |
| Main set | 2 × 20 min. (5 min. RI) | Crisscross, FTP to AC | 90–120 | 98–105 |
| | *30 sec.* | *Burst every 2 min.* | *120* | *102–103* |
| | 10 min. | Recover | 56–75 | 69–93 |
| | 2 × 5 min. (5 min. RI) | VO₂max | 115 | 103 |
| Cooldown | 15 min. | Easy riding | 56–75 | 69–83 |

## Weeks 1–4

In the first 4 weeks of Jill's plan, we'll build a powerful foundation of overall fitness, and she will focus on specific efforts in the last 4 weeks of the plan. Week 1 emphasizes threshold work, with a long, solid ride on Saturday to get in some "overdistance" (necessary to help aerobic development). The key workout during this week is the "Lactate Threshold Crisscross" workout (see Workout 9.E).

In this workout, Jill will use subthreshold intervals to improve her threshold. To understand the effect of this kind of workout, visualize a bathtub filled about three-quarters full, with the drain open. Every two minutes you will turn on the fire hose and fill the water level to its maximum capacity, stopping the hose just before water floods the bathroom floor. Let the water drain back down to three-quarters full, and then turn on the fire hose again. Unlike the tub, which will only let water drain at a constant speed, the body will (over time) begin to shed the fatigue from the high-capacity effort faster, therefore improving the rider's threshold. In other words, this workout can help to improve the size of your "drain."

| WORKOUT 9.F | Anaerobic Capacity (AC-W3) | | | |
|---|---|---|---|---|
| | Time | Description | % of FTP | % of FTHR |
| Warm-up | 15 min. | Easy riding | 56–75 | 69–83 |
| Main set | 8 × 2 min. (2 min. RI) | As hard as you can go (recover longer if needed) | avg. 130+ | >105 |
| | 3 × 1 min. (2 min. RI) | As hard as you can go | avg. 140+ | >105 |
| Cooldown | 15 min. | Easy riding | 56–75 | 69–83 |

After a 15-minute warm-up and some fast pedaling intervals, Jill will begin the criss-cross intervals, each of which will be 20 minutes in total. The crisscross interval begins at close to 90 percent of FTP. After 2 minutes, Jill will pop it up to 120 percent of FTP for 30 seconds, and then recover back to the initial pace, 85–90 percent of FTP, being careful not to let power drop below 85 percent in her 5-minute recovery leading up to the next 30-second effort at 120 percent. Jill will recover for 10 minutes after both crisscross intervals and finish with some VO₂max efforts and a cooldown.

Week 2 takes a "sharpening" approach to current fitness with a focus on shorter, more intense workouts, including a sprint workout early in the week, a critical Anaerobic Capacity workout on Thursday (Workout 9.F/AC-W3), and a very tough "race-winning" interval workout on Friday.

The goal of Thursday's workout is to improve Jill's ability to go hard and recover quickly. Jill will use the guidelines in Table 5.1 to know exactly when to stop doing intervals, but she will plan to do at least eight repeats. After a standard warm-up, Jill will adjust her power meter so she can view the average power in "interval" mode. She will begin her 2-minute intervals riding as hard as she can, pushing her average watts all the way to the end. Her goal will be an average that is over 130 percent of FTP. Jill will stop the intervals when she falls below 118 percent of FTP. After recovery (taking more than the recommended 2 minutes, if needed), Jill will finish with some hard 1-minute efforts where she pushes that average over 140 percent of FTP. She will do all three intervals unless her power fails to exceed 120 percent of FTP, and then cool down.

Week 3 is the final hard week before Jill gets a rest week in Week 4. Week 3 has two areas of focus: (1) during the week, the Anaerobic Capacity workout and the VO₂max workout on Tuesday and Wednesday, respectively, which are definite "must-do" workouts; and (2) two great workouts on the weekend emphasizing Level 3, Tempo. The key Level 5, VO₂max workout on Wednesday deals with what we call "race-winning intervals" and is designed to simulate making an attack in a race for the race win.

After a sensible warm-up, each effort begins with a 30-second sprint (15 seconds out of the saddle) in which Jill averages approximately 200 percent of her threshold wattage with a peak of at least 300 percent. She then rides for 3 minutes at 100–104 percent of her threshold wattage and finishes with an out-of-the-saddle 10-second burst, trying to reach 200 percent of her threshold wattage. She'll rest for 5–6 minutes between efforts and cool down for 15 minutes at Level 2.

In Week 3 of the training plan we included alternate plans for Jill to follow depending on whether she has a race on the weekend. Plan A is the plan Jill will follow if her race is on Saturday, while Plan B is the one she will use if the race is on Sunday. If she is just training through the weekend, she will follow Plan C.

The Level 3 Tempo ride on Sunday (Plan C, if you are not racing on the weekend) combines solid Tempo work with some FTP and VO$_2$max work. The goal of this ride is to improve Jill's endurance so that her muscles have the stamina for up to 3 hours of aggressive riding. She'll ride for at least 3 hours total, with the majority of the ride at between 76 and 90 percent of her FTP. Within this ride, she'll try for two efforts lasting 20 minutes each at FTP. If this is too tough for her right now, then she will start out with three 10-minute efforts, then go on to four 10-minute efforts, then three 15-minute efforts, and finally the two 20-minute efforts. In the second hour she will add three 3-minute efforts at VO$_2$max watts (230–260 watts), with 3 minutes of rest between efforts and a final cooldown of 15 minutes.

How do you know whether to use Plan A, Plan B, or Plan C? And what exactly is the flow of the workouts in each plan? Here are some guidelines:

- Plan A: You are racing on Saturday. Thursdays are easy rides to give yourself a rest two days before your race, and Friday is a tune-up workout to prep your legs for the hard effort that is coming up.
- Plan B: You are racing on Sunday, so Thursday will be an Endurance ride. You want to make sure not to overdo it before the weekend, but you want to include some short bursts to keep the legs sharp. Friday is an easy Active Recovery day, and Saturday is your tune-up day as you get those legs prepped for the race.
- Plan C: You are not racing this weekend. Thursday will be an Endurance ride, with some short bursts to keep the legs sharp. Friday is for easy, Active Recovery riding, Saturday is a solid Tempo ride with some shorter efforts, and Sunday is the great Level 3 Tempo ride (Workout 9.G/TEMP-W10).

Week 4, though not very glamorous, is an extremely important part of the plan. If Jill doesn't rest during this week, she won't reap the benefits of her hard work in the previous 3 weeks, and she won't recover enough from them to train optimally for the next 2. Jill will ride her bike this week, but when she does, she will ride easy. And when she rides easy, she must ride *really* easy, keeping her watts under 62 percent of her FTP—no speeding over 14 mph on a flat road.

Riding really easy is tough for many people. Too many of us ride at Endurance pace when we should actually be riding even easier. During Week 4, Jill will limit her riding to

| WORKOUT **9.G** | Tempo (TEMP-W10) | | | |
|---|---|---|---|---|
| | **Time** | **Description** | **% of FTP** | **% of FTHR** |
| Warm-up | 15 min. | Easy riding | 56–75 | 69–83 |
| Main set | 2 × 20 min. (10 min. RI) | Sweet spot | 88–93 | 92–98 |
| | 1 hr. | Cruise with VO₂max | 80–85 | 89–91 |
| | *4 × 3 min. (3 min. RI)* | *VO₂max efforts* | *115* | *>105* |
| | 1.5 hr. | Endurance/Tempo | 70–85 | 80–90 |
| Cooldown | 15 min. | Easy riding | 56–75 | 69–83 |

less than 2 hours per day, with her rides during the week lasting only an hour and 15 minutes. A rest week means that you also rest completely on some days, and Jill will relax around the house on Monday, Wednesday, and Sunday.

### Weeks 5–8

Training hard comes back with a vengeance during Week 5, with double workouts for Jill on Tuesday, a VO₂max workout on Wednesday, FTP work on Thursday, and a big 5-hour ride on Sunday—the longest ride in the entire training block.

Let's take a closer look at Jill's FTP workout (Workout 9.H/LT-W4). After warming up, Jill will ride two 20-minute intervals just below FTP, with 10 minutes to recover between them. Then she will begin a Tempo effort for 20–30 minutes with twenty 10-second bursts, riding out of the saddle and pushing her cadence to 110 rpm. She will attempt to shift only one gear, and she will rest for 50 seconds between the bursts. The workout will end with three 5-minute all-out intervals. As long as Jill keeps her power above 106 percent of FTP, she will reap the benefits.

Week 6 is the last hard week of Jill's training plan and features a combination of VO₂max work, to help bring on the peak of fitness, with some shorter but very intense threshold intervals. Thursday's workout is a critical one to help bring on this peak of fitness and starts out with a 20-minute warm-up, followed by five 1-minute fast pedaling efforts with 1 minute of rest between efforts. This prepares the muscles for the intensity of the next segment, which contains five 6-minute efforts at 240–250 watts. Jill pretends she is doing a time trial and really pushes hard for the entire 6 minutes at her self-selected cadence, resting for 5 minutes between efforts. She finishes with 20 minutes of Tempo riding (175–180 watts) and cools down for 15 minutes.

Saturday's ride is one of Hunter's favorites, as it provides a bit of everything in terms of training in each system (see Workout 9.I/WATTS-W5). This ride is around 4 hours long. The majority of the ride is in Level 2, but in the last 45 minutes Jill will be pushing at the sweet spot we talked about in Chapter 5. After a long warm-up, she will begin the first of two 20-minute intervals at just below threshold. These will be hard intervals and she will

| WORKOUT **9.H** | 2 × 20 with Bursts (LT-W4) | | | |
|---|---|---|---|---|
| | **Time** | **Description** | **% of FTP** | **% of FTHR** |
| Warm-up | 15 min. | Easy riding | 56–75 | 69–83 |
| Main set | 2 × 20 min. (10 min. RI) | Threshold | 90–95 | 98–103 |
| | 20–30 min. | Tempo with bursts | 80–85 | 90–98 |
| | *20 × 10 sec. (50 sec. RI)* | *Bursts, 110+ rpm* | *>140* | *N/A* |
| | 3 × 5 min. (5 min. RI) | All-out effort | 110–120 | >105 |
| Cooldown | 15 min. | Easy riding | 56–75 | 69–83 |

have to push it to maintain power, recovering for 10 minutes between the intervals. Jill will cruise for 30 minutes and then begin sprints: three in the small ring from a slow speed, spinning the gear, and three in the big ring from about 20 mph (300 m) and getting the 53:13 going. She will rest for 5 minutes between sprints. Then she will cruise for another 30 minutes or so.

Next, Jill will begin five hill repeats, riding multiple hills of different lengths. She will ride at $VO_2$max pace with good solid rests between intervals. Jill then will ride at Endurance pace for 30 minutes and do a short burst every 5 minutes, getting her cadence to 110 rpm for 20–30 seconds. With an hour to go, she will stop for some sugar and caffeine (soda or an energy drink). For the last 45 minutes she will push it in the sweet spot we talked about in Chapter 5. After her cooldown, it's important that Jill stretch to speed her recovery in the days that follow.

Hunter strongly believes in a rest week before the final week leading up to a big event, as this allows the athlete to become rested for the race. With a good result the weekend before her peak, Jill will go into her peak event with loads of confidence, and form plus confidence is always a winning combination. Week 7 is therefore very similar to Week 4, with the addition of a couple of workouts on the weekend. On Saturday she will do a relatively short Endurance ride of 2.5 hours, and on Sunday, an intense, shorter interval workout designed to put the finishing touches on her anaerobic capacity (see VO2-W5 in Appendix B). It starts with a 15-minute warm-up and four 1-minute fast pedaling intervals with a cadence of over 100 rpm. She won't worry too much about wattage but will focus more on cadence and pedaling smoothly. During a short (5-minute), easy spin, Jill mentally prepares herself for the next efforts, which are intense. For these six 2-minute efforts, she will ride as hard as she can, trying to average over 300 watts (135 percent of FTP). The goal is to go very hard, but to still pace herself so that she will just explode in the last 10 seconds. Jill will take a short rest (2 minutes) between intervals and finish with one 6-minute time trial simulation in order to max out her $VO_2$max system. She'll then cool down for 15 minutes and stretch afterward to help get the recovery process going.

The final week in Jill's plan is a "tune-up" week and starts off with an Anaerobic Capacity workout on Tuesday and a critical "race-winning workout" on Wednesday. Tuesday's work-

| WORKOUT 9.1 | Little Bit of Everything (WATTS-W5) | | | |
|---|---|---|---|---|
| | **Time** | **Description** | **% of FTP** | **% of FTHR** |
| Warm-up | 30 min. | Easy riding | 56–75 | 69–83 |
| Main set | 2 × 20 min. (10 min. RI) | Threshold | 93–100 | 98–103 |
| | 30 min. | Cruise | <75 | <83 |
| | 3 × 75 m (5 min. RI) | Small-ring sprints | max | N/A |
| | 3 × 300 m (5 min. RI) | Big-ring sprints (53:13) from 20 mph | max | N/A |
| | 30 min. | Cruise | <75 | <83 |
| | 5 varied hills | VO₂max | 110–120 | >105 |
| | 30 min. | Cruise with bursts at 5 min. | <75 | <83 |
| | *5 × 8 sec.* | *Bursts* | *>150* | *N/A* |
| | 45 min. | Sweet spot | 88–93 | 92–98 |
| Cooldown | 10 min. | Easy riding | 56–75 | 69–83 |

out is similar to the previous Anaerobic Capacity workout from Tuesday of Week 5, but this time with fewer intervals (see AC-W6 in Appendix B). There is no need for her to overdo it here, but the intensity will keep her legs prepped for the weekend. After a nice 15-minute warm-up, she will do three 2-minute efforts, striving for wattages similar to those of her previous Anaerobic Capacity workout (she'll review her power file from that workout to give herself a goal for the day). After the three efforts, Jill will ride for 5 minutes at an easy Endurance pace and then do three 1-minute efforts, striving for 330 watts (150 percent of FTP) with 1 minute of rest between. These 1-minute efforts are very intense: She will push it to the limit on each. A nice cooldown and stretching routine afterward will help her legs to recover and keep them supple for the weekend's peak.

The last couple of days before the state championship criterium must be easy days. Those final days are key to making sure that Jill is both fresh and rested, but also not becoming stale from too much rest. Her legs should be twitching with energy and ready to go off the front and win solo, in a break or in a sprint.

## DEVELOPING YOUR POWER-BASED TRAINING PLAN

We hope that by reading through these sample plans, you will begin to see how to develop a plan that addresses your own training needs. The workouts described in Chapter 5 should also give you ideas about how to do this and, of course, the rest of the workouts outlined above for Bob and Jill, which are presented in Appendix B.

There are a few traps that you should be wary of when writing your training plan. The first trap is entirely avoidable: Download your power following every ride. By now you should know how important it is to view the power-meter data, even from your recovery rides. For some athletes the prospect of riding without the feedback a power meter provides is cause for panic. If your power meter is in need of service during a critical time, don't panic. After all, you probably rode without all these gizmos for a long time, and now that you have more experience with power, you probably have a good sense of what 400 watts feels like going up a hill and how your heart rate responds to efforts. Fall back on your rate of perceived exertion (RPE) and heart rate, and you'll be able to weather the temporary horror of not having your power meter.

The most common trap facing most cyclists is the temptation to force the plan. Some athletes do this by "stacking" workouts to make up for missed workouts. "Stacking" is a term coined by Gale Bernhart. Busy athletes are prone to attempt stacking workouts over the weekend to make up for lost workouts earlier in the week. A stacker is a close relative to the weekend warrior. For example, the typical stacker completes the Tuesday workout but takes off the rest of the week because life and business are full throttle on those days. Stackers try to do their Level 4 work, their long group ride and hills, and their sprints all in the same day. The next day, they again go out and overdo it, with more intervals (because they didn't complete all of them on Saturday, most likely because they were too tired). Packing all or most of the work into 2 days is a recipe for illness or injury. Cycling is not a sport that allows you to "cram" the way you did back in your schooldays before your midterms.

If you miss a day, then it's generally better to move on to the next workout than to try to make it up. The only caveat to this is that if the workout was a highly specific one, and you

## 10 Steps to Develop a Power-Based Training Plan

1. Test for your functional threshold power.
2. Set your training levels.
3. Define your strengths and weaknesses and test your Power Profile time periods. Plot your Power Profile and Fatigue Profile.
4. Try sample workouts and collect data on your power meter.
5. Understand your data and what the charts/graphs are telling you.
6. Begin developing your power-based training plan.
7. Set a goal.
8. Understand your training time constraints.
9. Work on your weaknesses.
10. Write out a training plan!

look at your plan and see that you will not be performing that workout again for at least 2 weeks, then you should try to make up the workout as soon as possible.

A degree of flexibility is essential to any good training plan. It's okay to do your Tuesday and Wednesday workouts in the reverse order if you need to. The Thursday workout should be easier because it follows 2 hard days, and also because it's often 2 days before a big Saturday ride or race. If you are not racing on Saturday, or if you are not looking to be quite as sharp on the Saturday group ride, then you can switch your Thursday workouts with the Tuesday and Wednesday workouts, too.

If you begin to feel that you are overly tired at the end of a hard week of training, it might be advantageous to move up a rest week. On the other side of the coin, it's okay to push back a scheduled rest week if you are not tired. Many times athletes do not push themselves hard enough; as soon as they get a little tired, they assume they are overtraining. You have to push through these periods to avoid limiting your performance potential. Rest is incredibly important, but you should also challenge yourself to push beyond what you thought was possible. Do be sure to take the rest week in the week after it was scheduled.

Finally, cyclists are a competitive bunch. You might hear about the benefits of different training techniques or rides for other cyclists and be inclined to add them to your program. Keep in mind that your program should be driven by the strengths and weaknesses you identified in your Power Profile. In the case of Bob Rider's training, we planned some specific days for neuromuscular power work because one of his limiters was absolute power. In order to improve on this weakness, he'll need to do some work in this area. You might not need to incorporate such training in your training plan. If neuromuscular power is not one of your weaknesses, you might better use that time for additional miles on the bike.

You have now learned all the steps that are necessary for training effectively with your power meter. If you follow your training plan and make adjustments according to the feedback you get from your power-meter data, your training is sure to reach a new level of sophistication.

*You can purchase a training plan specific to your goals at www.trainingpeaks.com/hunter. If you are interested in trying an interactive online plan, please visit the site and choose the plan that fits your FTP. Bob Rider's training plan, as presented in this chapter, is a compilation of two plans: Weeks 1–8 are from the "Cycling Intermediate 250 Watts Threshold" plan, and Weeks 9–16 are from "Cycling Intermediate 250 Watts Threshold, Weeks 9–16." Jill Racer's plan in this chapter has been taken from "Eight Weeks to Peak 'A' Race—220 Watts." You'll find all of the details on the workouts for these plans in Appendix B.*

# Tracking Changes
# in Your Fitness

*Until the invention of the power meter,* it was difficult for coaches and athletes to accurately track changes in cycling fitness. Cycling is not like other sports where improvements can be easily measured. In football, for example, it is easy to track the number of successful catches in the end zone; in baseball, you can record the number of RBIs; and in golf, the number of birdies. But cyclists have usually judged their performances rather subjectively by comparing how they have placed in races or ridden against regular training partners. Some have gone further and regularly timed themselves on set courses or up specific climbs. These methods obviously have their limitations, however, as performance in races depends on tactics and good fortune as well as fitness, and even performance in the "race of truth" can vary significantly depending on environmental conditions such as wind.

With the introduction of the power meter, cyclists began to have the ability to easily track quantitative changes. You can see how much you have improved in your peak 5-minute power, for example, or your peak 60-minute power. With a few simple charts you can really see the fruits of your labor, as that little line on your graph continues to climb higher and higher. One of the benefits of this new technology is that seeing these changes is very exciting and motivating. There is no more guessing that maybe you are better. It's a definite. There's the number right there in your power-meter software. Unfortunately, the opposite can also apply, and when you are riding poorly, it can really be depressing. Quite simply, sometimes the truth hurts! Even in this case, however, it is worth knowing precisely how your fitness has declined, and by how much, so that you can make appropriate changes in your training program to get back on track.

It is important that you understand what the charts and graphs mean, so that with a few simple clicks of the mouse you can see your improvements. Each type of software has different options and ways to view the data. Some of these are more advanced than others, and going through each one is beyond the scope of this book. However, there are some key charts that you should understand and use on a daily basis. Though it is possible to perform some of these analyses using other programs, we have used TrainingPeaks WKO+ Software to illustrate the ideas.

## CHANGES IN MEAN MAXIMAL POWER

One of the most important charts for you to understand is the Mean Maximal Power (MMP) Periodic Chart. This chart compiles the data from every ride that you have done for a particular time duration. Each data point represents your mean maximal power (that is, average best power) for a particular ride for the time period you select. Figure 10.1 is a graph showing the peak 5 seconds, peak 1 minute, peak 5 minutes, and peak 20 minutes of a masters rider in his second season of training (his first year of training with a power meter). However, as you can tell by just glancing at this chart, there is too much data, and it is difficult to draw any conclusions about his fitness changes from it. Did he improve? It's hard to tell.

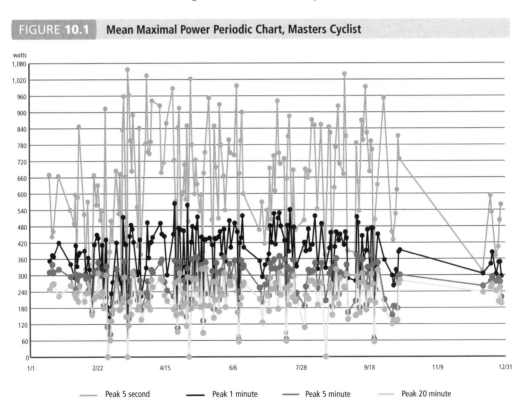

**FIGURE 10.1**    **Mean Maximal Power Periodic Chart, Masters Cyclist**

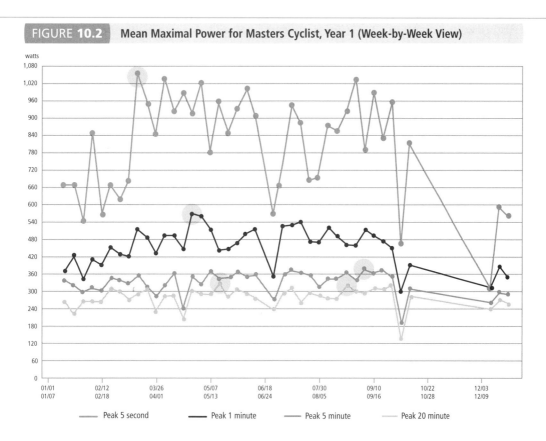

FIGURE **10.2**    **Mean Maximal Power for Masters Cyclist, Year 1 (Week-by-Week View)**

Peak 5 second    Peak 1 minute    Peak 5 minute    Peak 20 minute

How can we see the trees for the forest? By changing the "Days per Point," we can smooth the data over seven days and look at them week by week (Figure 10.2). This will help us to better see how the cyclist's fitness has changed over time. Now, each data point represents the peak wattage for each time period over the entire week. So the peak 5 seconds will be the peak 5 seconds for that entire week, the peak 1 minute will be the peak minute for the entire week, and so on.

Now we have a better picture of how this cyclist's fitness changed throughout the year and when it peaked in each of the different time periods. We see that his peak 5 seconds for the year was in early spring, when he almost cracked 1,080 watts. His peak 1 minute for the season was in early May, when he was able to produce 560 watts for 1 minute. Note how his peak 5-minute power stayed relatively the same throughout the entire racing season, finally peaking in early September at 375 watts. Now look at his peak 20-minute power. In fact, there are two peaks for this duration, one in May and one in August. Both are roughly the same wattage, at 327 and 323 watts, respectively.

A little background information might help to explain this double peak. This athlete wanted to do well in the spring races and also at Masters Nationals. His goal for Masters

Nationals was to achieve an FTP of 350 watts in August. He was right on track with his training, he was progressing well in the spring, and he had a great spring campaign, with eight race wins. Unfortunately, he crashed in early June, breaking his collarbone in four places. (Note the sharp drop across all power in June.) This effectively stalled his fitness growth for the season. When he came back to training at 100 percent, he was able to bring his fitness back to his previous level, but there was just not enough time to reach his goal of 350 watts at FTP for the Masters Nationals in August. He still placed in the top twenty of each event. In November, he took one month off completely in order to recharge his batteries and get ready for a strong winter of work.

Now, let's look at his performance in the following year (Figure 10.3). As the chart shows, in little more than one month he achieved his peak 5 seconds at 1,015 watts, his peak 1 minute at 575 watts, his peak 5 minutes at 387 watts, and his peak 20 minutes at 333 watts. Obviously, his fitness was the greatest in April and May, also evidenced by six race wins in this time period. Now, what this doesn't show is that he also did very well at Masters Nationals in year 2; however, since the event was held at altitude (at an elevation

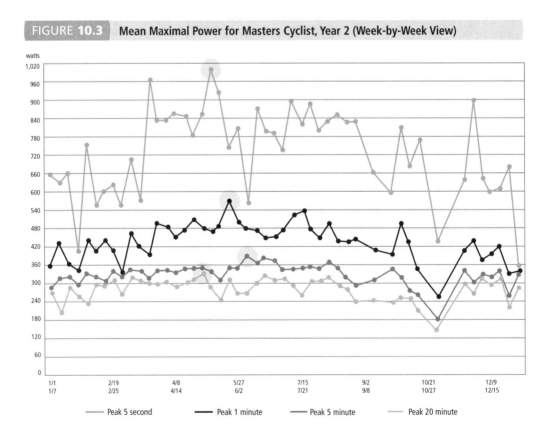

**FIGURE 10.3**    **Mean Maximal Power for Masters Cyclist, Year 2 (Week-by-Week View)**

of about 8,000 feet), his peak wattages were lower than what might have been expected at sea level. He finished fourth on the time trial and in the top fifteen in the other two events.

Finally, let's look at a third consecutive season (Figure 10.4). At the beginning of this season we changed his training so that he could really peak for Masters Nationals, aiming at an FTP of 375 watts. This year the Masters Nationals competition would be held in late June instead of early August, and we shifted his training accordingly. His fitness came up steadily at all levels throughout the season, peaking in mid-June with his peak 1 minute at 631 watts, his peak 5 minutes at 417 watts, and his peak 20 minutes at 375 watts. His peak 5 seconds was the highest in early April, as in previous years—almost exactly four weeks to the day after his winter weight training program was completed.

He did well throughout the season, coming to Masters Nationals with twelve wins under his belt. Masters Nationals was held at altitude, so his true peaks weren't reached in that event. However, his performance there was the best out of the three years. He took the Overall Omnium Win and a criterium championship and had the fastest time in the time trial for his age group (though, as seen in his downloaded power-meter file, he missed his start by 1:30!).

FIGURE **10.4**    **Mean Maximal Power for Masters Cyclist, Year 3 (Week-by-Week View)**

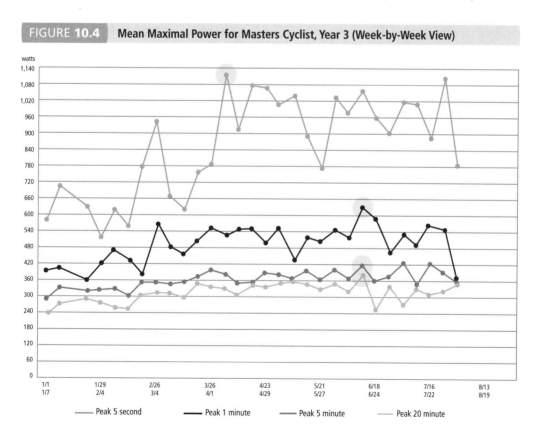

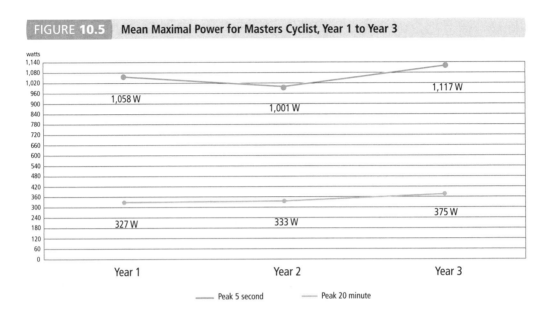

FIGURE **10.5**    **Mean Maximal Power for Masters Cyclist, Year 1 to Year 3**

Now let's compare all three years on a single chart (Figure 10.5). By charting them to-gether, we can see this athlete made some major improvements. His first season was very good, but in the second year he experienced even more dramatic growth. Some of this growth is obscured, because his peak occurred while at altitude. Nevertheless, having the opportunity to look at all three years of data is very powerful, not only for the athlete but also for the coach.

With the Mean Maximal Power Chart, we can see how an athlete has (or has not) im-proved in four different significant time periods. A related chart, called the Mean Maximal Power (MMP) Curve, shows how an athlete has (or has not) improved over *every* time pe-riod. With the MMP Curve, you can gain more insight into the type of rider you are.

The MMP Curve is a plot of *all* your "bests"—your best 39 seconds, your best 56 sec-onds, your best 1:38, your best 5:42, your best 1:15:32, and so on. By plotting all of your bests over the entire selected time span, you can grasp the rate of your wattage decay as the duration of the effort increases, and you can determine when it decays the fastest. By look-ing at the shape of the line and the areas of slope change in a rider's Mean Maximal Power Curve, we can also begin to distinguish the different training levels, their relative strengths and weaknesses, and possible areas for improvement. We can identify a rider as a sprinter, a time trialist, or a climber simply by reading the data.

Figure 10.6, for example, shows the Mean Maximal Power Curve of an all-rounder Category II female cyclist with a high $VO_2$max power. Note how little her power decreases from about 1 minute to 8 minutes, an indication that her strength would be in races em-phasizing hard $VO_2$max-type efforts. Figure 10.7 shows the curve for a sprinter. Notice the

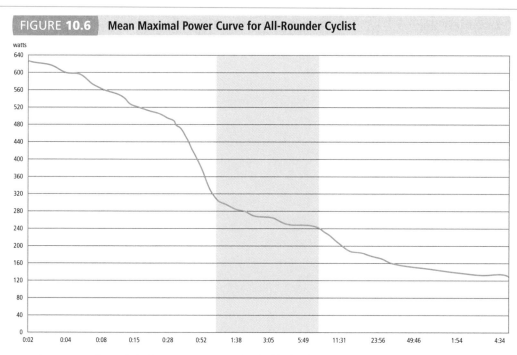

*Female Cat. II cyclist with high VO₂max power. The highlighted time frame (1–8 minutes) shows minimal decrease in power.*

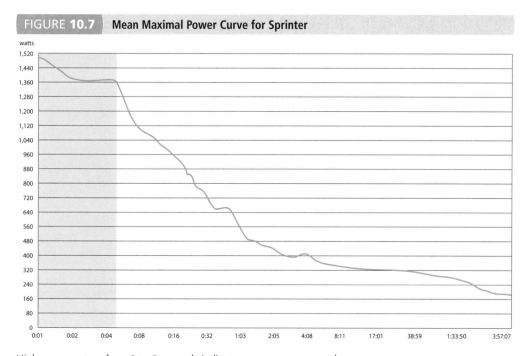

*High power output from 0 to 5 seconds indicates strong neuromuscular power.*

high power output from 0 to 5 seconds, indicating very good neuromuscular power. The power decay is very stable (the slope is constant) all the way to roughly 1 minute. Even at 30 seconds, this athlete is doing 700+ watts.

The MMP Curve is best viewed logarithmically, as this places the most emphasis on the data at the shorter time periods. Most fitness changes typically occur in time periods between 1 second and 30 minutes, so by placing a "log" on the data, you can bring out these small but important changes. Notice that in Figure 10.8, which shows a logarithmic view for a road racer, over half of the chart covers only the first 3 minutes of his mean maximal power data.

When you are viewing your own curve, note the exact time at which the slope of the line changes and how that relates to your different physiological systems. For example, in the MMP Curve shown in Figure 10.9, note that at 1 minute 25 seconds, the slope dramatically changes, and the new slope continues until about 7 minutes 25 seconds, at which point it flattens out even more. It could be that this slope shows the athlete moving from the

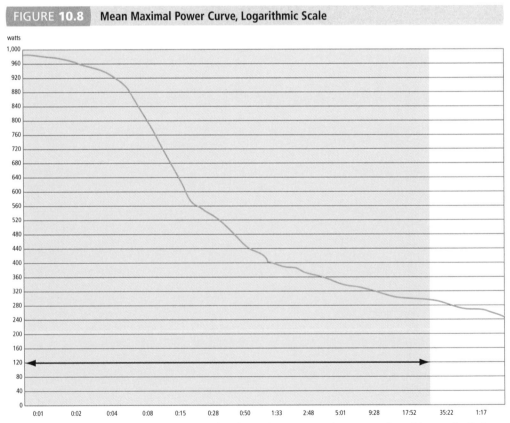

**FIGURE 10.8    Mean Maximal Power Curve, Logarithmic Scale**

*Most fitness changes occur between 1 second and 30 minutes, a good reason to draw this as a "log" plot.*

| FIGURE **10.9** | Mean Maximal Power Curve, Transitions Between Training Levels |

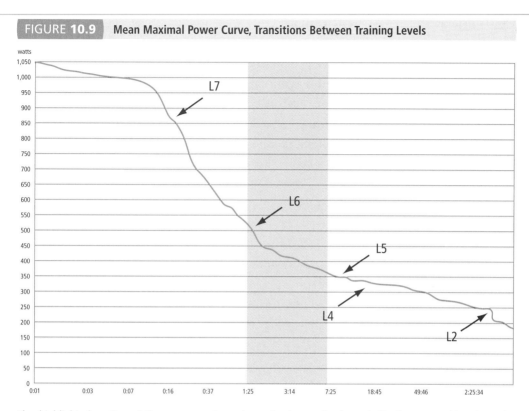

*The highlighted portion of the curve marks a dramatic change in slope, indicating a transition from the anaerobic capacity to the VO$_2$max system.*

anaerobic capacity system into the VO$_2$max system and then transitioning into the lactate threshold system around that 7:25 mark.

When you see the slope change, the steepness of the change could indicate a weakness in your cycling that you could address with some specific training for that time period. In addition, there will be some "dips" in the curve. Does this mean that you cannot do, say, 350 watts for 1:24, but you can do this same wattage for 1:45? No—that would not make sense. How could you produce more power at 1:45 than at 1:24? Remember: This is a curve of the best watts you produced for every 2–3 seconds over a long period of time. It's highly possible that you did a hard hill interval for 1:45 at about 350 watts but then did not do any maximal efforts for 1:24. Therefore, it's possible that your chart could show a higher wattage for that longer time period.

It is also important to note that, at longer durations, your average power will tend to be lower than the maximum wattage you can produce, in part because of the time you spend not pedaling. Thus, beyond about 1 hour (or beyond the longest, generally flat time trial that you have done), Normalized Power will be a more accurate measure of your true ability. In Figure

10.10, the upper line shows mean maximal power, while the lower line is the mean maximal Normalized Power. At about 7:25, they switch places and the Normalized Power becomes the upper line. This is an interesting curve because it shows that average power can obfuscate your true abilities. Theoretically, as this MMP line moves farther to the right, it would eventually hit zero, but in real life this most likely will be when you can't throw your leg over your bike and you are heading to the nursing home. For now, there is some level of wattage that you can maintain for even longer periods of time, almost indefinitely.

In year 1, the masters rider who was discussed earlier in this chapter lost many races in the final sprint when a competitor would just "nip" him, beating him by a hair. So in year 2, he changed his training in order to make his sprint longer, as evidenced by the flatter top portion of the MMP Curve (see Figure 10.11). From year 1 to year 2, the slope of the first 16 seconds of the line drastically changed, and although his overall watts were not as high in the second year, he was able to maintain a much higher wattage for 16+ seconds. Now, compare that first 16 seconds from year 1 and year 2 with year 3. The slope shifted back to a pattern that was similar to the one from year 1, but now the watts were higher overall. Did this athlete lose any of his sprinting ability in year 3? No, actually it got better! By year

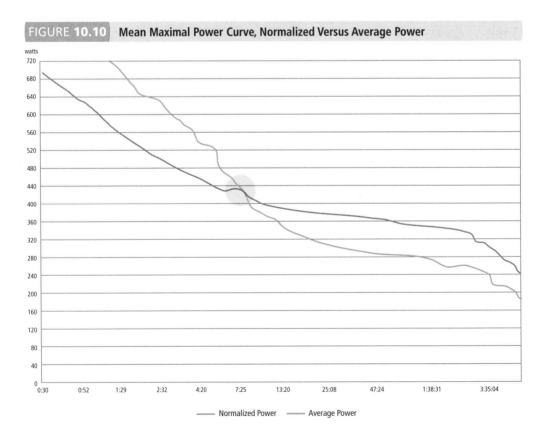

FIGURE **10.10**  **Mean Maximal Power Curve, Normalized Versus Average Power**

Normalized Power ——— Average Power

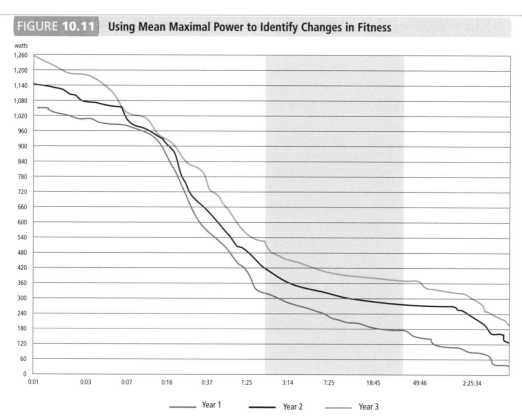

| FIGURE **10.11** | **Using Mean Maximal Power to Identify Changes in Fitness** |

*Over three years, this masters cyclist improved his sprinting ability in the first 16 seconds. The upward movement of the MMP Curve shows significant fitness gains, even where slope remained unchanged (see highlighted curve).*

3, he was able to produce more absolute peak watts and also could maintain them longer than in the preceding years. Now, take a closer look at the period from roughly 2 minutes to 30 minutes. The slope of this data did not change significantly from year to year, but it did move upward, indicating overall improvements in fitness.

## CHANGES IN THE DISTRIBUTION OF TRAINING LEVELS

You may notice that the areas you train in shift throughout the season. In the off-season, you might spend more time in Level 2 (Endurance), for example, and as spring approaches, you might spend more time in Levels 3 (Tempo) and 4 (Lactate Threshold). This is natural and indicates that you are indeed taking on more race-specific training as racing season approaches; you are building your fitness one piece at a time. By creating the power distribution charts for more than one duration, you can either confirm this shift in training levels or discover that you need to change your training and begin to address a different training level.

The power distribution chart in Figure 10.12 shows the percentage of time that a particular cyclist spent at each wattage level in January and February, and then the percentage of time that he spent in the different levels. In this example, the rider spent the majority of his time in Levels 1, 2, and 3 (Active Recovery, Endurance, and Tempo), just building a base of fitness. Figure 10.13 shows what happened in March through May. Notice how the amount of training begins to smooth out in the upper wattage bins. The rider is now spending more time at Level 3 (Tempo) and also in Level 5 (VO$_2$max) and Level 6 (Anaerobic Capacity).

By June, the amount of time he spends in Level 6 (Anaerobic Capacity) is really increasing (Figure 10.14). Also note the drastic increase in the amount of time that he spends in Level 1 (Active Recovery). As this rider begins to ride in more criteriums, he increases his emphasis on Anaerobic Capacity. The chart for July shows how much racing influences the amount of time spent at or near FTP (Figure 10.15). The big "step-down" after Level 4 (Lactate Threshold) is clearly evident now. Racing data, primarily road races and time trials, constitute much of the data. Although initially it appears that the increase in Level 4 riding is not that drastic, a 2 percent increase can be very significant in terms of creating chronic training stress. (Remember the caveat about the "time in levels" from Chapter 6.)

## CHANGES IN CADENCE

Although the main reason to invest in a power meter is to examine your power output in a variety of situations and make improvements accordingly, it is also extremely useful to examine your cadence in those situations. We know from all that Quadrant Analysis explained in earlier chapters that how you produce the watts is nearly as important as the number of watts you produce. Using cadence charts, you can track not only what your cadence was for one ride, but also how it changes over time.

One of the pro triathletes whom Hunter worked with pedaled at a very low cadence in both training and racing, and as a result, she had difficulty with the run portion of Ironman-distance races. Using Quadrant Analysis and comparing her files with those of other pro triathletes, he found that she spent much more time in Quadrant II than the other pros did. It became apparent that this high-force, low-velocity pedaling was contributing to her muscle fatigue in the runs. If she could reduce her reliance on force, thereby conserving precious muscular glycogen, he hypothesized, she would have a better chance of doing well throughout the entire 26.2-mile run.

Hunter encouraged her to concentrate on raising her cadence in all of her training and racing from her norm of 80 rpm up to 90 rpm. She would have to make a concerted, conscious effort to pedal faster. Figure 10.16 is a chart of her average cadence for a week of rides and her mean max cadence for 30 seconds, 20 minutes, and 60 minutes, after she made this change. The purpose of making this chart was to track her progress with this goal.

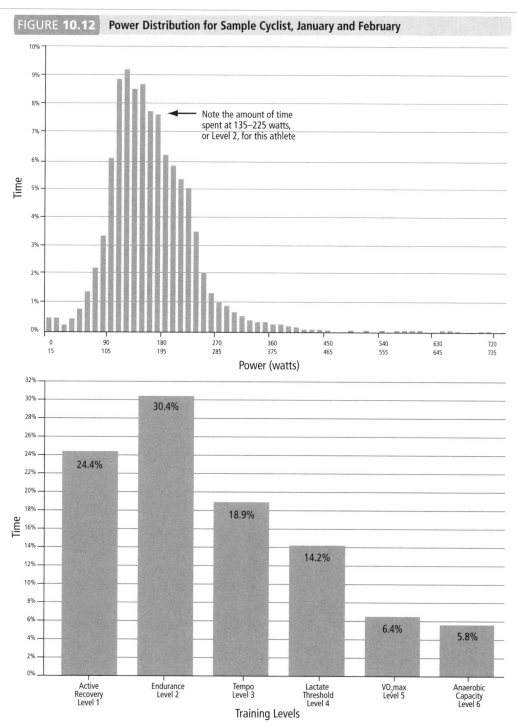

**FIGURE 10.12** | **Power Distribution for Sample Cyclist, January and February**

Note the amount of time spent at 135–225 watts, or Level 2, for this athlete

*Level 7, Neuromuscular Power, is not included in Figures 10.12–10.15 because time spent in this level is so insignificant.*

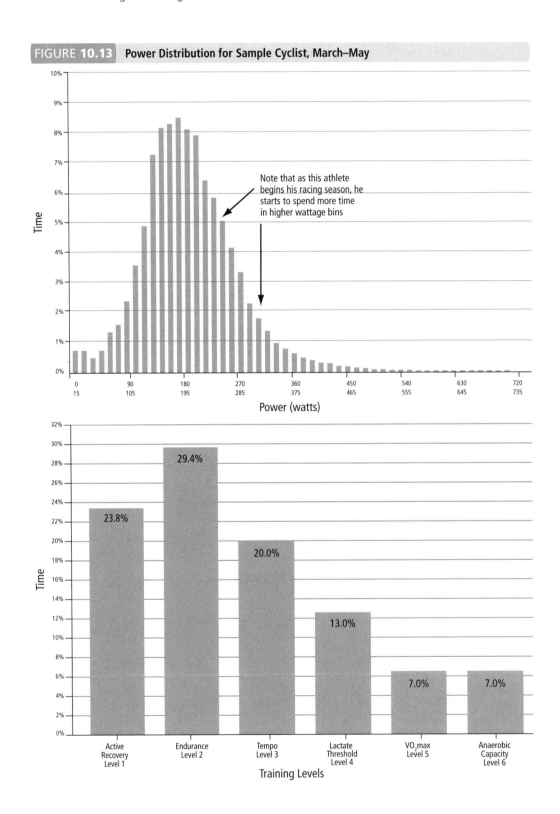

**FIGURE 10.13** **Power Distribution for Sample Cyclist, March–May**

Note that as this athlete begins his racing season, he starts to spend more time in higher wattage bins

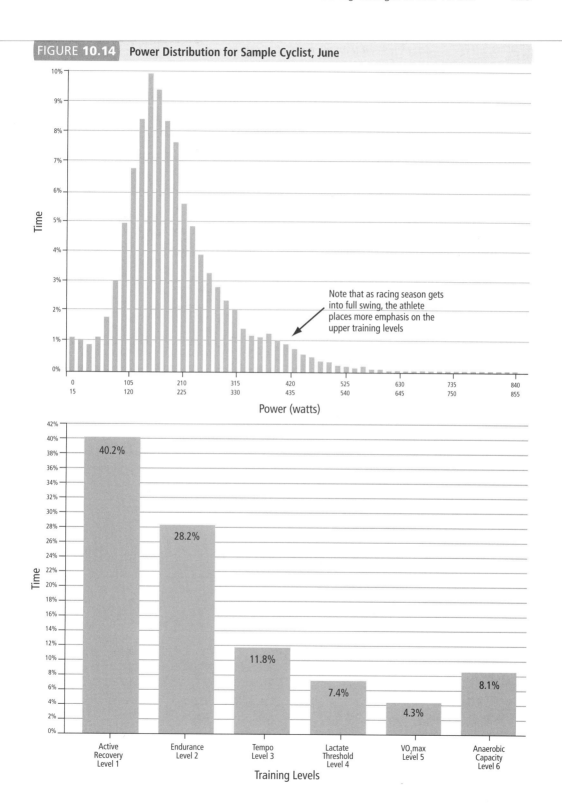

FIGURE **10.14**    **Power Distribution for Sample Cyclist, June**

Note that as racing season gets into full swing, the athlete places more emphasis on the upper training levels

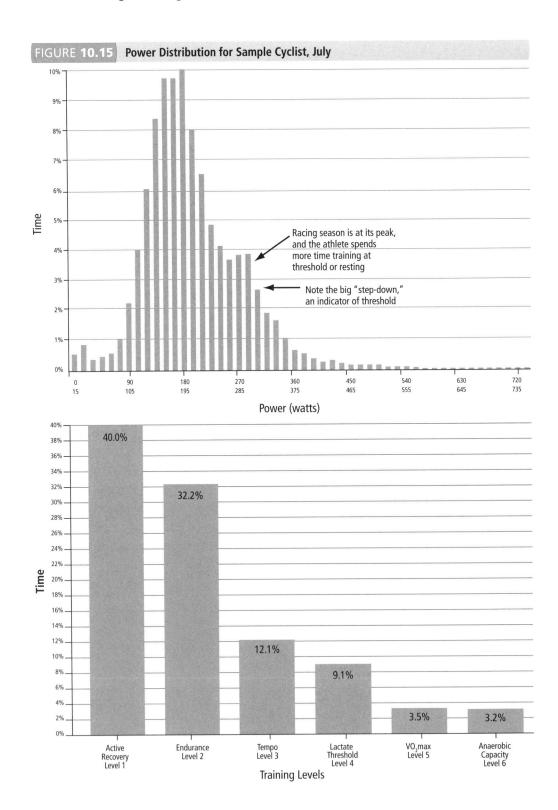

**FIGURE 10.15** Power Distribution for Sample Cyclist, July

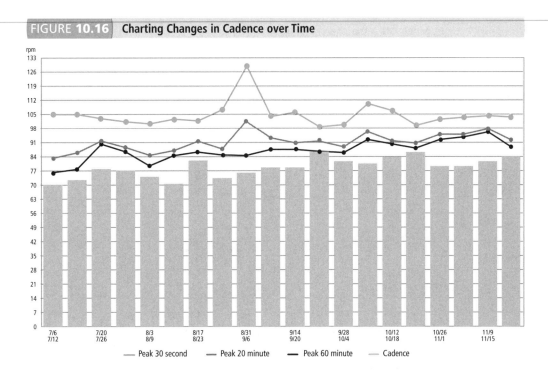

FIGURE **10.16**   **Charting Changes in Cadence over Time**

*Peak 30 second     — Peak 20 minute     — Peak 60 minute     ···· Cadence*

*A conscious effort by this pro woman triathlete to increase her cadence in training and in races is shown here. Each bar represents the average cadence for an entire week of rides, and the lines are the mean max cadence for 30 seconds, 20 minutes, and 60 minutes. Notice the trend to a faster cadence with some focused work.*

With cadence, you have to remember that the averages include all of the time spent not pedaling (when your cadence was zero), which can artificially drag the numbers down. But if you look for trends, you can still put this kind of analysis to good use. With enough data, you should be able to see the difference when you begin to change your cadence. Indeed, as you can see in Figure 10.16, which shows the cadence changes for this particular athlete, all of the lines, as well as the bar for average cadence per week, ended up rising, which was certainly a good sign that this rider's training had changed. The question remained as to whether she would be able to apply this new, faster cadence to a race and have a significant impact; at her next race, Hunter created a Multi-File Quadrant Analysis (MFQA) to make a "before-and-after" comparison.

By overlaying workouts, races, and intervals on top of one another, you can begin to understand more about your improvements over time. Reviewing your Mean Maximal Power Periodic Chart is a great way to instantly see any improvement in the overall wattage numbers. You might also want to take power data from the same exact ride done at different times—for example, two time trials done a year apart—and make comparisons. In this way

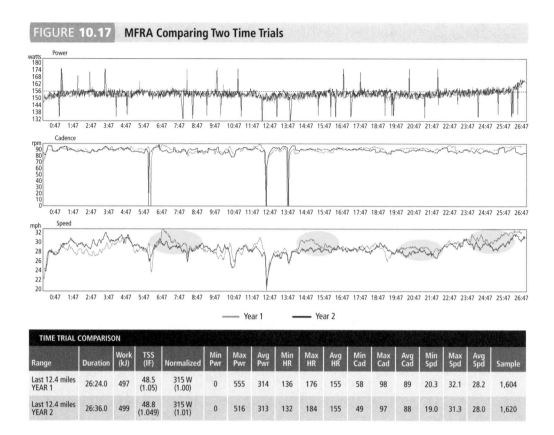

FIGURE **10.17** MFRA Comparing Two Time Trials

— Year 1 — Year 2

| TIME TRIAL COMPARISON | | | | | | | | | | | | | | | | | |
|---|---|---|---|---|---|---|---|---|---|---|---|---|---|---|---|---|---|
| Range | Duration | Work (kJ) | TSS (IF) | Normalized | Min Pwr | Max Pwr | Avg Pwr | Min HR | Max HR | Avg HR | Min Cad | Max Cad | Avg Cad | Min Spd | Max Spd | Avg Spd | Sample |
| Last 12.4 miles YEAR 1 | 26:24.0 | 497 | 48.5 (1.05) | 315 W (1.00) | 0 | 555 | 314 | 136 | 176 | 155 | 58 | 98 | 89 | 20.3 | 32.1 | 28.2 | 1,604 |
| Last 12.4 miles YEAR 2 | 26:36.0 | 499 | 48.8 (1.049) | 315 W (1.01) | 0 | 516 | 313 | 132 | 184 | 155 | 49 | 97 | 88 | 19.0 | 31.3 | 28.0 | 1,620 |

you can figure out exactly where you have improved over a particular section of a course. Maybe you just put out more watts, but as you get closer to that theoretical genetic potential, using the best possible aerodynamic position and becoming more efficient in the production of power will play bigger roles in making those incremental improvements that lead to optimal performance. You can gain a lot of insight into how these sorts of changes affect your performance by overlaying the same races or workouts from one year to the next. Just to illustrate this principle, let's examine a time trial from the same athlete on the same course that was done two years in a row.

The time trial results are shown in Figure 10.17. As you can see, the results are very similar in each of the three plots. The watts in the two rides (shown at the top) are nearly identical (within a watt of each other), as was the cadence (shown in the middle). The bottom line, showing speed, is just a bit different, however, from one year to the next. The darker line is the slower effort (by 10 seconds), and also the one representing year 2, so why did this cyclist go slower in the second year than in the first?

Upon further analysis, you'll notice that the peak speeds are higher in year 1 (the lighter line). This most likely was a result of the athlete trying to take advantage of a slight downhill to really push the speed up for a few seconds. You'll also notice that in the final 3 minutes, the speed in year 1 was a little higher than it was in year 2. Losing 10 seconds in a time trial may not sound like much, but certainly it could make the difference between a win and a second-place finish.

After analyzing the files and reviewing them with the athlete, it seemed most likely that the racer was just a little more focused in the first year than in the second. He was more focused not only in those crucial final 3 minutes, but also earlier on the slight downhill, where he pushed to get just that little bit of extra speed that the downhill could give him. The lack of focus in year 2 resulted in a time that was 20 seconds slower than the time achieved in the first year, despite nearly identical watts in both years.

––––––––––––––––––

Taking all the examples in this chapter as a guide, you can now begin to track your own fitness changes. Looking at your mean maximal power over the past 28 days is a reliable method of seeing how you are improving in different areas. Learning the intricacies of Quadrant Analysis and Multi-File comparisons is a little more complicated, but the tools are there and available for you. In any case, it should be clear that your power-meter data can help you to achieve more. The simple collection of data is one of the most "zen" ideas about training with power. Ride, collect data, do nothing extra. Even though this motto may sound simplistic, it also brings out a concept some cyclists may find helpful: a minimalist approach to training with a power meter. The interpretation of the charts and graphs is not complex in most cases, and we hope that this chapter has helped to illuminate the simplicity of tracking fitness changes.

# A Powerful Triathlete

*Pacing plays a leading role in triathlon;* in fact, it's the crux of the entire game. Sure, you need to know how to swim efficiently, ride your bike solidly, and run fast, but once you have those skills down, the event itself is about "metering" out your energy for the entire event so that you finish strong on the run. If you go too fast on your bike leg, you are going to be in serious trouble on the run, but if you hold back too much on the bike, it does not always translate to a faster run. In many ways, a power meter is even better suited for use with triathlon than for use with road racing. Most triathlons do not have complicated racing tactics—which increases the relative importance of pacing—and most are performed on the same course every year—which means that you can plan your pace in advance and test your pacing choices as you prepare for an event. Pacing, in short, is absolutely critical to triathlon success.

Using a power meter in triathlon training and racing can be very rewarding for the triathlete, not only because it can be used in triathlon in all the ways we have described already for cycling (figuring out your strengths and weaknesses, staying in training zones, and so on), but also because it can be used in specific ways tailored to triathlon. These specific ways include principles for both training and racing with a power meter, and you don't have to be a rocket scientist—or even an elite triathlete—to apply them. All the same concepts about training with power that we have discussed so far apply to triathletes, and you'll still have to do your 20-minute FTP test, complete your Power Profile and Fatigue Profile testing, figure out your power training zones, learn about how to analyze a power file, and, of course, get out there on the road and train correctly—all of which we have described in earlier chapters. In this chapter you will learn how to apply triathlon-specific principles to training and racing with a power meter.

These principles will be affected by the length of triathlon that you are doing and the type of training that you do. Training with power for a sprint race is very different from training with power for an Ironman-distance race. That difference plays a large role in your preparation for the event as well as during the event itself. Let's first take a look at how you can use your power meter effectively for training, and then we'll discuss principles of using a power meter during triathlon racing.

## TRAINING FOR TRIATHLON

Triathletes and triathlon coaches talk a lot about pacing yourself in the swim, pacing yourself on the bike, pacing your food intake, pacing your fluid intake, pacing your run times, and so on, and the longer the races, the more critical pacing becomes to your success. Pacing is a learned skill, and it is learned through your own trial-and-error experiences on the training grounds every day and at races, but you can speed up that learning process by using your power meter to give you an objective real-time view. One of the key uses of your power meter in training for triathlon is teaching yourself how to pace correctly.

### *Calibrating Your Power for Better Pacing*

The reason that pacing for triathlon is so difficult is that, for races at the Olympic distance and longer, the perceived exertion at the correct pace is much lower than you know you can do. It is important to be in tune with your rate of perceived exertion (RPE); every athlete needs to learn how to associate RPE with power output. One of the best ways that we have found to do this is to do longer and longer intervals at different intensities and simply be aware of what you are feeling physically at each level. As cycling coach Charles Howe said, "power calibrates perceived exertion, perceived exertion modulates power." Charles's statement sums up the underlying principle of pacing, and the key to proper pacing for triathlons is learning the wattage output that you must maintain for your bike leg so that you will have a good run leg, and then calibrating that with the correct perceived exertion.

The problem with this calibration is that your RPE changes daily and is impacted by your sleep, stress levels, hydration levels, and so on (just as your heart rate is). On race day, your RPE will likely be lower than it was in training for the same effort. This is where your power meter will play a significant role in your races, and we'll talk more about that in a moment. To learn to pace yourself on race day, you must go through what we call a "power calibration." To begin the process, you will do a series of intervals over ten days:

| Description | | % of FTP |
|---|---|---|
| Day 1 | 3–4 × 10 min. (5 min. RI) | 70–72 |
| Day 3 | 3–4 × 10 min. (5 min. RI) | 75–76 |
| Day 5 | 3–4 × 10 min. (5 min. RI) | 80–82 |
| Day 8 | 3–4 × 10 min. (5 min. RI) | 88–93 (sweet spot) |
| Day 10 | 3–4 × 10 min. (5 min. RI) | 100 |

For the power calibration to work, you must internalize the perceived exertion at each power level correctly—doing more than one session a day can cause you to confuse the physical responses to the different levels instead of learning how to distinguish them. If possible, however, do these efforts on the same road each time so that you minimize other factors that might influence how you feel at the different intensity levels. Make notes after each session.

Once you have done this exercise at each intensity at least twice, then lengthen the intervals and do two 20-minute efforts at each intensity level in order to recalibrate for the longer distance. While the prescribed intensities are the intensities you'll experience in the race (with the specific choices depending on the length of the race), the longer intervals will help you learn how to push yourself more consistently at higher intensities. Your RPE at the beginning of the interval will be different from your RPE at the end of the interval.

To complete the power calibration process, we recommend that you lengthen your efforts to 60 minutes and repeat the process at least two more times through each intensity level. After you have mastered the basics in pacing, then you need to get serious about training to the demands of the event. But you have not wasted any time; you are already training correctly for triathlon.

### Specific Training

First and foremost, triathlon is a highly aerobic sport, meaning that your functional threshold power is critical to your success. But your absolute stamina is also paramount. You might have a relatively high FTP because you train very intensely, but for only one-hour sessions at a time. This would be fine if you competed only in sprint triathlons, but for longer events you would need to be able to ride farther without major muscle fatigue—hence the need for exceptional endurance. We have devised workouts based on this two-pronged approach. The following two workouts address these key components separately, and then we'll introduce a third advanced workout that combines both, and still one more workout to help you train for short, high wattage efforts in unique events. You can find additional workouts in Appendix B.

### Functional Threshold Power

After a warm-up, start with two 20-minute intervals with watts at 95–100 percent of FTP (see Workout 11.A). Every 4 minutes (so, five times within each 20-minute interval), do a short "burst": Get out of the saddle and shift down one gear, sprint for 10 seconds, then return to your previous pace. Bursts simulate changes in pace that you might have to make in a race because of terrain or passing a slower rider. Rest 10 minutes between 20-minute efforts. Finish with 20 minutes at the sweet spot, and then cool down.

| WORKOUT **11.A** | | Functional Threshold Power | | |
|---|---|---|---|---|
| | **Time** | **Description** | **% of FTP** | **% of FTHR** |
| Warm-up | 15 min. | Easy riding | 56–75 | 69–83 |
| Main set | 2 × 20 min. (10 min. RI) | Threshold with 10-sec. bursts every 4 min. | 95–100 | 100–102 |
| | 20 min. | Sweet spot | 88–93 | 95–99 |
| Cooldown | 10 min. | Easy riding | 56–75 | 69–83 |

## Endurance

To address muscular endurance you will need to ride for a distance at least 50 percent longer than your normal distance and for a time period of at least 3 hours (see Workout 11.B). Within the first hour of riding, do at least two efforts at Tempo pace to get in some focused aerobic work. These efforts can be either on the flats or on climbs, and they must be at least 20 minutes long.

After the first hour, challenge yourself with ten efforts of 2–3 minutes each, preferably on hills that require you to push hard. If you live in a flat area, do your best to make these into the wind. Aim for 115 percent of FTP for each. Rest periods should be varied, and you can even spread these randomly throughout your ride. Between these short efforts, ride at the upper end of Endurance pace. After the hills, begin another 45 minutes at upper Endurance. Finally, with an hour to go, really push for 45 minutes at the sweet spot, stressing your muscles to the limit. Cool down for the last 15 minutes. The goal here is to fatigue the muscles in the legs so they adapt and gain more endurance for future rides.

| WORKOUT **11.B** | | Endurance | | |
|---|---|---|---|---|
| | **Time** | **Description** | **% of FTP** | **% of FTHR** |
| Warm-up | 15 min. | Easy riding | 56–75 | 69–83 |
| Main set | 2 × 20 min. (10 min. RI) | Tempo | 76–90 | 85–95 |
| | 45 min. | Upper Endurance | 70–75 | 80–85 |
| | 10 × 2–3 min. | Hard efforts | 115 | >105 |
| | 45 min. | Upper Endurance | 70–75 | 80–85 |
| | 45 min. | Sweet spot | 88–93 | 95–99 |
| Cooldown | 15 min. | Easy riding | 56–75 | 69–83 |

## FTP and Endurance

A combination of FTP work and endurance work, this workout extends the previous efforts even more (see Workout 11.C). Make sure you can easily do the above workout before attempting this one, as here it is your goal to ride for 100 miles (162 km).

For the first hour of riding in this workout, keep your watts under 76 percent of your FTP. In the second hour, keep your pace at 70–80 percent of FTP while staying in your aerobars, and every 5 minutes do a small burst at high power for 30 seconds. For each burst, increase your gear and drop your cadence 10 rpm to recruit more muscular strength.

In the third hour, do at least three efforts at your sweet spot to make sure you are continuing to stress the lactate threshold. These efforts can be either on the flats or on climbs. Rest for 10 minutes between efforts. After this set, fatigue will be settling in.

To recover, ride at Endurance pace for 15 minutes. Make sure you are eating and drinking. (A quick stop at a convenience store for a caffeinated soda can help refocus your mind and also give you a quick sugar boost before the last hard effort.) You will be tired as you near the end of the ride, but the final stretch will make you stronger and increase your endurance. During the last 45 minutes, increase your effort to 85–90 percent of FTP. Allow yourself time to cool down and stretch at the end of the ride.

| WORKOUT **11.C** | | **Functional Threshold Power and Endurance** | | |
|---|---|---|---|---|
| | **Time** | **Description** | **% of FTP** | **% of FTHR** |
| Warm-up | 60 min. | Easy riding | <76 | <83 |
| Main set | 60 min. | Ride in aero position with bursts every 5 min. | 70–80 | 80–84 |
| | *30 sec.* | *Bursts* | *120* | *100+* |
| | 3 × 20 min. (10 min. RI) | Hard efforts | 88–93 | 95–99 |
| | 45 min. | Sweet spot | 88–93 | 95–99 |
| Cooldown | 15 min. | Easy riding | 55–65 | 69–83 |

## Anaerobic Capacity

In road racing, the riders need to train their sprint and their ability to go very hard for short periods of time to bridge gaps. They also need the power to attack hills and the endurance to ride for 100-plus miles. Road racing incorporates many different physiological energy systems, and, as we wrote in Chapter 3 in the discussion of power training levels, Levels 5, 6, and 7 are as important to success in road racing as Levels 1, 2, 3, and 4. Triathlon, however, is a different story, as the demands of triathlon are more aerobic-based. We have never witnessed a "field sprint" in triathlon. In draft-legal races you might need to consider bridging short gaps to the next group, but in general a strong FTP will be the key determiner of your finishing position in triathlon events.

For this reason, it's not that important for a triathlete to train at the Neuromuscular Power level (Level 7), the Anaerobic Capacity level (Level 6), or even for $VO_2max$ (Level 5). Although if you are doing draft-legal races, you'll want to touch on these levels to promote a well-rounded level of fitness, the majority of multisport athletes do not need to train at these intensity levels. The only caveat (there are always caveats!) is that there may be courses that demand short, high-wattage efforts. An example would be the Ironman Wisconsin race, which contains over 100 hills, each taking from 10 seconds to 5 minutes to complete, with the majority in the 30- to 90-second range. The lesson here is that you always have to take the demands of the race into account. If you are competing on this type of course, consider adding the workout below (Workout 11.D) to your repertoire.

Start with a traditional warm-up to prepare your legs for an intense workout. Begin by doing one 5-minute effort at high intensity, then 5 minutes easy. If possible, set your power meter so you can see the average mode in "interval" mode. This will allow you to review each interval so that you can have a goal for the next one or know when to stop. Then do six to twelve (or possibly more) 2-minute intervals as hard as you can. Your goal is to average over 130 percent of your threshold power. Reach for that, but stop when your average falls below 118 percent of FTP. Recover for at least 3 minutes after each effort. Just choose your normal cadence for the recoveries—whatever feels right to you. Cool down.

| WORKOUT **11.D** | Anaerobic Capacity | | | |
|---|---|---|---|---|
| | **Time** | **Description** | **% of FTP** | **% of FTHR** |
| Warm-up | 15 min. | Easy riding | 56–70 | 69–83 |
| Main set | 5 min. | High intensity | 90–95 | 85–105 |
| | 5 min. | Recovery interval | <56 | <75 |
| | 6–12 × 2 min. (3 min. RI) | Hard as you can | avg. 130+ | >120 |
| Cooldown | 10 min. | Easy riding | 56–70 | 69–83 |

## Conserving Energy for the Run

When training for triathlon, keep in mind that you must also train your body to conserve precious muscle glycogen for the run. After you have consistently trained your muscles with workouts like the ones described above, you will be able to store more muscle glycogen and use it more efficiently. Still, you will need to spare as much of that glycogen as you can when you are out on the course itself, and practicing this in training is just as important as practicing your pacing. On days when you are not pushing yourself to the max with intervals at FTP and the like, make sure you are pedaling in the correct quadrant of the Quadrant Analysis chart (see Chapter 7 to review this concept). The better part of most triathlons should be completed in Quadrants III (low force, slow cadence) and IV (low force, fast cadence), which means low force on the pedals and adjusting your gearing to pedal either slower or faster. Quadrant Analysis can be used to confirm whether you are conserving enough energy on the bike leg. This topic is explored in some detail below.

## RACING TRIATHLONS

After training and pushing yourself to the limit, you will be prepared to take all of that hard-won fitness and do your best on race day. The most important thing on the bike will be

| TABLE 11.1 | General Guidelines for Triathlon Events | | | |
|---|---|---|---|---|
| Type of Triathlon | Distance | Intensity Factor (fraction of NP) | Average Power (% of FTP) | Training Level |
| Sprint | 10 km (6.2 mi.) | 1.03–1.07 | 100–103 | 4 |
| Olympic | 40 km (24.8 mi.) | 0.95–1.00 | 95–100 | 4 |
| Half-Ironman | 90 km (56 mi.) | 0.83–0.87 | 80–85 | 3 |
| Ironman | 180 km (112 mi.) | 0.70–0.76 | 68–78 | 2–3 |
| Double Ironman | 361 km (224 mi.) | 0.55–0.67 | 56–70 | 2 |

*Note: NP = Normalized Power*

pacing yourself correctly. Most triathletes do not understand how easy it is to ride too fast on the bike leg; it's the number one cause of DNFs in triathlons. The difference between a well-paced bike leg and a poorly paced one can be as little as 15 watts (normalized) for an average in the event. It's not just about average watts; it's about how you produce those watts, how many "surges" you make during the triathlon, and whether you go harder in the beginning or save some for the finish. All of these factors can dramatically impact your run time.

In pacing for a triathlon, no matter the distance, it is best to use Normalized Power because it accounts for the differences in terrain and allows you to focus on pedaling smoothly and steadily. If your power meter displays NP on the head unit, it can be a real advantage. If this isn't possible with your unit, you will need to pace yourself based on average power as a percentage of FTP.

See Table 11.1 for general pacing guidelines. But bear in mind that the levels provided in the table may not be exactly right for you. It is important for you to do some rehearsal rides in which you try to hold particular levels of intensity for the entire length of the event you are planning to enter. If your event is longer than Olympic distance, try to hold a particular pace for half the race distance, followed by a half-distance run, for a nice solid brick workout. Pacing at this distance will provide you with a good indication of exactly how much energy you will have left at the beginning of the run and at the end of the run.

## Wattage Creation: Are All Watts Created Equally?

How you will produce watts is the first consideration to think about when developing a tri racing strategy. "Not all watts are created equal." Recall the discussion in Chapter 7, where we covered Quadrant Analysis. You can create 1,000 watts by pedaling in the 53:12 gear at a very high force but slow cadence, or you can produce 1,000 watts by pedaling in the 39:21 gear at a low force but very fast cadence. The watts are the same in the end, but you called on very different muscle fiber types to produce them. More fast-twitch (Type II) muscle fibers are recruited when you are in Quadrant II or pedaling in a high-force, low-cadence situation, whereas more slow-twitch (Type I) fibers are recruited in a Quadrant IV, or low-force, high-cadence, situation.

Why does this matter in regard to triathlon? It matters because of the energy expenditure in both situations. When fast-twitch muscle fibers are recruited, more muscle glycogen is used in the contractions than when slow-twitch fibers are recruited. Pedaling as smoothly and steadily as possible is key in triathlon. By keeping the Normalized Power and average power as close to the same as you can, you save valuable energy for the run. When Normalized Power is very high relative to average power, or when the Variability Index is high, this means that your power fluctuated too much. By smoothing your effort on hills and avoiding bursts of wattage, you can keep your Variability Index low and therefore reduce the amount of muscle glycogen used on the bike leg.

When considering Quadrant Analysis and smooth pedaling, even an effort that isn't fully in Quadrant I or II will cost you more than you want to expend, and this is a critical waste of muscle glycogen and could impact you negatively on the run. Just as when you are driving a car your fuel consumption will be much higher if you are constantly "flooring" it

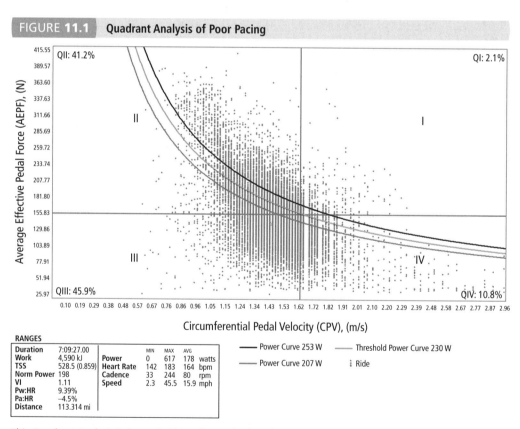

**FIGURE 11.1** **Quadrant Analysis of Poor Pacing**

*This Quadrant Analysis is for a triathlete who pushed too big a gear and rode too hard. He ended up walking on the run. Note that he spent 41.2 percent of his time in Quadrant II, showing high force and low cadence, which equals a lot of muscle glycogen usage.*

and accelerating hard at every chance you get than if you just drive smoothly and consistently, your muscle glycogen expenditure will be greatest on the bike when you are fluctuating your power between low and high forces. We are not necessarily advocating always using a high cadence in triathlon; we are, however, advising greater mindfulness about how you create your watts in a race. Stay light on the pedals, use your gearing to keep your cadence consistent, and if you are a "gear masher" spend plenty of time in training trying to achieve a more consistent, smoother pedaling stroke. Your pacing strategy should include being able to choose the correct gearing in such a way as to minimize excessive glycogen use.

Let's examine two different race files from an Ironman event to better illustrate this point. In Figure 11.1, the athlete spent over 41 percent of his race in Quadrant II, which represents high force and low cadence. From an energy standpoint, this is the worst quadrant for energy conservation. Quadrant II requires a particularly large amount of muscle glycogen.

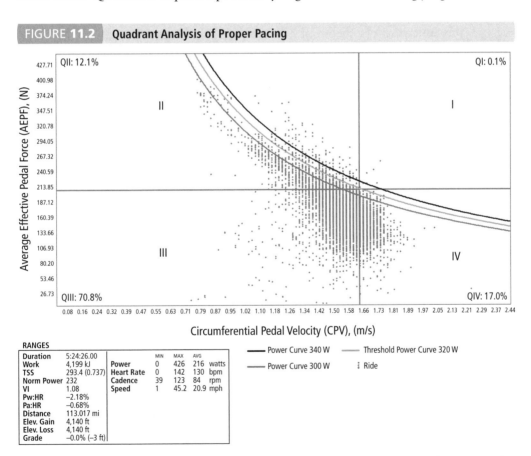

**FIGURE 11.2**   **Quadrant Analysis of Proper Pacing**

This Quadrant Analysis shows a well-paced Ironman-distance race with proper selection of gears. Note that this athlete spent only 12 percent of his time in Quadrant II and 70 percent in Quadrant III. He conserved a lot of glycogen in this way and consequently set a personal record on the run. He easily won in his age group.

In the Quadrant Analysis shown in Figure 11.2, we see a much better example of how an athlete can create watts. This athlete shows nearly perfect wattage creation for over 70 percent of the race. He pedaled with low force and a slower cadence as you would in a recovery/endurance ride, staying in Quadrant III. He avoided any hard power spikes and maintained a comfortable and steady pace throughout the ride, thus preserving his glycogen stores for the run. In fact, he was able to set a personal record on the run and easily won his age group as well, and this was in a tough event, the Ironman Canada. Riding as smoothly as possible, avoiding hard surges of power throughout the ride, and being sure not to push a big gear can dramatically enhance your ability to conserve energy for the run. The best triathletes not only ride fast but know exactly how to create watts in order to conserve energy—and the energy they conserve is energy that can be used on the run.

### The Mathematical Approach to Pacing

Pacing is such a huge part of successful triathlon racing that every tri coach makes it a priority. But they all have different ways of teaching this skill and then getting the athlete to apply it in races. A power meter makes a huge difference in how pacing skills are acquired. The power calibration process explained earlier in the chapter is just one example of how your power meter will help you pace yourself. Coaches and participants alike have developed some great tools and strategies to make sure you get to the run with plenty of energy.

Rich Strauss and Patrick McCrann from Endurance Nation (see EnduranceNation.us) have created an interesting mathematical approach to pacing. They give the triathlete a maximum "budget" of 300 Training Stress Score (TSS) points for an Ironman-distance event. From here, the athlete predicts his or her finishing time or sets a goal time for the event. With a known TSS and a known time, he or she can solve for the Intensity Factor (IF) and then calculate a precise wattage number. For example, if you are planning to finish your Ironman in 6 hours, and your budget is 300 TSS, with an FTP of 275 watts, then your IF for the event will be 0.71. However, according to Rich and Patrick, a 300-TSS Ironman is the maximum budget and puts you in the danger zone for not being able to run for the entire race. A more realistic TSS budget would be 280. When the TSS is 280, the IF is reduced to 0.68.

To do the calculations yourself, follow these steps:

1. **Figure out your TSS per hour**. This is the easy part. Simply divide the total TSS by the number of hours you will be racing (in our example, 280 divided by 6, which is 46.7).
2. **Solve for the Intensity Factor**. The TSS per hour (the number you just pinned down) is equal to the square of the Intensity Factor times 100. So, in our example,

$$IF^2 \times 100 = 46.7$$

Going back to Algebra I, you can go from there to figure out that $IF^2$ is equal to 46.7 divided by 100:

$$IF^2 = 46.7 \div 100, \text{ which means that } IF^2 = 0.47$$

So, again through algebra, you know that IF will be the square root of 0.47, or IF = 0.68.

3. **Calculate the average Normalized Power needed to maintain IF**. Intensity Factor is equal to average Normalized Power divided by FTP:

$$IF = \text{Average NP} \div \text{FTP}$$

Average NP is thus IF times FTP:

$$\text{Average NP} = IF \times \text{FTP}$$

So, in our example, multiply IF (0.68) by FTP (275) to calculate an average Normalized Power of 187 watts.

In this example, your pacing goal would therefore be 187 watts for an Ironman-distance race. It would be unrealistic to try to maintain exactly 187 watts for 6 hours, but fortunately there are some additional rules of thumb you can learn—again, thanks to Rich and Patrick at Endurance Nation. They prescribe a set of pacing guidelines for the Ironman and half-Ironman races.

For the first 30–45 minutes of the race, hold 95 percent of the goal wattage; thereafter, ride as close as you can to your goal wattage. If you encounter a hill, then base the level of intensity above your goal wattage on the length of the hill. If the hill is longer than a 3-minute climb, then ride at 105 percent of your goal wattage; if it's a 30-second to 120-second climb, then ride at 110 percent of your goal wattage.

Normally a 3-minute, all-out effort would be done at between 115 and 120 percent of FTP in Level 5, and a 30-second to 120-second effort would range from 120 to 150 percent of FTP. Rich and Patrick's guidelines to hold at 105 percent and 110 percent, respectively, are therefore nice conservative rules and should be good ones to consider when trying to minimize spikes in power on hills. Along with these pacing guidelines, they also use Variability Index as a key postmortem metric to determine how smoothly one pedaled on a ride or in a race. They maintain that a bike leg with a Variability Index of 1.04 to 1.07 signifies that a rider has done an excellent job of pedaling smoothly for the entire ride and has correctly limited his or her surges to a very low number (see Chapter 7 for more on Variability Index).

Every time you come to a hill, instead of attacking up the hill out of the saddle, smoothly transition your power from the flats to the hill and resist the temptation to accelerate to try to keep up with a faster rider passing you. This advice ties in nicely with the Quadrant

Analysis examples we wrote about earlier in the chapter and confirms the importance of muting power spikes and pedaling as smoothly as possible. A race with a low Variability Index when plotted on the Quadrant Analysis chart of TrainingPeaks WKO+ Software will show a majority of the ride in Quadrant III and Quadrant IV.

These guidelines are all designed around amateur athletes. The pros can ride at a much higher IF and also produce a larger TSS and still run at personal-record pace. Some elite triathletes create nearly 390 TSS at an IF of 0.83 and still finish with some of the best runs of their life, but that's why they're professional athletes, train 30-plus hours a week, and fall into the "genetic freak" category.

### Pacing in the Real Race

So far in racing, we have seen just how important a power meter can be in helping riders pace themselves correctly and smooth out those power surges. The power meter really comes into play on the execution of your strategy on race day. Having a strategy and using your power meter can make the difference between a good experience and a bad experience. The two case studies illustrated in Figures 11.3 and 11.4 will help you see the difference.

Let's start with an example of poor pacing. Figure 11.3 shows data from Lake Placid Ironman. This athlete is strong in her age group, 40–44. Her FTP is 215 watts, and her Power Profile slopes upward to the right, which is typical of most triathletes, who are often very fit aerobically but do not train their anaerobic system. This does not mean that she could not be a great sprinter; it's just that, since triathletes never have to sprint in their events, they do not usually train their anaerobic and neuromuscular capacities, and as a result they do not usually reach their full potential across all the different levels.

In this race, her goal was to qualify for the Hawaii Ironman World Championships. In her words, "I went all out on the bike course. My strategy was contrary to the advice of almost everyone I met. I felt that I had nothing to lose, except a slot in Hawaii. As it turned out, my body was spent and my run was about 10–15 minutes off where it should have been." Despite going all-out, she did have a strong run, and she still placed fourth and qualified for Hawaii!

Looking at her download, the first thing you may notice is just the sheer number of hills that were on this course. Every time the speed line goes up and down, that's an indicator of a big speed change—an uphill or downhill. What this means is that pacing is tougher than normal, but it is doubly important. If you go too hard on the hills, you risk using too much muscular glycogen and then not having any reserve for later. Second, notice that her IF was 0.75, which indicates that she held 75 percent of her Normalized Power. This figure falls near the upper limit in Table 11.1 for pacing in an Ironman. Notice, too, that her TSS was 306, which, according to Rick and Patrick, means that the athlete had better be

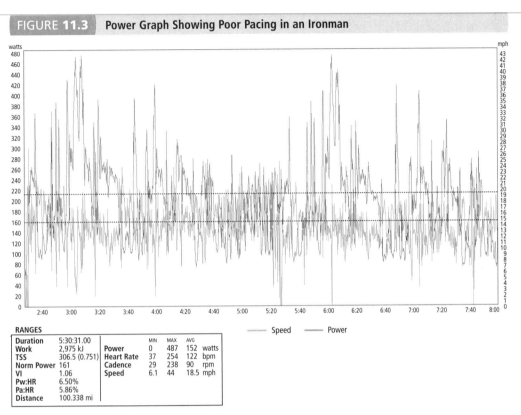

**FIGURE 11.3**   **Power Graph Showing Poor Pacing in an Ironman**

| RANGES | | | | MIN | MAX | AVG | |
|---|---|---|---|---|---|---|---|
| Duration | 5:30:31.00 | | | | | | |
| Work | 2,975 kJ | Power | | 0 | 487 | 152 | watts |
| TSS | 306.5 (0.751) | Heart Rate | | 37 | 254 | 122 | bpm |
| Norm Power | 161 | Cadence | | 29 | 238 | 90 | rpm |
| VI | 1.06 | Speed | | 6.1 | 44 | 18.5 | mph |
| Pw:HR | 6.50% | | | | | | |
| Pa:HR | 5.86% | | | | | | |
| Distance | 100.338 mi | | | | | | |

*The top gridline shows the FTP for this athlete at 215 W, and the bottom gridline shows the actual Normalized Power average at 161 W. The ranges box shows the rider's IF to be 0.751, which is 75 percent of her Normalized Power.*

*massively* prepared; it's a TSS for *proven* strong Ironman runners only. Although this competitor is indeed a talented athlete, by her own admission this pace was too much, and it left her without enough in the tank for the run.

There is not one clear area in the download that we can point to that was paced incorrectly, and even her Variability Index is 1.06, so she pedaled smoothly, but just too hard, for the entire race. She started out a little hot as, in the first 30 minutes, she averaged 170 watts, which is about 80 percent of her FTP. In the longer uphill portion (the second quarter of the race), her power was higher (with an average NP of 170 watts), and it stayed closer to her FTP at this point than during any other extended period in the race. Others might argue that she went too hard on this section, but instead we think that she paced this section correctly.

When riding uphill, in almost every situation, you can afford to produce more watts than you can in other parts of a triathlon or time trial. This is because you have more resistance to push against, and on the downhills, there isn't a big enough gear to allow you to produce

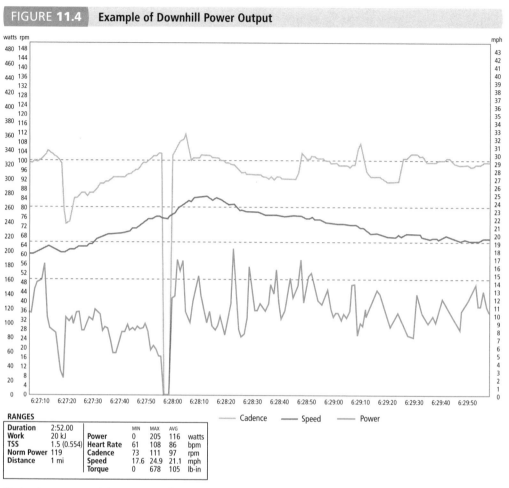

**FIGURE 11.4    Example of Downhill Power Output**

| RANGES | | | MIN | MAX | AVG | |
|---|---|---|---|---|---|---|
| Duration | 2:52.00 | | | | | |
| Work | 20 kJ | **Power** | 0 | 205 | 116 | watts |
| TSS | 1.5 (0.554) | **Heart Rate** | 61 | 108 | 86 | bpm |
| Norm Power | 119 | **Cadence** | 73 | 111 | 97 | rpm |
| Distance | 1 mi | **Speed** | 17.6 | 24.9 | 21.1 | mph |
| | | **Torque** | 0 | 678 | 105 | lb-in |

*Notice how as speed increases, cadence increases, but the watts plummet, demonstrating that producing power on a downhill is quite challenging.*

the same level of force no matter how hard you try. Even with your best effort, your muscles are recovering. Let's say that, as in this case, your FTP is 215 watts, and on the longer uphills you ride right at your FTP, or above it on the shorter ones (106 percent, or 230 watts); on the downhills, you might be lucky to be able to produce 120 watts. That would be roughly 55 percent of your FTP, which is Level 1, or Active Recovery pace.

Figure 11.4 illustrates the point that no matter how hard you try, it is difficult to produce wattage on a downhill. Therefore, although your pacing may be higher than FTP on the uphills, you will be able to recover on the downhills without losing any time to your competitors. With this Ironman file now in hand, we can go back to the drawing board and tweak her training so that she is better prepared for the number of hills, and also their

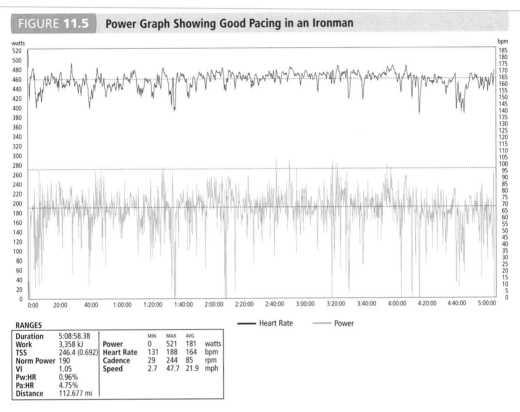

| FIGURE **11.5** | Power Graph Showing Good Pacing in an Ironman |

**RANGES**

| Duration | 5:08:58.38 | | MIN | MAX | AVG | |
|---|---|---|---|---|---|---|
| Work | 3,358 kJ | **Power** | 0 | 521 | 181 | watts |
| TSS | 246.4 (0.692) | **Heart Rate** | 131 | 188 | 164 | bpm |
| Norm Power | 190 | **Cadence** | 29 | 244 | 85 | rpm |
| VI | 1.05 | **Speed** | 2.7 | 47.7 | 21.9 | mph |
| Pw:HR | 0.96% | | | | | |
| Pa:HR | 4.75% | | | | | |
| Distance | 112.677 mi | | | | | |

— Heart Rate    — Power

*The middle gridline shows the rider's FTP at 275 W, and the bottom gridline shows his actual Normalized Power average at 190 W. Notice in the ranges bar, his IF is 0.692, which was his goal coming into the race and helped him win the 25–29 age group at the Ironman Wisconsin.*

length, and develop a finer point to her wattage goals. Practicing pacing before her trip to Hawaii will be important. She also needs to improve her FTP to have a chance of winning in her age group in Hawaii.

Now that you know what *not* to do, let's look at what *to* do. Figure 11.5 illustrates a well-paced Ironman Wisconsin race. This athlete had raced in this event the year previously and had gone too hard on the bike. He ended up walking during his run portion. Determined to come back the following year fitter, stronger, and with a smarter bike strategy, he budgeted for a 250-TSS day and therefore came into the event aiming for an IF of 0.70.

Notice how there are hardly any watts over his FTP power and that those that do go over FTP are short-lived. His Variability Index for the race was 1.05, which is very low given the incredibly hilly nature of this race, where the terrain usually causes the Variability Index to be over 1.10 without factoring in the rider's pacing. A Quadrant Analysis of his race

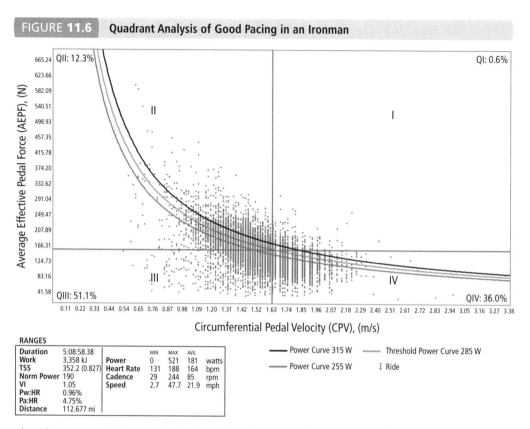

**FIGURE 11.6** | **Quadrant Analysis of Good Pacing in an Ironman**

| RANGES | | | | | | |
|---|---|---|---|---|---|---|
| Duration | 5:08:58.38 | | MIN | MAX | AVG | |
| Work | 3,358 kJ | Power | 0 | 521 | 181 | watts |
| TSS | 352.2 (0.827) | Heart Rate | 131 | 188 | 164 | bpm |
| Norm Power | 190 | Cadence | 29 | 244 | 85 | rpm |
| VI | 1.05 | Speed | 2.7 | 47.7 | 21.9 | mph |
| Pw:HR | 0.96% | | | | | |
| Pa:HR | 4.75% | | | | | |
| Distance | 112.677 mi | | | | | |

*The rider spent over 51 percent in Quadrant III and 36 percent in Quadrant IV. This really demonstrates the importance of how you create the watts.*

(see Figures 11.6) shows over 51 percent in Quadrant III and 36 percent in Quadrant IV, confirming his very low-force effort on the pedals, which allowed him to conserve precious glycogen for his run. He said, "While I wasn't scared of the bike and going too hard on it, I definitely was super careful this year not to push a big gear and hold fast to my wattage ceiling of 200 watts. My FTP was 20 watts higher than last year, so I knew I could go a bit faster, but I also knew that I had to pedal smoother this year. Last year, I really blew it by pushing too big of a gear and attacking the hills, and that sapped me for the run."

Another great way to confirm that he spent the correct amount of time in his training levels would be to check the power distribution chart by training level (see Figure 11.7). This chart displays the amount of time he spent in each of the training levels, as discussed extensively in Chapter 10. This athlete had had some big training sessions, but he excelled in this race largely because of his excellent pacing strategy, smooth pedaling, and smart use of the power meter. He won his age group pretty easily after setting a personal record on

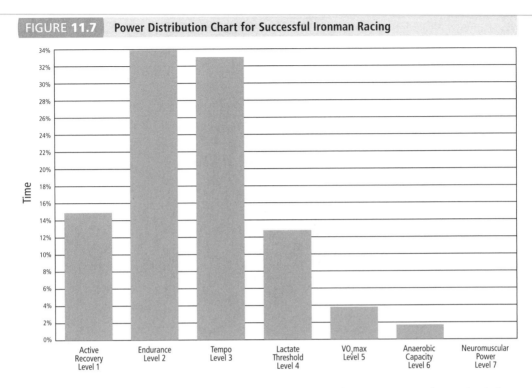

**FIGURE 11.7**  Power Distribution Chart for Successful Ironman Racing

*The power distribution chart by training level illustrates the amount of time spent in Levels 2 and 3 during a successful Ironman-distance triathlon event.*

the run leg, passing more than twenty competitors who had "great bike splits," and easily secured a slot for Hawaii.

## TIMING YOUR FITNESS PEAK

Coordinating a peak of fitness for your event is a great use of the power meter for a triathlete. One exciting aspect of triathlon is that you can record the data from both your bike ride and your run. Pace (minutes per mile) is very similar to power on the bike.

Dr. Stephen McGregor of Eastern Michigan University has developed "Running Training Stress Score" (rTSS) to quantify the training stress from runs. Based on coauthor Andrew Coggan's work on TSS, rTSS has become a common method for measuring training stress in the running world. Instead of using the one-hour scale used in TSS for cycling, Stephen took the approach of trying to create a level playing field, so that 100 TSS points on the bike would be the same amount of training stress as 100 points on the run. Since running has the additional musculoskeletal structural risk that comes from pounding your feet on the pavement (the additional gravitational forces of the weight of the body falling to the earth on each foot strike), an hour at functional threshold pace (FTp)—note the use

FIGURE **11.8**    **Performance Manager Chart for Cycling, Year 1**

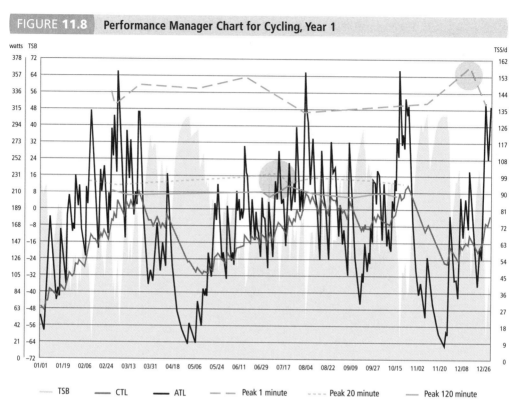

*The athlete's best efforts on the bike were at 368 W for peak 1-minute power, 235 W for peak 20-minute power, and 217 W for peak 120-minute power.*

of the lowercase "p" to denote pace instead of power) on the run would be more training stress than an hour on the bicycle, and consequently more recovery time would be required. Therefore, roughly 45 minutes of running at FTp, or a flat-out effort for 15 kilometers, would be equivalent to 1 hour at FTP on the bicycle.

Understanding the impact of TSS on cycling and running makes a huge difference in how much training a triathlete can handle and helps the athlete predict his or her perfect taper for a triathlon. In TrainingPeaks WKO+ Software, it's possible to input your data from your GPS device on your runs, and also power data from your bicycle rides, and then view the corresponding charts and graphs associated with each. Though discussing all of these graphs and charts is beyond the scope of this chapter, we would like to give you a case study on the Performance Manager Chart and provide some insight on how to use it for creating the right taper and the corresponding fitness peak for your upcoming triathlon.

The Performance Manager Charts shown in Figures 11.8, 11.9, and 11.10 belong to an age-group athlete who races primarily in Ironman-distance events. She is fortunate enough to be able to train nearly full-time, and she has been doing triathlons for many years. Highly

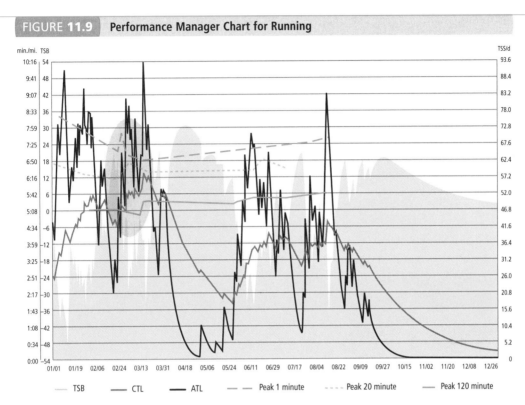

FIGURE **11.9**    **Performance Manager Chart for Running**

*This rider's best runs of the year all occurred leading up to her Ironman-distance event, giving her good evidence that she was "on form" for her main event of the season.*

dedicated to data, she also uses a power meter and a GPS device on nearly every workout, including sticking it in her swim cap on some open-water swims. With this vast repository of data, we were able to analyze each of her seasons since 2003, and we learned many things about what makes her tick.

As you read in previous chapters, the Performance Manager Chart can be a very useful tool in planning for a taper or peak of fitness. The first thing we needed to examine was the data from her previous year. We figured out what her best rides were and correlated that information with the Training Stress Balance (TSB), Chronic Training Load (CTL), and Acute Training Load (ATL). In this way we could determine the exact training load needed to create her best fitness and what her TSB is when she is riding and running at her best. As a triathlete, you will need to make three Performance Manager Charts inside the TrainingPeaks WKO+ Software: a PMC just for cycling, a PMC just for running, and then a combination PMC to include both running and cycling. This will allow you to get a better understanding of which workouts in which sports give you the best results in peak fitness; which workouts allow you to experience your highest level of training stress; where during the training year you experience your highest level of training stress; and finally, which sport contributes the most to the overall picture for you as a percentage of training stress.

In Figure 11.8 we see this athlete's cycling chart. We have added three additional sets of data to this chart in order to show her "bests." These mean maximal power numbers represent her 1-minute, 20-minute, and 120-minute Normalized Power and can be used to determine when her fitness and endurance were the highest. We like looking at the 1-minute power number even though it isn't a key factor in triathlon, because it gives us a picture of what was happening when she was the most rested and her anaerobic capacity was at its peak. This is useful in determining optimal training load; many times you will see a best 1-minute value at the same time you see a best 20-minute or 60-minute value. This would indicate that both the aerobic and anaerobic systems are at their maximum.

We also see in the chart that she had a peak 1-minute result on December 14 after a huge rest period, a peak 20-minute result on July 12, and a peak 120-minute result on July 20. The events that she was attempting to peak for were the Ironman Arizona (early April), the Ironman Wisconsin (early September), and the Ironman Hawaii (mid-October). Her peaks

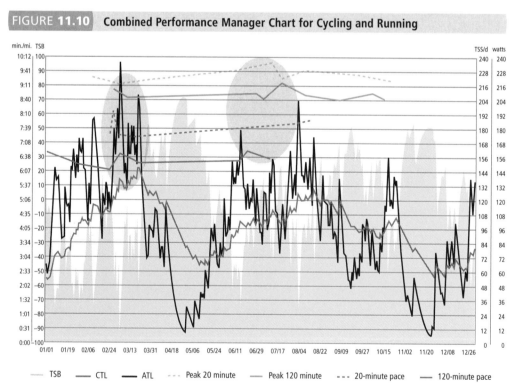

**FIGURE 11.10**    **Combined Performance Manager Chart for Cycling and Running**

*The two shorter gray lines represent pace, and the two orange lines represent power. All of this rider's personal bests for pace and power occurred during the lead-up to her peak events, but it's possible that she was "on form" too soon. When that happens, it can be difficult to maintain form for the goal event.*

therefore don't really correspond with her races in a way that you might be accustomed to seeing. Usually we see peak efforts on the days that the athlete wanted them, typically a race. However, an Ironman is more about endurance than about producing the highest wattage for 20 minutes. You cannot determine an Ironman triathlete's effort on the day of the event based on the 1-minute, 20-minute, and 120-minute values. So, even though we look at these numbers to get an idea of how the athlete's fitness changes throughout the season, the important thing to understand is what the athlete's TSB was, is, or will be on race day.

A high positive TSB would mean the athlete is too fresh and has lost fitness, and a negative TSB could mean the athlete will be too fatigued to perform well. So, for an Ironman triathlete, it is important to keep close tabs on the TSB metric. In Figure 11.8 it appears that the athlete peaked at the wrong times for her goal races. She was likely very close to her peak, as she had one of her best 20-minute wattages the week before her event in Arizona, but it was her third best of the year. Although it is possible to hold a peak for six to eight weeks, it's not advisable to attempt to do this; had she cracked out some big numbers two weeks before this event, we would be more confident that she would have hit her peak at just the right time. Though this example does not show an athlete successfully hitting her peak, it does show just how hard it is for even a very competitive athlete to peak at the right times. Given that there are three sports involved, it's not an easy thing to do even for the best in the business.

The triathlete must look at the PMC for running as well as for cycling. Fortunately, our triathlete in this example used her Garmin GPS for each of her runs leading up to Ironman Wisconsin and we have a good dataset to review.

When we examine her running chart (Figure 11.9), we see that she did a much better job of peaking for the run in April than for the run in August, as she had four of her ten best runs of the year all within fifteen days of the Ironman Arizona event. However, she did not have too many personal best runs for 20 minutes or 120 minutes until August, and it's possible that she then was close to a good run time for Ironman Wisconsin, but it's hard to be sure. One thing that reviewing the PMC for running has shown us, though, is that it's possible to peak for one event and not peak for another even though you are simultaneously training for both. Of course, the ideal is to merge these two peaks of fitness so that you will bike and run as fast as you ever have, but it's not always that easy.

Now that we have looked at both Performance Manager Charts separately, let's combine them to see how each sport impacted the big picture. Which sport contributed the most training stress? Was there a pattern to her fitness that we couldn't see separately? Did the combination of training stresses really impact her negatively?

From the screen shot shown in Figure 11.10, we begin to see a pattern in her personal bests for power and running pace. These occurred predominantly after her rest weeks during her hard training phases in the buildup to peak events. Nearly all of her bests happened right after her normal rest weeks during a hard week of training. This is very interesting for a couple of reasons. First, it could mean that this athlete keeps a relatively high load of fitness throughout the year and does not need much focused training to actually get into peak shape. Second, an Ironman event is largely endurance based, and it's very possible to have peak fitness for 20 minutes or 120 minutes but at the same time not have the requisite endurance fitness needed to complete an Ironman-length event. So, again, what the PMC doesn't tell us is important to understand and recognize.

If we were coaching this athlete, we would recommend plenty of endurance work for a long lead-up to the event, followed by four hard weeks of intensity, some rest, and then a week of endurance and intensity right before the Ironman event. This way, she could avoid peaking too early and build the needed aerobic fitness. With a high load of training stress right before the event, and with just enough rest, she would have both endurance and fitness on race day.

One last thought, and one that should be obvious here: We are not tracking the swimming part of tri training here, but this also plays a role in peaking and in cumulative training stress. Unfortunately, we don't have a good way to track this training stress yet, but we hope that in the future we'll be able to better account for this additional sport.

---

We have looked at many different aspects of triathlon in this chapter, and it's clear that a power meter can play a very large role in the success of a triathlete. Whether you are learning how to pace an Olympic-distance event, making sure you can create watts correctly in an Ironman, or coordinating a peak, a power meter and the data it provides are essential to a serious triathlete. By no means is this chapter definitive, and much still remains to be discovered and said about the world of triathlon and using a power meter, but we hope that this has given you a nice start to creating a successful race for yourself.

*For more workouts for triathletes, see TrainingPeaks.com.*

# Racing Faster with a Power Meter

**12**

*In bike racing, awards aren't given* to those who can produce the greatest number of watts per kilogram; they are given to those who finish first. It is exciting to think that more and more cyclists may be using power meters to help coordinate their racing strategy, their nutritional intake, and their pacing. Power meters can also serve as a post-race analysis tool and enable a racer to communicate more effectively with a coach about the race experience. Indeed, the data that you get from racing with your power meter are some of the most valuable data you will collect.

For starters, racing with your power meter is a great way to help pace yourself during very demanding times of the race. When you are riding in the breakaway, how do you know whether you should pull or just "sit on" (that is, draft behind the rider in front of you and never help in the workload)? How hard should you pull? If you pull too hard, you risk getting dropped, but if you don't pull hard enough, the peloton will inevitably catch your break. A power meter is a great pacing tool for any mass-start racing event or time trial. Second, racing with a power meter is a great way to define the physiological demands of the event. Just by capturing the data with your power meter while competing, you will begin to understand what it takes to ride in the peloton, to escape from the peloton, and even to win the race. Finally, by reviewing the data after the race, you will be able to better prepare yourself for your next race and for next year's racing season.

In the previous chapter we analyzed power-meter data from triathlon racing to consider how to plan a peak performance in not one, but three sports. In this chapter, we will take a look at power-meter files from different races and events and tell the stories behind them so that you can begin to understand how power meters can be used to achieve success. In fact, your own power-meter data are incomplete without the "story" behind each ride, so it's important for you to take a couple of minutes after each race to write the story of your ride in your ride diary. It does not need to be a dissertation, but it should contain the key points of your ride, any significant areas to review, and explanations of important moments of the race that you might want to have for future reference.

## PACING: THE SKILL WE NEVER TALK ABOUT

Pacing in cycling is probably one of the most overlooked areas for improvement. We are much too concerned with that latest carbon-fiber widget or the newest aero helmet to consider that if we don't have our pacing strategy dialed in, and possess an ability to "meter" out power smoothly, then that new aero helmet isn't going to do any good. Pacing your effort is definitely a learned skill. Yes, some people will be able to do it naturally, but they are the minority. In cycling, many races (and not just time trials) are lost because of poor pacing skills! Pacing plays such a large role in the sport that every racer needs to make it a priority. If you have not practiced your pacing skills, or if you do not think pacing is that big of a deal, think again. In this section we'll give you some examples of how important pacing is to success in cycling and how you can use your power meter to improve in this area.

How many times have you been out on a long group ride with your friends and felt great in the beginning, and as a consequence you hammered out the first 40 miles, only to fall to pieces in the last 20 miles? Meanwhile, another rider in the group (whom you consider not as strong as you) comes on stronger and stronger. All of a sudden, you are struggling, this other rider is driving the pace, and you are desperately hanging on. Is this rider really fitter than you? Or did he just pace himself better?

The importance of pacing may be most obvious in a century ride. Many newbies drive their pace high in the first 40–50 miles only to finish in 10 hours, after stopping at each rest stop in the last 50 miles and being reduced to 10 miles an hour. They used up all their energy in the first part of the ride.

The stakes are higher in stage races, such as the Tour de France, but the importance of pacing is the same. Are riders rewarded significantly for going off the front at the beginning of a stage? No—a rider taking this strategy would be more likely to get caught with 40 km to go and lose by 10 minutes. In fact, the winner of the Tour de France never undertakes that strategy. What about the Tour as a whole? Have you ever noticed that the riders who rip through the first five to eight stages are not the same ones who are in the top ten after Stage 8? Usually these riders have expended too much energy in the first third of the overall race, and in the latter third, they are in jeopardy of not finishing.

But pacing is important for racers at all levels, not just for the ones who make it to the Tour de France. And it is important for short events as well as long events. If you push yourself too hard in the beginning of a breakaway, for example, then you'll either "drop yourself" or the break will be caught because you and your companions cannot maintain your initial speedy pace. What about pacing for a pursuit on the track? Or even for an event lasting less than 4 minutes? Surely, you may think, pacing becomes less important in the shorter events. However, pacing may be even more critical in shorter events than in long stage races. In the pursuit, if you start out too hard and expend all your energy on the second lap, then your power will drop off too quickly and your time will suffer. Pacing in the pursuit and even in short track events can be critical to the outcome of the event. So critical, in fact, that we would dare to say that track racers should spend the most time of all on learning correct pacing strategies.

Good pacing is also essential in triathlons, as we talked about in Chapter 11. If you overdo your effort on the bike leg, then you'll be walking the "run," and that will definitely hurt your overall time. All you have to do is go to one triathlon and observe; the participants who started too hard on the bike will be the ones slowing down in the last 5 miles of the run. In a triathlon, pacing is so critical that even 10 watts—for example, riding at 240 watts instead of 250 over an Ironman distance—can make the difference between a steady run and a walk in the final leg.

### Pacing in a Criterium

Figure 12.1 shows the "story" of a criterium race and provides an example of how to use a power meter effectively in this type of event. This is a Category II racer with a very powerful sprint and a solid fitness level. His threshold power is 350 watts, he weighs 175 pounds, and his Power Profile slopes downward to the right, the classic shape for a sprinter.

In the first part of the race, this rider's heart rate was relatively low, but you can see a major spike in power at 2 hours into the ride file (time includes the warm-up). It was at this point that the bell for a preme was rung. This rider attacked out of the field and sprinted for the preme, and he was successful. At this point, he found himself off the front solo by 20 seconds, as the field really sat up after the preme sprint. Not wanting to ride solo for the rest of the race, but at the same time recognizing the opportunity presented by this nice 20-second "leash," he pedaled just below his threshold power.

Less than a lap later, three riders bridged up to him and were really drilling it. He jumped on the back of the train and instantly started to work in the rotation. However, after a couple of pulls, he realized that he was pulling at over 500 watts; when he was in the "recovery line," he was still having to put out 400 watts. Just doing some quick math and drawing on a keen understanding of his FTP, he realized that he was going to get dropped very quickly. He reasoned (and rightly so!) that if he was just sitting in on the break and over his FTP, then his time in the break was limited. So he did what every good rider should do at a point like this: sit on! It would make no sense to continue to pull in a breakaway that

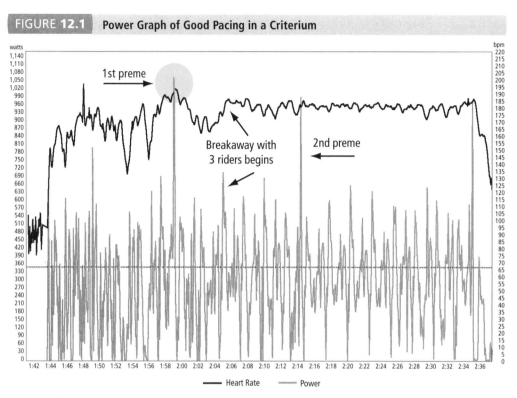

**FIGURE 12.1**   **Power Graph of Good Pacing in a Criterium**

*The rider has a major spike in power 2 hours into the ride. His first preme was at 1,065 max, averaging 913 for 13 seconds, while his second preme was at 1,007 max, averaging 711 for 11 seconds.*

was "over your head," and if you did, you would only succeed at spitting yourself out of the back of the breakaway. This rider had a hunch that the three riders were also riding above FTP and were in imminent danger of "blowing up."

Though he took some flak from the other riders for sitting on, he knew that was better than getting dropped from the breakaway at this point. The bell rang for the second preme, and like any good sprinter who has been sitting on, he blasted from the back of the trio and easily won the second preme (see Figure 12.2). After the preme, he looked around and the trio was nowhere to be found. They were rapidly falling back to the peloton. Now he was in quite a predicament: he was more than 45 seconds off the front of the field, solo, and a sprinter! He reasoned that the best he could do was to drill it on 350 watts for the rest of the race; if the field caught him, they caught him. He knew that if he tried to hold 360+ watts, he would only succeed in blowing up, and then the field would catch him for sure. In Figure 12.2, notice how much smoother his power became once he was solo off the front; his heart rate was also steady.

This was really his only viable strategy at this point. By using his power meter, he paced himself correctly to avoid overexertion, and luckily for him, he was able to hold off the charg-

| FIGURE **12.2** | **Power Graph of Maintaining Power and Pace in a Criterium** |

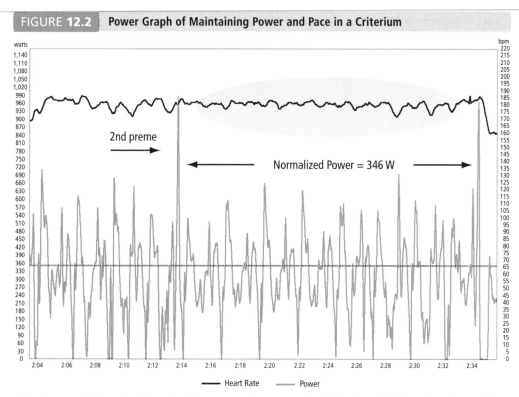

*Notice how stable the rider's heart rate becomes when he is solo off the front. His Normalized Power is just below his 350 FTP until the finish is in sight.*

ing field by about 10 seconds at the finish. Note his increase in power in the last 4–5 minutes. He knew he could hold his power output a little higher than his threshold for the last push, so he inched it up to the 360–370 range for the finish. This proved to be a crucial pacing move for his success. He was able to create a successful outcome because he used his power meter in almost every lap of the race to pace himself correctly for the phase that he was in.

## Pacing in a Time Trial

The "race of truth" is where your power meter can really shine. In a time trial you can use your power meter to regulate your watts in the first part of the event, pace yourself over hills or climbs, and figure out how much more intensity you can handle near the end of the event. There are many different kinds of time trials, from hill climbs, to dead flat, to rolling hills, and many different lengths as well. The type of time trial you are competing in will determine how you pace yourself throughout the event. Before we start to examine the different types of time trials and how each one will impact your pacing and racing strategy, let's look at a typical time trial situation.

Picture yourself 10 minutes before your time trial begins: your aero helmet is on, your shoe covers in place, the skinsuit that you barely squeezed into is already wet with the sweat from your warm-up, and you are excited, nervous, and caffeinated after drinking those shots of espresso. But you are ready to go, like a racehorse standing behind the gates at the start line, just bucking and pushing to be let go on the racecourse. As you approach the starter and your time, you take a few deep breaths to try to relax, but it's not much use, as the same amount of adrenaline is pumping through your veins as there would be if a bear was chasing you.

As the countdown approaches zero, you are even more ready to blast off the starting line. Then you hear it: "Go!" You accelerate, getting up to speed quickly, and with all that adrenaline and caffeine pumping through your veins, you can't even feel how hard you're pushing on the pedals. You look down at your speedometer and see 29 mph on it and think, "Oh, I am sooo going to win this TT. I am going to crush these people." Then you start to see your speed drop: 27 mph, 26.5 mph, 25, 23 . . . and finally you end up settling in at a rocketing fast 22.3 mph, even though you *know* you have done 24 mph for the same time period many times in training. What happened? Well, you made the same mistake that all of us have made. You started too hard. You see, in the beginning of a race, your rate of perceived exertion (RPE) does not match your actual exertion.

All the adrenaline, endorphins, caffeine, and general excitement mask the actual effort until about 4 to 5 minutes down the road, when it all catches up to you. By then it's too late to fix your pacing; you have dug yourself a nice hole in the pain cave and there is no way out. Yes, if you could stop pedaling for a couple of minutes, allow your body to recover, and then start over at a much more reasonable pace, maybe you'd have a chance of doing better—but of course that's impossible, because in a race you have only one shot at the start. You might recover, but your finish time cannot be saved.

The importance of pacing is summed up by the second rule of time trialing: "Don't start too hard, don't start too hard, don't start too hard." (The number one rule in time trialing is: "Get to your start time ON time.") If you start too hard in your time trial, it's highly likely that you will ride a slower time trial than if you had started off pacing yourself a bit more realistically. And this is where a power meter can really help. Your power meter doesn't lie.

When your power meter says you are doing 800 watts off the starting ramp and down the first 300 meters, it's not telling you that to make you feel good; it's telling you that because you are putting out 800 watts. There is no reason to go that hard in the start of a time trial. If your goal wattage is 250 watts for the time trial, then use the first 15 to 30 seconds to "get up to speed," and then nail your wattage at 250 to 260 for the rest of the time trial. Hold it there as best you can. This will allow you to pace your effort and average 24 mph for the entire TT, and not 22.3 mph. Begin to push a little harder in those last 5 minutes to finish strong, and then you can go as hard as you can on the finish line.

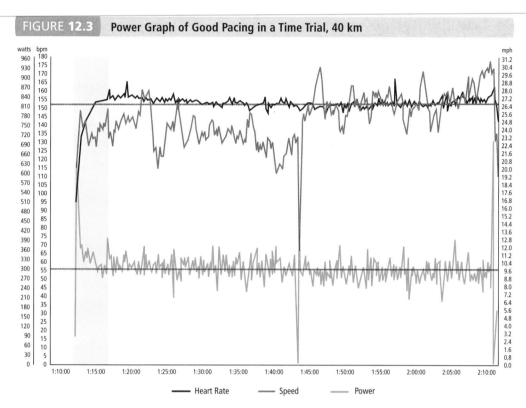

FIGURE **12.3**    **Power Graph of Good Pacing in a Time Trial, 40 km**

───── Heart Rate      ───── Speed      ───── Power

*The first 5 minutes were pivotal in establishing good pacing. Notice how heart rate slowly climbs to threshold, but power quickly settles at the rider's FTP.*

Figure 12.3 illustrates how one rider held his pace above threshold for just a few minutes before settling into a rhythm at his FTP. Notice how long it took for his heart rate to come up to his threshold heart rate—nearly 5 minutes, which indicates that he put out a good, regulated effort in the beginning of the time trial.

Correctly pacing yourself in the beginning of the time trial has a lot to do with the length of the time trial. If your time trial is a 40 km, as shown in the example above, then you should probably hold back a little for the first 5 minutes of the event. If it's shorter— such as a 10-miler—then you can't afford to hold back so much; you could still hold back for the first 2 minutes of the effort, however. And if you are doing a 4 km pursuit, there is almost no holding back; it's just a matter of how much you can hold on to at the end of the effort. In general, the shorter the event, the less you hold back.

But in addition to using your power meter to start correctly in a time trial, you can use it to pace yourself correctly during the rest of the effort. What's the ideal pace for a flat time trial or for a rolling time trial, and what about those downhills: how do you pace them? The impact of wind is another issue to consider.

## Flat Time Trials

First, let's tackle a flat time trial that doesn't have any wind, and make this our "control," so to speak, as well. This is where the pacing strategy is the simplest: ride at your FTP until there's only 3 to 5 minutes to go, and then bring that pace up until you reach the finish line. This "iso-power" strategy is always the default "go-to" strategy for any time trial: ride at your FTP, making it your goal to be as smooth and consistent as you possibly can be.

That said, there can be times when variable pacing might be beneficial, and though variable pacing is a very complicated subject—and this section is far too short to go into depth on the topic—there are some considerations you might want to make. If we introduce a headwind, for example, on the "out" leg of this flat time trial, it might be a good idea to change your pacing. When there is a headwind, there is also a tailwind, and when there is a tailwind, it has the effect of normalizing some of the fitness differences among riders. You might look down at your speedometer, see 32 mph, and think, "Wow, I am going to win this TT"; then you might relax a bit instead of focusing on what your strategy should be and working accordingly. As it turns out, though, because of the tailwind, everyone else is also going 32 mph, or very close to it, no matter what their FTP is.

In a tailwind, it's very difficult to produce watts even at your FTP. This is because (1) your gearing is too small and you can't spin the gear fast enough, or (2) you may not be accustomed to producing high power when traveling so rapidly. The net effect is that someone with an FTP of 340 watts can maybe put out 320 watts and rides at a speed of 32.5 mph in the tailwind, and a cyclist with an FTP of 320 watts can only put out about 300 watts in the tailwind and rides at an average speed of 32.1 mph. In a 40 km TT, this small speed difference for 20 km will result in the faster rider gaining only 17 seconds over the slower rider.

On the headwind section of the course, the rider with 340 watts can ride at 22 mph for the entire 20 km, and the rider with 320 watts averages only 20.5 mph for the same section. This gives the rider with 340 watts at FTP a 194-second advantage on that portion of the course. This shows that, all other things being equal, the time trial could be won in the headwind.

## Hilly Time Trials

In a time trial with a major hill, rolling hills, or perhaps a couple of significant but relatively short hills, there are other pacing strategies to use. It all depends on the kind of hills you will be encountering, however. What about a short, steep hill or a long, more gradual one? How about hills that plateau versus hills that have equal downhills on the other side?

First, let's think about how to pace yourself on a hill with an equal downhill on the other side of it. In this scenario, you can afford to push a little harder on the uphill section because you will get a chance to recover on the downhill. How much harder than FTP you pedal depends on the length and grade of the hill. For a hill that is less than 1 minute long and very steep, you can pedal much harder than you could for a hill that was as long as 5 minutes, yet more gradual. The reason is that a longer effort on the uphill will also take longer to recover from on the downhill, whereas a short, hard burst of power will create a quick burn in the legs, but also allow for a quick recovery.

You are riding at the absolute limit when you hit a hill, so be careful about how much harder you go over your FTP; it could also mean the end of your nice, consistent effort if you blow up spectacularly at the top of the hill. If you are unsure about how hard to go on a hill, think about power training levels: if it's a 3-minute hill, for example, then you know you can hold 115 percent of your FTP for that amount of time without cracking when you are fresh, so you could knock off, say, 5 to 10 percent of that and try for 105 percent of FTP. This strategy gives you a good place to start with your pacing, but it requires you to thoroughly understand the power training levels explained in earlier chapters.

On hills that have corresponding downhills, you can push a touch harder than you would in a flat time trial, but when you have a hill that flattens out at the top, or plateaus, then you have to be very careful to maintain FTP or just above it on the uphill portion. As soon as you crest the hill, you will want to get back on the gas and get back up to speed. The sooner you can do that, the better your time will be. These types of hills really throw some racers off; they hammer up the hill only to wear themselves out by the time they get to the top, and then they have to struggle to get back to speed. Make sure you meter out your effort on these kinds of hills. It's fine to be just at FTP on the hill. Remember: you won't have any time to recover afterward, and any time spent below FTP after the crest of the hill and on the flat will be time you are giving away to your competition.

Pacing in a time trial with your power meter gives you a definite advantage. You can regulate your effort in relation to the terrain, conditions, and length of the course, and you can pace yourself for certain sections within a course. At the start of a time trial, your RPE is not telling you the actual exertion rate, and you need to rely on your power meter to make sure you don't start too hard. Along with using our guidelines and tips, test pacing strategies in practice time trials over different types of courses, using your power meter to help you find the quickest time.

## COMPARING THE DEMANDS OF RACING AND TRAINING

Another way to improve your racing performance is to look at the demands of the events that you want to enter and train accordingly. Defining the specific demands of your event with power-meter data from the course itself is an excellent way to determine how you need to train. For example, if you know that you will have to do 20 laps of a criterium course, and that each lap has a 20-second hill on it, then you can train by doing 20 hill repeats of 20 seconds each. You can also look at the Quadrant Analysis chart of a race and compare this with a typical day of training. If you look at the number of hills or accelerations that you might have to produce, but do not take account of the neuromuscular demands, then you could be missing a very critical component.

Be sure also to think about how many kilojoules of energy you will need to produce for the event. If you are not aware of this factor during a race, you may begin to tire prematurely. The key thing here is to mark this point on your power meter with the beginning of an interval (many times you can still find this point in your data after you have downloaded the data). When you download racing data, you can see how many kilojoules of energy and TSS points you scored before you became tired, and in this way you can determine how many calories you need to consume during your next race. For example, if you did a 2.5-hour race and consumed 500 kcals during the race, but then downloaded your race file and found out that you expended 2,000 kJ, or roughly 2,200 kcals, you might plan to eat more during your next race or load up on carbs in the days leading up to the race.

In this section we will look at a typical training file from a mountain-bike rider, then a race file from the same cyclist, and use the Quadrant Analysis spreadsheet in order to compare the actual neuromuscular demands of the race with the athlete's training.

**FIGURE 12.4    Mountain Biker's Training File**

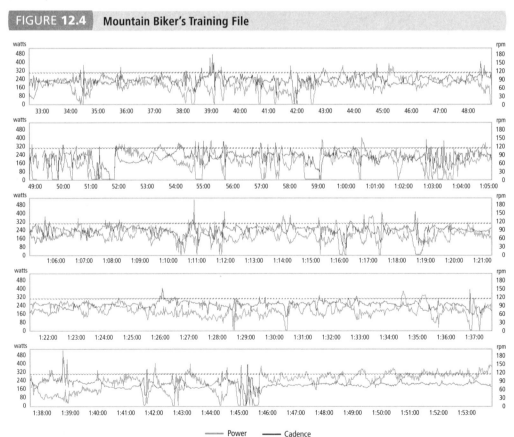

Figure 12.4 shows the graph of the athlete's training ride, and it's easy to see that there is a lot of power fluctuation. He was definitely riding near his threshold for a good portion of the time, and slightly above it at other times. In the words of the athlete, "I felt good today! I was kind of dreading the workout Hunter slated for me because I was feeling tired and weary. Wow, I felt good power and excellent ability to maintain it. After the up tempo at Bob's place, we cruised over to the steepest hill you have ever seen, called Upper Springs. I ramped it up to 350 watts for the beginning 2 minutes, and then it got steep—in fact, so steep that the 32:27 I was riding was not enough gear! Ouch! The climb pitched to over 20 percent in spots and I was going over power just trying to keep the wheels turning. I really tried to focus on low cadence and high force in this workout, but I'm not sure if I got enough in."

Let's compare that with his race file around the same time period (Figure 12.5). Immediately, you can see how much more stochastic the race was than the training ride. In the race, there are fluctuations in cadence and wattage; the cadence and power lines in the training file look almost smooth by comparison. The comment from the athlete was "Awesome day!! 80 degrees and clear skies at Flat Rock Ranch in Texas. Way fun race! More open Texas hill

FIGURE **12.5**    **Mountain Biker's Race File**

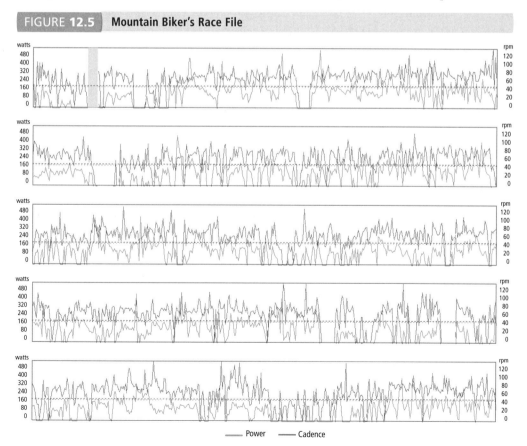

Power — Cadence

country like I had seen on TV. Hard race with lots of rocks up on top of the hills, and sweet single track. More technical than I would have thought for Texas. Good win and was still feeling strong at the end despite having drilled it for the whole race."

Now let's compare the same two power files using Quadrant Analysis and see if the athlete is training in the correct quadrants to specifically address the neuromuscular system (Figures 12.6 and 12.7). To review: Quadrant I is high force and high cadence; Quadrant II is high force and low cadence; Quadrant III is low force and low cadence; and Quadrant IV is low force and high cadence. Overall, it is easy to see that in the training ride, this mountain biker's goal was to do plenty of subthreshold work, and from that perspective it was a great success. Almost all of the points fall just below the line representing functional threshold power. However, the majority of his time pedaling fell into Quadrants III and IV, which are relatively low force but require both fast and slow cadence. Thus, although this training ride accomplished the goal of stressing his metabolic fitness, it did not place much emphasis on the use of his Type II, or fast-twitch, muscle fibers.

It is apparent that the race put a much larger demand on multiple neuromuscular capabilities than the training ride did. The "shotgun blast" of the race indicates a high degree of variability in the neuromuscular and cardiovascular capacities needed to win the event. Although the majority of the ride was in Quadrant III, it also contained quite a lot of effort in Quadrant II. This makes sense because in a mountain-bike race, many times you have to push hard and fast in order to get over obstacles, maintain traction on steep slopes, and keep your momentum going. This distribution also shows approximately how much effort the rider spent over his threshold power and exactly how his muscles were working at those times. In this race, when he was riding over his threshold, it appears that he was spending a majority of his time in Quadrant II, which gives us further insight into the demands of the event.

What should this athlete do in order to train more specifically for the races that he enters? For starters, he needs to develop some workouts that will focus on Quadrant II. He needs to be better prepared, come race time, to produce a large amount of force at a low cadence, and with a high degree of cardiovascular strain. Second, he should introduce more variability into his ride to be ready for the speed and force changes required by mountain biking. Perhaps the easiest and most logical way to accomplish this would be to do more racelike efforts while riding off-road—for example, he could perform time trials on a technically challenging loop. Alternatively, he could do specific interval workouts—such as microbursts using a large gear, or perhaps motorpacing—to achieve this goal.

## GAUGING AEROBIC AND ANAEROBIC ENERGY PRODUCTION

There are other numerous opportunities for a rider to use data from a power meter to, quite simply, go faster than ever before. Let's consider the individual pursuit—one of track

| FIGURE **12.6** | Quadrant Analysis of a Mountain Biker's Training File |

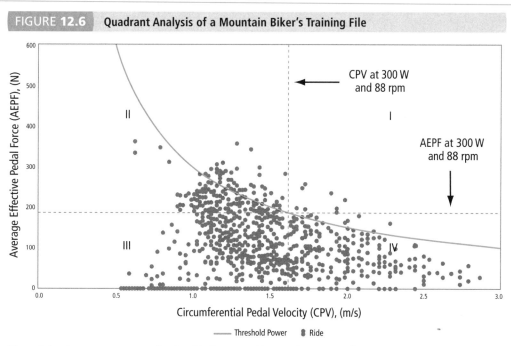

*Most of the data were spent under the rider's FTP and in Quadrants III and IV.*

| FIGURE **12.7** | Quadrant Analysis of a Mountain Biker's Race File |

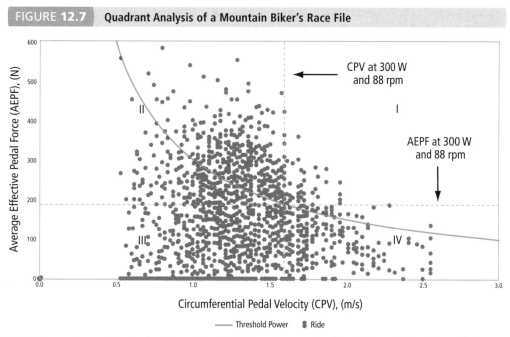

*The rider spent more time in Quadrants II and III during the race than in training and also plenty of time above threshold. Note the much wider distribution of data in this file than in the training file. This indicates that the race required a much higher degree of power fluctuation.*

## On-Site Post-Event Performance Analysis

Using the information from your power meter for immediate on-site analysis of your performance can be very helpful because it can allow you and your coach to make quick adjustments in your pacing or racing strategy, or even in your gearing combination. At a velodrome track event, for example, you might be competing in eight different races, and in those events, you would have heats, qualifiers, and then a final. You could have up to 30 minutes of downtime between events, leaving you with ample time to download your data and make adjustments before your next race.

From training and testing with a power meter, you would know what cadence you generally use in your best performances. But you might discover when looking at your data that your cadence in the first qualifying round was faster. The track could be quicker than you anticipated, or the air density could be radically different from what you are used to in your training. With the power-meter data, you would know immediately how to adjust your pace and your gearing.

cycling's classic races. At first glance, it may seem to be a fairly straightforward event, as it is just a short time trial contested on a banked velodrome (4 km for men, 3 km for women). In reality, however, this appearance of simplicity is deceptive, as the margin of victory in such races is often very small, and there are numerous physical and physiological factors that can have a significant influence on a rider's performance.

Although it is possible for a rider to learn how to pace himself or herself correctly using only lap times for feedback, post-race analysis of power-meter files can speed up the feedback process by providing the rider with objective data regarding the distribution of his or her effort throughout the race. A power meter can also be used to optimize the rider's position from an aerodynamic perspective, which is crucial, since approximately 85 percent of a pursuiter's power output is used to overcome wind resistance (which we'll explore in more detail later in this chapter). (The other sources of resistance—inertia, rolling resistance, and drivetrain and bearing friction, account for approximately 8 percent, 5 percent, and 2 percent, respectively.)

Of course, data from a power meter can also be used to determine whether the rider's training program is having the desired effect—that is, whether his or her ability to produce power for various periods of time, especially over the 3.5- to 5-minute duration of a pursuit, is indeed increasing. Just as important, however, is that power-meter data can be used to determine *how* a particular rider produces his or her power—the individual's relative reliance on aerobic and anaerobic energy metabolism during this predominantly, but by no means exclusively, aerobic event. In turn, this information can be used to fine-tune the rider's training program by consolidating strengths while improving on weaknesses.

Consider the two riders whose data are shown in Figure 12.8. Rider A, on the one hand, is a male masters racer who excels in road races and longer time trials but has a very poor sprint and a limited anaerobic capacity. Rider B, on the other hand, is an elite female track cyclist whose specialty is the pursuit. As shown in the figure, their average powers during a pursuit are quite comparable, as are their personal best performances—3-kilometer times on the same outdoor concrete 333.3-meter velodrome. (Although Rider A does not produce quite as much power as Rider B, Rider A is a bit more aerodynamic and thus goes slightly faster.) However, how they go about generating their power and thus achieving their performances *is* significantly different. Specifically, Rider A apparently produces more of his power via aerobic metabolism, whereas Rider B relies more on her superior anaerobic capacity.

These differences in power can be determined by comparing the areas under the lines shown in the figure: The lower, smoother lines in the two graphs represent the riders' theoretical maximal aerobic power output, as calculated from laboratory-determined $VO_2$max and efficiency, whereas the more jagged lines represent their total power output as directly measured using an SRM crank during their pursuit. For Rider A, the area under the power-meter line represents 80 percent of the total area (i.e., 80 percent of the *work* was performed aerobically), which leaves only 20 percent unaccounted for, meaning that it must have come

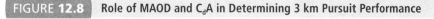

**FIGURE 12.8**  **Role of MAOD and C$_d$A in Determining 3 km Pursuit Performance**

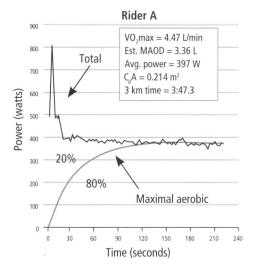
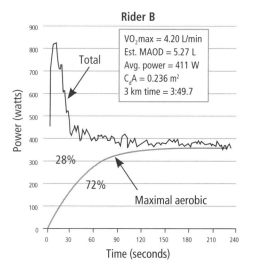

*$VO_2$max = Maximal oxygen uptake*
*MAOD = Maximal accumulated oxygen deficit*
*C$_d$A = Aerodynamic Drag Characteristics*

from anaerobic sources (i.e., phosphate creatine/adenosine triphosphate, or PCr/ATP, and lactate production). Expressed in terms of the amount of additional oxygen that would have to be taken up to generate this energy aerobically, this anaerobic energy production is equivalent to 3.36 liters (L) of $O_2$—in other words, Rider A's maximal accumulated $O_2$ deficit (MAOD) can be estimated at 3.36 L.

In contrast, for Rider B the area under the maximal aerobic power output line represents only 72 percent of the total area (at most she could have generated only 72 percent of her energy aerobically). The remaining 28 percent therefore must have come from anaerobic sources, leading to an estimated MAOD of 5.27 L, which is significantly greater than that of Rider A. Or, to put it another way: despite the fact that her $VO_2$max is 4 percent lower (4.20 L/min versus 4.47 L/min), Rider B is able to produce 4 percent more power (411 watts versus 397 watts) during a 3 km pursuit because her anaerobic capacity is much larger. (This difference is even more striking when you consider that, on average, anaerobic capacity is generally lower in women than in men, even when expressed relative to muscle mass.) If Rider B were as aerodynamic as Rider A, the additional power that she could generate anaerobically would enable her to complete the 3 km in approximately 3 minutes and 43 seconds, or approximately 4 seconds faster than Rider A.

Given the differences between Riders A and B in how they generate their power during a pursuit, we can conclude that even though they might be training for the same event, their training programs should be different. Specifically, since Rider A's weakness as a pursuiter is his anaerobic capacity, his performance would likely be improved the most if he focused on very high-intensity (i.e., Level 6) intervals, especially during the run-up to his goal event (for example, district championships). Rider B, by contrast, has a tremendous anaerobic capacity that seems unlikely to improve dramatically with additional high-intensity training. Thus, she should place a greater emphasis on improving her $VO_2$max (and also her functional threshold power, since this is an important determinant of muscle fatigue resistance, even during maximal/supra-maximal exercise) via training at Levels 3, 4, and 5 (especially in the off-season and preseason periods). Indeed, after making precisely this change in her training program, Rider B improved her personal-best time by more than 4 seconds and won the national championship in the pursuit.

In this example we used laboratory-based measurements of $VO_2$max and efficiency to calculate the riders' maximal aerobic power output, but you could just as easily use the quasi-plateau in power that occurs after the 1.5- to 2.5-minute mark of a well-paced pursuit. As shown in the figure, this is essentially the rider's power at $VO_2$max, as would be expected, since anaerobic capacity (as measured by maximal accumulated oxygen deficit) is generally completely used up after that period of time. So from that point, further exercise can only be performed on a "pay as you go" basis (i.e., 100 percent aerobically).

## AERODYNAMIC TESTING WITH A POWER METER

If you are a road time trialist, track racer (e.g., pursuiter, kilometer, or 500-meter rider), or triathlete, one of the benefits of owning a power meter is that it enables you to determine your aerodynamic drag via field testing. Indeed, with an optimal venue and careful attention to detail, it is possible to measure your effective frontal area, or $C_dA$ (i.e., the product of the dimensionless coefficient of drag, $C_d$, and frontal area, A, measured in square meters, or m²), just as precisely (albeit much less conveniently) as when using a wind tunnel. Data obtained using a power meter can therefore be used to make decisions about rider positioning or possibly even choice of equipment so as to maximize performance at any given power output—in other words, it can enable you to buy "free speed." A detailed description of how best to perform such testing is beyond the scope of this book, but in general, three different approaches may be used: the constant speed (or constant power) method, the regression method, or the "virtual elevation" method.

### *Constant Speed (or Constant Power) Method*

The simplest way to determine $C_dA$ is to have a rider perform one or more passes, or test runs, in both directions along a section of windless road (or better still, on a running track or velodrome, especially indoors) of known grade or slope (perfectly flat is ideal, but not absolutely necessary) at a constant speed while measuring the power output (or at constant power while measuring speed). The measurements should be made over a distance of at least 500 meters, and the power data should be corrected (after downloading) for any slight variations in starting and ending speed (to correct for changes in stored kinetic energy). This is most easily achieved by simply selecting as starting and ending points of each run moments when the speed was the same (and if testing on a track, select a straightaway and not a turn). If the road is not perfectly flat, the data also need to be corrected for changes in potential energy during each run. Finally, if an SRM, Quarq, or Polar power meter is used, the data also need to be corrected for the assumed efficiency of the drivetrain (since the PowerTap measures power "downstream" of the chain, the power value it provides can be considered equal to that of driving the bicycle forward).

As a first approximation, the corrected power itself can be viewed as a rough indicator of the rider's aerodynamic drag (or changes in his or her aerodynamic drag), provided that the speed, air density, and rolling resistance are constant across trials. It can be difficult to achieve precisely the same average speed during all trials. Furthermore, when testing outdoors, the environmental conditions—that is, barometric pressure, temperature, humidity, and wind—are subject to considerable change, which in turn will influence the air density and hence the power requirement. Consequently, it's best to complete all of the measurements in a rather short period of time. If this can't be done, it is necessary to record the precise environmental conditions to determine the air density and then calculate the rider's actual $C_dA$ (for example, check out the free calculators available at Tom Compton's excellent website, www.analyticcycling.com). Perhaps more importantly, when using this approach it is necessary to assume a value for the coefficient of rolling resistance, or Crr, and to accurately weigh the rider and all of his or her equipment in order to account for the power required to overcome rolling drag. This complicates interpretation of the results should different tires or wheels be used in different tests, or if the tire pressure or temperature should vary significantly (since rolling resistance varies with both tire pressure and temperature).

### Regression Method

A somewhat more complicated approach for determining $C_dA$ is to have a rider make multiple passes (six to nine) along the same type of course at a variety of speeds, ranging from perhaps 5 to 15 meters per second, or m/s (or the highest that the rider can sustain and reproduce for the required distance and duration). If the course is not level or if there may be residual wind, it may be a good idea to make an equal number of runs in each direction to try to account for, or at least detect, such effects. When the corrected steady-state power (in watts) from such trials is plotted on the Y-axis of a graph against speed on the X-axis, the relationship is well described by a curvilinear equation of the form:

$$Y = aX + bX^3$$

where a is a constant representing the rolling resistance (in newtons, N) and b is proportional to one-half times the air density (in grams per liter, or g/L) times $C_dA$.

Alternatively, this equation can be transformed into a linear equivalent by dividing the power during each trial by the speed and plotting this result on the Y-axis against the square of the speed (in $m^2/s^2$) on the X-axis. The resultant data should form a straight line, the intercept of which will again be the rolling resistance and the slope of which will again be proportional to one-half times the air density times $C_dA$. Based on the environmental conditions at the time of the testing, it is therefore possible to calculate the air density, and thus in turn, to derive the $C_dA$. Compared to the constant speed (or constant power) approach, there are two advantages to using the regression method. First, it distinguishes between changes in rolling resistance and changes in aerodynamic drag, which can be useful in equipment selection. If you seem to be faster using a particular set of wheels, for example, using the regression method will enable you to determine whether it is because they are more aerodynamic or because the tires roll better. Second, the regression method may provide a more precise estimate of $C_dA$, since the value derived is automatically based on multiple measurements.

### Robert Chung's "Virtual Elevation" Method

This approach was developed largely as a means of estimating $C_dA$ when an idealized venue such as the one described before is not readily available. Rather than placing any constraints on speed or power, as in the first two methods described above, in this method the rider simply collects speed and power data while repeatedly riding over the same stretch of road as he or she normally would. These data are then used along with the total mass and other factors to solve for the apparent, or virtual, elevation profile based on the physics of cycling, assuming reasonable starting values for $C_dA$ and Crr. The latter two parameters are then adjusted as needed to visually "level the plot," that is, to force the repeated measurements made at each point along the route to appear to be at a constant elevation.

Alternatively, more formal mathematical and statistical (rather than graphical) methods can be used to arrive at the combination of $C_dA$ and Crr that best explains such data. While this method can be applied to estimate $C_dA$ from data collected during, for example, longer time trials (as can the constant speed or power method described above), shorter out-and-back or loop courses work best, as they provide more estimates of the virtual elevation of any particular point. Because braking must be avoided (or data collected during such braking events excluded from the analysis), one particularly useful approach has been to use a "half-pipe" course—a short section of road with moderately steep hills at each end—as this eliminates, or at least minimizes, the need for braking while also providing the variation in speed required to truly "pry apart" $C_dA$ and Crr.

As indicated above, the primary advantage of this method is that the slope of the road does not have to be zero or even constant—in fact, the exact profile of the path traveled does not even need to be known (indeed, estimating course profiles from data collected using a power meter is another application of the "virtual elevation" method). In addition, because the data are utilized on a point-by-point basis rather than averaged together, it may be easier to identify anomalies due to, for example, a gust of wind or a change in rider position. However, it can sometimes be difficult to differentiate changes in $C_dA$ from changes in Crr and vice versa. While this problem can be avoided by testing under conditions where Crr can be assumed to be constant (i.e., using the same set of tires inflated to the same pressure rolling over the same surface at the same temperature while carrying the same mass), it does tend to complicate comparison of different tires or wheels, or data collected at one location with data collected at another.

### Precision in Aerodynamic Testing

Regardless of which approach is used, under ideal conditions it is possible to quantify $C_dA$ via such field testing with a coefficient of variation (i.e., reproducibility) of less than 2 percent. This is comparable to that obtained in wind-tunnel testing and approaches the limits of resolution of power meters themselves. To obtain this degree of precision, however, testing generally needs to be performed in the absence of any significant wind or automobile traffic, as a single car can disturb the air enough to affect measurements for several minutes after the car has passed.

Assuming that you can find a suitable location, you should plan to perform this field test very early in the morning, immediately after the sun has risen but before the wind starts to pick up or traffic begins to develop. It could require many days of testing to obtain the data necessary to, for example, determine the optimal aerobar height, as uncooperative weather or other conditions could make your data unusable. If you want to check the accuracy of your data, measure the reproducibility of trials by comparing your data for outbound versus inbound within a given session and comparing data across sessions.

Since it is necessary to perform such testing only when there is minimal wind, the value obtained for $C_dA$ reflects only that for when the wind is coming from straight ahead (i.e., at or near zero degrees of yaw). This is in contrast to measurements made in a wind tunnel, where it is possible to measure $C_dA$ quickly and conveniently across multiple yaw angles. This distinction is important, since the benefits of aerodynamically designed cycling equipment are usually greatest when the wind is coming from an angle rather than from straight ahead. Nonetheless, if you are a dedicated racer interested in wringing out every last drop of speed, a field test to determine $C_dA$ becomes a very useful application of a power meter.

––––––––––

When you begin to race with your power meter, you will be taking full advantage of all it has to offer. The information that you will collect while you are on the bike in a race will help you with many aspects of creating a peak performance. It will help you learn how to pace yourself efficiently whether you are in a 40 km time trial, off the front of a criterium soloing to the line, or simply drafting in the peloton. In shorter events such as track racing it is easy to make adjustments to your pacing and/or racing strategy, along with your gearing, based on your power-meter data, so that in your next heat you'll have the advantage you need to perform your best.

Using your power meter to guide your energy expenditure in a race can make the difference between standing on the podium as a champion and being just another rider in the field. As you learn more about the demands of your events and the requirements for success, you will be able to train more specifically and efficiently for each event. From knowing how to coordinate your nutrition for optimal energy conservation to understanding the neuromuscular demands of your discipline, defining the demands of your event can also make a big impact on your ability to make the winning move.

# 13

# Power for Other Disciplines: BMX, Cyclocross, Track, Ultra-Endurance

*Though more and more cyclists have begun using power meters* on the road and for mountain biking over the past few years, there are many other disciplines in cycling, and enthusiasts in all of these specialties could benefit from using power meters to train with wattage. BMX, ultra-endurance mountain biking, cyclocross, and track riding are all areas of cycling where the potential for power meters is very promising.

In any sport, a great recipe for properly utilizing a power meter is to:

1. Determine the demands of the event. Using the power meter as a recording device and just recording data and the effort that it takes to complete the event successfully is a good start.

2. Understand your strengths and weaknesses relative to the demands of the event.

3. Train for both the demands of the event and your weaknesses (as long as your weaknesses could impact the success of the event).

4. Review the results of those training sessions and compare them with data collected in races.

Keep these steps in mind as we discuss the four disciplines covered in this chapter. One goal of the chapter is to show how competitors can use a power meter effectively in a given event. For each discipline we have therefore given examples of how the power meter has been used by actual riders. Although you might not be interested in all of these disciplines, it will still be useful for you to read through the chapter, as the ideas shared can also be applied across most of the cycling disciplines.

## BMX

Bicycle Motocross, or BMX, has been around since the late 1970s, and thousands of people, kids and adults alike, now take part in these short races each year. BMX has a very high skill component, as being able to do the jumps, to navigate the berms (tight, banked curves), and to have good timing off the start gate are determining factors in a racer's success. The demands of BMX events are high, as any first-time spectator can immediately see. The sheer number of jumps, the height and angle of the berms, and the gate drop speed combine to make it a challenging sport.

When the International Olympic Committee approved BMX as an Olympic sport for the 2008 Games, Olympic hopefuls on the U.S. team were outfitted with SRM power meters. The event in Beijing was going to be held on a Super Cross (SX) course, which was very different from the tracks that BMX riders around the world were used to practicing and racing on. The SX course had a starting ramp 10 meters tall with a steep drop (a gradient of up to 53 percent!). It also contained jumps from as high as 8 meters, as well as gaps spanning between the jumps 15 meters long. This was a stark departure from standard BMX tracks, which usually have starting ramps only 3 meters tall, jumps from as high as 3 meters, and gaps no longer than 5 meters. A standard BMX track is built for all ages, from five-year-old kids to the pros, whereas the Super Cross track was built for the new BMX elite.

When first exposed to the Super Cross track, though, even some of the elite BMX racers reacted with disbelief. Many were unwilling to ride the track, citing the fact that it was so big and intimidating. Since there were no permanent Super Cross tracks in the United States, USA Cycling and the U.S. Olympic Committee built an exact replica of the Beijing track at the Olympic Training Center in Chula Vista, California. This was the only replica track in existence, and as technical coach for the 2008 Olympic team, Hunter was able to do extensive testing on it with many racers, with Dr. Stephen McGregor conducting some of the data analysis.

Before we started collecting data on the Super Cross track, we collected data on regular tracks in order to learn more about the demands of normal BMX racing and find out what the best pros in the world of BMX could do. One limitation we faced was that, because the SRM's fastest sampling rate was half a second, it was possible to miss some critical information. BMX is a sport where changes happen very rapidly, and recording at half-second intervals was not always enough. Nevertheless, we gathered some very good data over a variety of courses and conditions. We learned from the initial testing, for example, that elite BMX men can put out over 24.5 watts per kilogram (W/kg) at the initial drop of the gate, with the best women averaging over 19 W/kg on the start. This forced us to revise the Power Profiling table in Chapter 4, integrating these new records.

Elite male BMX racers produce over 20 W/kg for the entire first straightaway, with cadences averaging over 150 rpm. Clearly, the technical aspects of BMX are important, but the ability to translate sheer neuromuscular power into force on the pedals of the bike is also required for success. One thing that surprised us about the best BMXers was their ability to accelerate out of the turns with tremendous wattage and cadence. A typical exit would be over 22 W/kg for the men, with a cadence of 170–190 rpm, and the women would exit the turns at over 16 W/kg and at a cadence of 150–170 rpm. For a 175-pound male, that's 1,750 watts at 170+ rpm—an astonishing figure.

The ability to "corner start," or replicate nearly the same wattage and technical motion as if starting from the gate, was also found to be a key indicator of success—something the very top athletes selected for the Olympic team had mastered but the hopefuls had not. Each race in fact was a series of micro-bursts and micro-rests. The micro-bursts were anywhere from 2 to 5 seconds long, and the micro-rests could be from half a second to 3 seconds long (see Figure 13.1). While the micro-bursts were obviously

Power Meter on BMX Bike

done on the ground, the micro-rest periods could come while in the air over a jump or while riding over an obstacle that did not allow pedaling. These micro-rest periods, which seemed so small as to be insignificant, really weren't, as they gave the racer just enough rest to recover slightly and sprint to the next obstacle.

The data from the elite riders on the Super Cross track and the data from riders on standard BMX tracks were similar in some ways, but a few key differences did emerge. An SX track, with its large starting hill, necessitates a bigger gear, as speeds are much higher than on regular tracks. The upper limit for cadence appeared to be in the 190 rpm range, so it was important for riders to have a gear that allowed them to keep a cadence of between 140 and 180 rpm. Because of the steep starting ramp and higher speeds, an SX rider actually pedals less than a rider at a normal BMX track, and the extra momentum gained from the start hill can be carried throughout the track.

Balancing the need for a bigger gear is the need to get the "hole shot" out of the starting gate, and this priority ranked higher than we had anticipated. The start hill was composed of three distinct sections: the upper section just after the starting gate, only 4.2 meters long and with a gradient of 32 percent; the middle section, 11 meters long with a harrowing 53 percent gradient; and finally, a short "transition" at the bottom, 9 meters long, leveling off to the ground with a gradient that goes from 53 percent to 0 percent. Since the upper section

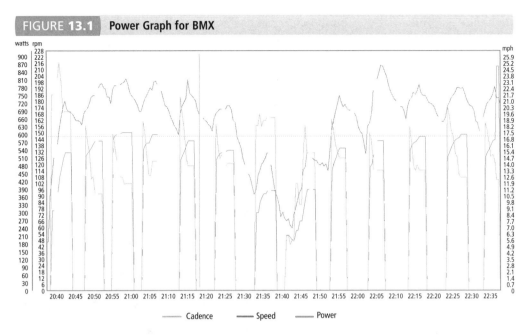

**FIGURE 13.1**  Power Graph for BMX

*Micro-bursts for BMX had to be modified to meet the demands of the event. This 2-minute graph shows 5 seconds on and 5 seconds off, making this a tough workout for a BMXer.*

includes a transition from 6 percent to 27 percent, there comes a point about two-thirds of the way down the hill where pedaling is no longer possible. This makes the initial start even more critical than at a normal track, where racers can make up for a poor start by powering down the front straight section. With this discovery, we advised one USA Olympic team member to use an easier gear than he had been using in order to get a better "hole shot," and then to use his superior leg speed to maintain that momentum throughout the rest of the track. This strategy was successful for him.

With the discoveries of the demands of BMX races in both standard BMX and SX tracks, we were able to optimize training for many racers. The gearing recommendation cited above is one example. Training specifically for the micro-rests and micro-bursts also turned out to be key (see Workout 13.A). To develop this workout, we started from the micro-burst workout outlined in Chapter 5 (see Level 7 workouts in Appendix B) but reduced the "on" and "off" time periods to 5 seconds from 15 seconds. This allowed the workout to more correctly mimic a BMX race. Doing these very intense micro-bursts for a total of 1 minute, before resting for 5 minutes, effectively prepared the athletes for their race, and in fact for even more than what might be needed. One thing that should be kept in mind as you try the workout below is that basing the workout on percentages of FTP is problematic at best, as BMXers don't ride long enough even to do an FTP test. Therefore, the percentages in the workout are a best guess.

| WORKOUT **13.A** | Micro-Burst Workout for BMX | | | |
|---|---|---|---|---|
| | **Time** | **Description** | **% of FTP** | **% of FTHR** |
| Warm-up | 20 min. | Easy riding | 76–85* | 80–90 |
| Main set | 1 min. (5 min. RI) | Micro-bursts | | N/A |
| | 5 sec. | "On" | 300–500+* | N/A |
| | 5 sec. | "Off" | 50%* | N/A |
| Cooldown | 15 min. | Easy riding | <56 | <69 |

*The FTP numbers here are only estimates since FTP isn't usually a known metric for most BMXers.*

The athletes who excel at BMX are comparable to some of the top professional track cyclists in the world (better in many cases), combining their cycling skills with the coordination of elite Olympic gymnasts. Elite BMX racers are indeed highly tuned athletes who have engaged in extremely hard, focused training, but the top racers in the sport are likely to continue to improve in the coming years as more scientific training methods are put to use—especially with the help of the power meter. As power meters designed specifically for BMX become more prevalent, such as the recently introduced G-Cog, we expect that new and exciting discoveries will be made that will continue to change the way BMX riders train and race.

## CYCLOCROSS

In recent years, cyclocross (CX) has become the fastest-growing sport in cycling in the United States, now boasting some of the largest numbers for attendance at bicycle races in any specialty throughout the country. With field limits selling out and events such as Cross-Vegas drawing more than 30,000 spectators, it's rapidly becoming *the* sport to do within the cycling community both here and in Europe.

Cyclocross brings its own set of demands, in that competitors must be able to create quick bursts of effort over small obstacles, or leap off the bicycle and run while carrying it for sections as long as 30 seconds, all the while maintaining a pace at FTP (and above) for 40 to 75 minutes. Power-meter files from CX races typically show an average of 20 to 40 watts below what the actual FTP of the athlete is, however, and there are two main reasons for this. One is that there is so much downtime when the athlete is either coasting down a technical hill or off the bike and running. The other is that many of the courses lack good traction, as they traverse mud, sandpits, and the like.

The ability to put the power to the ground skews the power down, and one has to take this into consideration when reviewing CX power files. Because of the running and coasting sections of the course, it's also hard to determine the exact muscular demands of CX. When viewed in a Quadrant Analysis plot, a CX race turns out to be largely in Quadrant II, which represents slow pedaling and higher force, but Quadrants III and IV are also heavily involved in CX (see Figure 13.2).

In some ways the power file from a CX race can resemble the power file from a criterium: stochastic power spikes, easily discernible laps, and big "race-winning" types of efforts are all common in both. Other aspects of a CX power file that are interesting are the power bursts, the amount of rest in each lap, and the overall training stress accumulated. One thing that is important to identify in a CX power file is the number of watts above FTP and the length of each of these efforts; in other words, how many "matches" the cross racer has to burn. A CX match is a little different from a match in a road race or a criterium, however, because most likely the racer is already at his or her FTP when the need to do a hard effort arises. In this case, the matches are more like bursts of flames coming up from an already raging fire! Identifying these "flames" and being aware of their intensity will allow you to train more specifically for the kind of effort that cyclocross requires. (Use the FAST FIND feature in TrainingPeaks WKO+ Software in order to help identify them. Figure 13.3 shows an example.)

After reviewing hundreds of cyclocross race and training power files, we began advising that CX racers work yet another variation of the Level 7 "Micro-Burst Workout" into their training plan (see Workout 13.B). This workout, which we call the 30-30-30 workout, involves 30 seconds at 150 percent of FTP, 30 seconds of coasting (0 percent of FTP), and 30 seconds of running. By extending the intervals to 30 seconds (instead of 15 seconds), we take the workout from Level 7 to Level 6. At 30 seconds, the anaerobic capacity system is utilized, but the neuromuscular power requirements are reduced. The 30-30-30 workout is done continuously for 10 minutes. Rest for 5 minutes between intervals, completing three to five 10-minute intervals, and then cool down.

| WORKOUT 13.B | 30-30-30 Workout for Cyclocross | | | |
|---|---|---|---|---|
| | Time | Description | % of FTP | % of FTHR |
| Warm-up | 20 min. | Easy riding | 56–75 | 69–83 |
| Main set | 3–5 × 10 min. (5 min. RI) | Micro-bursts | | |
| | 30 sec. | "On" | 150 | 90–100 |
| | 30 sec. | "Off"/coasting | 0 | 90–100 |
| | 30 sec. | Running (quick pace, but not sprinting) | N/A | 90–100 |
| Cooldown | 15 min. | Easy riding | <56 | <69 |

Rule 3 from the four steps for utilizing a power meter effectively—training to the demands of the event—is highly applicable here. The 30-30-30 workout is good training for cyclocross because it addresses the specific need for strong anaerobic capacity along with the need for highly tuned technical skills (dismounting and running with the bike and remounting smoothly). In addition, cyclocross demands a strong FTP, so the traditional Level 4 FTP workouts are important for the successful CX racer. We recommend doing four efforts at

| FIGURE **13.2** | **Quadrant Analysis of a Typical Cyclocross Race** |
|---|---|

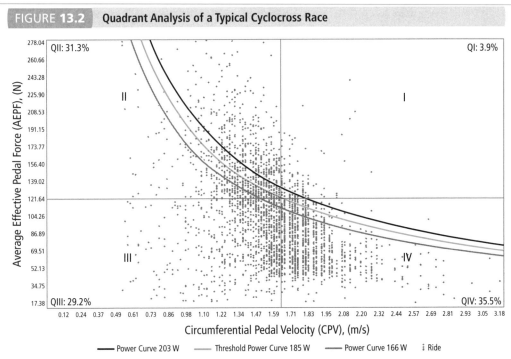

This graph shows a typical cyclocross race. Note that there are about equal amounts of work in Quadrants II, III, and IV.

| FIGURE **13.3** | **Matches Burned in a Cyclocross Race** |
|---|---|

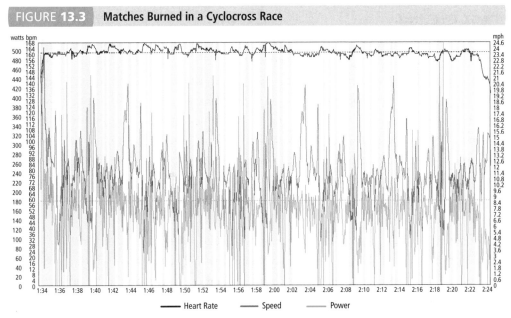

Using the FAST FIND feature in WKO+ Software, we see not only the "matches" burned, but the "flames" of a cyclocross race. A hard, sustained effort with hard bursts on top of it creates flames of leg burns.

FTP for 10 minutes each, or three for 15 minutes each, or two for 20 minutes each, in order to get in the needed threshold work in one of your workouts each week.

The 30-30-30 workout is a favorite of Sam Krieg's, a coach for the Peaks Coaching Group and an elite 'cross racer, who likes "the structure it provides" and "the nearly identical similarities" to his 'cross races. "It forces me to go hard for the entire 10-minute set," he said. Kris Walker, the national champion in the 2009 masters (45–49) time trial and the 2008 and 2009 masters cyclocross event, also found these workouts helpful, saying, "As a classic steady-state rider, my forte is my ability to hold a constant power for the entire event, and cyclocross is very challenging to me because I have to train my weakness, anaerobic capacity. After reviewing my power files with Hunter, we were able to determine just exactly how much anaerobic work I was going to need in order to be on the top step of the cyclocross national championship podium."

Cyclocross is another discipline in cycling where racers are using power meters to train more quantitatively and also more specifically to the demands of the race. To a large degree, the improvement that can be made with power meters in CX hinges on the athlete's ability to mimic the demands of upcoming CX races and develop training routines for them accordingly. As the popularity of cyclocross continues to gain momentum, more and more racers will be using power meters to collect data, analyze the demands of the events, and change the way they train.

## TRACK CYCLING

Track cyclists have, in general, been slower to adopt power meters than road racers and triathletes. In part this is because, until recently, the only power meter commercially available in a track-specific version was the most expensive one, the SRM (although a fixed-gear version of the Saris PowerTap hub is now available from Wheelbuilder.com). Perhaps more importantly, however, it is because track racers perform a significant portion of their training, and all of their racing, under comparatively well-controlled conditions—on an indoor or outdoor velodrome track. This makes a simple stopwatch more useful for quantifying a rider's training and performance than is often the case in cycling. Unfortunately, this has led to the belief by some track cyclists and coaches that there is little, if anything, to be gained from using a power meter.

Contrary to that perspective, it is our opinion that track cyclists can benefit from the use of a power meter just as much as, if not more than, other types of cyclists. Why? First, the short distances and durations of most track cycling events mean that the difference between winning and losing is often exceedingly small; gaining even a tiny advantage over the competition can often tip the balance in a racer's favor. Furthermore, at least at the elite level, many races are conducted using a time trial (TT) format, which places more emphasis on the rider's physical ability and less upon, for example, tactics. Finally, even on an indoor track, the environmental conditions (for example, air density) can vary enough to result in a significant difference in a rider's TT time even when actual performance—that is, power output—remains constant. For all of these reasons, a power meter can be a very useful tool even for a "trackie."

Track cyclists can clearly benefit from using a power meter, although the actual *ways* in which they use it will tend to be somewhat different from, say, the ways that a road racer employs it. For example, a track cyclist is unlikely to find much use for a power meter for pacing purposes, as (1) track training and racing quite often entail short, high-intensity, unpaced effort; and (2) the high speed and frequent turns on the track can make it difficult to read the power-meter display even during longer intervals or races where some degree of pacing is desirable (for example, individual pursuit). In addition, with the exception of some endurance events (such as a points race or a Madison), most races on the track are too short for Normalized Power data to be readily interpretable.

On the other hand, data from a power meter can be absolutely invaluable for determining the precise demands of a particular event, and hence for optimizing a racer's training program and/or position, his or her equipment, and the strategy he or she will use when racing. Indeed, there are so many opportunities for fine-tuning your preparation for track racing using data from a power meter that it is simply impossible to describe them all in this short section. Instead, below we have simply listed a number of different potential applications to illustrate some of the various ways in which a track cyclist can employ a power meter.

### Aerodynamic Testing

The high speeds typical of track cycling mean that aerodynamic drag often represents an even greater fraction of the total resistance a rider faces than is true in other branches of the sport. Because of this, it is common for track racers to use the most aerodynamically designed equipment they can (for example, disc wheels), even in mass-start events. With a power meter and some careful testing (see "Aerodynamic Testing with a Power Meter" in Chapter 12), however, it is possible to make equipment choices based on actual data instead of theory and manufacturers' claims. More importantly, such testing can be used to refine a rider's position, thus potentially saving those critical tenths of a second in a flying 200-meter race, or many seconds in a team pursuit.

The controlled, or at least semicontrolled, environment of a velodrome also provides an excellent venue for such testing, in part because the testing can be performed under precisely the same conditions that will exist during the race. This minimizes concerns over differences in wind angles and aerodynamic drag characteristics that arise when testing and racing are done in different settings. When testing on a track, other factors that can influence the outcome are also eliminated: you don't have to worry about cars, dogs, bumps in the road, and so on. It is important, however, to conduct such testing only when the track is empty, or nearly so, not only for safety reasons but also because the presence of many riders on the track at once can disturb the air enough to affect the data.

### Monitoring and Managing Training Load

As mentioned above, it is often difficult to interpret Normalized Power data from track races, simply because these races are usually so short. The general concepts behind Training Stress Score, however, remain valid, and the Performance Manager approach can still be effectively used to monitor a rider's overall training load, to plan and execute an appropriate taper, and so on. (Indeed, the very first use of this method was to quantify the training of a national champion pursuiter.) Care must be taken when analyzing track workouts to delete any significant portions of the file where the rider was not actively pedaling; otherwise the TSS score may be artificially inflated.

### Determining Race Demands

A power meter is obviously useful for recording the power associated with a particular level of performance (such as time or placement) as well as the cadence at which it was achieved. This information can then be used to adjust your training and gear selection to better meet the demands of a particular event. For example, Dr. Jim Martin of the University of Utah, working in conjunction with the Australian Institute of Sport, has shown that world-class match sprinters tend to initiate their "jump" during a flying 200-meter time trial essentially right at the cadence that results in maximal power output—beyond this point, power declines continuously because of increases in cadence beyond this optimum as well as fatigue. Such data demonstrate why it is important for such riders to train not only to increase their peak power, but also to be as fatigue-resistant as possible at very high cadences (for example, 140–160 rpm). They also suggest, however, that riders may benefit from using larger gears in qualifying (versus the actual match-sprint rounds), so as to stay closer to their optimal cadence for more of the effort.

Although simply measuring power and cadence can provide significant insight into race demands, even greater understanding can often be achieved by analyzing power-meter data using tools such as Quadrant Analysis. Consider, for example, the data shown in Figure 13.4, a Quadrant Analysis of average effective pedal force against circumferential pedal velocity for the same rider performing two different events: a 20 km points race on the track and a criterium of approximately 30 minutes on the road. These races were specifically chosen for analysis because the average power and cadence were nearly identical.

FIGURE **13.4**    **Quadrant Analysis of Points Race and 30-minute Criterium**

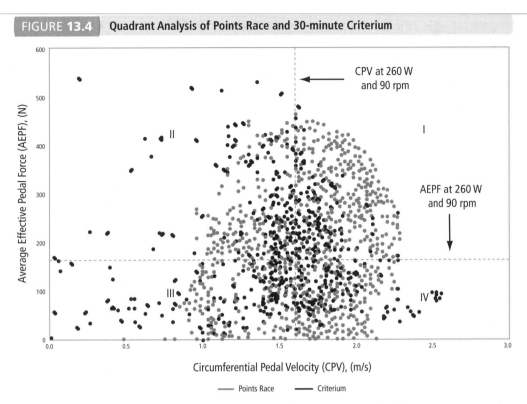

Quadrant Analysis plot of power-meter data from a national-caliber female track cyclist competing in a 20 km points race on the track and a 30-minute criterium on the road. The average power and cadence during these two races were nearly identical, but the pattern of the AEPF and CPV was dramatically different.

As is immediately evident from the plot, however, the points race on the track entailed considerably more variation than the criterium in both the force applied to the pedals and the speed at which they moved, because of the use of a fixed gear. In fact, if the data points from the track race file were connected sequentially with lines, the result would be a consistent, clockwise pattern, as the rider went from pedaling easily and relatively slowly during lulls in the action (Quadrant III), to generating high forces at a lower cadence when initiating or following a sudden attack (Quadrant II), to producing high forces at high cadence while sprinting or in a breakaway (Quadrant I), to easing off on the pedals but continuing to pedal rapidly while slowing down afterward (Quadrant IV), and so on.

Connecting the data points from the criterium in the same manner would not reveal any consistent pattern; instead it would just result in what would appear to be a tangled knot. Although this difference in the "power expansion path" between track and road racing may seem intuitively obvious to some individuals, analysis of data from a power meter makes it abundantly clear and illustrates the importance of specifically training on the track—or at least performing specific training—to meet the specific demands of track racing—that is, to gain one's "track legs." As we saw in Chapter 12, a power meter can also be used in other ways to determine the demands of a particular event (see "Gauging Aerobic and Anaerobic Energy Production").

### Evaluating Physical Performance

Performance has historically been defined on the basis of a rider's time or placement, and indeed, that is how the outcome of races is determined. As alluded to earlier, however, there can be significant differences from track to track, or even at different times on the same track, in the way that an athlete's power output—that is, *physical* performance—translates into speed. This can make it difficult to determine with confidence whether a particular change in your approach to training, equipment selection, and other factors had a positive, neutral, or even negative effect. However, this is much less of an issue for cyclists who train with a power meter, and especially those who race with one, as the power data themselves demonstrate how well you functioned as an "engine" on any given occasion. Furthermore, by carefully recording the conditions under which a particular performance was achieved, it is often possible to compare results from different tracks, even if they vary markedly in their inherent "speed."

An example of the latter approach is shown in Table 13.1, in which the results of two 3 km pursuits performed by the same rider are compared. The race at sea level took place on a concrete, 333.3-meter track, and the race at altitude took place on a very similar track. The rider went nearly 6 seconds faster at altitude. But when the data are adjusted for the effects of the reduced atmospheric pressure on both aerodynamic drag and aerobic power output, the predicted power—and hence time—are *identical* to what was achieved at sea level. The two performances are therefore essentially equivalent, despite the significant difference in time re-quired to cover the same distance. Of course, a similar conclusion might be reached by simply examining the times achieved by a large number of riders who have also raced on both tracks. But such data are not always available, and that kind of data would only provide a measure of the *average* difference, which may or may not be applicable to the performances of a given individual.

**TABLE 13.1 Performance Comparison for Track Cyclist, 3 km Pursuit**

| | Sea Level | Altitude |
| --- | --- | --- |
| Total time (min.:sec.) | 03:55.9 | 03:50.2 |
| Average power (W) | 386 | 360 |
| Time for 1st lap (min.:sec.) | 00:30.0 | 00:30.0 |
| Time laps 2–9 (min.:sec.) | 03:25.9 | 03:20.2 |
| Average power laps 2–9 (W) | 358 | 333 |
| Air density (g/mL) | 1.159 | 0.97 |
| $C_dA$ (m²) | 0.24 | 0.24 |
| Sea-level equivalent power (W) | 358 | 358 |
| Sea-level equivalent time (min.:sec.) | 03:55.9 | 03:55.9 |

## *Evaluating Technical Performance*

Racing on the track requires a unique set of skills, with the importance of a given skill varying with the event. For example, team sprint cyclists must be highly proficient at performing standing starts, especially if they will be lead riders, but there's essentially no need for them to learn how to pace themselves during such a violent, all-out event. The opposite is true for individual pursuiters, whose final times depend very little on starting skills (as long as they don't fall over!) but who are heavily influenced by how well they can pace themselves. In this context, a power meter can once again be a useful tool.

For example, recording power-meter data (including not only power and cadence but also speed) at a high frequency during a standing start can often provide more insight into the impact of changes in technique (for example, the position of the hips relative to the crank) on a rider's performance than simply looking at split times, even if the latter are recorded over very short distances (such as 25 meters) using an electronic timing tape. Somewhat along the same lines, knowing a rider's actual power during an individual pursuit and, in particular, how it changes over time can be more useful in evaluating pacing strategy than knowing the rider's splits, especially if environmental conditions are variable (either from one occasion to the next or during an actual race—for example, there could be variations in wind on an outdoor track).

Yet another example of how a power meter can be used to evaluate a rider's technical performance comes from data collected by Dr. Jeff Broker (now at the University of Colorado–Colorado Springs) and others as part of Project 96, USA Cycling's program to prepare for the 1996 Atlanta Olympics. Jeff and his colleagues measured the power that team pursuit riders produced in various positions in the pace line as well as their power during exchanges. They observed that riders in the second, third, or fourth position required only 64–71 percent of the power required for the lead rider. This is not surprising, but they also found that the power requirement varied significantly with the rider's skill at drafting.

The amount of power a rider had to produce to remain on the wheel in front of him was initially quite high, but it decreased dramatically as a rider became more comfortable drafting and was able to draft more closely behind his teammates. More surprisingly, Jeff and his team determined, using power meters, that what coaches had typically considered a bad exchange proved not to be so bad after all. Dropping back down the track too early after completing a turn at the front, such that you briefly overlap the third rider in the line before drifting back slightly to slot onto his wheel, does not require any more power than a "perfect" exchange in which you drop directly into the line. (On the other hand, coming down too late, such that you lose some of the draft and have to accelerate to get back onto the wheel ahead, proved to be much more costly, just as you might expect.) Of course, overlapping wheels during an exchange in a team pursuit can be dangerous, so riders should at least aim for a "perfect" exchange, regardless of the power requirements of the alternatives.

### Evaluating Training Methods

Just as the demands of track cycling tend to be different from those found in other disciplines—and more diverse—so, too, are the various workouts to address these demands. Fortunately, a power meter can be an extremely useful tool for determining whether a particular workout is likely to achieve its intended goals. For example, data from a power meter can be used to assess whether sufficient rest is taken between, say, the efforts in a 2,000-meter flying-start workout, so that each effort will adequately stress the rider's anaerobic capacity as intended. Otherwise, cumulative fatigue can cause the workout to deteriorate into a suboptimal $VO_2max$ training session. The critical power approach (see Chapter 3) could then be used to track changes in the rider's anaerobic capacity over time, just to be certain that this aspect of his or her fitness was improving.

Continuing along this theme, it is not uncommon for track cyclists to perform standing-start efforts in a gear that is larger than normally used when racing, under the assumption that this creates a greater overload on the neuromuscular system and hence increases

| FIGURE 13.5 | Force-Velocity Curve During Standing Starts |

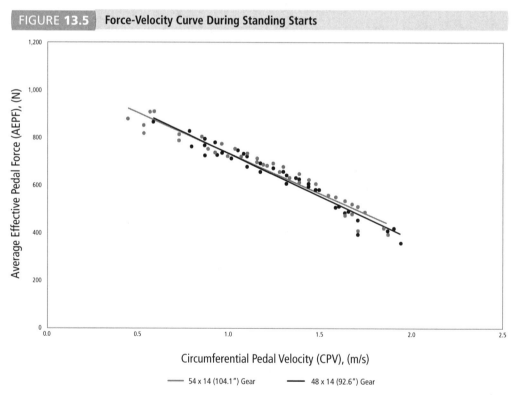

54 x 14 (104.1") Gear          48 x 14 (92.6") Gear

*Plot of AEPF against CPV for a track cyclist performing standing-start efforts when using two different gear ratios. As can be seen in the figure, the force-velocity curve is essentially identical for the two training sessions, demonstrating that the choice of gearing had no impact on the demands of the workout.*

cycling-specific strength and/or power more effectively than if such efforts were done using typical race gearing. As shown in Figure 13.5, however, this is not the case. Instead, within fairly broad limits, the gear that is used when performing a standing start has no impact on the force applied to the cranks at any particular cadence. This is because during maximal efforts it is primarily the contractile properties of the cyclist's muscles (and to a lesser extent his or her technique) that determine the force-velocity relationship when pedaling; the exact conditions under which the test (that is, the standing start) is performed are far less important.

To put it another way: within reason, varying the gear ratio has no effect on the force that a rider's muscles can produce at a particular speed, but only determines how quickly the rider will "hop, skip, and jump" down his or her maximal force-velocity line—pedal stroke by pedal stroke—when accelerating away from the starting point. Armed with this knowledge, astute riders and coaches can focus their energies on something other than constantly swapping chainrings or cogs in training, such as manipulating the motivation of the rider(s) when performing standing-start efforts (by, for example, pairing riders together or using a handicapped start with one rider chasing another). The standing-start efforts could also be performed in a manner that would greatly increase the "dwell time" at high forces and low cadences. For example, an *extremely* large gear could be used, or the rider could climb up the banking, thus using gravity as well as inertia to slow his or her rate of acceleration.

## ULTRA-ENDURANCE MOUNTAIN BIKING

Mountain biking has its own set of unique challenges, from long rocky climbs, to narrow muddy tracks, to hair-raising descents over drop-offs. Serious mountain bikers are already utilizing power meters to train. Mountain biking is extreme in its demand for high-force, low-cadence efforts (Quadrant II), and a power meter can help mountain bikers train in the correct quadrant and apply the appropriate amount of training stress.

In the past few years, longer and longer mountain-bike races have become popular in the United States. The Shenandoah 100, Leadville 100, 24 Hours of Moab, and 24 Hours of Old Pueblo are extremely demanding in terms of both muscular and aerobic fitness. An epic stage race in Costa Rica, La Ruta de los Conquistadores, is a multiday event with stages that are over 6 hours long. These longer events contain the same technical demands as short mountain-biking events but add in the demands of ultra-endurance races, thus putting a high premium on muscular and aerobic fitness along with technical cycling skills. Here we'll examine the ultra-endurance mountain-biking event, determine how best to train for one, and look at strategies for the event itself. We'll focus on how to use your power meter as a pacing device, how to use software for training and participating in these events, and what the Quadrant Analysis diagram looks like for these events.

In some ways, ultra-endurance mountain biking is similar to time trialing. The mountain-bike course is very seldom about drafting; in fact, after about the first 15 minutes, each mountain-bike racer is in his or her own little world of time trialing to the finish. Pacing—holding back your effort in the beginning to conserve energy for the end—however, does not work the same way in these two specialties. The time trialing rule about not starting too hard, in order to conserve energy for the finish, does not apply here.

Consider the "Allen effect." The Allen effect occurs when a competitor accelerates through a slow section of a course, knowing that a much faster section is coming up. As the competitor reaches the faster section and increases his speed, a larger gap can be created between him and the competitors behind him. Meanwhile, the competitors behind him are still stuck riding in a slower section of the course. A common place to see this effect is when a competitor attacks on a steep hill in order to get over the climb first, and then averages over 30 miles per hour on the back side of the hill while other riders are pacing themselves carefully up the final part of the hill, but averaging only 4 miles per hour. Because of the Allen effect, it can become impossible for the riders still climbing that hill to close the gap.

This gap initially begins as a distance gap, and it is true that the distances between riders can fluctuate while the time gap remains the same. It can be a psychological strength for the riders who are following to realize that the gap is indeed only a distance gap and not a time gap. However, in most forms of bicycle racing, it's the distance between riders that determines the winners. In any case, holding back your effort in the beginning of a mountain-bike race is rarely going to help you in the end. The Allen effect will continue to accumulate throughout the race. The front-runner in this scenario will find his pace slowing dramatically near the end of the race, but there just isn't enough time or space left by then for the other riders to make up the difference. The Allen effect that occurred in the first half of the race will keep that rider in the lead during the second half. This effect is exaggerated in ultra-endurance mountain-bike races.

## 24–Hour Races

Power files of 24-hour racers have shown that putting out more wattage in the first 4 hours of a race and creating a gap on the competition can be a huge advantage later in the event. In an ultra race (a race longer than 6 hours), most athletes fatigue at the same rate over the next 18 hours, so a gap of 45 minutes from Rider 1 to Rider 2 at the 6-hour mark is most likely going to hold for the next 18 hours. Of course, poor hydration, improper nutrition, and bike mechanicals can change this—but take those things out of the equation, and a solid time gap established in those critical first 6 hours will most likely hold for the rest of the race.

In Figure 13.6, you can see the power from the first 6 hours, which this rider (professional ultra-endurance mountain-biker Dave Harris) held at just above what he thought he could for the entire event. In fact, Dave's power over the first four laps was almost identical from one lap to the next, which demonstrates excellent discipline and ability to pace himself using his power meter. Figure 13.7 shows this same ride as a Quadrant Analysis. Table 13.2 shows the first five laps of the race. The TrainingPeaks WKO+ Multi-File/Range Analysis

| TABLE 13.2 | Multi-File/Range Analysis of First 5 Laps of 24-Hour Mountain Bike Race | | | | | | | | | | | | | | | |
|---|---|---|---|---|---|---|---|---|---|---|---|---|---|---|---|---|
| **MT. BIKE RACE** | | | | | | | | | | | | | | | | |
| Range | Duration | Work (kJ) | TSS (IF) | Normalized | Min Pwr | Max Pwr | Avg Pwr | Min HR | Max HR | Avg HR | Min Cad | Max Cad | Avg Cad | Min Spd | Max Spd | Avg Spd |
| Lap 1 | 1:05:26.16 | 814 | 51 (0.684) | 226 W (1.09) | 0 | 568 | 208 | 130 | 134 | 146 | 30 | 174 | 85 | 5.3 | 31.3 | 15.3 |
| Lap 2 | 1:08:07.44 (1:09:26.08) | 839 | 50.8 (0.67) | 221 W (1.07) | 0 | 650 | 206 | 115 | 161 | 146 | 29 | 152 | 86 | 2.7 | 31.8 | 15.0 |
| Lap 3 | 1:08:57.84 (1:09:10.36) | 852 | 53.7 (0.684) | 226 W (1.09) | 0 | 553 | 206 | 125 | 166 | 150 | 29 | 146 | 85 | 2.9 | 29.7 | 14.9 |
| Lap 4 | 1:08:57.84 (1:13:10.96) | 855 | 53.1 (0.68) | 224 W (1.08) | 0 | 735 | 207 | 117 | 160 | 150 | 29 | 159 | 84 | 2.2 | 29.3 | 14.8 |
| Lap 5 | 1:13:35.04 (1.19:53.00) | 827 | 47.5 (0.623) | 206 W (1.10) | 0 | 497 | 188 | 113 | 157 | 144 | 29 | 163 | 83 | 4.4 | 28.2 | 13.9 |

| FIGURE 13.6 | Power Graph of Good Pacing in a 24-Hour Mountain Bike Race |
|---|---|

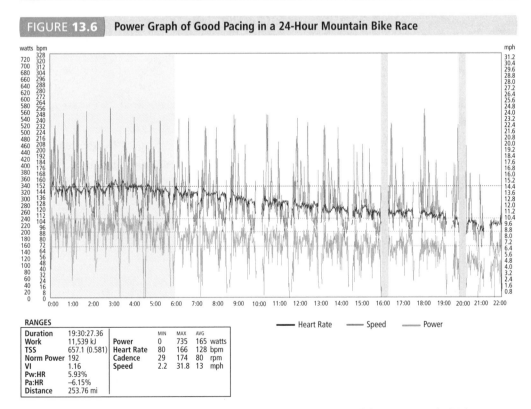

**RANGES**

| Duration | 19:30:27.36 | | MIN | MAX | AVG | |
|---|---|---|---|---|---|---|
| Work | 11,539 kJ | Power | 0 | 735 | 165 | watts |
| TSS | 657.1 (0.581) | Heart Rate | 80 | 166 | 128 | bpm |
| Norm Power | 192 | Cadence | 29 | 174 | 80 | rpm |
| VI | 1.16 | Speed | 2.2 | 31.8 | 13 | mph |
| Pw:HR | 5.93% | | | | | |
| Pa:HR | −6.15% | | | | | |
| Distance | 253.76 mi | | | | | |

—— Heart Rate    —— Speed    —— Power

*This is Dave Harris's power file from a 24-hour ultra-endurance mountain-bike race. Note the higher wattage in the first 6 hours of the race. This was done in order to create a gap between Dave and the riders behind him that Dave could hold to the finish.*

**FIGURE 13.7**    **Quadrant Analysis of Good Pacing in a 24-Hour Mountain Bike Race**

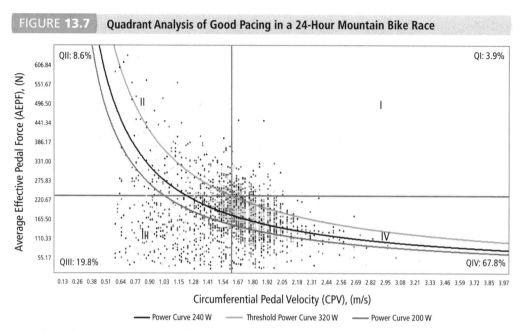

*In 24-hour ultra-endurance mountain-bike races, the best riders are able to modulate their power output to spend the majority of their time (50 percent or more) in Quadrant IV, which is relatively low force, high cadence. This spares muscle glycogen for use later in the event.*

makes it easy to do this comparison. Dave's Normalized Power averaged 224 watts for the first four laps (1 hour, 7 minutes to 1 hour, 9 minutes), dropping to 206 watts (1 hour, 10 minutes) in lap 5. This will be closer to the power that can be sustained for the remaining 19 hours of the race. This is a textbook example of how a racer can create a distance gap between himself and his next competitor as part of his overall race-winning strategy. Initially, the idea of going harder than you know you will be able to sustain for a 24-hour race seems highly suspect, but when we consider the cumulative impact of the Allen effects, we see that this strategy is a sound one.

### 100-Mile Races

Let's examine a power file from Jeremiah Bishop, an elite pro mountain biker, 2008 national marathon mountain-bike champion, and winner of multiple ultra-endurance mountain-bike races, including the Shenandoah 100-mile event. This event is considerably shorter than a 24-hour mountain-bike race, although still considered an ultra-endurance event. The power file from Jeremiah's record-breaking time in the 2009 Shenandoah 100 (see Figure 13.8) can teach us many lessons. Jeremiah had done this race many times before, so he had intimate knowledge of the course.

| FIGURE 13.8 | Power Graph of a 100-Mile Mountain Bike Race |
| --- | --- |

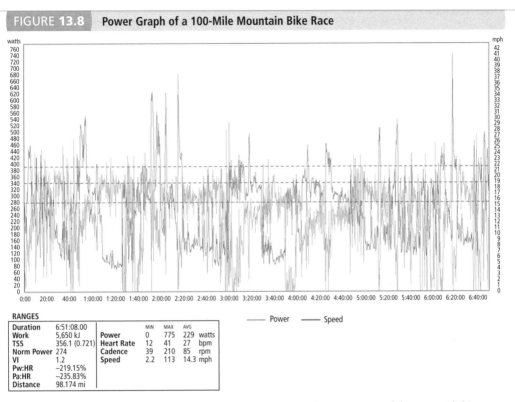

**RANGES**

| Duration | 6:51:08.00 | | MIN | MAX | AVG | |
| --- | --- | --- | --- | --- | --- | --- |
| Work | 5,650 kJ | **Power** | 0 | 775 | 229 | watts |
| TSS | 356.1 (0.721) | **Heart Rate** | 12 | 41 | 27 | bpm |
| Norm Power | 274 | **Cadence** | 39 | 210 | 85 | rpm |
| VI | 1.2 | **Speed** | 2.2 | 113 | 14.3 | mph |
| Pw:HR | −219.15% | | | | | |
| Pa:HR | −235.83% | | | | | |
| Distance | 98.174 mi | | | | | |

——— Power    ——— Speed

*Jeremiah Bishop's record-breaking power file from the Shenandoah 100 mountain-bike race. With his FTP at 390 (upper dashed line) and a grid line at 340 watts, this file demonstrates just how intense a shorter ultra-endurance race can be. The stats inside the ranges bar also show the level of difficulty.*

As a pro, Jeremiah's FTP is an impressive 390 watts, which is the higher of the three dashed gridlines in Figure 13.8. The middle gridline is at 340 watts. If we look at the number of times Jeremiah's intensity fell within this range, we can see how incredibly intense a shorter ultra-endurance race can be. With Normalized Power at 274 watts (see lower gridline) and a TSS of 356 over close to 7 hours, this win was just as difficult as (if not more difficult than) winning a stage in the Tour de France.

To understand Jeremiah's pacing strategy it's helpful to know that in this race, he had some stiff competition. After the first 2 hours of racing, there was a front group of five riders. Jeremiah and the four others rotated in a paceline on gravel road sections, averaging speeds of over 30 miles per hour. The essential work done by a team of riders during early fast sections is the key to a record-breaking performance in many types of races. During these faster-than-normal early 2 to 3 hours, Jeremiah tried to limit hard efforts and sharp bursts, and in this way he avoided early glycogen depletion. He pedaled as smoothly as he could,

**FIGURE 13.9** **Power Graph Showing Conservation of Effort in 100-Mile Mountain-Bike Race**

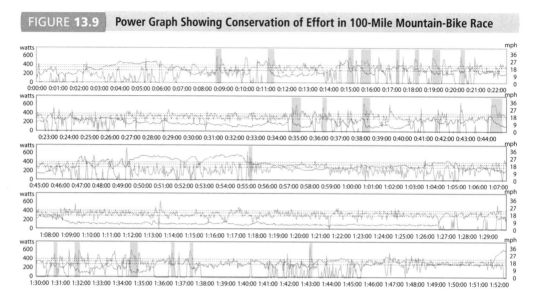

*Conservation of effort: Using the FAST FIND feature in WKO+ Software, we find that Jeremiah only exceeds 500 watts thirty-three times in the 100-mile race, and nineteen of these occur in the first 2 hours. Not only is this a very small number of efforts for a race this long, but each effort was only between 10 and 60 seconds long. In a 1-hour criterium, there might be 100 power spikes.*

spinning a higher cadence when necessary to minimize fatigue. In fact, by examining his power file we can see that he went over 500 watts numerous times during the entire record-breaking 6-hour, 51-minute ride, and he held each of those efforts for less than 60 seconds.

The conservation of effort illustrated in Figure 13.9 was based on a few different insights that Jeremiah could explain: "From using my power meter in races from short tracks to cross-country, to these epic 100 milers, I have found that what you have in the 'tank,' so to speak, in the last 30 miles of the race determines the winner, especially in a tightly fought race. For sure, the higher-than-average pacing that occurs in the first 4 hours can be the difference between winning and losing (especially so in a long 24-hour race), but races in the 6- to 8-hour range are more competitive and similar to long road races, where the winning attacks come near the end of the event."

Even with this key conservation strategy in mind, an ultra-endurance mountain-bike race requires a tremendous amount of force, as do regular mountain-bike races. The physiological demands of ultra-endurance mountain biking are not that different from those of a normal cross-country race, but those demands have increased in volume. This increase in volume, in terms of muscular endurance and power as well as cardiovascular fitness, is a key aspect of the ultra-endurance mountain-bike event, and it is something that every rider must take into consideration. A Quadrant Analysis of Jeremiah's race shows that 21 percent of his

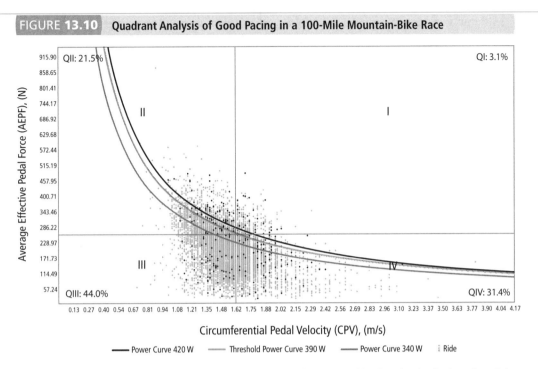

FIGURE **13.10** Quadrant Analysis of Good Pacing in a 100-Mile Mountain-Bike Race

*With the majority of his efforts in Quadrants III and IV, Jeremiah conserved his legs for the final section of the race. The darker points represent the last hour of the 100-mile race. Note that most of them are over his FTP and a large number (21 percent) are in Quadrant II. You must have muscular strength in the final miles of a race of this type in order to have a chance at winning.*

ride was spent in Quadrant II, which represents slower cadence and higher force, and therefore we know that fatigue resistance of Type II fibers was a determining factor in his success.

Circling back to the conservation strategy, we can examine the amount of data in Quadrants III and IV, which represent nearly 75 percent of his ride. This confirms that Jeremiah did a very good job of pacing himself over the entire ride. In Figure 13.10, the darker points represent the last 36 minutes of the race. You'll notice that the majority of the darker points (21 percent) fall in Quadrant II, drawing attention to Jeremiah's herculean effort to drop the second-place rider. The final miles of the event required tremendous force. Notice also the sheer volume of data points in this Quadrant Analysis. At the risk of pointing out the obvious, this shows us that more riding equals more data equals more muscular fatigue.

Clearly, ultra-endurance mountain biking is becoming more and more popular, and its demands are such that specific training will be needed. Cyclists hoping to excel in this type of event must push their muscular endurance further and further in order to be able to handle the sheer volume of muscular contractions. In addition, they must do solid force work in

Quadrant II and finish off with threshold work, then package all this together with a careful pacing strategy and an understanding of how to conserve energy throughout a race. For all these reasons, a power meter is an essential tool for the ultra-endurance mountain biker.

# Putting It All Together

**Our goal in this book has been** to take you from being a novice at using a power meter to being a savvy user of this new technology in training and racing. If your initial feeling about your power meter was "Oh no, now what do I do with this thing?" we hope you are well on your way to becoming an advanced user who is more likely to ask, "Hey, my Power Profile says that I am a sprinter and I can do 4.55 watts per kilogram at FTP, so how do I increase my $VO_2max$ power?" Ultimately, we hope that this book, along with your power meter, will help you to achieve your fitness goals.

## A REVIEW OF THE STEPS

We have covered the steps that you can take to get started with using your power meter, and we've discussed some advanced tools and techniques that you can use as you become more familiar with it. Now it's time to put it all together. The main steps are as follows.

### Step 1: Data Collection and Determination of Threshold Power

Testing your FTP as you begin using a power meter will be one of the most important steps you take. This will define the intensity of all your training from here on out. As you gather ride data over your local routes and races, you'll learn even more about what it means when you ride at a particular wattage during particular types of rides. Remember to repeat this test every six to eight weeks, or whenever you think your fitness has changed. (Chapter 3)

### Step 2: Determine Your Training Levels

Once you know your threshold power, training in the correct levels will guide you to success. By understanding what happens physiologically when you train in each level, you will be able to easily target any weaknesses that need to be addressed. (Chapter 3)

### Step 3: Determining Your Strengths and Weaknesses

How you define your strengths and weaknesses will also be a guiding factor in your training. When you plot your Power Profile, you will not only know how you stack up against your peers but will learn even more precisely the physiological systems that you need to train. The Fatigue Profile is also critical, as it will help you determine whether there is a specific area in which your fatigue resistance needs to be improved. That knowledge can help you change your training to make that final 10 percent leap in improvement. (Chapter 4)

### Step 4: Creating Workouts and Beginning Training

The work must be done. So use your new knowledge to create workouts that address your own fitness needs and goals and that are aimed at specific power levels, and go for it. In order to really improve, you will have to train, and you will have to train hard. It will hurt and you will want to quit. But one of Hunter's favorite sayings applies here: "Quitters never win, and winners never quit." Go ride your bike . . . faster. (Chapter 5)

### Step 5: Interpreting Your Data

Download every ride, every race, every time you throw a leg over that bike. Your data are important, and interpreting them correctly will help you to make the right decisions about the next day's training, the next month's training, and even the next year's training. Spend the time that you need to understand what the data are telling you. (Chapter 6)

### Step 6: Learning Analysis Tools

The advanced tools of Training Stress Score, Intensity Factor, Normalized Power, and Quadrant Analysis can give you even more insight into your cycling and help you to fine-tune your training and racing. They can help you define the demands of your events and shed light on the additional factors that are necessary for success. Cycling is an incredibly complicated sport with many unknowns, and the more unknowns you can eliminate, the better your chance of success. (Chapters 7, 8, and 9)

### Step 7: Racing with Your Power Meter

Your best data will come from races, your best efforts will come in races, and you stand to learn the most from your race data. Contrary to what you might think, some of the very best data will come from your failures. You'll learn exactly why you failed, and then you'll be able to take steps to avoid making the same mistakes again. You will also learn why pacing is the most important component of success in this sport. (Chapters 11, 12, and 13)

### *Step 8: Making Changes to Achieve Your Goals*

Training with a power meter is about results. It is worth doing only if you have a clear understanding of what needs to be done. Now that you have a good working knowledge of what needs to be done, you must be ready and willing to change. So, based on what you've learned in taking the steps listed above, go ahead and make the needed changes, and watch your cycling improve.

## SOME FINAL THOUGHTS

While training and racing with your power meter, avoid the "paralysis by analysis" syndrome. Training with a power meter can be very easy to do, but it can also be very frustrating, especially if you have trouble with your unit or encounter some initial technical difficulties. Sometimes your power meter may seem to be more of a hassle than it's worth. But remember to keep an eye on the big picture. Each training day fits into an overall set of objectives. Sometimes you may want to download your ride, keep it in your database, and not even look at the actual workout file. That's fine once in a while. But keep looking at the long-term graphs to get a sense of how all your systems are improving. You may even decide that ultimately you are not all that interested in the data, or may choose not to spend hours poring over your data files. And that's fine, too. You can still benefit from using the power meter on your bike as the ultimate pacing tool. You can still have fun driving a Ferrari even if you never test its limits on the racetrack!

Change is tough for all of us. Whether it is change in a job or change in a daily routine, it is always a challenge. However, in order to grow, you have to change. Be open to making changes in your training based on new information. When you begin making these changes, you will see your fitness improve, and this will be very satisfying and rewarding. Having the ability to quantify that improvement is doubly rewarding. Training and racing with a power meter will allow you to truly know that your hard work is paying off and worth it all.

# APPENDIX A

## Additional Resources

### POWER-METER MANUFACTURERS

#### ergomo
Germany:
  Pariser Str. 50
  55286 Wörrstadt
  Germany
  Phone: +49 (0)6732 / 94 7 94 44
  buero-powermeter@gmx.de
USA:
  JDS Sportcoaching, LLC
  2164 S. Grant St.
  Denver, CO 80210
  Phone: (877) 698-5835
  www.ErgomoUSA.com
  info@jdssportcoaching.com

#### iBike
Velocomp LLP
1747 Avenida del Sol
Boca Raton, FL 33432
Phone: (214) 801-9895
www.ibikesports.com
info@velocomp.com

#### MetriGear
MetriGear, Inc.
500 Laurelwood Road, Suite 12
Santa Clara, CA 95054
Phone: (408) 850-2981
www.metrigear.com
info@metrigear.com

#### Polar
Polar Electro Inc.
1111 Marcus Avenue, Suite M15
Lake Success, NY 11042
Phone: (800) 227-1314
Fax: (516) 364-5454
www.polarusa.com
customer.service.usa@polar.fi

#### PowerTap
Saris Cycling Group
5253 Verona Road
Madison, WI 53711
Phone: (800) 783-7257
www.saris.com

#### Quarq
Quarq Technology
3100 1st Avenue
Spearfish, SD 57783
Phone: (800) 660-6853
Fax: (800) 660-3589
www.quarq.com
thinkfast@quarq.us

#### SRM
SRM Service Center, Inc.
720 W. Monument Street
Colorado Springs, CO 80904
Phone: (719) 266-4127
Fax: (719) 266-4284
www.srm.de
usa@srm.de

## THIRD-PARTY POWER-METER SOFTWARE

### CyclingPeaks ERG+
www.trainingpeaks.com

### GoldenCheetah
www.goldencheetah.org

### PowerCoach
www.powercoach.ch

### RaceDay
www.physfarm.com/inside/raceday.html

### TrainingPeaks WKO+
www.trainingpeaks.com

## BOOKS

Friel, Joe. *The Cyclist's Training Bible,* 4th ed. Boulder: VeloPress, 2009.

Skiba, Philip. *The Triathlete's Guide to Training with Power.* Available at www.physfarm.com.

Wharton, Richard. *Watts per Kilogram: Using the CompuTrainer™ Indoor Ergometer to Improve Your Performance.* Available at www.onlinebikecoach.com.

## ARTICLES

Coggan, Andrew. "Training and Racing Using a Power Meter: An Introduction." Available at home.trainingpeaks.com/power411.aspx.

Howe, Charles. "The Road Cyclist's Guide to Training by Power." Available at velodynamics2.webs.com/rcgtp1.pdf.

## WEBSITES

### Analytic Cycling
www.analyticcycling.com

### FAQ for Power-Based Training
http://midweekclub.ca/powerFAQ.htm

### Train with Power.net

www.trainwithpower.net

### Training and Racing with a Power Meter Journal

www.trainingandracingwithapowermeter.com

### Wattage online forum

groups.google.com/group/wattage

*Hunter Allen's workouts and training plans are available for purchase at trainingpeaks.com/hunter.*

# APPENDIX B

## Workout Guide

### Level 1: Active Recovery (<55% of FTP)

**AR-W1     Active Recovery: Spin**                    APPROX. TIME: 1 HR.

Just spin the legs at a normal cadence (neither fast nor slow) at Active Recovery pace. Do not place force on the pedals or allow lactate to build up in the legs. The goal is to preserve the "feel" for the legs and muscles, but to go really easy. Power and heart rate should remain low.

|  | Time | Description | % of FTP | % of FTHR |
|---|---|---|---|---|
| Ride | 1 hr. (or as specified in plan) | Spinning | <55 | <68 |

### Level 2: Endurance (56–75% of FTP)

**END-W1     Endurance: Active Recovery**                    APPROX. TIME: 1 HR.

Warm up and ride at a nice, steady pace. Keep cadence high, at 85–95 rpm. Occasional hills might increase your power, but generally average between 56 and 75 percent of FTP. Cool down.

|  | Time | Description | % of FTP | % of FTHR |
|---|---|---|---|---|
| Warm-up | 15 min. | Easy riding | 56–75 | 69–83 |
| Main set | 45 min.–1 hr. | Endurance | <75 | 69–83 |
| Cooldown | 15 min. | Easy riding | 56–75 | 69–83 |

**END-W2     Endurance: Basic Ride 1**                    APPROX. TIME: 2 HR.

This is almost like an Active Recovery day, but a touch too long for that. Warm up to get the legs loose. Try for a solid 2- to 2.5-hour ride today. Still, just ride easy and do not push it. Keep cadence high, at 85–95 rpm. Power should not exceed 80 percent of FTP. It's okay if power tips past 80 percent on the occasional hill, but keep the ride focused on building endurance. Cool down with easy pedaling.

|  | Time | Description | % of FTP | % of FTHR |
|---|---|---|---|---|
| Warm-up | 10–15 min. | Easy riding | 56–75 | 69–83 |
| Main set | 1.5–2 hr. | Endurance | <80 | <85 |
| Cooldown | 10–15 min. | Easy riding | 56–75 | 69–83 |

END-W3     **Endurance: Basic Ride 2**                           APPROX. TIME: 3 HR.

This ride will extend your mileage slightly and build your "engine." Solid Endurance/Tempo miles will improve your aerobic capacity.

After warming up, ride for about 2.5 hours with power between 60 and 70 percent of FTP and cadence in the 90–95 rpm range. At times this is an easy effort, and other times it's a solid, fast pace. Try not to spend much time at over 70 percent of FTP. Cool down with 10–15 minutes of easy riding before making that recovery shake and stretching.

|  | Time | Description | % of FTP | % of FTHR |
|---|---|---|---|---|
| Warm-up | 15 min. | Easy riding | 56–75 | 69–83 |
| Main set | 2.5–3.5 hr. | Endurance, 90–95 rpm | 60–70 | 75–80 |
| Cooldown | 10–15 min. | Easy riding | 56–75 | 69–83 |

END-W4     **Endurance: 8-Second Bursts**                        APPROX. TIME: 2.5 HR.

Warm up with cadence at 90–100 rpm. Then begin 2.5 hours of riding at a nice, steady pace with watts in Levels 2–3. This is a great Endurance pace that will allow you to finish strong and also get some solid aerobic benefit. Within the Endurance set do ten short 8-second bursts out of the saddle. This burst effort is 80 percent of what a full sprint would be. Cadence should be high (over 105 rpm) to create a hard, sharp effort that will begin to improve your neuromuscular capacity. Do these bursts randomly throughout the ride. Cool down.

|  | Time | Description | % of FTP | % of FTHR |
|---|---|---|---|---|
| Warm-up | 15 min. | Easy riding, 90–100 rpm | 56–75 | 69–83 |
| Main set | 2–2.5 hr. | Endurance/Tempo with bursts, 90–95 rpm | 70–85 | 84–90 |
|  | *10 × 8 sec.* | *Bursts at hard effort, 105+ rpm* | *150* | *N/A* |
| Cooldown | 10–15 min. | Easy riding | 56–75 | 69–83 |

END-W5     **Endurance: Tempo Drills**                           APPROX. TIME: 4.25 HR.

The main set is 3.5 hours today. Just ride and have fun. Complete the work, and make sure to stay hydrated and strong throughout.

Warm up and begin the first hour with power under 75 percent of FTP. For the next 2 hours, try to stay within 80–85 percent, including a short 10-second sprint (in the 53:17 gear) every 5 minutes. This will add up to 24 sprints over the 2 hours of riding.

With 1 hour to go, stop at a convenience store for a caffeinated drink. In the last hour, try to ride at your sweet spot, keeping a nice, strong pace. To cool down, pedal easy for 15 minutes before you get home.

| END-W5 | Time | Description | % of FTP | % of FTHR |
|---|---|---|---|---|
| Warm-up | 30 min. | Easy riding | 56–75 | 69–83 |
| Main set | 30 min. | Endurance | <75 | <78 |
| | 2 hr. | Tempo with bursts | 80–85 | 90–93 |
| | *10 sec.* | *Burst every 5 min.* | *150* | *N/A* |
| | 1 hr. | Sweet spot | 88–93 | 92–98 |
| Cooldown | 15 min. | Easy riding | 56–75 | 69–83 |

## END-W6   Endurance: Cadence Drills

APPROX. TIME: 1.25 HR.

Cadence drills are intended to improve your pedaling. Don't worry about speed, power, or heart rate. Ultimately, you are hoping power and heart rate remain low at the higher cadence so you can become more efficient at harder efforts. Build cadence steadily to avoid fading too fast.

Warm up with cadence in the 90–95 rpm range. Start the main set with six 1-minute "on," 1-minute "off" fast pedaling cadence efforts. Ride 10 minutes easy, and then do two 5-minute efforts, trying to get wattage to FTP and hold it there. RPE should be 5; keep cadence at 100 rpm. Rest for 5 minutes between intervals. Finish with two more 1-minute "on" and 1-minute "off" cadence drills. Cool down.

| | Time | Description | % of FTP | % of FTHR |
|---|---|---|---|---|
| Warm-up | 15 min. | Fast riding, 90–95 rpm | 70–75 | 69–83 |
| Main set | 6 × 2 min. | Cadence drill | | |
| | | *1 min. "on": 105 rpm* | *<90* | *<85* |
| | | *1 min. "off": 85 rpm* | *<56* | *<69* |
| | 10 min. | Easy riding | 56–75 | 69–83 |
| | 2 × 5 min. (5 min. RI) | Threshold, 100 rpm | 91–105 | 95–105 |
| | 2 × 2 min. | Cadence drill | | |
| | | *1 min. "on": 105 rpm* | *<90* | *<85* |
| | | *1 min. "off": 85 rpm* | *<56* | *<69* |
| Cooldown | 10–15 min. | Easy riding | 56–75 | 69–83 |

## END-W7   Endurance: FTP Hills

APPROX. TIME: 4.5 HR.

Make this a hilly ride. Rolling hills, one long hill (more than 20 min.), or several short hills should accommodate 30 minutes of Threshold work over the course of the 3.5–4 hours. If you don't have hills, simulate hills by riding into the wind. For the majority of the ride, pace should be at Level 2, Endurance. Cool down and stretch.

| | Time | Description | % of FTP | % of FTHR |
|---|---|---|---|---|
| Warm-up | 15 min. | Easy riding | 56–75 | 69–83 |
| Main set | 3–3.5 hr. | Endurance/Tempo, with Threshold intervals | 64–94 | 70–98 |
| | *30 min. (10 min. RI)* | *Threshold* | *100–105* | *95–105* |
| Cooldown | 15 min. | Easy riding | 56–75 | 69–83 |

**END-W8**    **Endurance: Tempo and VO$_2$max Intervals**    APPROX. TIME: 4 HR.

This will be a 4-hour solid Endurance/Tempo ride on varied terrain. If you live in a hilly area, then meter your efforts on the hills. Ride at Endurance/Tempo pace and have fun with some variety of work. Getting in a long ride with VO$_2$max efforts will hit the watts that will work your cardiovascular system and also fatigue the muscles.

After warming up, begin an hour of riding in the sweet spot, then get in 20–30 minutes of Endurance riding. Next, do two 20-minute intervals and maintain power right at your FTP. Cruise for another 30 minutes at Endurance pace. With an hour to go, stop for a caffeine boost (Coke, Red Bull, etc.). Now start six 3-minute VO$_2$max intervals, riding at Endurance pace for 5 minutes between them. Cool down.

|  | Time | Description | % of FTP | % of FTHR |
|---|---|---|---|---|
| Warm-up | 15 min. | Easy riding | 56–75 | 69–83 |
| Main set | 1 hr. | Sweet spot | 88–93 | 93–95 |
|  | 20–30 min. | Endurance | 56–75 | 69–83 |
|  | 2 × 20 min. (10 min. RI) | Threshold | 100–105 | 95–105 |
|  | 30 min. | Endurance | 56–75 | 69–83 |
|  | 6 × 3 min. (5 min. RI) | VO$_2$max | >110 | 102–104 |
| Cooldown | 15 min. | Easy riding | 56–75 | 69–83 |

**END-W9**    **Endurance: 100 miles**    APPROX. TIME: 5+ HR.

Get out there and spend time in the saddle today, riding toward a goal of 100 miles (162 km).

In the first hour, keep watts under 220. In the second hour, include 15-second sprints, resting for 4 minutes between sprints. Keep your pace at Threshold between the sprints.

In hours 3 and 4, it's key that you do at least three 20-minute efforts in the sweet spot to make sure you are continuing to develop that system. Do these either on the flats or on climbs. Rest for 10 minutes between efforts.

The last 45 minutes will be the most important part of the ride—this is where you become a stronger, better rider. Motor at 85–90 percent of FTP. Cool down and stretch.

|  | Time | Description | % of FTP | % of FTHR |
|---|---|---|---|---|
| Warm-up | 10 min. | Easy riding | 56–75 | 69–83 |
| Main set | 50 min. | Endurance pace | <75 | <83 |
|  | 1 hr. | Steady with sprints every 4 min. | 70–80 | 84–90 |
|  | 15 × 15 sec. | Sprints | 120 | N/A |
|  | 2 hr. | Tempo with sweet spot efforts | 76–90 | 84–93 |
|  | 3 × 20 min. (10 min. RI) | Sweet spot | 88–93 | 92–98 |
|  | 45 min. | Tempo | 85–90 | 90–93 |
| Cooldown | 15 min. | Easy riding | 56–75 | 69–83 |

## Level 3: Tempo (76–90% of FTP)

TEMP-W1     **Tempo: Basic Ride 1**                                          APPROX. TIME: 1 HR.

Warm up at a high cadence, 95–105 rpm. Begin a solid 35-minute Tempo effort. Keep the pressure on and have fun—this is a fast but achievable pace. Keep your cadence in the 90–95 rpm range and make sure you get into a nice breathing rhythm. After the Tempo set, ride at Level 2, Endurance pace. Spin to cool down.

|          | Time           | Description             | % of FTP | % of FTHR |
|----------|----------------|-------------------------|----------|-----------|
| Warm-up  | 15 min.        | Fast pedaling, 95–105 rpm | <75    | <83       |
| Main set | 35 min.        | Tempo, 90–95 rpm        | 76–90    | 84–93     |
|          | Remaining time | Endurance               | 56–75    | 69–83     |
| Cooldown | 15 min.        | Easy riding             | <68      | <75       |

TEMP-W2     **Tempo: Basic Ride 2**                                          APPROX. TIME: 2 HR.

This ride will improve your aerobic capacity with some solid Endurance/Tempo miles.

Warm up at a high cadence, 95–105 rpm. The goal is to ride 2–3 hours with power between 70 and 90 percent of FTP and cadence at 90–95 rpm. Try not to spend any time above 90 percent FTP. Cool down and stretch.

|          | Time        | Description               | % of FTP | % of FTHR |
|----------|-------------|---------------------------|----------|-----------|
| Warm-up  | 15–20 min.  | Fast pedaling, 95–105 rpm | 70–75    | <83       |
| Main set | 1.5–2.5 hr. | Endurance/Tempo, 90–95 rpm | 70–90   | 85–95     |
| Cooldown | 15 min.     | Easy riding               | <75      | <83       |

TEMP-W3     **Tempo: Anaerobic Capacity Intervals**                          APPROX. TIME: 1.5 HR.

Work on smooth, efficient pedaling on this ride: When your foot is at the bottom of the pedal stroke, pretend you are scraping mud off the bottom of your shoe. At the top of the pedal stroke, try to contract your quadriceps muscles and drive your knee forward toward the handlebar.

Warm up at a high cadence. Begin a solid 45-minute effort with watts at 76–94 percent of FTP. It's a fast pace, but it should feel achievable. Keep your cadence in the 90–95 rpm range and make sure you get into a nice breathing rhythm. If this feels good, then begin three 2-minute hard intervals. Recover at 80 percent of FTP and not lower. Cool down.

|          | Time                     | Description             | % of FTP | % of FTHR |
|----------|--------------------------|-------------------------|----------|-----------|
| Warm-up  | 15 min.                  | Fast pedaling, 95–105 rpm | <75    | <83       |
| Main set | 45 min.                  | Tempo pace              | 76–94    | 84–94     |
|          | 3 × 2 min. (3 min. RI)   | Anaerobic Capacity      | 120–150  | N/A       |
| Cooldown | 15 min.                  | Easy riding             | 56–75    | 69–83     |

TEMP-W4    **Tempo: 10-minute FTP Intervals**    APPROX. TIME: 2 HR.

After warming up, begin a solid 45-minute effort with watts at 76–94 percent of FTP. Then ride for 10 minutes at Active Recovery pace. Next ride at least one Threshold effort for a full 10 minutes, with Active Recovery as needed. Do a second interval if possible. Cool down with 15 minutes of easy riding.

|  | Time | Description | % of FTP | % of FTHR |
|---|---|---|---|---|
| Warm-up | 15 min. | Fast pedaling, 95–105 rpm | <75 | <83 |
| Main set | 45 min. | Tempo pace | 76–94 | 84–94 |
|  | 10 min. | Active Recovery | <55 | <68 |
|  | 1–2 × 10 min. (RI as needed) | Threshold, +5 rpm | 100–105 | 99–105 |
| Cooldown | 15 min. | Easy riding | 56–75 | 69–83 |

TEMP-W5    **Tempo: Anaerobic Capacity Bursts**    APPROX. TIME: 2 HR.

Riding at your Tempo pace will increase speed! Focus on your pedaling stroke—"scrape the mud off the bottom of your foot" as you pull back across the bottom of the stroke and drive your knee toward the handlebar at the top of the stroke.

Warm up and then do a 3-minute all-out effort to get the carbon out of the legs. Next begin five 1-minute fast pedaling intervals with 1 minute of rest between intervals. Ride for 20 minutes at Endurance pace, increasing cadence by 5 rpm. Legs should be spinning a little faster than they want to be! Next ride for 1 hour at Tempo pace, not race pace—this should feel challenging but not quite uncomfortable. Within this 60 minutes, do twenty bursts to FTP and hold it there for 20 seconds, then recover to your previous pace. Cool down for at least 10 minutes.

|  | Time | Description | % of FTP | % of FTHR |
|---|---|---|---|---|
| Warm-up | 15 min. | Easy riding | 56–75 | 69–83 |
| Main set | 3 min. | All-out | 115–120 | >105 |
|  | 5 × 1 min. (1 min. RI) | Fast pedaling, 110+ rpm | 56–75 | 69–83 |
|  | 20 min. | Endurance pace, +5 rpm | 56–75 | 69–83 |
|  | 1 hr. | Tempo with bursts | 76–90 | 85–94 |
|  | *20 × 20 sec. (2.5 min. RI)* | *Bursts* | *100* | *N/A* |
| Cooldown | 10 min. | Easy riding | 56–75 | 69–83 |

TEMP-W6    **Tempo: Anaerobic Capacity Bursts and Hills**    APPROX. TIME: 4 HR.

Begin by riding at Endurance pace for 1 hour, smooth and steady. In the second hour, pick up the intensity to Tempo pace. Include fifteen 30-second bursts to 150 percent of FTP within this hour and then return to 80–85 percent FTP—no lower! Finish the last hour by attacking eight hills and sprinting until you reach 15 meters over the crest. Cool down for 20 minutes.

| TEMP-W6 | Time | Description | % of FTP | % of FTHR |
|---------|------|-------------|----------|-----------|
| Warm-up | 15 min. | Easy riding | 56–75 | 69–83 |
| Main set | 1 hr. | Endurance | <75 | <83 |
| | 1 hr. | Tempo with bursts | 80–85 | 84–92 |
| | *15 × 30 sec.* | *Bursts* | *150* | *N/A* |
| | 1 hr. | Hill intervals, sprint over crest | 76–90 | 84–94 |
| Cooldown | 20 min. | Easy riding | 56–75 | 69–83 |

## TEMP-W7    Tempo: Endurance Intervals                                    APPROX. TIME: 4 HR.

After warming up, keep your power at under 90 percent of FTP for the first hour of riding. For the long interval (1.5–2 hr.), keep the effort within 64–80 percent of FTP. In the final hour, push a strong pace, between 90 and 94 percent of FTP. Cool down.

| | Time | Description | % of FTP | % of FTHR |
|---------|------|-------------|----------|-----------|
| Warm-up | 15 min. | Easy riding | 56–75 | 69–83 |
| Main set | 1 hr. | Tempo | <90 | <95 |
| | 1.5–2 hr. | Endurance/Tempo | 64–80 | 75–94 |
| | 1 hr. | Tempo | 90–94 | 94–98 |
| Cooldown | 10–15 min. | Easy riding | 56–75 | 69–83 |

## TEMP-W8    Tempo: VO$_2$max and Neuromuscular Power Intervals          APPROX. TIME: 1.5 HR.

Warm up with 15 minutes of fast pedaling at 90–100 rpm. Next, begin a 5-minute Threshold interval to prepare the legs for the rest of the ride. Increase the intensity in the last 30 seconds to push the effort over your threshold. Over the next hour in the saddle, every 5 minutes start a hard 20-second effort in the 53:13 gear, increasing your cadence with each second. Cool down with 10–20 minutes of small-ring spinning.

| | Time | Description | % of FTP | % of FTHR |
|---------|------|-------------|----------|-----------|
| Warm-up | 15 min. | Fast pedaling, 90–100 rpm | <75 | <83 |
| Main set | 5 min. | Hard effort, burst in last 30 sec. | 100–110 | N/A |
| | 5 min. | Recover | <68 | <75 |
| | 1 hr. | Tempo with 20-sec. sprints every 5 min. | 68–80 | 80–90 |
| | *12 × 20 sec.* | *Seated big-ring sprint (53:13)* | *160–200* | *N/A* |
| Cooldown | 10–20 min. | Spinning in small ring | <55 | <68 |

## TEMP-W9    Tempo: Aerobic Building, Ride 1                              APPROX. TIME: 4 HR.

If this ride is scheduled early in your training, this will likely be a breakthrough ride. Be sure to eat and drink enough to sustain the final Tempo interval.

Warm up, loosening the legs for 3–3.5 hours of riding. To begin, try two 15-minute intervals at threshold. Rest for 10 minutes between intervals with easy pedaling. In the final hour, ride for 40 minutes at Tempo pace. Have fun getting in the time! Cool down and stretch.

| TEMP-W9 | Time | Description | % of FTP | % of FTHR |
|---------|------|-------------|----------|-----------|
| Warm-up | 15 min. | Easy riding | 56–75 | 69–83 |
| Main set | 2.5–3 hr. | Endurance, with Threshold and Tempo intervals | 70–84 | 80–90 |
| | *2 × 15 min. (10 min. RI)* | *Threshold* | *95–100* | *98–103* |
| | *40 min.* | *Tempo* | *76–90* | *84–94* |
| Cooldown | 15 min. | Easy riding | 56–75 | 69–83 |

### TEMP-W10    Tempo: Aerobic Building, Ride 2                    APPROX. TIME: 4 HR.

For this ride choose a steady and relatively flat route where you will have to push the whole time.

Warm up, loosening the legs for 4 hours of riding. To begin, try two 20-minute intervals at the sweet spot and push those. Rest for 10 minutes between each. Then cruise for 60 minutes, adding in four 3-minute efforts at VO$_2$max to give that system a little charge. Rest for 3 minutes between intervals. Now it's hammer time—ride at Endurance/Tempo pace and have fun getting in the time! Cool down and stretch.

| | Time | Description | % of FTP | % of FTHR |
|---------|------|-------------|----------|-----------|
| Warm-up | 15 min. | Easy riding | 56–75 | 69–83 |
| Main set | 2 × 20 min. (10 min. RI) | Sweet spot | 88–93 | 92–98 |
| | 1 hr. | Cruise with VO$_2$max | 80–85 | 89–91 |
| | *4–6 × 3 min. (3 min. RI)* | *VO$_2$max efforts* | *115* | *>105* |
| | 30 min.–1.5 hr. | Endurance/Tempo | 70–85 | 80–90 |
| Cooldown | 15 min. | Easy riding | 56–75 | 69–83 |

## *Levels 3 and 4: Sweet Spot (88–93% of FTP)*

### SubLT-W1    Subthreshold: Basic Ride 1                    APPROX. TIME: 1.25 HR.

After warming up, start with a 5-minute "blow-out" effort, pushing power to above threshold, and then recovering with 5 minutes of easy riding. Follow this with two 10-minute intervals either at or just under threshold, keeping cadence at 90–100 rpm. Be careful not to start out too fast on these intervals. Take the first minute to build up to speed. Rest for 5 minutes between intervals. Cool down.

| | Time | Description | % of FTP | % of FTHR |
|---------|------|-------------|----------|-----------|
| Warm-up | 15 min. | Easy riding | 56–75 | 69–83 |
| Main set | 5 min. (5 min. RI) | Blow-out effort | 100–105 | >105 |
| | 2 × 10 min. (5 min. RI) | Sub-Lactate Threshold | 95–100 | 95–98 |
| Cooldown | 15 min. | Easy riding | 56–75 | 69–83 |

**SubLT-W2     Sweet Spot: Basic Ride 2**                    APPROX. TIME: 2.25 HR.

After warming up, begin a set of five 1-minute fast pedaling intervals, keeping your cadence over 110 rpm, with a 1-minute recovery between efforts. Next do two 20-minute sweet spot intervals, with a rest interval of 5 minutes. Finish with a nice, but not hard, 45-minute Tempo ride. Cool down.

|  | Time | Description | % of FTP | % of FTHR |
|---|---|---|---|---|
| Warm-up | 15 min. | Easy riding | 56–75 | 69–83 |
| Main set | 5 × 1 min. (1 min. RI) | Fast pedaling, 110+ rpm | <80 | <90 |
|  | 2 × 20 min. (5 min. RI) | Sweet spot | 88–93 | 92–98 |
|  | 45 min. | Tempo | 76–80 | 84–89 |
| Cooldown | 15 min. | Easy riding | 56–75 | 69–83 |

**SubLT-W3     Sweet Spot: Cadence and Tempo**              APPROX. TIME: 2.25 HR.

Start with a steady warm-up before moving into a set of five 1-minute fast pedaling intervals, keeping your cadence over 110 rpm, with a 1-minute recovery between efforts. Move into three 10-minute sweet spot intervals, with a rest interval of 5 minutes. Finish with a nice, but not hard, Tempo ride for 45 minutes. Cool down.

|  | Time | Description | % of FTP | % of FTHR |
|---|---|---|---|---|
| Warm-up | 15 min. | Easy riding | 56–75 | 69–83 |
| Main set | 5 × 1 min. (1 min. RI) | Fast pedaling, 110+ rpm | <80 | <90 |
|  | 3 × 10 min. (5 min. RI) | Sweet spot | 88–93 | 92–98 |
|  | 45 min. | Tempo | 76–80 | 84–88 |
| Cooldown | 15 min. | Easy riding | 56–75 | 69–83 |

**SubLT-W4     Subthreshold: Single-Leg Drills**              APPROX. TIME: 1.5 HR.

After a brief warm-up, ride at a smooth, steady pace for 30 minutes, keeping your cadence at 85–90 rpm. Then do ten 1-minute, single-leg pedaling efforts with each leg, alternating left and right to allow for 1-minute recoveries. Identify your weaker leg by noting which one starts to "burn" the soonest. Try to complete five extra intervals with that leg. Cool down with 15 minutes of smooth and steady riding, focusing on getting your legs back in "balance." Cadence (at least 90 rpm) supercedes power in these drills.

|  | Time | Description | % of FTP | % of FTHR |
|---|---|---|---|---|
| Warm-up | 10 min. | Easy riding | 56–75 | 69–83 |
| Main set | 30 min. | Tempo, 85–90 rpm | 80–85 | 88–92 |
|  | 10 × 1 min. | Single-leg drill, right leg, 90+ rpm | 80 | <90 |
|  | 10 × 1 min. | Single-leg drill, left leg, 90+ rpm | 80 | <90 |
|  | 5 × 1 min. (1 min. RI) | Single-leg drill, weaker leg, 90+ rpm | 80 | <90 |
| Cooldown | 15 min. | Easy riding | 56–75 | 69–83 |

SubLT-W5    **Subthreshold: Downhill Intervals**                              APPROX. TIME: 1.5 HR.

For this ride you'll want to have access to some gradual downhill stretches where you can still push the effort hard, but also go fast and keep a fast cadence.

After warming up, begin a hard 5-minute effort to increase your heart rate. Ride for 10 minutes easy. Jump into (i.e., sprint start) six downhill 1-minute intervals, pushing your cadence to over 105 rpm for each effort. To recover, pedal easy between downhill efforts for 20–40 seconds. Then go again. After completing the set, take 10 minutes to ride easy and then begin six more downhill efforts. This time do 45-second intervals. Ride for 10 minutes easy and then do six 30-second downhill intervals. Finish with three 2-minute efforts on a flat road, pushing hard. Rest for 2 minutes between intervals. Ride home at Tempo pace—this last push will get your top-end speed higher and work on your anaerobic capacity without stressing the muscles too much. Cool down.

| | Time | Description | % of FTP | % of FTHR |
|---|---|---|---|---|
| Warm-up | 15 min. | Easy riding | 56–75 | 69–83 |
| Main set | 5 min. (10 min. RI) | All-out | 115–120 | >105 |
| | 6 × 1 min. (20–40 sec. RI) | Downhill, 105+ rpm | 88–93 | 95–98 |
| | 10 min. | Easy riding | 56–75 | 69–83 |
| | 6 × 45 sec. (20–40 sec. RI) | Downhill, 105+ rpm | 88–93 | 95–98 |
| | 10 min. | Easy riding | 56–75 | 69–83 |
| | 6 × 30 sec. (20–40 sec. RI) | Downhill, 105+ rpm | 88–93 | 95–98 |
| | 3 × 2 min. (2 min. RI) | Hard | >120 | >105 |
| | Remaining time | Tempo | 80–85 | 88–92 |
| Cooldown | 15 min. | Easy riding | 56–75 | 69–83 |

SubLT-W6    **Sweet Spot: Crisscross and Neuromuscular Power Sprints**    APPROX. TIME: 1.5 HR.

Warm up and jump into a 3-minute hard effort, followed by 5 minutes easy. Get your power to the sweet spot and hold for 20 minutes, with seven 10-second bursts to 150 percent of FTP, returning to the sweet spot after each burst. Try to recover within the 2 minutes allotted—initially reducing the effort drastically, but turning the gas back on so your power doesn't drop too much before the next burst. Ride for 5 minutes easy after the 20-minute interval is complete. Finish with five big-gear (53:13) sprints going from 12 to 31 mph. Remain seated and tighten the core before beginning the effort. Don't worry about heart rate. Finish with 10 minutes of easy spinning.

| | Time | Description | % of FTP | % of FTHR |
|---|---|---|---|---|
| Warm-up | 15 min. | Easy riding | 56–75 | 69–83 |
| Main set | 3 min. (5 min. RI) | All-out | 115–120 | >105 |
| | 20 min. | Sweet spot with bursts | 88–93 | 92–98 |
| | *7 × 10 sec. (2 min. RI)* | *Bursts* | *56–75* | *69–83* |
| | 5 min. | Easy riding | 56–75 | 69–83 |
| | 5 × 300 m (3–5 min. RI) | Big-ring sprints (53:13) from 12 to 31 mph | >150 | N/A |
| Cooldown | 10 min. | Easy riding | 56–75 | 69–83 |

**SubLT-W7    Sweet Spot: Hill Repeats**                    APPROX. TIME: 1.75 HR.

Warm up and begin three 10-minute intervals at the sweet spot. To recover, pedal easy for 3 minutes between intervals. Then do four repeats of a hill that will take 3 or 4 minutes. On the downhill, pedal slowly with the brakes on and in a big gear to better "flush" the legs. Allow for a solid 4 minutes between efforts. Finish with five 1-minute fast pedaling intervals, resting for 1 minute between intervals. Cool down.

|  | Time | Description | % of FTP | % of FTHR |
|---|---|---|---|---|
| Warm-up | 15 min. | Easy riding | 56–75 | 69–83 |
| Main set | 3 × 10 min. (3 min. RI) | Sweet spot | 88–93 | 92–98 |
|  | 4 × 3–4 min. (4 min. RI) | Hill | 76–80 | 84–88 |
|  | 5 × 1 min. (1 min. RI) | Fast pedaling, 110+ rpm | <90 | <80 |
| Cooldown | 10 min. | Easy riding | 56–75 | 69–83 |

## Level 4: Lactate Threshold (91–105% of FTP)

**LT-W1    Lactate Threshold: Basic Ride 1**              APPROX. TIME: 1.5 HR.

Warm up for 15 minutes, then do three 1-minute fast pedaling intervals. Stay seated for these. Rest for 1 minute between efforts. Follow this with 10 minutes of pedaling at 80–90 percent FTP. Begin two 10-minute Lactate Threshold intervals, resting for 5 minutes between intervals. These efforts should be right at Threshold and can be done on a 10-minute hill if you prefer. Cool down.

|  | Time | Description | % of FTP | % of FTHR |
|---|---|---|---|---|
| Warm-up | 15 min. | Endurance | 56–75 | 69–83 |
| Main set | 3 × 1 min. (1 min. RI) | Fast pedaling, 100+ rpm | <80 | <90 |
|  | 10 min. | Cruise | 80–90 | 85–94 |
|  | 2 × 10 min. (5 min. RI) | Threshold, +5 rpm | 100–105 | >105 |
| Cooldown | 15 min. | Easy riding | 56–75 | 69–83 |

**LT-W2    Lactate Threshold: Basic Ride 2**              APPROX. TIME: 1.25 HR.

Fast pedaling intervals teach your muscles to be ready for changes in speed at any time. They are also a good warm-up when you want a hard interval set that does not cause too much fatigue. Since the goal is based on cadence and not wattage, be sure to keep your power lower when doing these.

After warming up, spin those legs fast for five 1-minute intervals. Keep your cadence over 100 rpm, resting for 1 minute between intervals. To recover, ride easy for 10 minutes. Next, do two 15-minute intervals at Lactate Threshold with a 5-minute rest interval between efforts. Cool down.

(Note: Intervals mentioned in text reflect the minimums. As the season progresses, or as time allows, add intervals to develop your abilities.)

| LT-W2 | Time | Description | % of FTP | % of FTHR |
|---|---|---|---|---|
| Warm-up | 10 min. | Easy riding | 56–75 | 69–83 |
| Main set | 5–10 × 1 min. (1 min. RI) | Fast pedaling, 100+ rpm | <80 | <90 |
| | 10 min. | Easy pace | 56–75 | 69–83 |
| | 2–3 × 15 min. (5 min. RI) | Lactate Threshold | 100–105 | 100–103 |
| Cooldown | 10–15 min. | Easy riding | 56–75 | 69–83 |

### LT-W3    Lactate Threshold: Tempo and Sweet Spot        APPROX. TIME: 4 HR.

Warm up for a solid hour at Endurance pace. Hammer eight 1-minute all-out intervals, recovering for 1 minute between intervals. Cruise for 15 minutes or so and then begin four 10-minute intervals at threshold, increasing your cadence by 5 rpm. Rest for 10 minutes between intervals. Finish with 45 minutes in the sweet spot, riding just below Threshold. Cool down.

| | Time | Description | % of FTP | % of FTHR |
|---|---|---|---|---|
| Warm-up | 1 hr. | Endurance | 56–75 | 69–83 |
| Main set | 8 × 1 min. (1 min. RI) | All-out | >150 | N/A |
| | 15 min. | Cruise | 75–85 | 84–88 |
| | 4 × 10 min. (10 min. RI) | Threshold, +5 rpm | 100–105 | 98–103 |
| | 45 min. | Sweet spot | 88–93 | 92–98 |
| Cooldown | 15 min. | Easy riding | 56–75 | 69–83 |

### LT-W4    Lactate Threshold: Tempo with Neuromuscular Power Bursts
###            and VO$_2$max Intervals        APPROX. TIME: 3 HR.

After a warm-up, do two 20-minute intervals at Threshold, resting for 10 minutes after each one. Then ride at Tempo for 20–30 minutes, including twenty 10-second bursts. For the bursts, start out of the saddle and push your cadence to 110 rpm, maybe shifting just once. Rest for 50 seconds after each one before starting the next burst. Finally, finish with three 5-minute all-out intervals. Hammer these, trying to hold 110–115 percent of FTP, but just do your best. As long as you are above 106 percent of FTP, you are doing them correctly. Rest for 5 minutes between intervals. Cool down.

| | Time | Description | % of FTP | % of FTHR |
|---|---|---|---|---|
| Warm-up | 15 min. | Easy riding | 56–75 | 69–83 |
| Main set | 2 × 20 min. (10 min. RI) | Lactate Threshold | 90–95 | 98–103 |
| | 20–30 min. | Tempo with bursts | 80–85 | 90–98 |
| | *20 × 10 sec. (50 sec. RI)* | *Bursts, 110+ rpm* | *>140* | *N/A* |
| | 3 × 5 min. (5 min. RI) | All-out effort | 110–115 | >105 |
| Cooldown | 15 min. | Easy riding | 56–75 | 69–83 |

**LT-W5**      **Lactate Threshold: 2 × 20-minute Intervals with**
**Neuromuscular Power Bursts**              APPROX. TIME: 1.5 HR.

After a warm-up, do one 10-minute interval at Threshold, followed by 10 minutes of recovery. Then ride at Threshold for 20–30 minutes, followed by ten 20-second bursts. For the bursts, start out of the saddle and push your cadence to 100 rpm in all-out intervals—hammer these. Rest 2–3 minutes between intervals. Cool down.

|          | Time                          | Description                | % of FTP | % of FTHR |
|----------|-------------------------------|----------------------------|----------|-----------|
| Warm-up  | 15 min.                       | Easy riding                | 56–75    | 69–83     |
| Main set | 10 min.                       | Lactate Threshold, TT effort | 98–105 | 98–103    |
|          | 10 min.                       | Easy riding                | 56–75    | 69–83     |
|          | 20–30 min.                    | Threshold with bursts      | 100–105  | 98–103    |
|          | 10 × 20 sec. (2–3 min. RI)    | Bursts, 100+ rpm           | >135     | N/A       |
| Cooldown | 10–15 min.                    | Easy riding                | 56–75    | 69–83     |

**LT-W6**      **Lactate Threshold: 4 × 10-minute Intervals with**
**Sub–Lactate Threshold and Neuromuscular Power Bursts**   APPROX. TIME: 2.75 HR.

Warm up for 20 minutes, then do four 10-minute intervals at Threshold, with 5 minutes of recovery after each one. Then ride for 20 minutes easy. Next, push your power to the sweet spot for 20 minutes, including ten 10-second bursts to 200 percent of FTP, and back down to your previous effort. Cruise for 30 minutes and cool down.

|          | Time                      | Description              | % of FTP | % of FTHR |
|----------|---------------------------|--------------------------|----------|-----------|
| Warm-up  | 20 min.                   | Easy riding              | 56–75    | 69–83     |
| Main set | 4 × 10 min. (5 min. RI)   | Lactate Threshold        | 100–105  | 98–103    |
|          | 20 min.                   | Easy riding              | 80–85    | 88–91     |
|          | 20 min.                   | Sweet spot with bursts   | 88–93    | 92–98     |
|          | 10 × 10 sec.              | Bursts                   | 200      | N/A       |
|          | 30 min.                   | Cruise                   | 70–85    | 80–88     |
| Cooldown | 15 min.                   | Easy riding              | 56–75    | 69–83     |

**LT-W7**      **Lactate Threshold: Cadence Drills and Hills**          APPROX. TIME: 4 HR.

Warm up and ride smooth and steady for the first hour with five 1-minute fast pedaling intervals and then two hard 3-minute hills. At the start of the second hour, do the two 20-minute Lactate Threshold testing and give it your best! Next, hit ten shorter 2-minute hills. Your wattage should be at least 130 percent of FTP—these are not all-out hills. Rest at least 2–3 minutes after each one. Finish with 30–45 minutes in the sweet spot. Cool down.

| LT-W7 | Time | Description | % of FTP | % of FTHR |
|---|---|---|---|---|
| Warm-up | 15 min. | Easy riding | 56–75 | 69–83 |
| Main set | 1 hr. | Smooth with cadence and hill work | 80–95 | 90–98 |
| | *5 × 1 min. (1 min. RI)* | *Fast pedaling, 100+ rpm* | *<80* | *<90* |
| | *2 × 3 min.* | *Hard hills* | *>115* | *>105* |
| | 2 × 20 min. (10 min. RI) | Lactate Threshold | 90–95 | 98–102 |
| | 10 × 2 min. (2–3 min. RI) | Short hills | >130 | >105 |
| | 30–45 min. | Sweet spot | 88–93 | 92–98 |
| Cooldown | 10 min. | Easy riding | 56–75 | 69–83 |

## LT-W8    Lactate Threshold: Mountain Passes and Short Hills    APPROX. TIME: 5 HR.

Warm up and ride smooth and steady for the first hour or so. If possible, plan to ride over two mountain passes, riding both at Threshold power. These should be 30-minute efforts. Later in the ride, hit ten solid hill jams, each lasting from 30 seconds to 2 minutes. Wattage should be at least 120 percent of FTP—these are not all-out hills. Rest for 2–3 minutes between hills. (This ride can be done into the wind if hills or mountains are not accessible.) Cool down.

| | Time | Description | % of FTP | % of FTHR |
|---|---|---|---|---|
| Warm-up | 30 min. | Easy riding | 56–75 | 69–83 |
| Main set | 4 hr. | Smooth with hill work | 70–85 | 80–92 |
| | *2 × 30 min. (10 min. RI)* | *Lactate Threshold* | *98–100* | *99–103* |
| | *10 × 30 sec.–2 min. (2–3 min. RI)* | *Short hills* | *>120* | *>105* |
| Cooldown | 30 min. | Easy riding | 56–75 | 69–83 |

## LT-W9    Lactate Threshold: Crisscross to Anaerobic Capacity    APPROX. TIME: 2 HR.

Warm up for 15 minutes, then do three 1-minute fast pedaling intervals. Begin two 20-minute crisscross FTP intervals, and every 2 minutes do a burst for 30 seconds, which will swing your power from FTP to Anaerobic Capacity and back to FTP. Be careful to keep your power from slipping below 90 percent of FTP and try to come back to 95–100 percent. Recover for 5 minutes after each 20-minute crisscross interval. Finish with two 5-minute VO$_2$max intervals, resting for 5 minutes after each one. Cool down for 15 minutes.

| | Time | Description | % of FTP | % of FTHR |
|---|---|---|---|---|
| Warm-up | 15 min. | Easy riding | 56–75 | 69–83 |
| | 3 × 1 min. (1 min. RI) | Fast pedaling, >110 rpm | <80 | <90 |
| Main set | 2 × 20 min. (5 min. RI) | Crisscross, FTP to AC | 90–120 | 98–105 |
| | *30 sec.* | *Burst every 2 min.* | *120* | *102–103* |
| | 10 min. | Recover | 56–75 | 69–83 |
| | 2 × 5 min. (5 min. RI) | VO$_2$max | 115 | 103 |
| Cooldown | 15 min. | Easy riding | 56–75 | 69–83 |

LT-W10      **Lactate Threshold: Anaerobic Capacity**
**Intervals and Cadence Drills**                           APPROX. TIME: 2 HR.

Warm up for 15 minutes in Level 2. Begin fast pedaling intervals with the goal of pedaling at 110+ rpm for the entire minute. Don't worry about power or heart rate. Recover for 1 minute between intervals. Then push hard and increase your cadence by 5 rpm for four 10-minute intervals at 100 percent of FTP. Rest for 5–10 minutes between efforts. Finish with four 1-minute intervals. Attack at the beginning of each interval, pushing as hard as you can. Rest for 2 minutes between efforts. Finish the ride with a 15-minute cooldown.

|          | Time                       | Description             | % of FTP | % of FTHR |
|----------|----------------------------|-------------------------|----------|-----------|
| Warm-up  | 15 min.                    | Easy riding             | 56–75    | 69–83     |
|          | 3 × 1 min. (1 min. RI)     | Fast pedaling, 110+ rpm | <80      | <90       |
| Main set | 4 × 10 min. (5–10 min. RI) | FTP, +5 rpm             | 100–103  | 100–105   |
|          | 4 × 1 min. (2 min. RI)     | All-out effort          | >140     | >105      |
| Cooldown | 15 min.                    | Easy riding             | 56–75    | 69–83     |

## Level 5: VO₂max (106–120% of FTP)

VO2-W1      **VO₂max: 6-minute Time Trial**                           APPROX. TIME: 1.75 HR.

If you have a time trial bike, use it for this ride. These time trials will help you develop pacing and deliver solid work at Threshold power.

After warming up, move into the time trial simulation. Keeping FTP between 96 and 102 percent of FTP, do six 6-minute time trial simulations. Ride fast at max pace, but avoid hammering. Rest for at least 6–8 minutes between intervals, being sure to ride at your normal self-selected cadence. Finish with a 15-minute cooldown.

|          | Time                   | Description      | % of FTP | % of FTHR |
|----------|------------------------|------------------|----------|-----------|
| Warm-up  | 15 min.                | Endurance pace   | 56–75    | 69–83     |
| Main set | 6 × 6 min. (6–8 min. RI) | VO₂max TT, fast  | 96–102   | 100–105   |
| Cooldown | 15 min.                | Easy riding      | 56–75    | 69–83     |

VO2-W2      **VO₂max: 6-minute Time Trial with Tempo**                APPROX. TIME: 3 HR.

If you have a time trial bike, use it for this ride. Because this ride is a simulation of pushing through a time trial, it is important to nail the FTP as much as possible.

Start with a brisk 20-minute warm-up and then go right into five 1-minute fast pedaling efforts, resting for 1 minute between efforts. Ride easy for 10 minutes and then move into the time trial simulation. Do five 6-minute pushes. Rest for 5 minutes between intervals, being sure to ride at your normal, self-selected cadence. Finish with 20 minutes of Tempo riding and a 15-minute cooldown.

| VO2-W2 | Time | Description | % of FTP | % of FTHR |
|---|---|---|---|---|
| Warm-up | 20 min. | Endurance pace | 56–75 | 69–83 |
| Main set | 5 × 1 min. (1 min. RI) | Fast pedaling, 100+ rpm | <80 | <90 |
| | 10 min. | Easy riding | 56–75 | 69–83 |
| | 5 × 6 min. (5 min. RI) | TT simulation | 110–115 | >105 |
| | 20 min. | Tempo riding | 80–90 | 90–94 |
| Cooldown | 15 min. | Easy riding | 56–75 | 69–83 |

### VO2-W3    VO$_2$max: 3-minute Time Trial                    APPROX. TIME: 1 HR.

Go for it on this ride. Try to do six 3-minute hard pushes, holding your power at over 115 percent of FTP for the entire interval—so don't start your interval on a section of road that will include a downhill. Be sure to rest for 5 minutes after each push, keeping your FTP at 75 percent (with FTHR at 85 percent). Keep a Tempo pace when you're not pushing, staying around 80 percent of FTP.

| | Time | Description | % of FTP | % of FTHR |
|---|---|---|---|---|
| Warm-up | 15 min. | Easy riding | 56–75 | 69–83 |
| Main set | 6 × 3 min. (5 min. RI) | Hard efforts at VO$_2$max | >115 | >105 |
| | Rest of the ride | Tempo pace | 80–85 | 88–90 |
| Cooldown | 10 min. | Easy riding | 56–75 | 69–83 |

### VO2-W4    VO$_2$max: 3-minute and 2-minute Time Trial        APPROX. TIME: 1.5 HR.

Warm up, then complete a 5-minute VO$_2$max interval, followed by 5 minutes of easy riding. Do six 3-minute intervals next, trying to average the highest possible power—shoot for 120 percent of FTP. Rest for 3 minutes between intervals. Cruise easy for 10 minutes, and then do four 2-minute intervals with 4 minutes of rest after each one. These are hard efforts. Cool down.

| | Time | Description | % of FTP | % of FTHR |
|---|---|---|---|---|
| Warm-up | 15 min. | Easy riding | 56–75 | 69–83 |
| Main set | 5 min. (5 min. RI) | VO$_2$max | 106–115 | >105 |
| | 6 × 3 min. (3 min. RI) | VO$_2$max | 120 | >105 |
| | 10 min. | Cruise | 56–75 | 69–83 |
| | 4 × 2 min. (4 min. RI) | VO$_2$max time trial | 135 | >105 |
| Cooldown | 15 min. | Easy riding | 56–75 | 69–83 |

### VO2-W5    VO$_2$max: 2-minute Time Trial                     APPROX. TIME: 1.25 HR.

You should be fresh for this ride. As you can see from the big numbers, this is not a long workout, just a hard one.

After warming up, it's hammer time! Do four 1-minute fast pedaling intervals with your cadence over 100 rpm. Don't worry too much about wattage, but focus on cadence and pedaling smoothly. Ride for 5 minutes easy and then do six 2-minute time trial intervals, starting from a speed of 23–25 mph, pushing steady for the entire effort, and building to a hard push at the end. Rest for 2 minutes between intervals. Ride easy for 10 minutes and finish with one 6-minute time trial—really push it! Cool down.

| VO2-W5 | Time | Description | % of FTP | % of FTHR |
|---|---|---|---|---|
| Warm-up | 15 min. | Easy riding | 56–75 | 69–83 |
| Main set | 4 × 1 min. (1 min. RI) | Fast pedaling, 100+ rpm | <80 | <90 |
| | 5 min. | Easy riding | 56–75 | 69–83 |
| | 6 × 2 min. (2 min. RI) | VO₂max time trial | avg. 135+ | avg. 105 |
| | 10 min. | Easy riding | 56–75 | 69–83 |
| | 6 min. | VO₂max time trial | avg. 135+ | >105 |
| Cooldown | 15 min. | Easy riding | 56–75 | 69–83 |

## VO2-W6   VO₂max: Race-Winning Intervals, Ride 1                       APPROX. TIME: 1.5 HR.

These intervals will improve your VO₂max and your ability to win races because the workout simulates the power graph of a rider attacking for the race win.

Begin the workout with a 20-minute warm-up at Endurance pace. Next begin five 1-minute fast pedaling efforts, keeping the amount of force on the pedals relatively low to prevent bouncing in the saddle. Ride at Endurance pace for 5 minutes and then get ready for the race-winning intervals, trying to complete at least five efforts in one session.

Begin intervals with a 30-second sprint (spend 15 seconds out of the saddle), averaging 200 percent of FTP and peaking at 300 percent of your Threshold wattage. Try to reach a speed of 28–30 mph and hold it for 30 seconds. Ride for 3 minutes and really hammer at 100–110 percent of FTP (or the best speed you think you can maintain for 1 hour), and finish with a 10-second out-of-the-saddle burst, trying to reach 200 percent of FTP wattage again. Rest for 5–6 minutes between sets.

If you can push yourself, finish with eight 1-minute fast pedaling efforts (over 110 rpm), resting for 1 minute after each effort. Cool down.

| | Time | Description | % of FTP | % of FTHR |
|---|---|---|---|---|
| Warm-up | 20 min. | Easy riding | 56–75 | 69–83 |
| | 5 × 1 min. (1 min. RI) | Fast pedaling, 110+ rpm | <80 | <90 |
| | 5 min. | Endurance pace | 56–75 | 69–83 |
| Main set | 5–8 × 5 min. (5–6 min. RI) | Race-winning intervals | 100–110 | 100–105 |
| | 30 sec. | Sprints, peak at 300% FTP | 200+ | N/A |
| | 3 min. | Steady effort | 100–110 | 100–105 |
| | 10 sec. | Burst | 200+ | N/A |
| | 8 × 1 min. (1 min. RI) | Fast pedaling effort, 110+ rpm | <80 | <90 |
| Cooldown | 15 min. | Easy riding | 56–75 | 69–83 |

VO2-W7    **VO₂max: Race-Winning Intervals, Ride 2**                    APPROX. TIME: 2.5 HR.

Complete a 30-minute warm-up. Build from Tempo to Threshold for 10 minutes, so the last minute is at Threshold. Then ride easy for 10 minutes.

For the main set, start out with 5 minutes at Threshold, then ride for 2 minutes at just above Threshold (your heart rate will rise about 5 bpm). Bring it back down to Threshold pace. For example, if your Threshold power is 300 watts and your Threshold heart rate is 170 bpm, ride at 300 watts for 5 minutes, then bring up the power to 320 watts for 2 minutes, raising your heart rate to 175 bpm, then back off to a power of 300 watts again. When your heart rate reaches 170 bpm again, or when 3 minutes is up, bring it back up to 320 watts (175 bpm).

Each set of race intervals begins with 3 minutes at Threshold, then 2 minutes just above, repeating three times in 15 minutes. Then rest for 10 minutes. Do three 15-minute sets of race intervals. Cool down for 20 minutes.

|  | Time | Description | % of FTP | % of FTHR |
|---|---|---|---|---|
| Warm-up | 10 min. | Easy riding | 56–75 | 69–83 |
|  | 10 min. | Build to Threshold | 75–100 | 85–100 |
|  | 10 min. | Easy riding | 56–75 | 69–83 |
| Main set | 5 min. | Threshold | 100–105 | 98–103 |
|  | 2 min. | Just above Threshold | 105–110 | >105 |
|  | 3 × 5 min. | Race-winning intervals |  |  |
|  |  | *3 min. at Threshold* | *100* | *100–103* |
|  |  | *2 min. above Threshold* | *105–110* | *>105* |
|  | 10 min. | Recovery | 56–75 | 69–83 |
|  | Repeat set of race-winning intervals two more times |  |  |  |
| Cooldown | 20 min. | Easy riding | 56–75 | 69–83 |

## Level 6: Anaerobic Capacity (121–150% of FTP)

AC-W1    **Anaerobic Capacity: Hills, Ride 1**                    APPROX. TIME: 1 HR.

Make this ride a very hilly one or simulate hills by riding into the wind. The hills can range from 30 seconds to 2 minutes in length.

After warming up, let the fun begin. Ride at a fast pace. Your legs should be burning by the time you reach the top.

|  | Time | Description | % of FTP | % of FTHR |
|---|---|---|---|---|
| Warm-up | 20 min. | Easy riding | 56–75 | 69–83 |
| Main set | 10 × 30 sec.–2 min. | Hill repeats | >120 | >105 |
| Cooldown | 15–20 min. | Easy riding | 56–75 | 69–83 |

~~AC-W2~~     **Anaerobic Capacity: Hills, Ride 2**     ~~APPROX. TIME: 2 HR.~~

This is a hill-repeat workout. Find a hill that is similar to the hills in an upcoming race, requiring 2–3 minutes to climb.

Warm up with at least 20 miles at a steady pace before beginning the hill intervals. Do ten repeats, hammering all the way and exploding at the top. Rest between efforts. These should hurt. Cool down.

| | Time | Description | % of FTP | % of FTHR |
|---|---|---|---|---|
| Warm-up | 20 min. | Easy riding | 56–75 | 69–83 |
| Main set | 1.5 hr. | Tempo with hill repeats | 70–85 | 88–91 |
| | 10 × 30 sec.–2 min. | Hill repeats | >120 | >105 |
| Cooldown | 15–20 min. | Easy riding | 56–75 | 69–83 |

**AC-W3**     **Anaerobic Capacity: 1-minute and 2-minute Intervals**     APPROX. TIME: 1.5 HR.

The goal of this workout is to improve your ability to go hard and recover quickly. Use the guidelines in Table 5.1 to know exactly when to stop doing intervals, but do at least eight intervals.

Get the legs moving with a standard warm-up and then set your power meter to "interval mode" so you can see the average. You want to go as hard as you can in your main sets, using your average watts as a "carrot" to push all the way until the end. Reach for over 130 percent of your Threshold power, but stop when you can no longer reach 118 percent in your average. After recovering for at least 2 minutes (more if needed), finish with three 1-minute efforts, trying to average over 140 percent, and stopping when you fall below 120 percent. Cool down.

| | Time | Description | % of FTP | % of FTHR |
|---|---|---|---|---|
| Warm-up | 15 min. | Easy riding | 56–75 | 69–83 |
| Main set | 8 × 2 min. (2 min. RI) | Hard as you can<br>Recover longer if needed | avg. 130+ | >105 |
| | 3 × 1 min. (2 min. RI) | Hard as you can | avg. 140+ | >105 |
| Cooldown | 15 min. | Easy riding | 56–75 | 69–83 |

**AC-W4**     **Anaerobic Capacity: FTP and Sweet Spot**     APPROX. TIME: 1.5 HR.

Get the legs moving with a low-intensity 15-minute warm-up, and then set your power meter to "interval mode" so you can see the average. This will allow you also to review each interval after it is completed, so you can have a goal for the next one or know when to stop.

Begin the 45-minute main set by hitting 100 percent of your FTHR in a 5-minute effort to get the legs ready. Do another 5-minute effort at 80 percent of your FTHR, and then really push it, doing six 2-minute sets as hard as you can go, using your average watts as a "carrot" to push yourself to the end. Try to average over 130 percent of your Threshold power, but stop when you can't reach 118 percent of FTP. Recover for at least 3 minutes, and then finish with a 20-minute sweet spot ride. Cool down.

| AC-W4 | Time | Description | % of FTP | % of FTHR |
|---|---|---|---|---|
| Warm-up | 15 min. | Easy riding | >56 | >69 |
| Main set | 5 min. | Threshold effort | 91–105 | 99–103 |
| | 5 min. | Recover | <75 | 80 |
| | 6 × 2 min. (3 min. RI) | Hard as you can | avg. 130 | >105 |
| | 20 min. | Sweet spot | 88–93 | 92–98 |
| Cooldown | 10 min. | Easy riding, watts <100 | 56–75 | 69–83 |

### AC-W5    Anaerobic Capacity: Tempo with Neuromuscular Power Bursts    APPROX. TIME: 2 HR.

Warm up and ride for 1 hour at your sweet spot, smooth and steady, including ten 15-second bursts at 150 percent of FTP within the hour. Next, do eight 2-minute intervals at an average of at least 135 percent of FTP. Stop when the intervals fall below 122 percent. Rest for 2 minutes between intervals. Use the interval guidelines to decide when to stop doing repeats. Cool down.

| | Time | Description | % of FTP | % of FTHR |
|---|---|---|---|---|
| Warm-up | 15 min. | Easy riding | 56–75 | 69–83 |
| Main set | 1 hr. | Sweet spot with bursts | 88–93 | 92–98 |
| | *10 × 15 sec.* | *Bursts* | *150* | *N/A* |
| | 8 × 2 min. (2 min. RI) | Hard as you can | avg. 135 | >105 |
| Cooldown | 15 min. | Easy riding | 56–75 | 69–83 |

### AC-W6    Anaerobic Capacity: All AC Intervals, Ride 1    APPROX. TIME: 1 HR.

There are fewer Level 6 intervals in this workout. There is no need to overdo it, but the intensity should be good.

After warming up, do three 2-minute intervals at Anaerobic Capacity with 1-minute rests between intervals. Then ride easy for 5 minutes. Begin three 1-minute intervals, pushing harder still, again resting for 1 minute between intervals. Ride at an easy pace for 5 minutes. Finally, do three 30-second intervals, riding all-out, with 1-minute rest intervals. Cool down.

| | Time | Description | % of FTP | % of FTHR |
|---|---|---|---|---|
| Warm-up | 15 min. | Easy riding | 56–75 | 69–83 |
| Main set | 3 × 2 min. (1 min. RI) | Anaerobic Capacity | 135 | 105 |
| | 5 min. | Easy riding | <75 | <83 |
| | 3 × 1 min. (1 min. RI) | Anaerobic Capacity | 150 | >105 |
| | 5 min. | Easy riding | <75 | <83 |
| | 3 × 30 sec. (1 min. RI) | All-out | 200 | N/A |
| Cooldown | 15 min. | Easy riding | 56–75 | 69–83 |

AC-W7    **Anaerobic Capacity: All AC Intervals, Ride 2**    APPROX. TIME: 1.25 HR.

After warming up, do six 2-minute intervals at Anaerobic Capacity with 1-minute rests after each one. Then ride easy for 5 minutes. Begin six 1-minute intervals, pushing harder still, again resting for 1 minute between intervals. Ride easy for 5 minutes. Finally, do six 30-second intervals, riding all-out, with 1-minute rest intervals. Cool down.

|  | Time | Description | % of FTP | % of FTHR |
|---|---|---|---|---|
| Warm-up | 20 min. | Easy riding | 56–75 | 69–83 |
| Main set | 6 × 2 min. (1 min. RI) | Anaerobic Capacity | >135 | >105 |
|  | 5 min. | Easy riding | <75 | <83 |
|  | 6 × 1 min. (1 min. RI) | Anaerobic Capacity | >150 | >105 |
|  | 5 min. | Easy riding | <75 | <83 |
|  | 6 × 30 sec. (1 min. RI) | All-out | 200 | N/A |
| Cooldown | 15 min. | Easy riding | 56–75 | 69–83 |

## Level 7: Neuromuscular Power

NP-W1    **Neuromuscular Power: Microbursts**    APPROX. TIME: 1.25 HR.

This workout will teach your muscles how to change speeds by improving contraction and relaxation responses.

After warming up, begin three 10-minute microburst intervals. Your power will be continuously switching from 15 seconds "on" (150 percent of FTP) to 15 seconds "off" (spinning easy). Rest for 5 minutes between intervals. Cool down.

|  | Time | Description | % of FTP | % of FTHR |
|---|---|---|---|---|
| Warm-up | 15 min. | Easy riding | <56 | <69 |
| Main set | 3 × 10 min. (5 min. RI) | Continuous 15-sec. microbursts | 91–105 | 95–103 |
|  | *15 sec.* | *"On": hard microburst* | *150* | *N/A* |
|  | *15 sec.* | *"Off": recovery* | *50* | *N/A* |
| Cooldown | 15 min. | Easy riding | 56–75 | 69–83 |

NP-W2    **Neuromuscular Power: Microbursts and Sprints**    APPROX. TIME: 2 HR.

After a standard 15-minute warm-up, do three 10-minute microbursts with 15 seconds "on" (150 percent of FTP) and 15 seconds "off" (50 percent of FTP). Repeat continually for 10 minutes. Recover for 5 minutes after intervals. Cruise for 15 minutes easy, and then do ten 10-second sprint intervals out of the saddle, with at least 2 minutes between efforts. Try to reach 300–350 percent of Threshold power on the sprints. Cool down.

| NP-W2 | Time | Description | % of FTP | % of FTHR |
|---|---|---|---|---|
| Warm-up | 15 min. | Easy riding | 56–75 | 69–83 |
| Main set | 3 × 10 min. (5 min. RI) | Continuous 15 sec. microbursts | 91–105 | 95–103 |
| | *15 sec.* | *"On": hard microburst* | *150* | *N/A* |
| | *15 sec.* | *"Off": recovery* | *50* | *N/A* |
| | 15 min. | Cruise | 56–75 | 69–83 |
| | 10 × 10 sec. (2 min. RI) | Sprint intervals | 300–350 | N/A |
| Cooldown | 15 min. | Easy riding | 56–75 | 69–83 |

### NP-W3    Neuromuscular Power: 10-second Bursts                APPROX. TIME: 1.5 HR.

After a standard warm-up, set a pace in the lower end of Level 3 (76–80 percent of FTP) and hold it steady for the next hour. Within this hour, do a 10-second, out-of-the-saddle burst every 3 minutes, trying to reach 180 percent of FTP wattage, and hold it there with no more than two gear changes, if any. Make sure your cadence stays high. Cruise the rest of the ride at below 80 percent of FTP. Cool down.

| | Time | Description | % of FTP | % of FTHR |
|---|---|---|---|---|
| Warm-up | 15 min. | Easy riding | <56 | <69 |
| Main set | 1 hr. | Tempo riding with bursts every 3 min. | 76–80 | 84–88 |
| | *10 sec.* | *Bursts, 100+ rpm* | *180* | *N/A* |
| | Remaining time | Cruise | <80 | <90 |
| Cooldown | 15 min. | Easy riding | 56–75 | 69–83 |

### NP-W4    Neuromuscular Power: Big Gear Uphill                APPROX. TIME: 1.75 HR.

This is a great ride for an indoor trainer. Place the front wheel of the bike on some blocks to lift it about 2–4 inches above horizontal. Alternatively, find a 2-minute hill nearby and ride outdoors.

Warm up for 20 minutes. While remaining seated, begin six big-ring efforts in 53:14, starting from 12 mph. Bring your cadence up to 80 rpm to finish the effort and begin a 3-minute recovery interval. Recover from the set with 15 minutes of spinning. Start the next set of sprints in 53:19 or 53:17. Get out of the saddle and ride for 2 minutes, visualizing that you are taking off at the bottom of a hill and muscling the gear over the top. Do six to eight sprints total, keeping your cadence at 50–60 rpm. Be careful on the knees. Rest for 3 minutes after each interval. Spin to cool down.

| | Time | Description | % of FTP | % of FTHR |
|---|---|---|---|---|
| Warm-up | 20 min. | Easy riding | 56–75 | 69–83 |
| Main set | 6 × 30 sec. (3 min. RI) | Seated big-ring sprints (53:14) from 12 mph, finish at 80 rpm | N/A | <80 |
| | 15 min. | Spinning | <75 | <83 |
| | 6–8 × 2 min. (3 min. RI) | Standing small-ring sprints (53:19 or 53:17), 50–60 rpm | >115 | >105 |
| Cooldown | 15 min. | Easy riding | 56–75 | 69–83 |

**NP-W5**     **Neuromuscular Power: Small- and Big-Ring Sprints, Ride 1**   APPROX. TIME: 1.25 HR.
One of the goals of this workout is to avoid "dumping the chain" into the hardest gear for a sprint. Sprinting starts out with a hard jump. As you "wind" out each gear, you shift down one. Just like driving a stick-shift car, you work down the gears when the rpms reach the correct range.

After warming up, begin six sprints in the small chainring with no gear changes, riding 50 meters and winding the gears out. Rest for 2–3 minutes between sprints.

Then do three sprints in the big chainring, jumping in the 53:17 from 20 mph and shifting once. Rest for 3–5 minutes after each sprint. Next, do three big-ring sprints from 53:16 at 23 mph with two gear changes. Finish with one big-ring sprint from 53:15 at 28 mph, jumping hard and winding out both the 53:14 and 53:13 gears. (This can be on a slight downhill grade to help you get up to speed.) Cool down.

|  | Time | Description | % of FTP | % of FTHR |
|---|---|---|---|---|
| Warm-up | 15 min. | Easy riding | 56–75 | 69–83 |
| Main set | 6 × 50 m (2–3 min. RI) | Small-ring sprints from 10 mph, finish at 120 rpm | max | N/A |
|  | 3 × 250 m (3–5 min. RI) | Big-ring sprints in 53:17 from 20 mph<br>Wind out the gear and shift once<br>Finish at 110–120 rpm | max | N/A |
|  | 3 × 250 m (3–5 min. RI) | Big-ring sprints in 53:16 from 23 mph<br>Wind out the gear and shift twice<br>Finish at 110–120 rpm | max | N/A |
|  | 250 m | Big-ring sprint in 53:15 from 26 to 28 mph (downhill)<br>Wind out the gear and shift twice<br>Finish at 110–120 rpm | max | N/A |
| Cooldown | 20–30 min. | Easy riding | 56–75 | 69–83 |

**NP-W6**     **Neuromuscular Power: Small- and Big-Ring Sprints, Ride 2**     APPROX. TIME: 2 HR.
To improve your sprint for this season, try this workout. Make sure you have a smooth road with plenty of visibility—ideally a flat to gentle downhill section of straight road.

Warm up for 20 minutes, keeping your effort at Endurance pace. Start out with three 1-minute fast pedaling efforts in which you get your cadence to 110+ rpm, holding it there for 1 minute. Force on the pedals is relatively low, but avoid bouncing in the saddle. Recover for 1 minute between intervals. Ride at Endurance pace for 5 minutes, then get ready for the sprints.

Start out with small-ring sprints from a slow speed, about 10 mph. Emphasize the initial "jump" and then wind out that gear as best you can and spin the legs. Do six 50-meter small-ring sprints in your small ring and two cogs down from the top gear on the rear wheel, without shifting gears. Wind the gears out. Rest for 1–2 minutes after intervals (which is usually just the time it takes for a leisurely ride back to the starting line of your sprint).

Next, do six big-ring sprints with only one gear change. Try to start out at 53:17 from 20 mph, and when you wind out this gear, shift to the 53:16 and wind it out to the finish line. Again, rest for at least 2 minutes, if not longer, for these intervals.

Finish with four more sprints, but now starting from a slightly harder gear and from a faster speed. Do three big-ring sprints from the 53:16 at 23 mph, and this time you can shift gears two times, so you finish in the 53:14. The final sprint of the day is in the big ring from 30 mph and starting in the 53:15, and then giving yourself two gear changes so you finish in the 53:13. Remember that for each sprint, you need to wind out each gear until you have nothing left to wind out. Cool down for at least 20 minutes.

| NP-W6 | Time | Description | % of FTP | % of FTHR |
|---|---|---|---|---|
| Warm-up | 20 min. | Easy riding | 56–75 | 69–83 |
| Main set | 3 × 1 min. (1 min. RI) | Fast pedaling, 110+ rpm | <80 | <90 |
| | 5 min. | Easy riding | 56–75 | 69–83 |
| | 6 × 50 m (1–2 min. RI) | Small-ring sprints from 10 mph<br>Finish at 120 rpm | max | N/A |
| | 6 × 250 m (2–3 min. RI) | Big-ring sprints in 53:17 from 20 mph<br>Finish at 110–120 rpm, shifting once (53:16) | max | N/A |
| | 3 × 250 m (2–3 min. RI) | Big-ring sprints in 53:16 from 23 mph<br>Wind out the gear and shift twice (53:15, 53:14)<br>Finish at 110–120 rpm | max | N/A |
| | 250 m | Big-ring sprint in 53:15 from 30 mph (downhill)<br>Wind out the gear and shift twice (53:14, 53:13)<br>Finish at 110–120 rpm | max | N/A |
| Cooldown | 20–30 min. | Easy riding | 56–75 | 69–83 |

### All Levels: Kitchen Sink

Many of the rides work multiple energy systems at once, yet there is typically emphasis on one system. The rides that follow throw in "everything but the kitchen sink." They are challenging workouts and a good test of overall fatigue resistance.

**WATTS-W1    Kitchen Sink: Mountains**                    APPROX. TIME: 4 HR.

Try for a solid 4 hours of riding in the mountains. Make sure to maintain cadence on steep grades.

Ease into the ride and in the first two hours do at least three major climbs. Ride at Threshold over two of them. Ride the other climb at Tempo pace. Watch cadence and power, and maximize efficiency!

On each of the downhills, try to fit in two 3-minute fast pedaling efforts. Keep your cadence above 120 rpm, braking as needed to keep pressure on the pedals, and pedal fast. Rest for 3 minutes between intervals. If the climbs are not long enough to fit in two intervals, make them up later in the ride on flatter sections.

In the third hour, ride steady, incorporating eight 2-minute intervals on flat to rolling terrain.

Stop for a recovery drink or caffeine boost with 20 miles to go. Hammer for the last 30–40 minutes, riding fast. Cool down.

| WATTS-W1 | Time | Description | % of FTP | % of FTHR |
|---|---|---|---|---|
| Warm up | 30 min. | Easy riding | 56–75 | 69–83 |
| Main set | 1.5 hr. | Endurance/Tempo with hills | 70–85 | 80–92 |
| | 2 × 20 min. | Hills at Threshold | 100–105 | 99–103 |
| | 2 × 3 min. (3 min RI) | Downhills, fast pedaling, 120+ rpm | <100 | <100 |
| | 20 min. | Hill at Tempo | 76–90 | 84–94 |
| | 2 × 3 min. (3 min RI) | Downhills, fast pedaling, 120+ rpm | <100 | <100 |
| | 1 hr. | Endurance/Tempo with hard 2 min. efforts | 70–85 | 80–92 |
| | 8 × 2 min. | Anaerobic Capacity | 120–140 | >105 |
| | 30–40 min. | Fast | 80–95 | 90–98 |
| Cooldown | 30 min. | Easy riding | 56–75 | 69–83 |

## WATTS-W2    Kitchen Sink: Anaerobic Capacity, Neuromuscular Power, FTP, and Motorpacing

APPROX. TIME: 5 HR.

The Training Stress Score for this ride is 300. Warm up and do four 1-minute fast pedaling intervals. Then do six 2-minute all-out efforts on a flat road. Recover fully, riding for about 4 minutes at Endurance pace. Then do six 30-second efforts with a hard sprint at the start. Recover fully, riding for about 3 minutes. Cruise easy for 20 minutes.

Next, do six 75-meter small-ring sprints, starting from 10 mph and winding out the 39:16 and 39:17 gears to 135 rpm. Then do six 250-meter big-ring sprints, starting from 18 mph and winding out the 53:16, 53:15, and 53:14 gears.

Finally, choose a hill that will take 10–12 minutes to ride. You'll be riding in the sweet spot, completing five repeats. Your intensity should approach the edge of Threshold up the hill (100–105 percent of FTP). Rest for 5–10 minutes between the climbs. Motorpace home and cooldown.

| | Time | Description | % of FTP | % of FTHR |
|---|---|---|---|---|
| Warm up | 30 min. | Easy riding | 56–75 | 69–83 |
| Main set | 4 × 1 min. | Fast pedaling | <80 | <90 |
| | 6 × 2 min. (4 min. RI) | All-out effort | 120+ | >105 |
| | 6 × 30 sec. (3 min. RI) | Hard sprint | 150+ | >105 |
| | 20 min. | Easy riding | 56–75 | 69–83 |
| | 6 × 75 m | Small-ring sprints (39:16, 39:17) from 10 mph, finish at 135 rpm | max | N/A |
| | 6 × 250 m | Big-ring sprints (53:16, 53:15, 53:14) from 18 mph | max | N/A |
| | 5 × 10–12 min. (5–10 min. RI) | Hill repeats in sweet spot | 88–93 | 92–98 |
| | Remaining time (2+ hr.) | Motorpace home | 85–110 | 90–105 |
| Cooldown | 15 min. | Easy riding | 56–75 | 69–83 |

WATTS-W3   **Kitchen Sink: FTP, Anaerobic Capacity,**
**and Neuromuscular Power Sprints, Ride 1**                    APPROX. TIME: 3 HR.

This is a great Saturday workout. By the end of the ride, you should be tired and ready for the ride to be over.

Warm up, including three 1-minute fast pedaling intervals. Begin with four sprints in the big chain-ring (53:15) from 22 mph, shifting just twice to finish at 53:13. Rest for 3–4 minutes after each sprint. Then do two 12-minute intervals at just above Threshold, doing your best to hold it. Rest for 5 minutes after intervals.

Finally, do four 2-minute intervals on the flats, with 1-minute recoveries. Try to hold 130 percent of FTP. Finish with 20 minutes at Endurance pace. Cool down.

|  | Time | Description | % of FTP | % of FTHR |
|---|---|---|---|---|
| Warm-up | 15 min. | Easy riding | 56–75 | 69–83 |
|  | 3 × 1 min. | Fast pedaling, 100+ rpm | <80 | <90 |
| Main set | 4 × 300 m (3–4 min. RI) | Big-ring sprints (53:15), from 22 mph, shifting twice (53:14, 53:13) | max | N/A |
|  | 2 × 12 min. (5 min. RI) | Above Threshold | 100–105 | 100–105 |
|  | 4 × 2 min. (1 min. RI) | Anaerobic Capacity | 130 | >105 |
|  | 20 min. | Endurance | 56–75 | 69–83 |
| Cooldown | 5 min. | Easy riding | 56–75 | 69–83 |

WATTS-W4   **Kitchen Sink: FTP, Anaerobic Capacity,**
**and Neuromuscular Power Sprints, Ride 2**                  APPROX. TIME: 3.5 HR.

This is a great Saturday workout with everything but the kitchen sink thrown in. By the end of the ride, you should be tired and ready for the ride to be over.

Warm up, including three 1-minute fast pedaling intervals. Begin with four sprints in the big chain-ring (53:15) from 22 mph, shifting just twice to finish at 53:13. Rest for 3–4 minutes after each sprint. Then do four 12-minute intervals at just above Threshold, doing your best to hold it. Rest for 5 minutes after each interval.

Finally, do four 2-minute intervals on the flats, with 1-minute recoveries. Try to hold 130–140 percent of FTP on the 2-minute efforts. Next, cruise for 45 minutes at upper Endurance pace. Finish with 20 minutes in the sweet spot. Cool down.

|  | Time | Description | % of FTP | % of FTHR |
|---|---|---|---|---|
| Warm-up | 15 min. | Easy riding | 56–75 | 69–83 |
|  | 3 × 1 min. (1 min. RI) | Fast pedaling, 100+ rpm | <80 | <90 |
| Main set | 4 × 300 m (3–4 min. RI) | Big-ring sprints (53:15) from 22 mph, shifting twice (53:14, 53:13) | max | N/A |
|  | 4 × 12 min. (5 min. RI) | Above Threshold | 100–103 | 100–105 |
|  | 4 × 2 min. (1 min. RI) | Anaerobic Capacity | 130–140 | >105 |
|  | 45 min. | Upper Endurance | 70–75 | 80–85 |
|  | 20 min. | Sweet spot | 88–93 | 92–98 |
| Cooldown | 5 min. | Easy riding | 56–75 | 69–83 |

WATTS-W5   **Kitchen Sink: The Great Workout**                    APPROX. TIME: 4 HR.

This 4-hour ride includes a bit of training in all the physiological zones. Endurance will be the focus, but with the added work throughout the ride, this is a great all-around workout. You should be feeling fatigued at the end of the ride, but in the last 45 minutes, push at the sweet spot.

After a 30-minute warm-up, do two 20-minute intervals at or just below Threshold. This will be challenging. Rest for 10 minutes after each effort.

Cruise for 30 minutes and then do six sprints—three 75-meter sprints in the small chainring from a slow speed, spinning the gear, followed by three 300-meter sprints in the big chainring, starting from about 20 mph in the 53:13 gear. Rest for 5 minutes after each sprint.

Cruise for another 30 minutes or so. Next, ride five hills of various lengths and grades at VO$_2$max pace, with good solid rests after each hill.

Cruise for another 30 minutes, adding in some 8-second bursts every 5 minutes or so. With an hour to go, stop at a convenience store to drink something with sugar and caffeine. Finish with 45 minutes of riding in the sweet spot. Cool down and stretch.

|  | Time | Description | % of FTP | % of FTHR |
|---|---|---|---|---|
| Warm-up | 30 min. | Easy riding | 56–75 | 69–83 |
| Main set | 2 × 20 min. (10 min. RI) | Threshold | 93–100 | 98–103 |
|  | 30 min. | Cruise | <75 | <83 |
|  | 3 × 75 m (5 min. RI) | Small-ring sprints | max | N/A |
|  | 3 × 300 m (5 min. RI) | Big-ring sprints (53:13) from 20 mph | max | N/A |
|  | 30 min. | Cruise | <75 | <83 |
|  | 5 varied hills (RI) | VO$_2$max | 110–120 | >105 |
|  | 30 min. | Cruise with bursts at 5 min. | <75 | <83 |
|  | *5 × 8 sec.* | *Bursts* | *>150* | *N/A* |
|  | 45 min. | Sweet spot | 88–93 | 92–98 |
| Cooldown | 10 min. | Easy riding | 56–75 | 69–83 |

## *Performance Testing*
TEST          **Monthly Testing Protocol**                    APPROX. TIME: 2.75 HR.

After warming up, begin three 1-minute fast pedaling efforts, resting for 1 minute after each one. Then ride for 3 minutes easy. Next, do a 5-minute all-out effort, followed by 10 minutes at an easy pace.

The next set of intervals will test your aerobic capacity. Do two 1-minute efforts with 5 minutes between them. Ride for 5 minutes easy.

The third set of intervals will test neuromuscular power. Do three 20-second "super jumps." Jump hard out of the saddle and sprint for the full 20 seconds. Rest for 3 minutes after each sprint, and after the final sprint pedal easy for 10 minutes. Finally, complete a 20-minute time trial. Cool down.

| TEST | Time | Description | % of FTP | % of FTHR |
|------|------|-------------|----------|-----------|
| Warm-up | 15 min. | Easy riding | 56–75 | 69–83 |
| | 3 × 1 min. (1 min. RI) | Fast pedaling, 100+ rpm | <80 | <90 |
| | 3 min. | Easy riding | <68 | <75 |
| Main set | 5 min. | All-out | max | >105 |
| | 10 min. | Endurance | 68–75 | 69–83 |
| | 2 × 1 min. (5 min. RI) | Anaerobic Capacity | 125–150 | >105 |
| | 5 min. | Recovery | <68 | <75 |
| | 3 × 20 sec. (3 min. RI) | Super jumps | max | N/A |
| | 10 min. | Easy riding | 56–75 | 69–83 |
| | 20 min. | TT Test | 100 | 99–103 |
| Cooldown | 15 min. | Easy riding | 56–75 | 69–83 |

## Race Preparation

**RACE-W1    Race Preparation: 20 km Time Trial**                    APPROX. TIME: 1.75 HR.

This ride is a good race rehearsal for a 20 km time trial.

Start with 15 minutes at Level 2, Endurance. Then begin a 10-minute "ramp" where you gradually build from Level 2 to Level 4, Threshold. By the last minute, you will be riding flat-out, at time trial pace. Then ride at an easy pace for 5 minutes. Next, do four 1-minute fast pedaling efforts. For each effort, keep your cadence over 100 rpm. Don't worry about power, but focus on fast, smooth pedaling and getting the muscles to "open up" and the blood pumping. Rest for 1 minute between intervals, pedaling easy. Ride for 5 minutes at Level 2. Follow this up with one 5-minute effort at Level 5, VO₂max. Pedal at an easy pace for 5–10 minutes.

Next, start your 20 km time trial, starting your time from about 3 mph. To avoid starting out too hard, take the first 4–5 minutes to build up to Threshold power. On the way into the turnaround, get a sip of water, and then get back up to speed, making sure power is applied throughout the turnaround. Get right back into your rhythm and remain focused. In the last 5 kilometers, pick up the pace and push a little harder. In the last kilometer, push your effort to the max.

Take 30 minutes of easy riding to cool down and do a solid stretching session.

| | Time | Description | % of FTP | % of FTHR |
|------|------|-------------|----------|-----------|
| Warm-up | 15 min. | Easy riding | 56–75 | 69–83 |
| | 10 min. | Build to Threshold | 75–100 | 85–100 |
| | 5 min. | Easy riding | 56–75 | 69–83 |
| | 4 × 1 min. (1 min. RI) | Fast pedaling, 100+ rpm | <80 | <90 |
| | 5 min. | Easy riding | 56–75 | 69–83 |
| | 5 min. | VO₂max | 106–120 | >105 |
| | 5–10 min. | Easy riding | 56–75 | 69–83 |
| Main set | 20 km TT | Start timer at 3 mph | 91–105 | 95–105 |
| | *1st 4–5 min.* | *Build to Threshold* | *75–100* | *85–100* |
| Cooldown | 30 min. | Easy riding | 56–75 | 69–83 |

**RACE-W2     Race Preparation: Classic Race Tune-up**                              APPROX. TIME: 2 HR.

The purpose of a tune-up is to prepare your muscles and the cardiovascular system for an upcoming race or big effort. With some hard, short intervals, the legs will become a bit more supple and responsive the following day. Riding too hard could create some muscle trauma and cause muscle soreness.

After warming up, begin the main set. Over the next hour or more, cruise at Endurance pace, working in two sets of sprints. The first set consists of three hard 1-minute intervals, with 5-minute rest intervals. Next, begin three 30-second all-out sprints, again resting for 5 minutes between intervals. These intervals can be done at any point during the ride, on hills or on flats. Cool down.

|         | Time | Description | % of FTP | % of FTHR |
|---------|------|-------------|----------|-----------|
| Warm-up | 15 min. | Easy riding | 56–75 | 69–83 |
| Main set | 1–1.5 hr. | Endurance riding, including intervals | 65–75 | 75–83 |
|         | 3 × 1 min. (5 min. RI) | Anaerobic Capacity | >150 | >105 |
|         | 3 × 30 sec. (5 min. RI) | All-out | max | N/A |
| Cooldown | 15 min. | Easy riding | 56–75 | 69–83 |

**RACE-W3     Race Preparation: Warm-up for Road Race or Crit**                     APPROX. TIME: 1 HR.

This is a great warm-up for a road race or criterium. Be sure you know the course and have surveyed the turns and your lines in advance. If it's a road race, take it easy for the first half unless it's windy—in which case you should try out some moves near the end and give it a shot to win! If it's a criterium, be sure to warm up really well, get a great start, and try to stay up front!

For the warm-up, start with a 5-minute Endurance set and then do four 1-minute fast pedaling efforts, shooting for a cadence of over 100 rpm. Don't focus on the wattage; focus on fast, smooth pedaling to really open up the muscles and get the blood pumping. Rest for 1 minute between intervals. Take an additional 5-minute rest before moving into "ramps."

For the ramp intervals, gradually take your wattage from Level 2 to Level 4. You should be at Threshold in the last minute of each ramp. Take a rest, riding for 5 minutes at Endurance level before beginning the next interval. Finish with 5–10 minutes of easy pedaling, and then start the race.

|         | Time | Description | % of FTP | % of FTHR |
|---------|------|-------------|----------|-----------|
| Warm-up | 5 min. | Easy riding | 56–75 | 69–83 |
|         | 4 × 1 min. (1 min. RI) | Fast pedaling, 100+ rpm | <80 | <90 |
|         | 5 min. | Endurance | 56–75 | 69–83 |
| Main set | 2 × 5 min. (5 min. RI) | Ramps, build to Threshold | 56–105 | 75–100 |
| Cooldown | 5–10 min. | Easy pedaling before race starts | 75–80 | 83–87 |

# Glossary

**Acute Training Load (ATL)**   The overall quantity (i.e., combination of frequency, duration, and intensity) of training that you have performed recently (during the past week or two). See also Chronic Training Load (CTL).

**Aliasing**   Distortion or artifact in data (such as from a power meter) that occurs when an analog signal is sampled at too low of frequency

**Anaerobic capacity/anaerobic work capacity**   The overall quantity of work (not the rate of doing such work, which is power) that you can perform by relying on anaerobic metabolism. Usually trained by performing short (e.g., 30-second to 3-minute), very high-intensity intervals.

**Anaerobic threshold (AT)**   More correctly termed "ventilatory threshold"; the exercise intensity at which there is a nonlinear increase in ventilation relative to metabolic rate—that is, the rate of oxygen uptake ($VO_2$). Although they are not mechanistically related (i.e., not related as cause and effect), "anaerobic" or ventilatory threshold is often used to estimate lactate threshold.

**Athlete Home Page**   The main screen that shows the user long-term changes in your fitness in CyclingPeaks Software.

**Average Effective Pedal Force (AEPF)**   The average force applied to the pedal that causes the crank to turn.

**Big-ring sprint**   A maximal effort completed in the largest chain-ring of the bicycle. Usually this large chain-ring is made up of 53 teeth.

**BMX (Bicycle Motocross)**   A form of bicycle racing in which the competitors ride bicycles with 20-inch to 24-inch wheels and jump over obstacles. They compete against a maximum of seven other riders at a time. The races are very short, usually less than 1 minute.

**Cadence**   The revolutions per minute (rpm) of the cranks at which you pedal.

**Cardiovascular fitness**   The capability of the cardiovascular system to transport $O_2$ to tissues (e.g., contracting muscles), aid thermoregulation by increasing blood flow to the skin, and so on. It is traditionally quantified by measuring a person's maximal oxygen uptake, or $VO_2$max.

**$C_dA$**   A measure of an object's aerodynamic drag characteristics. In the context of this book, the object is the cyclist and his or her bike. $C_dA$ is the product of the coefficient of drag,

$C_d$, and frontal area, A. Though $C_dA$ is best measured in a wind tunnel, it can also be estimated via field tests performed using a power meter.

**Chronic Training Load (CTL)**    The overall quantity (i.e., combination of frequency, duration, and intensity) of training that you have been performing over a substantial period of time—for example, several months or more. See also Acute Training Load (ATL).

**Circumferential Pedal Velocity (CPV)**    The speed at which the pedal travels around the circle. CPV determines the speed at which your muscles must contract to produce force and thus power.

**CompuTrainer**    An indoor trainer in which you place the back wheel of your bicycle. It uses an electronic brake to modulate resistance on the wheel and can measure wattage.

**Critical Power**    Defined in scientific literature as the slope of the work-time relationship. Critical power is an inherent characteristic of the aerobic energy supply system and as such represents a power that can be sustained for a very long time without fatigue. When measured using exercise bouts that are 3 minutes to perhaps 30 minutes in duration, critical power is essentially the same as functional threshold power. See also Mean Maximal Power.

**ergomo**    A power meter that measures the torsion of the bottom bracket axle.

**Fartlek**    See Tempo.

**Fast Find**    A feature in CyclingPeaks software that allows the user to easily find specified efforts based on the starting and ending wattage of each effort.

**Fatigue Profile**    The measure of a cyclist's resistance to fatigue over Levels 4–7, pinpointing specific areas of weakness when considered alongside the power profile.

**40 kilometer TT**    A 40 km (24.8-mile) solo race against the clock. Time trials are often referred to as "the race of truth."

**Functional threshold power (FTP)**    The highest power that a rider can maintain in a quasi–steady state without fatiguing for approximately one hour. When power exceeds FTP, fatigue will occur much sooner, whereas power just below FTP can be maintained considerably longer.

**Intellicoach Erg+**    Software designed to be used in conjunction with a CompuTrainer.

**Intensity Factor (IF)**    For any workout or part of a workout, the ratio of the Normalized Power to the rider's functional threshold power.

**Kilocalorie (k/cal)**    The amount of energy required to raise 1 kilogram of water by 1 degree Celsius. In common vernacular, 1 kilocalorie is typically referred to as one Calorie (note the capital C).

**Kilojoule (kJ)**    Like the kilocalorie, the kilojoule is a measure of energy. One joule is equal to 1 watt-second, or the work done by exerting 1 watt of power for 1 second. One kilojoule is therefore equal to 1,000 joules.

**Lactate Threshold (LT)**    The exercise intensity at which the release of lactate into the blood first begins to exceed its rate of removal, such that blood lactate levels begin to rise. From the perspective of most athletes and coaches, LT is a relatively low intensity, approximately corresponding to the transition between Levels 2 and 3.

**Match**    A reference to expending a tremendous amount of energy in a short period of time when, for example, attacking during a race. "Burning a match" is when you actually expend the energy.

**Maximal Accumulated $O_2$ Deficit (MOAD)**    The difference between the rate of oxygen uptake ($VO_2$) and the rate of $O_2$ demand at the onset of supra-maximal (i.e., requiring more than 100 percent of $VO_2$max) exercise continued to fatigue. MAOD is currently considered the "gold standard" for measuring a person's anaerobic capacity.

**Maximal heart rate**    The maximal rate at which your heart can beat per minute.

**Maximal Lactate Steady State (MLSS)**    The highest exercise intensity at which blood lactate levels remain essentially constant over time. MLSS is comparable to functional threshold power and is closer to what most coaches and athletes mistakenly call "LT."

**Maximal neuromuscular power**    The maximal power that you can generate under optimal conditions (e.g., at the right cadence).

**Mean maximal power**    Your highest average power for a particular duration. Referred to by Joe Friel as "critical power."

**Mean Maximal Power (MMP) Curve**    The curve of all your average best watts over each second of time, starting from zero seconds and extending to the longest ride you have completed.

**Mean Maximal Power (MMP) Periodic Chart**    A chart of specific average best power for a certain time period. For example, a line graph of your best 5 seconds for each ride you have completed over the entire year.

**Metabolic fitness**    The ability of your muscles to balance aerobic energy production with energy demand, which in turns determines the rate of muscle glycogen utilization, blood lactate levels, and so on.

**Micro-burst**    Intervals with very short work and rest periods (e.g., 15 seconds "on", 15 seconds "off"). Sometimes also referred to as "micro-intervals."

**Normalized Power (NP)**    An estimate of the power that you could have maintained for the same physiological "cost" if your power had been perfectly constant, such as on an ergometer, instead of variable.

**Onset of Blood Lactate (OBLA)**    The exercise intensity corresponding to a blood lactate concentration of 4 millimoles per liter. An individual's OBLA is generally close to, but may be significantly higher than, his or her MLSS or FTP.

**Overreached**    An acute state of fatigue and hence diminished performance resulting from a brief period of excessive training relative to what you normally perform. Although many times riders describe themselves as being "overtrained," in reality they have usually simply overreached and their performance will recover after just a few days of rest or reduced training.

**Overtrained**    A chronic state of overreaching from which recovery takes a long period of time.

**Performance Manager**    Analysis available in WKO+ and other software that allows you to quantify changes in your acute and chronic training load and hence training stress balance over time, thus helping you to build fitness and peak at the appropriate time while minimizing the risk of overtraining, illness, or injury.

**Periodic Chart**    A chart in CyclingPeaks Software that allows the user to view data over a certain period of time.

**Power**    The rate of doing work, where work is equal to force times distance.

**Power Profile**    The specific measurements of power (watts) per kilogram generated at 5 seconds, 1 minute, 5 minutes, and functional threshold power that reveal the relative strengths and weaknesses of a cyclist.

**Power Profile table**    A table that categorizes the watts per kilogram needed to be successful in each category of racing.

**PowerTap**    A power meter that measures the torsion in the rear hub of the bicycle wheel.

**Preme**    A special prize given to the winner of a designated lap in a bike race.

**Quadrant Analysis**    A graphical means of analyzing data from a power meter to visualize specific demands placed upon the neuromuscular system.

**Rate of perceived exertion (RPE)**    An individual's subjective evaluation of how intense or strenuous a particular exercise intensity feels. Typically rated on either a linear 20-point or a nonlinear 10-point scale, both of which were developed by Dr. Gunnar Borg.

**Repeatability**    The ability of an athlete to repeat a certain effort many times without a loss in power.

**Scientifically Computer Aided Training Era**    The time that we are now in, in which we are using microcomputers to help us to scientifically apply training principles for peak performance.

**Self-selected cadence**    The cadence range in which you naturally will pedal without consciously thinking about your cadence.

**Small-ring sprint**    A maximal effort completed in the smallest inner chain-ring of the bicycle. Usually this small inner chain-ring is composed of 39 to 42 teeth.

**Specificity**    An important concept of exercise physiology that takes account of the fact that the adaptations to training tend to specific, or unique, to the particular demands that are imposed.

**SRM PowerControl**   The actual microcomputer that mounts on the bicycle handlebar that comes with the SRM power meter system.

**SRM (Schoberer Rad Messtechnik)**   Power meter invented by Ulrich Schoberer that measures the torsion in the "spyder" of the right crank arm.

**Stochastic**   Technically, "varying randomly."Often used to refer to the marked fluctuations in power that occur when riding a bicycle outdoors. In fact, such variations are generally not really random but occur because of the ever-changing resistances (e.g., hills, wind) that must be overcome.

**Strain gauges**   Small foil leaflets that, when incorporated into an electronic circuit and bonded to a surface, can be used to measure the amount of strain, or deformation, occurring in the underlying material. This deformation is related to the magnitude of the force that is applied; hence, strain gauges are used to measure force (or torque).

**Sweet spot**   A small area of intensity characterized by 88–93 percent of one's FTP.

**Tempo (or "fartlek")**   From Swedish, meaning "speed play"; workouts performed at an intensity that is "up tempo" from what a rider normally trains at when riding at a comfortable level.

**Threshold heart rate**   The heart rate corresponding to functional threshold power.

**Training Stress Score (TSS)**   A composite number that takes into account the duration and intensity of a workout to arrive at a single estimate of the overall training load and physiological stress created by that session. It is conceptually modeled after the heart rate–based training impulse (TRIMP).

**Variability Index (VI)**   The ratio of Normalized Power to average power, Variability Index provides an indicator of just how variable, or "stochastic," a rider's power output was during a particular workout.

**$VO_2$max**   The maximal rate of whole-body oxygen uptake that can be achieved during exercise.$VO_2$max is primarily limited by the ability of the cardiovascular system to deliver $O_2$-carrying blood to exercising muscle; hence,$VO_2$max is considered the best measure of a person's cardiovascular fitness and sets the upper limit to aerobic power production.

**Zero offset**   A task that needs to be done when using the SRM and ergomo power meters. For the SRM, it must be done before every ride. For the ergomo, it needs to be done every 600 miles.

# Index

# About the Authors

***Hunter Allen*** is a USA Cycling Level 1 Cycling Coach, owner of the Peaks Coaching Group, and a former professional cyclist with the Navigators Team. He has been coaching endurance athletes of varied experience levels since 1995, and his athletes have achieved more than 1,000 victories and numerous national and world championship titles and medals.

Having analyzed thousands of power-meter files and furthered the capabilities of power-meter software, Hunter is considered an authority on power meters. TrainingPeaks WKO+ Software emerged from his efforts to help athlete and coach be in closer communication with a simple yet robust program that identifies true weaknesses, quantitatively assesses training improvements, and continually refines training. Hunter has been teaching USA Cycling power certification courses since 2005. Contact Hunter at www.peakscoachinggroup.com.

Hunter resides in Bedford,Virginia, with his wife, Kate, and their children, Thomas, Jack, and Susannah.

***Andrew Coggan, PhD,*** is an internationally renowned exercise physiologist. Andrew has published numerous scientific articles on a diverse range of topics, including the effects of carbohydrates on cycling performance, physiological adaptations to endurance training, and the effects of aging on muscle metabolism during exercise.

A national-caliber masters cyclist, Andrew is also widely recognized as one of the leading experts on the use of power meters in training. Many of the concepts introduced in this book and featured in the WKO+ software (Normalized Power, Intensity Factor, Training Stress Score, Power Profiling, and the Performance Manager) are the result of Andrew's work with cyclists and coaches. As a result of his contributions, in 2006 he was honored by USA Cycling with their Sport Science Award and named a Finalist for the US Olympic Committee's Doc Councilman Award.

Andrew Coggan earned his PhD in exercise physiology from the University of Texas and an MS in human bioenergetics from Ball State University. He lives in Ballwin, Missouri with his wife, Angela (a former elite national champion track cyclist), and children, Madeleine and Gavin.